FRANÇOIS GUARY
Agrégé de l'Université
Lycée Jean Macé (Vitry)

GENEVIÈVE COHEN-CHEMINET
Agrégée de l'Université
Collège P. Éluard (Vigneux-sur-Seine)

DOMINIQUE MELLANO-GUARY
Professeur certifié
Collège C. Debussy (Aulnay-sous-Bois)

JOSETTE STARCK
Agrégée de l'Université
Collège-Lycée A. Renoir (Asnières)

DOMINIQUE DAUGERAS
Agrégée de l'Université
Lycée de Vilgénis (Massy)

JACQUES ROGGERO
Agrégé de l'Université
Université de Provence

ARIEL STROMBONI
Professeur certifié
Maison de la Légion d'Honneur
(Saint-Germain-en-Laye)

Avec la collaboration de

KATSY BLAMONT-NEWMAN
B.A. (Honours) - Agrégée de l'Université
Collège Maupassant (Houilles)

GORDON GOLDING
Master of Arts (Honours)

WAYS AND MEANS

Classe de Seconde

NATHAN

AUX ÉLÈVES DE SECONDE

Ways and Means, Classes de Seconde, est le fruit de nombreuses rencontres, recherches, réflexions et discussions avec des élèves et des professeurs. Son objectif est de vous proposer des supports et un environnement pédagogique riches et abondants afin de vous aider à développer le mieux possible vos capacités de **compréhension orale et écrite, d'expression orale et écrite, de réflexion et d'imagination.** Il est donc important que vous en connaissiez les éléments principaux.

MANUEL : 1re PARTIE

UNITÉ 1

Cette unité de **tests** et de **révisions** vous permettra de voir ou de revoir, en début d'année, les **points essentiels** dont vous avez besoin pour bien commencer votre classe de seconde. Elle fait en quelque sorte le **lien entre la troisième et la seconde.**

UNITÉS 2 À 8

1. Textes
Quatre textes principaux vous sont proposés par unité. Ils sont extraits de la littérature et de la presse anglaises, américaines et africaines, et accompagnés d'activités propres à vous permettre d'exercer votre **réflexion** et votre **imagination.**

2. Main topics
Cette rubrique propose les **principaux sujets de discussion** qui peuvent se présenter lors de l'étude du texte, et vous servira de base pour un travail oral comme pour un travail écrit.

3. A few guidelines
Les **points de grammaire** les plus intéressants du texte ont été relevés dans cette rubrique et sont accompagnés d'**exercices en contexte,** naturellement liés aux *Main topics*. Des références claires vous renverront aux paragraphes du précis grammatical correspondants.

4. Follow-up work
Activités orales ou écrites, ces travaux de *Follow-up work* sont très importants : ils vous permettront d'exercer votre **imagination** (beaucoup d'activités s'appuient sur des **images**), d'acquérir et d'utiliser un **anglais plus vivant et naturel.**

5. Useful functions / Useful vocabulary
Ces deux rubriques suivent les *Main topics* et chaque activité de *Follow-up work*, et **renvoient aux index fonctionnel et lexical** de la deuxième partie du manuel. Les **principaux outils de communication** y sont suggérés. Il vous appartiendra donc, avant ou pendant une activité orale ou écrite, seul ou avec votre professeur, de privilégier les quelques fonctions ou zones de vocabulaire qui vous sembleront particulièrement utiles.

READ AND SPEAK
Ce sont des **nouvelles,** donc des textes plus longs que les autres. L'activité est orientée ici vers la **lecture,** la **compréhension écrite,** l'**expression orale et écrite.** Les nouvelles sont également suivies des rubriques *Main topics, A few guidelines* et *Follow-up work.*

LISTEN AND SPEAK
Vous ne verrez apparaître, dans la table des matières, que les titres de cette activité. Elle consiste en effet en une **série d'interviews réelles,** de **discours, pièces de théâtre,** etc., destinés à l'audition et non à la lecture. Les enregistrements sont liés aux thèmes des textes et développeront vos **capacités de compréhension orale.**

ILLUSTRATIONS
Elles ont été pour la plupart choisies dans une **optique symbolique.** Elles vous serviront de base pour un travail oral ou écrit, individuel ou collectif. Elles concourent à vous enrichir linguistiquement et culturellement.

MANUEL : 2e PARTIE

PRÉCIS GRAMMATICAL
Avant, pendant ou après une étude de texte ou une activité, ce précis vous permet un travail systématique sur tel ou tel point.
De **nombreux exercices** suivent chaque point de grammaire afin de vous entraîner à un travail d'expression guidée et, dans une certaine mesure, de traduction.
Un **index-glossaire** simplifie ces recherches, mais vous permet également, grâce à quelques développements, de mieux comprendre le langage de la description grammaticale.

INDEX FONCTIONNEL ET LEXICAL
L'essentiel des outils de communication s'y trouve. Ce sont donc des « boîtes à outils » précieuses que vous consulterez toujours avec profit avant, pendant, et après une activité. N'oubliez pas de lire les conseils d'utilisation qui précèdent ces index.

FICHIER DE L'ÉLÈVE

Vous y trouverez des **fiches de compréhension écrite et orale** qui proposent une quantité importante d'exercices. Elles vous permettront d'effectuer une première approche d'un texte ou d'une activité de *Listen and speak*, d'éliminer les plus grosses difficultés, de cerner les points essentiels, donc de vous sentir et d'être plus compétents avant une étude approfondie. De plus, elles vous aideront à comprendre et à acquérir dès le départ un certain nombre de moyens linguistiques.

Voilà tous les outils que nous vous proposons. Ils sont nombreux, bien rangés et prêts à vous servir et à vous aider. Bon courage !

Les auteurs

ISBN.2.09.175 122.7

CONTENTS

RÉFÉRENCES PHOTOGRAPHIQUES

AMNESTY INTERNATIONAL : Mordillo : 150. CAHIERS DU CINÉMA : 121 m. CHARMET : 25, 36, 54, 63, 75, 85 d, 111, 154. CINÉMATHÈQUE FRANÇAISE : 121 h, 121 b. CINESTAR : 23, 26 h, 26 md, 26 b, 76 bg, 133. COSMOS : Gorgoni : 55 ; Reininger : 114. EXPLORER : Ferrero : 39 b ; Lanceau : 39 mg. GAMMA : Francolon : 122. GIRAUDON : 43. MAGNUM : Fusco : 67 ; Haas : 130 ; Steele : 128 g ; Uzzle : 45 h. NATHAN : 26 mg, 102. NEF : 46. NEWSWEEK : Wilkinson : 40. RAPHO : Arcis : 45 b ; Duroy : 87 g ; Hamilton : 58 ; Pick : 39 ; Rouland : 39 h. SAUDI BANK : 66 h. SAUNDERS : 83. SMITH : 128 d. SYGMA : Hennings : 83 h. TOP : Desjardins : 79 ; Ionesco : 91. TRANSWORLD : 74 bd ; Kahana : 12, 74 h. VLOO : Brown : 62 ; Hood : 51 ; Young Artist : 59, 108, 132, 134. WAX : 90. WELZENBACH : 142.

Recherches iconographiques : BRIGITTE RICHON
Dessins : GABS
Maquette : LÉA VERDUN

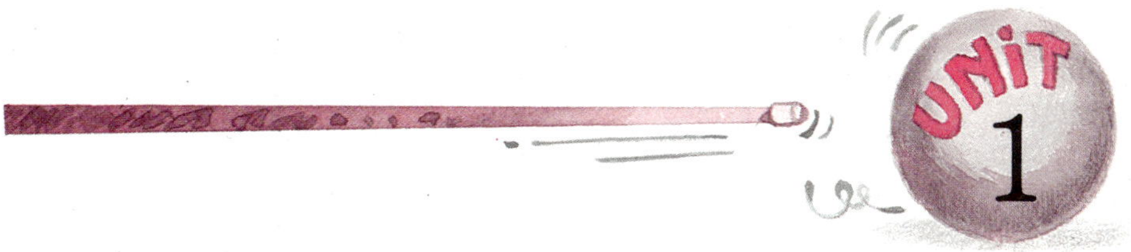

TESTEZ-VOUS...

A - GRAMMAIRE

Vous devez écrire les réponses aux exercices suivants soit sur les grilles qui se trouvent dans le fichier de l'élève, soit sur des grilles que vous donnera votre professeur. Vous n'avez donc rien à écrire sur votre livre.

Le signe Ø qui vous est parfois proposé parmi les choix signifie que cette solution consiste à ne rien mettre à la place des trois points.

Exemple : I went to... school yesterday.

a) *the* **b)** *an* **c)** *Ø*

La bonne réponse est **c)** *car il ne faut rien mettre à la place des trois points :* I went to school yesterday.

SHE'S VERY FOND OF...OLD CASTLES. I'M NOT!

1

1 - My father 's . . . architect. What's *your* father's job?
a) *a* **b)** *the* **c)** *an* **d)** *Ø*

2 - . . . alligators are awful animals, aren't they?
a) *A* **b)** *The* **c)** *An* **d)** *Ø*

3 - She's very fond of . . . old castles. I'm not.
a) *a* **b)** *the* **c)** *an* **d)** *Ø*

4 - More than 60 years later, I still remember . . . terrible winter of 1922.
a) *this* **b)** *that* **c)** *Ø* **d)** *a*

5 - I like . . . apples! Did you buy them at the supermarket?
a) *this* **b)** *that* **c)** *these* **d)** *those*

6 - I've just found a watch. Is it . . . ?
a) *you* **b)** *yours* **c)** *your* **d)** *yourself*

7 - She's one of . . . best friends.
a) *my mother* **b)** *Jennifer's* **c)** *mine* **d)** *hers*

8 - Is John a relative of ... ?
a) *you* **b)** *your* **c)** *yours* **d)** *yourself*

9 - Are you going to ... this afternoon?
a) *the doctor* **b)** *the doctor's* **c)** *the doctors*
d) *a doctor*

10 - My car is American, whereas ... is Japanese.
a) *mine* **b)** *my* **c)** *her* **d)** *hers*

2 *Remplissez les blancs avec* some, any, no *ou leurs composés* (-thing, -one *ou* -body, -where).

1 - Sorry, there aren't ... sandwiches left.
2 - Would you like ... more cake?
3 - I feel lost in this town: I don't know ... .
4 - I'm sure I've left my book ... .
5 - I'm very sorry, but there's ... I can do for you.

3 1 - I can't go to the pictures tonight because I've got ... time.
a) *too little* **b)** *too few* **c)** *a little* **d)** *a few*

2 - She's ... clever to marry such a stupid boy!
a) *too* **b)** *too much* **c)** *too many* **d)** *little*

3 - Don't worry. We've got ... time.
a) *few* **b)** *many* **c)** *several* **d)** *plenty of*

4 - I only need ... time to finish this exercise.
a) *a few* **b)** *a little* **c)** *several* **d)** *many*

5 - ... people think that Alfred Hitchcock was American. He was British!
a) *Each* **b)** *Every* **c)** *Most* **d)** *Much*

4 1 - John is ... than his brother.
a) *old* **b)** *the oldest* **c)** *the elder* **d)** *older*

2 - This is ... film I've ever seen in my life!
a) *worst* **b)** *better* **c)** *worse* **d)** *the worst*

3 - Now that I live in a big city, I've got ... before.
a) *fewer friends than* **b)** *fewer friends* **c)** *better friends*
d) *so many friends that*

4 - I really believe she is not so rich ... she pretends.
a) *as* **b)** *than* **c)** *Ø* **d)** *that*

5 - These days, life is getting ... expensive!
a) *the most* **b)** *the least* **c)** *the more*
d) *more and more*

5 1 - Are you sure she is the girl ... car is parked over there?
a) *which* **b)** *of whom* **c)** *whose* **d)** *of which*

2 - The world needs people ... can speak a foreign language.
a) *who* **b)** *Ø* **c)** *whose* **d)** *whom*

3 - This is exactly the car ... I'm looking for!
a) *for which* **b)** *whom* **c)** *Ø* **d)** *whose*

4 - I didn't understand ... you said. Could you repeat, please?
a) *that* **b)** *Ø* **c)** *what* **d)** *which*

5 - Mummy, this is the boy ... I want to live.
a) *with whom* **b)** *whom* **c)** *who* **d)** *whose*

6 *Posez la question qui correspond à l'élément souligné. Vous devez commencer toutes vos questions par un* pronom interrogatif.

Exemple 1 : I live in Bexley, Kent.
Question : **Where** do you live?

Exemple 2 : I see my grandmother twice a month.
Question : **How often** do you see your grandmother?

1 - She plays football every day.
2 - I paid very little for that record.
3 - We were looking for a place to park the car.
4 - I left before the end because I was too tired.
5 - There will be 200 friends at my birthday party!
6 - Suzy told me that Peter was ill.
7 - I'm going to visit my parents' friends.
8 - She's been living in Australia for 10 years now.
9 - He broke his leg by slipping on his soap.
10 - They were listening to Jeremy's father.

7 *Remplacez les 3 points par les verbes entre parenthèses mis selon le cas au prétérit, au parfait (*have + *participe passé) ou au plus-que-parfait (*had + *participe passé). Utilisez la forme progressive chaque fois que cela est nécessaire.*

1 - You seem very happy together. How long ... her? *(you - know)*
2 - He ... TV for two hours when his parents came back. *(watch)*
3 - ... to their party yesterday? *(you - go)*
4 - ... when we phoned last night? *(you - sleep)*
5 - When I see them, I can't imagine that they ... 30 years ago! *(get married)*
6 - Look at the dog. He's all wet. He ... in the rain again! *(run)*
7 - I can go out with you now. I ... my essay. *(just - finish)*
8 - She ... ill for 3 weeks, since that famous party when she drank so much whiskey. *(be)*
9 - Don't worry. I ... the baby while you were asleep. *(change)*
10 - The maths teacher gave us such a difficult problem that I ... on it for five hours yesterday. *(work)*

8 **1** - I didn't want to, but my mother . . . me clean my room.
a) *wanted* **b)** *made* **c)** *expected* **d)** *forced*

2 - Do you really want . . . with you?
a) *that I go* **b)** *I go* **c)** *me to go* **d)** *that I'm going*

3 - You . . . go to bed at 10.
a) *are expected to* **b)** *are wanted* **c)** *expect to* **d)** *want*

4 - I wouldn't like . . . alone.
a) *that he travels* **b)** *him to travel*
c) *that he would travel* **d)** *that he travelled*

5 - I'll have my car . . . next week.
a) *repairing* **b)** *will be repaired* **c)** *repaired* **d)** *repair*

9 *Mettez le verbe entre parenthèses à l'infinitif sans* to, *à l'infinitif avec* to, *ou à la forme en* -ing *selon le cas.*

1 - Will you stop . . . like that! *(shout)*
2 - I saw the car . . . suddenly. *(stop)*

3 - He enjoys ... in cold rivers. *(swim)*
4 - Would you like ... your holidays in Greece? *(spend)*
5 - Do you mind ... your car elsewhere? *(park)*
6 - He kept ... about his new car. *(talk)*
7 - How about ... out tonight? *(dine)*
8 - He left without ... a word. *(say)*
9 - I can't help ... the good old days. *(remember)*
10 - Why don't you go to the cinema instead of ... TV? *(watch)*

10 1 - I'll tell you when ... ready.
a) *I had been* **b)** *I was* **c)** *I am* **d)** *I'd be*
2 - Let's go to the restaurant, ...
a) *shall we?* **b)** *will we?* **c)** *don't we?* **d)** *won't we?*
3 - I ... leave when the phone rang suddenly.
a) *Ø* **b)** *shall* **c)** *am about to* **d)** *was about to*
4 - As soon as you ..., don't forget to call me.
a) *had finished* **b)** *will finish* **c)** *have finished*
d) *will have finished*
5 - They say they ... to spend their holidays in Italy next year.
a) *are about* **b)** *are going* **c)** *will go* **d)** *will be going*

11 1 - She was asleep when I left at 8, and when I came back at 12, she was ... sleeping!
a) *still* **b)** *always* **c)** *again* **d)** *yet*
2 - Have you ... finished your exercise?
a) *still* **b)** *already* **c)** *again* **d)** *always*
3 - I ... get up at 6, even on Sundays.
a) *yet* **b)** *again* **c)** *always* **d)** *already*
4 - My maths problem was so full of mistakes that I had to do it ... .
a) *always* **b)** *yet* **c)** *still* **d)** *again*
5 - A: Have you had your dinner, Genevieve?
B: Not ... , Mum!
a) *yet* **b)** *again* **c)** *still* **d)** *already*

12 *Mettez les phrases suivantes au passif. (Inutile de mettre* by + *complément d'agent dans la phrase passive).*
1 - My father gave me a car for Christmas!
2 - We'll take him to the nearest hospital.
3 - They're painting the bedroom.
4 - I can't see my house from the beach.
5 - He's repaired our TV set at last!

HE'S REPAIRED OUR TV SET AT LAST!

13 1 - She speaks good English, ... ?
a) *does she* **b)** *doesn't she* **c)** *is she* **d)** *isn't it*
2 - A: I won't go out tonight. I'm too tired.
B: Neither ... .
a) *I will* **b)** *will I* **c)** *I won't* **d)** *won't I*

3 - A: I was very happy to see her.
B: So . . . .
a) *am I* **b)** *was I* **c)** *I am* **d)** *I was*

4 - Help me carry this suitcase, . . . you?
a) *do* **b)** *don't* **c)** *are* **d)** *will*

5 - Everybody went to the party, . . . ?
a) *didn't he* **b)** *didn't they* **c)** *was he* **d)** *were they*

14 1 - I wish I . . . richer than I am.
a) *am* **b)** *would be* **c)** *were* **d)** *will be*

2 - If you asked me to jump out of the window, . . . do it!
a) *I'd* **b)** *I'll* **c)** *I would have* **d)** *I can*

3 - If only . . . smoking that awful pipe, Frankie!
a) *you stop* **b)** *you'll stop* **c)** *you stopped*
d) *you should stop*

4 - If she . . . a baby so soon, she'd have kept her job.
a) *hasn't had* **b)** *wouldn't have* **c)** *hadn't had*
d) *wouldn't have had*

5 - . . . the car, if it had been repaired on time.
a) *I'll use* **b)** *I've used* **c)** *I had used* **d)** *I'd have used*

15 1 - You . . . smoke in class. It's forbidden.
a) *needn't* **b)** *may* **c)** *can't* **d)** *must*

2 - We . . . this house when it was only $10,000! Now it's too expensive.
a) *should buy* **b)** *can't buy* **c)** *can't have bought*
d) *should have bought*

3 - You . . . send your aunt a letter. She'd be so pleased.
a) *ought to* **b)** *'d rather* **c)** *would* **d)** *mustn't*

4 - Look! The lights are on at the Starks'. They . . . have come back home.
a) *must* **b)** *need* **c)** *would* **d)** *can't*

5 - You . . . him in London yesterday! He's been in New York for a week now!
a) *can't see* **b)** *mustn't see* **c)** *mustn't have seen*
d) *can't have seen*

6 - If I had known his phone number, I . . . him immediately.
a) *must have called* **b)** *can't call*
c) *could have called* **d)** *needn't call*

7 - It's already 6 o'clock and she's not here. She . . . her train.
a) *can't have missed* **b)** *must have missed*
c) *would miss* **d)** *should have missed*

8 - . . . you be kind enough to stop arguing all the time!
a) *May* **b)** *Would* **c)** *Must* **d)** *Should*

9 - No wine for me, please. . . . have tomato juice.
a) *I'd rather* **b)** *I can't* **c)** *I shouldn't* **d)** *I mustn't*

10 - . . . bring anything to the party. I'll have prepared everything.
a) *You needn't* **b)** *You'd better* **c)** *You'd rather*
d) *You might not*

B - FONCTIONS

There are lots of things you can do with the following pictures! Describe and imagine the characters' feelings, their thoughts, what they are saying, the reasons why they are doing or saying something, etc. It's up to you now...

9

10

11

12

13

14

15

16

17

18

C - COMPRÉHENSION ÉCRITE

Toutes les réponses aux questions se font sur les grilles qui se trouvent dans le cahier de l'élève, ou sur celles que vous donnera votre professeur. N'écrivez donc rien sur votre livre.

Avant de répondre aux questions, lisez d'abord attentivement le texte une fois en essayant de comprendre le sens général, puis répondez aux questions de compréhension globale. Lisez ensuite paragraphe par paragraphe et répondez au fur et à mesure aux questions de compréhension détaillée.

Ghosts and all that...

Ghosts are great dividers. Half the world declares that they cannot possibly exist. The other half believes that, although arguments and logic are against them, one's feelings and instincts are for them.

The trouble is that ghosts do not work to a routine. Nobody knows when they are going to turn up and so they are difficult to investigate. But they still make the front pages from time to time, like the ghost that the *Guardian* reported which drove a new vicar[1] and his wife out of their rectory after a single night. The wallpaper in their freshly decorated bedroom, they said, peeled off, wrinkled and aged 20 years in that short time.

A poltergeist is a particular sort of ghost that never actually appears. Plates may fly across the room, books fall off shelves. There is often a lot of noise, banging of doors, thumping on ceilings, drumming on windows. Sceptics can dismiss[2] all these happenings with explanations of wind noise, earth tremors or foundations of the house shifting. Such natural things are indeed often the cause, but sometimes they are not.

1. vicar: *pasteur*

2. to dismiss: *rejeter*

One odd[3] thing is that kids are often involved in poltergeist activity. That does not mean they are actually throwing the furniture about or jumping up and down on the floor, but that some kids, especially teenagers, generate a particular sort of force which causes the trouble. They don't know they are doing it and it can't be captured or measured, so this 'energy' theory remains unproved.

Proof[4] of any kind is (1) to get with ghosts. They seem not to appear if they know (2) are waiting for them with cameras. There's the (3) of a vicar in Newby, Yorkshire, who took some (4) of the altar[5] inside his church. When the film came back, one picture clearly (5) a tall draped figure with the (6) of face you'd (7) in a nightmare, standing by the altar rail. The vicar had not felt or seen anything odd at the time (8) film experts could not find any evidence of a fake[6]. Very bizarre...

Anna PAVORD, in *Observer Magazine*, October 28, 1979.

3. odd: *étrange*

4. proof: *preuve*

5. altar: *autel*

6. fake: *fraude*

I. Compréhension globale

1 - This text is

a) a journalist's report.
b) a fictional story.
c) a scientific study.
d) a science-fiction story.

2 - This text is mainly about

a) people who believe in ghosts.
b) people who do not believe in ghosts.
c) the existence of ghosts.
d) the relationships between children and ghosts.

3 - The writer of this text

a) is convinced that ghosts exist.
b) definitely believes that ghosts do not exist.
c) does not try to prove anything.
d) would like to convince the reader that ghosts exist.

II. Compréhension détaillée

Paragraphe 1

1 - *"Ghosts are great dividers"* means that

a) ghosts love to appear in different places.
b) opinions are divided on ghosts.
c) ghosts are able to cut into walls.
d) ghosts often appear in pairs.

2 - The people who believe in ghosts

a) admit they cannot possibly exist.
b) refuse to listen to arguments and logic.
c) feel that everyone is against them.
d) never follow their feelings and instincts.

Paragraphe 2

Right or wrong?

1 - It is not so easy to guess when and where ghosts will appear.

2 - Apart from the *Guardian,* newspapers are not interested at all in ghost stories.

3 - A vicar and his wife refused to spend the night in a bedroom which was haunted by a ghost.

4 - Because of a ghost, the vicar and his wife got 20 years older in a very short time.

Paragraphe 3

Right or wrong?

1 - Poltergeists are ghosts who used to appear long ago, but no longer today.

2 - When there is a poltergeist in a room, he can be driven away by making a lot of noise.

3 - The phenomena caused by poltergeists can always be explained in a logical way.

Paragraphe 4

1 - Poltergeists
- **a)** are generally the ghosts of children.
- **b)** like persecuting children.
- **c)** are afraid of children.
- **d)** often act through children.

2 - The children who get involved in poltergeist activity
- **a)** are not conscious of what they are doing.
- **b)** are generally arrested by the police.
- **c)** throw objects everywhere and jump up and down.
- **d)** suddenly become stronger than adults.

Paragraphe 5

8 words are missing. Which ones?

D - COMPRÉHENSION ORALE

Tout le travail de compréhension orale se fait sur les grilles du cahier de l'élève ou sur les grilles que vous donnera votre professeur.

QUELQUES RAPPELS ESSENTIELS...

A - PASSÉ / PRÉSENT / FUTUR

Avant de faire les exercices des pages 17-18, regardez très attentivement cette histoire.

Extrait de *Vive les femmes*, Reiser,
Éditions du Square.

Rappel

- Le **présent simple** exprime une **action habituelle** ou un **état.**
- Le **présent progressif** est composé de l'auxiliaire ***be*** au présent et de la forme en ***-ing*** du verbe. Il exprime une **action en cours de déroulement.**

1 *Ask one another questions about what this woman does every day, then answer them.*

Example:

Question: *What does she do every day?*
Answer: *She works a lot!*

Now, ask one another...

... what time she gets up every morning.
... where she rushes to as soon as she gets up.
... why she gets up so early.
... what she prepares as soon as she is up.
... whom she wakes up.
... whom she gives breakfast to.
... who feeds the baby.
... what they have for breakfast.
... what she usually does after breakfast.
... if her husband helps her.
... how she goes to work.
... why she always runs.
... how she feels when she arrives at her office.
... etc.

2 *Now, imagine that this woman is fed up with her husband and complains about him (and men in general) to a neighbour. What could she say?*

Example:

Every morning, I get up at six, my husband doesn't help me, he never gets up before seven, ...

Hints: always, usually, all the time, most of the time, often, rarely, etc., hurry, rush, feed, do the housework, sweep the floor, hoover the room, do the washing, look after, etc.

3 *Now, ask one another "wrong" questions about what this woman is doing in the various pictures and answer these questions. (This must be done* very quickly.*)*

Example:

Question: *In picture 1, is she getting up?*
Answer: *No, she's not (she isn't). She's waking up.*

4 *Now, describe (as quickly as possible) what the husband is* not *doing in pictures 1, 2, 6, 21, 22, 23, 24 and 25.*

Example:

In picture 1, he's not (he isn't) waking up, he's still sleeping.

Rappel

- Le **futur** est très souvent exprimé par l'auxiliaire modal ***will*** (ou ***'ll***) suivi de l'**infinitif sans *to*.**

5 *What will this woman do this evening, after 6 p.m.?*
Hints: collect the children from school, prepare the evening meal, lay the table, clear the table, give the baby a bath, etc.

6 *Ask one another "wrong" questions about what this woman will do tomorrow and answer these questions.*
Example:
Question: *Will she dress the children after doing the washing?*
Answer: *No, she won't. She'll wash and dress first.*

Rappel

- Le **prétérit simple** sert à raconter, à rapporter des **événements** et des **états du passé.**
- Le **prétérit progressif** sert à décrire une **action en cours de déroulement à un moment du passé.** Il est composé de ***was*** ou ***were*** suivis de la forme en ***-ing*** du verbe.

7 *Ask one another questions about what this woman did yesterday and answer the questions.*
Example:
Question: *What did she do at 6.30 a.m.?*
Answer: *She woke up.*

Now, ask one another...

... what she did just after waking up.
... where she went when she got up.
... why she went to the kitchen.
... what she did in the kitchen.
... whom she gave breakfast to.
... what she did in the house after breakfast.
... what she did after cleaning the house.
... what she did at her office.
... what time she left her office.
... where she rushed to after leaving her office.

8 *Ask one another "wrong" questions about what the woman did yesterday in the various pictures.*
Example:
Question: *Did she do the washing after giving breakfast to the family?*
Answer: *No, she didn't. She swept the floor first.*

9 *Compare the husband and the wife in pictures 1, 2, 6, 21, 22, 23, 24 and 25. Use the following pattern:*
Picture 1... *The woman woke up while her husband was sleeping.*

B - LES PRONOMS PERSONNELS

Rappel

- Pronoms personnels **sujets:**
  I You He/She/It We You They
- Pronoms personnels **compléments:**
  Me You Him/Her/It Us You Them

Read the following dialogue and find for each blank the appropriate personal pronoun.

Coming home

The scene takes place in a small village in England. Steven, 21, is back home after spending three years in an American university. Brenda, 19, is one of his old schoolfriends.

STEVEN: Brenda! Brenda!

BRENDA: Who's that calling … ? Oh! Is that …, Steven McGuire? … 'd never have recognized … ! … didn't know … were back home!

STEVEN: … arrived late last night. … took the 9 o'clock train.

BRENDA: … suppose your Mum and Dad were waiting for … at the station, weren't … ?

STEVEN: Of course, … were! … was so happy to see .., and … were so happy to see .., their only son. Can … imagine that? Three long years without seeing …, without Mum's steak and kidney pie! When … saw Dad, … hardly recognized …, poor old Dad.

BRENDA: … know what? … met … yesterday outside the pub, drinking his lager as usual. … didn't say anything to … about your coming back home!

STEVEN: Well, here … am at last. … should have seen … at the station! Kissing each other and crying! Quite a moving scene!

BRENDA: What was … like in the States? Is … really so different? Does … look like what … show on TV?

STEVEN: …'s an entirely different world! Especially the people. … aren't like …, … know. First, …'re always in a hurry. Everybody rushes all the time, … seem unable to slow down at all. … sometimes wonder what pushes … .

BRENDA: Did … meet interesting people?

STEVEN: … bet … did! Well, … shouldn't tell …, but—

BRENDA: Oh, come on!

STEVEN: All right, but … must promise … that … won't tell my parents.

BRENDA: … promise!

STEVEN: Well, between … and …, … won't be staying long in England. … met a girl in the States, at a party. … had never seen a girl like … ! … intend to marry … as soon as … have finished my studies. … is the most gorgeous girl in the world! Tall, fair-haired, and—

BRENDA: Well, … has been a pleasure seeing …, Steven McGuire. … must rush now, my parents must be waiting for …, and … wouldn't want … to worry. So long, cowboy!

STEVEN: But Brenda, … haven't let … finish!

C - LA POSSESSION

Rappel

- Les déterminants (ou adjectifs) possessifs et les pronoms possessifs s'**accordent avec le(s) possesseur(s).**
- Les **déterminants possessifs** sont :
  My Your His/Her/Its Our Your Their
- Les **pronoms possessifs** sont :
  Mine Yours His/Hers Ours Yours Theirs
- La possession peut aussi être exprimée par le **génitif,** le plus souvent lorsque le possesseur est un **animé.** La marque du génitif est :
  - **'s** après un nom **singulier,** même terminé par « s » ou au pluriel irrégulier.
  - **'** après un **pluriel** régulier.

Read the following dialogue and find for each blank the appropriate possessive.

The frog

The scene takes place in a classroom. A nice little green frog suddenly jumps on the teacher ... desk right in the middle of the lesson.

TEACHER: Jenkins! I suppose this is one of ... tricks again! Could you tell me what ... frog is doing on ... desk?

JENKINS: ... frog, sir? It isn't ..., it's Stutter ...!

STUTTER: You dirty little sneak!

TEACHER: Well, Stutter, since this frog is apparently ... and not Jenkins ..., I'm waiting for ... explanation!

STUTTER: Well, you see, sir, I found her yesterday on ... way home and—

TEACHER: Because ... frog is a she!

STUTTER: I think so, sir. Obviously, she had lost ... mother or ... father, I don't know exactly which one. Anyway, I put her in ... bag, took her home and hid her in ... father ... attaché-case.

TEACHER: In ... father ... what? I guess ... father must have been very pleased to discover this new friend of ... in ... attaché-case!

STUTTER: Well, er—not exactly, sir. Especially when he found that ... frog had eaten all ... flies.

TEACHER: ... flies?

STUTTER: Yes, well, you see, sir, ... father always keeps a few dead flies in a box in ... attaché-case. Just in case he feels like going fishing after work and—

TEACHER: All right, all right, Stutter. I imagine you had ... reasons for bringing ... frog to school, but I've got ... for wanting her out! This desk is not ... frog ...—although she seems to believe it is! It's ...!

STUTTER: Couldn't we adopt her, sir?

TEACHER: Adopt her? What do you mean?

STUTTER: ... form could have a pet, sir. The 5th B have ... pet! A gold fish! Couldn't we have ...?

TEACHER: A frog as a pet? Have you lost ... mind, Stutter? Who will feed her? You or ... friends?

JENKINS: Stutter will, sir. After all, this frog is ..., not ...!

TEACHER: Well, Stutter, you've heard Jenkins ... opinion. What's ...?

STUTTER: Do you mind ... going out a few minutes, sir?

TEACHER: May I ask you why?

STUTTER: I'd like to find this damned frog ... mother, sir. After all, it's not ... job to feed her! It's ..., isn't it?

D - L'INTERROGATION

Rappel

- Les principaux **pronoms interrogatifs** sont :
  - ***Where*** (lieu)
  - ***When*** (moment)
  - ***Why*** (raison/cause)
  - ***Who*** (personne : sujet)
  - ***Who(m)*** (personne : complément)
  - ***What*** (chose/action)
  - ***Which*** (choix limité)
  - ***Whose*** (possesseur)
  - ***How*** (manière)
  - ***How long*** (durée)
  - ***How often*** (fréquence)
  - ***How far*** (distance)
  - ***How much*** (quantité)
  - ***How many*** (nombre)
  - ***How old*** (age)
- Lorsqu'un verbe est utilisé avec une **préposition,** celle-ci se place **après le verbe** ou **après le complément** dans la question.
  Who(m) did you play with?
  Who(m) did you play tennis with?
- **Attention :** *Who(m) did you play tennis with yesterday?*

You are watching a very interesting programme on TV: a famous explorer tells his adventures in Africa. Unfortunately, your TV set does not work well and words are sometimes blurred by "beeps". *You are so frustrated at the end of the programme that you decide to write to the explorer to ask him a few questions about what you could not hear.*

Example:

Explorer: *We then saw the* - beep -.
Question: *What did you see?*

... so we decided to leave our camp early because - *beep* - and we didn't want to miss the - *beep* - of the lions. There were at least - *beep* - African porters ready to go, chatting and laughing. - *beep* - was shouting and swearing as usual because he couldn't find his - *beep* -. As for Forrester, he had drunk - *beep* - whisky the night before because of - *beep* - and he seemed not to know where he was!

I took - *beep* -'s map out of his rucksack and started to - *beep* - carefully. First, we had to cross the - *beep* - River before - *beep* - o'clock. Afterwards it would be too late ... The crocodiles would be

ready for breakfast and we would have to go to - *beep* - to find a suitable bridge. I decided to travel with - *beep* - in front of the column; I got on well with him and he always made me laugh by constantly - *beep* -ing and - *beep* -ing, even in the worst circumstances! My only worry was the choice of a gun ... I hesitated between a Remchester and a Winnington. I finally decided to take the - *beep* -; it would be better if we were attacked by elephants.

The long walk began ... Although I had already explored this part of Africa - *beep* - times, I was still fascinated by - *beep* -. But there was no time to lose playing at tourists. Our first goal, the Genejo reservation, was at least - *beep* - miles from the camp and I knew it would be difficult for Forrester: he hadn't been in Africa for - *beep* - and he had behaved strangely ever since - *beep* - the two snakes. I could understand that! ...

E - LE DISCOURS INDIRECT

Rappel

- Lorsqu'on rapporte au passé les paroles de quelqu'un *(he said that ..., she asked if ..., etc.)*, on observe les correspondances suivantes :
  - « ... **présent ...** » → *He said that* ...**prétérit ...**
  - « ... **parfait ...** » → *He said that* ...**plus-que-parfait ...**
    (*have* + part. passé) (*had* + part. passé)
  - « ... **prétérit** ... » → *He said that* ... **plus-que-parfait** ...
  - « ... ***will*** ... » → *He said that* ... ***would*** ...
- Changeront également lorsque ce sera nécessaire : les **pronoms,** les **possessifs,** les **interrogations directes** (qui deviendront des interrogations indirectes), certaines **indications de temps** *(yesterday → the day before; tomorrow → the day after, etc.).*

You are listening to a political speech, but unfortunately there is an old man sitting beside you who cannot hear the speaker and keeps asking you "what did he say?". As you are very polite, you cannot but answer: "He said that ... He asked if ..."

My dear friends,

... and I'm here today to try to convince you ...
... of course, you're not obliged to believe me ...
... Now, I want to ask you a question ...
... Do you know what your problem is? And ...
... I've never seen such a situation ...
... I know that many of you will understand what I mean ...
... Did you try to change your lives? No! You didn't! ...
... and it's precisely because you're not really trying ...
... that's why I feel it is my duty to help you ...
... but can't you see it's time to react? ...
... I've often said this before ...
... I won't ask you to give up your convictions ...
... Have I convinced you? I hope I have, and now ...

UNIT 2

1. The time machine

Dr. Grainger said solemnly, "Gentlemen, the first time machine."

His three friends stared[1] at it.

It was a box about six inches[2] square, with dials[3] and a switch.

"You need only to hold it in your hand," said Dr. Grainger, "set the dials for the date you want, press the button—and you are there."

Smedley, one of the doctor's three friends, reached for the box, held it and studied it. "Does it really work?"

"I tested it briefly," said the doctor. "I set it one day back and pushed the button. Saw myself—my own back—just walking out of the room. Gave me a bit of a turn[4]."

"What would have happened if you'd rushed to the door and kicked yourself in the seat of the pants[5]?"

Dr. Grainger laughed. "Maybe I couldn't have—because it would have changed the past. That's the old paradox of time travel, you know. What would happen if one went back in time and killed one's own grandfather before he met one's grandmother?"

1. to stare: *regarder fixement*
2. inch: *pouce = 2,5 cm*
3. dial: *cadran*
4. (it) gave me a bit of a turn: *ça m'a fait un choc*
5. to kick s.o. in the seat of the pants: *donner à qqn un coup de pied au derrière*

6. to back away: *reculer*
7. to grin: *sourire*
8. otherwise: *sinon, autrement*
9. bully: *brute*
10. hell: *enfer*
11. there was a blur: *tout se brouilla*
12. spot: *endroit*
13. club: *gourdin*
14. whip: *fouet*
15. to yell: *hurler*
16. to lash: *cingler*
17. to swing (swung, swung): *asséner*

Smedley, the box still in his hand, suddenly was backing away[6] from the three other men. He grinned[7] at them. "That," he said, "is just what I'm going to do. I've been setting the date dials sixty years back while you've been talking."

"Smedley! Don't!" Dr. Grainger started forward.

"Stop, Doc. Or I'll press the button now. Otherwise[8] I'll explain to you." Grainger stopped. "I've heard of that paradox too. And it's always interested me because I knew I *would* kill my grandfather if I ever had a chance to. I hated him. He was a cruel bully[9], made life a hell[10] for my grandmother and my parents. So this is a chance I've been waiting for."

Smedley's hand reached for the button and pressed it.

There was a sudden blur[11]... Smedley was standing in a field. It took him only a moment to orient himself. If this spot[12] was where Dr. Grainger's house would some day be built, then his great-grandfather's farm would be only a mile south. He started walking. En route he found a piece of wood that made a fine club[13].

Near the farm, he saw a red-headed young man beating a dog with a whip[14].

"Stop that!" Smedley yelled[15], rushing up.

"Mind your own damn business," said the young man as he lashed[16] with the whip again.

Smedley swung[17] the club.

Sixty years later, Dr. Grainger said solemnly, "Gentlemen, the first time machine."

His two friends stared at it.

Fredric BROWN, *Honeymoon in Hell* (1958),

MAIN TOPICS

1 Who are the characters? Where are they? When does the story take place? What happens throughout the whole story?

2 What do you learn about the machine and what it can do?

3 Describe the various characters and their reactions to the machine.

4 Try to imagine Doctor Grainger's life and character.

5 What do you learn about the relationship between Smedley and his grandfather? What are the causes and consequences of this relationship?

6 What are *your* feelings at the end of the story?

7 Travelling in time... Try to list as many advantages and disadvantages as you can.

Useful functions

CONDITION AND HYPOTHESIS — DESIRE AND WISHES — DISLIKING — PROBABILITY — SURPRISE.

Useful vocabulary

4. PEOPLE, THEIR WAYS AND CHARACTERS — 5. EMOTIONS — 7. FEELINGS AND APPRECIATION — 8. JUDGEMENTS AND EVALUATION — 14. EDUCATION AND SCIENCES.

A few guidelines

1

→ ***"What would happen if one went back in time and killed one's own grandfather?"*** (Gr: **9,** § 11)

A. Imagine Smedley's thoughts while looking at the time machine at the beginning of the story. Use the following pattern:

If I had this time machine, I would/I'd go back in time.
If I went back in time, I would/I'd...

Hints: travel 60 years back, go to my grandfather's farm, look for a weapon, try to find my grandfather, kill my grandfather, avenge my parents, etc.

B. Now, imagine what *you* would do if you had a time machine. Use the following pattern:

If I had a time machine, I would/I'd...

2

→ ***"What would have happened if you'd rushed to the door and kicked yourself in the seat of the pants?"*** (Gr: **9,** § 11)

Use the following pattern to imagine what would have happened if Dr. Grainger had used his machine to change the past.

Q: *What would have happened if Dr. Grainger had killed Bonaparte in 1790?*
A: *If he had killed Bonaparte in 1790, Bonaparte wouldn't have become Emperor, he wouldn't have married Marie-Louise, he wouldn't have...*

Hints: ...if Dr. Grainger had killed Adolf Hitler when he was a young boy?
...if Dr. Grainger had convinced Christopher Columbus not to leave for "India"?
...if Dr. Grainger had convinced Charlemagne not to invent school?
...if Dr. Grainger had given Vercingetorix a machine-gun and plenty of ammunition?

3

→ ***"Saw myself just walking out of the room./Near the farm, he saw a red-headed young man beating a dog with a whip."*** (Gr: **19,** § 2)

Use the following pattern to imagine what you'd see or hear if you travelled back in time.

If I went back to the 1880's, in a small Texas town, I'd see horses galloping in the streets, cowboys drinking in a saloon bar, Lucky Luke...

Hints: ...if you went back to 1789, in Paris?
...if you went back to 30,000 B.C.?
...if you went back to Rome, in 50 B.C.?
...if you went back to 50 B.C., in a small village in Gaul?

4

→ ***"Smedley, one of the doctor's three friends..."*** (Gr: **3,** §§ 1, 2, 3)
→ ***"...and kicked yourself.../Saw myself..."*** (Gr: **5,** §§ 2, 3)
→ ***"I've been setting the date dials.../...you've been talking. / ...I've been waiting for."*** (Gr: **11,** §§ 1, 2, 5)
→ ***"I knew I would kill my grandfather..."*** (Gr: **17,** § 3 - **8,** § 3e)

FOLLOW-UP WORK

1. Oral or written work: An old family photograph

You have found this old photograph in the attic. It is a photo of your family a century ago... Either in groups or individually, write each member's identity card. Each "card" should include:
— Name and age (if possible date of birth).
— Life and job, past and future.
— Character and personality.
— Relationships with the family.

Useful functions

COMPARISON — CONTRAST AND CONTRADICTION — DISLIKING — LIKING — PAST.

Useful vocabulary

4. PEOPLE, THEIR WAYS AND CHARACTERS. 11. HUMAN COMMUNITIES.

2. Oral or written work: Travelling in time

Thanks to Dr. Grainger's time machine, you have been able to travel back in time and have found yourself in one of these scenes. When you come back to the XXth century, you will talk about what you saw, the people you met, what they did, what *you* did, what they told you, the adventures (or misadventures) you had, etc.

You can either work in groups and be interviewed by the rest of the class or relate your adventures in a letter to a friend or in a newspaper article.

Useful functions

ADMIRATION — OBLIGATION — QUANTITY — REPORTING — SURPRISE.

Useful vocabulary

1. LIGHT, SOUNDS AND THE SENSES — 2. LANDSCAPES — 3. THE BODY AND ITS ACTIVITIES — 5. EMOTIONS — 9. SOCIAL ATTITUDES.

1

2

3

4

3. Translation

1 - Voici la machine à explorer le temps que vous attendez depuis tant d'années.
2 - Vous n'avez qu'à appuyer sur le bouton.
3 - Si je l'avais épousée, cela aurait changé ma vie.
4 - J'étais encore dans mon bain lorsque le téléphone se mit à sonner.
5 - Si jamais j'avais de l'argent, j'achèterais une ferme.
6 - Je me suis vue à la télévision et ça m'a effrayée.
7 - Si j'avais été plus riche, je serais allé aux États-Unis cet été.
8 - J'ai vu un des deux enfants de Jean qui conduisait la voiture de son père.
9 - Est-ce qu'il savait que nous serions en retard?

2. Help!

"Sergeant Riley, Fifth Precinct[1], Homicide Division, speaking."

"Sergeant, I would like to report a crime. Someone tried to poison my entire family."

"Are you sure?"

"I'm certain. I had my water and food analyzed by a laboratory and they were full of pesticides. Someone dumped[2] the poison in our wells[3] and rivers and not only my loved ones but all our neighbors may be croaking[4] at this very moment."

"Let me get this straight[5]. You think there is a mass murderer in your neighborhood?"

1. precinct (U.S.): *circonscription*
2. to dump: *déverser*
3. well: *puits*
4. to croak (pop.): *passer l'arme à gauche*
5. let me get this straight: *soyons clairs*

Dessin de NAPO, extrait de *A ma mer*, © Édition Greenpeace.

"Sergeant, I think there is a mass murderer in the county[6]."

"Okay, do you have suspects?"

"Well, the Frankenstein Chemical Co. is about two miles from my house and they've been dumping all sorts of sludge[7] in the river. Sometimes it's green, sometimes a dark red and other times it's a deep brown. They do it mostly at night so no one will see them."

"Wait a minute. The Frankenstein Chemical Co. is a multi-million dollar corporation with plants[8] all over the United States. I know the men running[9] the one in this county. Are you accusing them of poisoning people?"

"I know it sounds hard to believe, Sergeant, but I have this niece who works in the company's office and she has memos[10] signed by two of the officers instructing the Frankenstein employes to dump all the waste[11] in the river at night. The memos say that if anyone questions them about it to deny[12] they did it, because if they get caught Frankenstein will have to close down the plant and they'll all be out of jobs."

"So what's the crime?"

"They're knowingly poisoning all of us. Isn't that a felony[13]?"

"No, that's an environmental problem."

"Let me ask you something, Sergeant. If someone came into your house and started sprinkling[14] arsenic on your food and fed your dog DDT and poured cyanide into your children's milk, would you arrest him?"

"Damn right I would, and I'd see he got sent up[15] for life."

"What's the difference between that and a company doing the same thing to an entire community?"

"The police only deal with[16] individual crime. We have no authority to arrest company officials just because they have no way of getting rid of[17] their pesticides."

"Then you mean the average[18] citizen[19] has no recourse when a large corporation knowingly tries to kill him?"

"If the government thinks they're doing anything wrong they have ways of punishing people who dump their waste in the wrong place."

"What's the punishment?"

"I think it's a $5,000 fine[20]. It could be less. But you better be careful before you make wild[21] charges[22] such as you have."

"Why?"

"I can arrest you for harassing[23] a respectable business establishment."

Art BUCHWALD (1979), reprinted by permission of the author.

6. county: *comté (U.S.: division administrative)*
7. sludge: *produits chimiques (= boues)*
8. plant: *usine*
9. to run (ran, run): *diriger*
10. memo: *note de service*
11. waste: *déchets*
12. to deny: *nier*
13. felony: *crime*
14. to sprinkle: *saupoudrer*
15. to get sent up (got, got) (pop.): *se faire coffrer* (G.B.: to get sent down)
16. to deal with (dealt, dealt): *s'occuper de*
17. to get rid of (got, got): *se débarrasser de*
18. average: *moyen*
19. citizen: *citoyen*
20. fine: *amende*
21. wild: *insensé*
22. charge: *accusation*
23. to harass: *harceler*

MAIN TOPICS

1 Who are the characters? Where are they? When does the story take place? Try to sum up the story in a few words.

2 What are the writer's various reasons for calling the police?

3 Describe the Sergeant's reactions. How do they change? Why? What can you guess about the consequences of the writer's phone call?

4 Art Buchwald's humour: Would you say that this story is comic, tragic or both? Why? How

does Art Buchwald manage to make us laugh or smile? How does he want us to react to the story?

5 Industrial growth... Try to find the advantages and drawbacks for the environment in particular and society in general.

6 Consumers vs pollution: What are the various ways of fighting against pollution? How could the following people act and react? The police force? The media (which ones)? Political leaders? Citizens? Intellectuals? etc.

Useful functions

ADVICE — CONDITION AND HYPOTHESIS — DESIRE AND WISHES — GETTING S.O. TO DO S.THING — REPROACH.

Useful vocabulary

2. LANDSCAPES — 8. JUDGEMENT AND EVALUATION — 12. TOWNS, SMALL AND LARGE — 13. DEVELOPED AND DEVELOPING COUNTRIES.

A few guidelines

1

→ ***"Are you accusing them of poisoning people?"*** (Gr: **20,** § 3)

Use the following pattern to imagine on what grounds (= for what reasons) the local Citizen Defense Committee would attack the Frankenstein Chemical Co.

They could accuse them of polluting the river, of...

Hints: kill the wild life, damage the environment, etc.

2

→ ***...by V-ing.*** (Gr: **20,** § 3)

Imagine as many ways as you can of fighting against a plant which is endangering *your* life. Use the following pattern:

We could fight the plant by writing to local newspapers, by...

Hints: boycott the plant, buy and run the plant, blow up the plant, move to another district, etc.

3

→ ***"If someone came into your house, and started... and fed... and poured..., would you arrest him?"*** (Gr: **9,** § 11)

You intend to have your own plant built near a small village. Imagine what you would do if you were an ecology-minded plant manager and wanted the villagers to accept your plant. Use the following pattern:

If I wanted to build a plant, I would first see the mayor, I would...

Hints: ask people to visit the plant, swim every day in the river, etc.

4

→ ***"I had my water and food analyzed..."*** (Gr: **19,** § 1 - **14,** § 6)

→ ***"...all our neighbors may be croaking..."*** (Gr: **9,** § 3)

→ ***"... they've been dumping..."*** (Gr: **11,** §§ 1, 2, 5)

→ ***"...they have no way of getting rid of their pesticides. / ...they have ways of punishing..."*** (Gr: **20,** § 3)

→ ***"...you better be careful..."*** (Gr: **10,** § 1b)

→ ***"I can arrest you for harassing..."*** (Gr: **20,** § 3)

FOLLOW-UP WORK

1. Translation

1 - J'aimerais me faire construire une maison à la campagne.
2 - La police n'a aucun moyen de le faire arrêter.
3 - Tu ferais mieux d'arrêter de le harceler.
4 - Elle est peut-être en train de téléphoner à la police.
5 - Cela peut sembler difficile à croire, mais j'ai entendu dire qu'en Écosse, des compagnies déversent du whisky dans le Loch Ness depuis le

mois dernier et cela fait quinze jours que le monstre est invisible.

6 - Si elle se faisait prendre, elle se ferait certainement coffrer.

7 - On m'a accusé d'essayer de me débarrasser de ma femme en saupoudrant sa nourriture avec de l'arsenic.

2. Oral or written work: After the phone call

Once he has put the receiver down, Art Buchwald tells his wife what he said to Sergeant Riley and what the Sergeant said. (Art Buchwald's wife was away while he was phoning.) Imagine their conversation.

Useful function

REPORTING.

3. Oral or written work: Ronald Searle on man and nature

After looking at these pictures very carefully,

1) Describe each picture in detail: characters, setting, facts, feelings, colours, contrasts, etc.

2) What do you think of Ronald Searle's view of man and nature? How does he use colours? Try to find what each picture symbolizes. What does Searle want to prove? Are you convinced or not? Why?

3) Find as original a title as you can for each picture, then justify it.

Useful functions

COMPARISON — CONTRAST AND CONTRADICTION — PURPOSE — REFUSAL — REGRET.

Useful vocabulary

1. LIGHT, SOUNDS AND THE SENSES — 3. THE BODY AND ITS ACTIVITIES — 4. PEOPLE, THEIR WAYS AND CHARACTERS — 7. FEELINGS AND APPRECIATION.

1

2

3

4. Oral or written work: We shall overcome...

After his phone call, Art Buchwald realizes that the time has come for immediate action against the Frankenstein Chemical Co. and the local police force. He invites a few neighbours round and they decide to write a protest letter. (To the President of the U.S.A.? To the local newspaper? To the Governor of the state? To their Congressman? A petition?... It's up to you to decide...).

1) Imagine the meeting. (It would be interesting to draw up each character's portrait first: name, age, occupation, etc.).

2) Write the letter or the petition. You will naturally make use of the text, but also write in quite a different style. Remember that you want to get people's attention by putting forward forceful arguments. They will read your letter or sign your petition only if they are convinced!

Useful functions

DETERMINATION — EMPHASIS — GETTING S.O. TO DO S.THING — INCAPACITY — REFUSAL — REPROACH — REQUESTS.

Useful vocabulary

2. LANDSCAPES — 7. FEELINGS AND APPRECIATION — 8. JUDGEMENTS AND EVALUATION — 12. TOWNS, SMALL AND LARGE.

5. Oral and written work: Frankenstein goes to court

Let us imagine that Art Buchwald has succeeded in taking the Frankenstein Chemical Co. to court and is backed by the local Consumer Defence Society. The trial will include the defence, the prosecution, a judge and several jurors, witnesses, experts from both sides, etc. You will have to find all the possible arguments for or against put forward in this case and reach a verdict.

Hints: In order to make the trial sound more realistic, you could first imagine the various characters' identity cards: name, age, job, sex, where he/she lives, how and why he/she got involved in this trial, etc.

After the trial, you could also write a short article in the local newspaper. (Your article should not exceed 200 words.)

Useful functions

CONDITION AND HYPOTHESIS — GETTING S.O. TO DO S.THING — OBLIGATION — REPORTING — REPROACH.

Useful vocabulary

2. LANDSCAPES — 4. PEOPLE, THEIR WAYS AND CHARACTERS — 7. FEELINGS AND APPRECIATION — 12. TOWNS, SMALL AND LARGE.

3. Jazz vs Greek

Professor Coleman's son, Jeremy, 17, wants to become a jazz pianist. At the moment he is playing the "Memphis Blues" instead of studying Greek grammar as his father has ordered him to.

I heard the door open behind me. I could just see, in one prophetic flash, what the situation must look like to him. Here was that problem son again, not having any tea (how did he hope to keep up his strength for Greek grammar without tea?). Going into the music room instead. That might be condoned[1] once in a way, but on top of it, not even getting on with his music. Just making that awful undignified row[2].

I swear[3] I wasn't doing it to needle[4] him. I was in revolt, yes, but not necessarily personal revolt against the old man. I wanted to play the "Memphis Blues". It was welling out[5] of me. But how do you explain that sort of thing to someone like my old man? Answer: You don't. So, in a kind of desperation, I kept on playing.

"Jeremy," I heard the old man saying. Quiet, full of dignity. Only he probably thought it was a bit too quiet, with the racket[6] I was making. So he upped it[7] a bit and sang out a bit louder, "Jeremy".

1. to condone: *pardonner*
2. row: *tintamarre*
3. to swear (swore, sworn): *jurer*
4. to needle: *agacer*
5. to well out: *jaillir*
6. racket: *boucan*
7. he upped it: *il haussa la voix*

I was within four bars[8] of finishing a chorus[9], so I played them out. Not offensively, just as a person who was reading might finish the sentence he was on before he laid the book down. Then I swivelled[10] the stool[11] round.

I could see he was annoyed. His face had that brick-red colour.

"Hello, Dad", I said.

"Are you quite sure you've got time for *that?*", he asked, very short and stiff[12]. On the word "that", he nodded[13] towards the piano. I opened my mouth, but a great weariness[14] descended on me. What was the use of chewing the fat[15] with him?

I swung[16] the stool and faced the keys[17] again. My hands moved forward of their own volition[18] and struck out a chord[19]. Just one rich, rolling chord. It was a beautiful sound: full of colour, life, depth. Without moving away from the keyboard[20], I spoke to him over my shoulder.

"Time?", I said. "Yes, I've got time. Thanks," I added to make it seem a bit more polite.

He muttered[21] something like, "I'm glad to hear it", and I heard the door close. I started to slam[22] the keys again, in fast tempo this time. But suddenly, I found I was trembling. My hands wouldn't go to the right keys; I began to hit wrong notes. The room felt oppressive. I knew I had to get out of the trap[23] I was in, but I just didn't know what to do. Tears came into my eyes.

John WAIN, *Strike the Father Dead* (1962), © Macmillan Ltd.

8. bar: *mesure*
9. chorus: *refrain*
10. to swivel round: *faire pivoter*
11. stool: *tabouret*
12. stiff: *raide*
13. to nod: *faire un signe de la tête*
14. weariness: *lassitude*
15. to chew the fat (pop.): *discuter le bout de gras*
16. to swing (swung, swung): *faire tourner*
17. key: *touche*
18. of their own volition: *d'elles-mêmes*
19. chord: *accord*
20. keyboard: *clavier*
21. to mutter: *marmonner*
22. to slam: *marteler*
23. trap: *piège*

MAIN TOPICS

1 Who are the characters? Where are they? Sum up the story briefly.

2 What can you guess about Jeremy's personality, tastes, relationships with others?

3 Describe Jeremy's feelings and attitude towards his father.

4 *"I had to get out of the trap I was in...":* What sort of "trap" is it? How could he get out of it?

5 What can you imagine about Professor Coleman's life, his general behaviour, what he believes in?

6 Describe Professor Coleman's feelings and attitude towards Jeremy.

7 What can we guess about the usual relationships between Professor Coleman and his son? Would you say that they are typical of today's parent-child relationships? Why?

8 Analyse the part played by music and school work in Jeremy's life in particular and in teenagers' lives in general. Are they antagonistic or complementary?

9 Teenagers and music... What kind of music? What is its role in a teenager's life?

Useful functions

COMPARISON — DESIRE AND WISHES — LIKING — PROBABILITY — REPROACH.

Useful vocabulary

4. PEOPLE, THEIR WAYS AND CHARACTERS — 5. EMOTIONS — 7. FEELINGS AND APPRECIATION — 8. JUDGEMENTS AND EVALUATION — 15. THE ARTS.

A few guidelines

1

→ ***"What was the use of chewing the fat with him?"*** (Gr: **20,** § 3)

Use the following pattern to imagine Jeremy's thoughts while playing the piano.

What's the use of studying Greek grammar?
What's the use of...

2

→ ***You should V... You shouldn't V...*** (Gr: **9,** § 8)

Using *should* and *shouldn't,* imagine Jeremy's reproaches to his father and Professor Coleman's reproaches to his son.

FATHER: *You should study your grammar!*
SON: *You should let me play the piano!*
FATHER: *You...*

3

→ ***I wish V (preterite)...*** (Gr: **9,** § 7 - **8,** § 2d)

Use the following pattern and hints to describe Jeremy's regrets and wishes.

A: *I'm never alone.* B: *I wish I were alone sometimes.*
A: *My father doesn't leave me alone.* B: *I wish my father left me alone.*
A: *I have an awful piano.* B: *I wish...*

Hints: I can't play the "Memphis Blues" properly.
My father won't stop harassing me.
I'm only 17. I can't leave home.
I don't have enough money to study with a good teacher.
I don't have enough jazz records.
I can't take the plane to New Orleans, it's too expensive.
My father doesn't understand me.
My father never lets me do what I really want.
I...

4

→ ***"I heard the door open behind me. / ...I heard the door close. / ...I heard the old man saying."*** (Gr: **19,** § 2)

→ ***"...I kept on playing. / Without moving away..."*** (Gr: **20,** § 3)

→ ***"I knew I had to get out of the trap..."*** (Gr: **17,** § 3 - **8,** § 3e)

1. Oral or written work: Sophie, the falling star

First, look at all the pictures very carefully. You will then:

1) Tell the whole story, i.e. describe what happens, the various characters' attitudes, reactions, probable feelings, etc;

2) Imagine what the different characters are saying or thinking in each picture (this should be done in *direct* speech).

3) Would you say that this story is entirely fictional, or does it correspond to real situations? What does Sempé criticize through this story?

Useful functions

ADMIRATION — ADVICE — CONDITION AND HYPOTHESIS — REGRET — REPROACH.

Useful vocabulary

3. THE BODY AND ITS ACTIVITIES — 4. PEOPLE, THEIR WAYS AND CHARACTERS — 7. FEELINGS AND APPRECIATION — 8. JUDGEMENTS AND EVALUATION — 15. THE ARTS.

Extrait de *La grande panique*, SEMPÉ, © Christiane Charillon.

2. Written or oral work: Answering an ad

ATHLETIC SWISS CANADIAN to work in Paris with children or in fitness. Apartment wanted. Mrs Steinberg, Call: 068/55 43 33

US GOVERNMENT SECURITIES BROKERS

London Eurobond broker seeks experienced US government securities brokers to staff new desk. Will consider bright ambitious trainees with related market experience. Good compensation and benefits for the right individuals. Box: 59866, I.H.T., 32 Long Street, London WC 3H 9 IG.

BODY GUARD, professional protection, 34, handsome. Languages: English, Russian, Polish, Yugoslavian, Italian, seeks long term serious employment—anywhere. Please write: Box 2065, I.H.T., Friedrichstr. 19, 7000 Frankfurt/Main.

COPY TYPIST with 50 WPM sought by Paris organization. English mother tongue. Salary F7100 per month/13x. Write with CV & photo to Personnel Section, 3 rue Paul-Bert 75008 Paris.

JAZZ PIANIST WANTED
We are a new jazz group and we intend to tour around the world (Japan first, then Australia and Canada). If you love jazz and are a good pianist, please write: Peter Richards, 49 Bedford Rd., London SE8 LG9 or call Crayford 297421.

EXPERIENCED SWISS BUTLER
with educated background, 40, good presentation, excellent driver. German, English and French, also skilled in secretarial work, takes care of You and Your Home. Free to travel. First class references. Please write: Hans Burger, Cottage 6, Ch. 2007, Genève.

ENGLISH NANNIES, GOVERNESSES, ladies maids, butlers, house couples and chauffeurs, highly experienced in private households, excellent references, free now for positions world-wide. Fly Staff Consultants, 15 Low St, Aldershot, Berks, UK. Tel: 1612/451964. UK licensed.

ALWAYS AVAILABLE AU PAIRS
Children's nanny, mum's helpers & all branches of 1st class live-in domestic help worldwide. Call Weigel Bureau, London 630 92 237642 (24 hours), MAC.AGY. Tex: 99 16120 FG WEIGELG.

NEEDED IMMEDIATELY
For An International Investment Company Based in Geneva
A BOND TRADER
With at least 4 to 10 years experience in the Eurobond and U.S. Treasury bond markets. Knowledge of Japanese market will be an asset. Swiss work permit. Attractive salary, excellent conditions.

This is an ad Jeremy has read in a newspaper... You can choose one of the following activities:

1) Jeremy is quite interested in taking this job and writes a letter to Peter Richards in which he tells him about his love for jazz and piano playing, his desires and wishes, his longing to travel around the world, etc. Write this letter.

2) Jeremy chooses to call Peter Richards to tell him how much he is interested in the job. You can either write or act out the telephone conversation.

3) Jeremy is so anxious to get the job that he decides to pay Peter Richards a visit in his London flat. You can either write or act out the dialogue.

Useful functions

CAPACITY — DESIRE AND WISHES — DETERMINATION — INTENTION — LIKING.

Useful vocabulary

4. PEOPLE, THEIR WAYS AND CHARACTERS — 5. EMOTIONS — 7. FEELINGS AND APPRECIATION — 15. THE ARTS.

3. Oral or written work: A family discussion

Jeremy has eventually got the job advertised in the previous activity. But he does not know how to break the news to his parents. He manages to convince Peter Richards to come home with him and support him against his father. Imagine the discussion which might take place among the various members of the family and Peter Richards. You can invent as many members as you wish (but not too many!): father, mother, younger sister, grandmother, etc.

Useful functions

DESIRE AND WISHES — DETERMINATION — DISAGREEMENT TO CRITICISM — REFUSAL — REPROACH.

Useful vocabulary

4. PEOPLE, THEIR WAYS AND CHARACTERS — 5. EMOTIONS — 7. FEELINGS AND APPRECIATION — 15. THE ARTS.

4. Translation

1 - Es-tu bien certain qu'il savait que nous devions prendre ce train ? Tu devrais lui téléphoner...

2 - Je voyais bien qu'il était fatigué, mais il continuait à courir.

3 - Il entendit la porte s'ouvrir brusquement et vit son père qui se tenait là sans rien dire.

4 - A quoi cela servait-il de lui dire que je ne pouvais pas l'aider ? Il ne voulait pas m'écouter, et par-dessus le marché, je ne savais même pas quoi faire...

5 - J'aimerais pouvoir jouer du piano sans être dérangé !

4. The children of the forest

Newsweek's Ray Wilkinson spent seven days with a Pygmy group of northeast Zaïre.

For the Pygmies of the Ituri rain forest—the "children of the forest," as they call themselves—little has changed since explorer Henry Morton Stanley first paddled[1] down the Congo River in 1876. Nomadic bands of Pygmies—averaging[2] just 4 feet 7 inches tall—still roam[3] the seemingly impenetrable wilderness[4], gathering[5] mushrooms[6], nuts and berries[7] and hunting game[8]. They have had contact with the outside world for several generations, but the Pygmies have refused to adopt customs that conflict too sharply[9] with their own. They do know when to compromise, however. "The Pygmies adapt what they want and quietly drop everything they dislike," says John Hart, an American anthropologist who has lived among them for three years.

1. to paddle: *pagayer*
2. averaging: *en moyenne*
3. to roam: *sillonner*
4. wilderness: *jungle*
5. to gather: *ramasser*
6. mushroom: *champignon*
7. berry: *baie*
8. game: *gibier*
9. sharply: *radicalement*

The band of about 70 that I traveled with was typical of the 50,000 Pygmies living in the Ituri region. Before the hunt began, the group cleared[10] a small area on the banks[11] of the Ekare River and built *endus*—igloo-shaped family huts made from saplings[12] and the broad, heavy leaves of the mongongo tree. Except for some fire-blackened pots and a few hunting knives, traces of civilization were conspicuously[13] absent. Both men and women wore nothing more than ragged[14] shorts made from softened[15] tree bark[16].

Like most Pygmies, the band also spends time in the villages surrounding the forest, selling game and working for the pastoral Bantu[17] and Sudanic townspeople. There they exchange their forest garb[18] for more modern attire: men wear shirts and trousers and women wear wraparounds[19]. The result can be wildly incongruous. In one of the most remote[20] parts of Africa, I saw Pygmies wearing T shirts emblazoned with the Harvard logo[21] or pictures of kung fu heroes. Pygmies sometimes adopt town names to match their jobs. "Bwana Mercedes," for instance, cleans vehicles, and "Bwana Bangi" sells locally grown marijuana.

The Pygmies' flexibility has helped them survive, but that alone may not be enough to save them. Zaïre has nearly half of Africa's 210 million acres of rain forest, and private businessmen are pressuring the government to let them begin clearing the land. For now, however, the government lacks[22] the resources to attempt a large-scale exploitation of the area's valuable hardwood and potentially rich farmland, and the Ituri Pygmies appear relatively safe. "As long as the Ituri region remains intact," says Hart, "there may not be any fundamental change in their position for another 30 years." Given[23] the centuries of Pygmy culture and tradition, 30 years is not a long time.

Ray WILKINSON, in *Newsweek*, September 21, 1981.

10. to clear: *défricher*
11. bank: *rive*
12. sapling: *arbrisseau*
13. conspicuously: *visiblement*
14. ragged: *en lambeaux*
15. to soften: *ramollir*
16. bark: *écorce*
17. pastoral Bantu: *bergers Bantous*
18. garb: *habits*
19. wraparound: *boubou, pagne*
20. remote: *reculé*
21. logo: *emblème, logo*
22. to lack: *manquer de*
23. given: *étant donné*

MAIN TOPICS

1 Who are the various characters? When and where does the story take place? Try to locate Northeast Zaïre on a map.

2 What do you learn about the Pygmies, their probable history, their way of life, their activities, their values, their education, etc.?

3 Guess how the Pygmies were discovered by Europeans: Where? When? How? What were the Whites' probable reactions? What were the Pygmies' probable reactions?

4 Imagine how the Pygmies may have had contacts with the outside world. With whom? Why? Where? What can you guess about the consequences of these contacts?

5 Imagine the anthropologist's identity card: his name, age, family, probable background, values, education, goals, etc.

6 What could you say about the roles of explorers and anthropologists? Have they got similar or different roles? What are the consequences of their actions?

7 What can be imagined about the Pygmies' future? What are their hopes? What are the dangers? Do *you* know any other Third World tribal peoples in danger? Which ones? Where? Why are they in danger? What can you guess about the probable consequences of these dangers on their way of life?

Useful functions

CAPACITY — CONTRAST AND CONTRADICTION — DESIRE AND WISHES — DURATION — PROBABILITY.

Useful vocabulary

3. THE BODY AND ITS ACTIVITIES — 4. PEOPLE, THEIR WAYS AND CHARACTERS — 9. SOCIAL ATTITUDES — 11. HUMAN COMMUNITIES — 13. DEVELOPED AND DEVELOPING COUNTRIES.

A few guidelines

1

→ ***"...little has changed since... / They have had contacts for... / ...who has lived among them for three years."*** (Gr: **11,** § 4)

Imagine John Hart's life among the Pygmies for three years (since 1978). Use the following pattern:

For three years (since 1978) John Hart has been working among the Pygmies, he has been eating with them, he has...

2

→ ***"...to let them begin..."*** (Gr: **19,** § 3)

Try to think of all the things the Western world should let the tribal peoples do. Use the following pattern:

We should let them live in peace, we should let them do what they want, we should let them...

3

→ ***"...the band also spends time selling game and working..."*** (Gr: **20,** § 3)

Compare the Pygmies' life and that of the Westerners, using the following pattern:

The Pygmies spend their time hunting in the forest whereas the Westerners spend their time working in offices. The Pygmies...

4

→ ***"As long as the Ituri region remains intact..."***

What can we guess about the Pygmies' future? Finish these sentences, using the following pattern:

The Pygmies will carry on hunting as long as there is game in the forest.

Hints: The Pygmies will be happy as long as...
The Pygmies' life will remain the same as long as...
The Pygmies' lands will remain virgin as long as...
Pygmy children will spend their time playing as long as...
The Westerners won't try to force the Pygmies out of their lands as long as...
The Pygmies will keep on building huts as long as...
The Pygmies will dress with softened tree bark as long as...
The Pygmies will drink pure water as long as...
The Pygmies...

5

→ ***"...still roam the wilderness..."***

→ ***"They do know when..."***

→ ***"...that may not be enough to save them... / ...there may not be any fundamental change..."*** (Gr: **9,** § 3)

FOLLOW-UP WORK

1. Oral or written work: Tribal life

Either collectively, in groups, or individually, compare these pictures and try to analyse these tribes' ways of life, customs, activities, values, etc. You might find it useful to draw (and complete) a grid of the following kind.

	Characters	Environment	Activities	etc.
1				
etc.				

Useful functions

CAPACITY — COMPARISON — CONTRAST AND CONTRADICTION — INCAPACITY — PROBABILITY.

Useful vocabulary

2. LANDSCAPES — 3. THE BODY AND ITS ACTIVITIES — 4. PEOPLE, THEIR WAYS AND CHARACTERS — 9. SOCIAL ATTITUDES — 11. HUMAN COMMUNITIES.

1

2

3

4

2. Oral or written work: Three articles in the *London Herald*

The *London Herald,* an important newspaper, has decided to publish several articles on Henry M. Stanley's discovery of the Pygmies. Three people are being interviewed: Stanley himself, a scientist from the British Museum who was with the expedition, and a soldier whose role was to protect the members of the expedition. You can either write one of these interviews or prepare it in groups and be interviewed by the rest of the class.

Hints: You must not forget to give the explorer's, soldier's and scientist's identity cards: name, age, social and professional background, etc.

Useful functions

CAUSE — INTENTION — OBLIGATION — PURPOSE — QUANTITY.

Useful vocabulary

1. LIGHT, SOUNDS AND THE SENSES — 2. LANDSCAPES — 3. THE BODY AND ITS ACTIVITIES — 4. PEOPLE, THEIR WAYS AND CHARACTERS — 5. EMOTIONS.

3. Written work: Essay on tribal people

"We were robbed of what pathetic little we had. Now we have nothing." (Negande, a chief of Zimbabwe's Batonga tribe.)

The death of an Indian tribe is *"like destroying a library of information. A range of culture enriches us all. If we get rid of these people we are effectively destroying a part of ourselves."* (Mr. Bentley, from *Survival International.)*

Use these two quotations to analyse what the tribal peoples have to offer the modern world, why and how they should be protected, giving precise examples.

Useful functions

ADVICE — COMPARISON — OBLIGATION — PROHIBITION — PROPOSING.

Useful vocabulary

4. PEOPLE, THEIR WAYS AND CHARACTERS — 7. FEELINGS AND APPRECIATION — 11. HUMAN COMMUNITIES — 13. DEVELOPED AND DEVELOPING COUNTRIES.

4. Translation

1 - Je me demande ce qui a changé depuis que j'ai quitté l'Afrique.
2 - Il y a trente ans, il y avait encore quelques parcs où on pouvait laisser son chien courir librement.
3 - Ce film nous a permis de comprendre comment Tarzan a survécu dans la jungle.
4 - Il passait son temps à courir et à chasser.
5 - Il se peut que nous ayons des problèmes sous peu.
6 - Tant que tu resteras avec moi, tout ira bien.
7 - Tu comprends bien ce que je te dis, n'est-ce pas ?
8 - J'habite dans une ville depuis tant d'années que je rêve parfois de partir dans une île déserte...
9 - Il se pourrait qu'elle n'ait pas assez d'argent pour s'acheter une nouvelle robe.

© *Newsweek,* September 21, 1981.

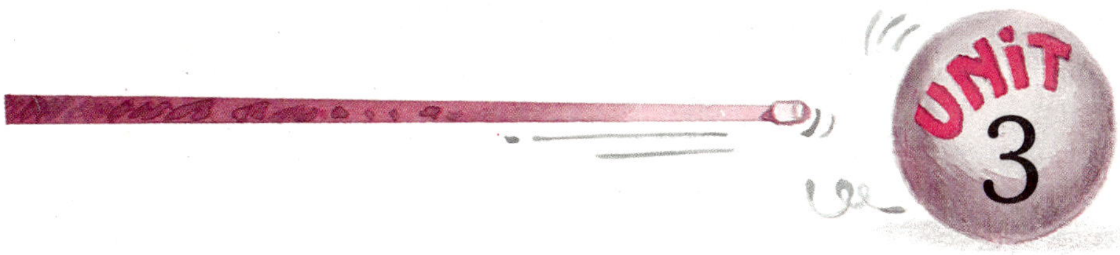

1. Of friendship, flowers and flour[1]

Once upon a time, there was an honest little fellow named Hans. He lived in a tiny[2] cottage all by himself, and every day he worked in his garden. In all the country-side there was no garden so lovely as his.

Little Hans had a great many friends, but the most devoted[3] friend of all was big Hugh the Miller[4]. Indeed, so devoted was the rich Miller to little Hans, that he would never go by his garden without leaning over the wall and plucking[5] a large nosegay[6], or a handful of sweet herbs, or filling his pockets with plums[7] and cherries if it was the fruit season.

"Real friends should have everything in common," the Miller used to say, and little Hans nodded[8] and smiled, and felt very proud of having a friend with such noble ideas.

Sometimes, indeed, the neighbours thought it strange that the rich Miller never gave little Hans anything in return, though he had a hundred sacks of flour stored away[9] in his mill, and six cows, and a large flock[10] of sheep; but Hans never troubled his head about these things, and nothing gave him greater pleasure than to listen to all the wonderful things the Miller used to say about the unselfishness[11] of true friendship.

So little Hans worked away[12] in his garden. During the spring, the summer, and the autumn he was very happy, but when the winter came, and he had no fruit or flowers to bring to the market, he suffered a good deal from cold and hunger, and often had to go to bed without any supper but a few dried[13] pears or some hard nuts. In the winter, also, he was extremely lonely, as the Miller never came to see him then.

"There is no good in my going to see little Hans as long as the snow lasts[14]," the Miller used to say to his wife, "for when people are in trouble they should be left alone and not be bothered[15] by visitors. That at least is my idea about friendship, and I am sure I am right. So I shall wait till the spring comes, and then I shall pay him a visit, and he will be able to give me a large basket of primroses[16], and that will make him so happy."

1. flour: *farine*
2. tiny: *minuscule*
3. devoted: *dévoué*
4. miller: *meunier*
5. to pluck: *cueillir*
6. nosegay: *bouquet*
7. plum: *prune*
8. to nod: *acquiescer*
9. to store away: *mettre de côté*
10. flock: *troupeau*
11. unselfishness: *générosité*
12. to work away: *continuer à travailler*
13. dried: *séché*
14. to last: *durer*
15. to bother: *déranger*
16. primrose : *primevère*

17. why: *ici, tu penses bien*
18. cask: *tonneau*
19. to spoil: *gâcher*
20. besides: *de plus*
21. to spell (spelt, spelt): *épeler*

"But could we not ask little Hans up here?" said the Miller's youngest son. "If poor Hans is in trouble I will give him half my porridge, and show him my white rabbits."

"What a silly boy you are!" cried the Miller; "I really don't know what is the use of sending you to school. You seem not to learn anything. Why[17], if little Hans came up here, and saw our warm fire, and our good supper, and our great cask[18] of red wine, he might get envious, and envy is a most terrible thing, and would spoil[19] anybody's nature. I certainly will not allow Hans' nature to be spoiled. I am his best friend, and I will always watch over him, and see that he is not led into any temptations. Besides[20], if Hans came here, he might ask me to let him have some flour on credit, and that I could not do. Flour is one thing, and friendship is another, and they should not be confused. Why, the words are spelt[21] differently, and mean quite different things. Everybody can see that."

Oscar WILDE, *The Happy Prince and other Tales* (1888).

MAIN TOPICS

1 Who are the main characters? Where do they live? What are their jobs? Try to sum up the story in a few words.

2 Could you describe Little Hans' physical appearance and his character? Try to guess his likes and dislikes (if any).

3 What do we learn about Hugh the Miller? What sort of man is he? Draw up his portrait, imagining his physical appearance, the sort of education he had, his family life, his likes and dislikes. Could you sum up his moral values?

4 Hans and Hugh... Guess how they met. Why did they become friends? What did they see in each other? Try to compare what each one says to and does for the other.

5 The winter episode: Imagine Little Hans' problems. Why is his situation difficult? Who could help him? How? How does the Miller react to Hans' situation? Explain his reactions and the reasons he gives. How do Hugh's wife and child react? Why? What would *you* have suggested if you had known Hans and Hugh?

6 Who does Oscar Wilde side with? How does he want the reader to react? Why?

7 Tales like this one often have a moral ending. Try to imagine one in a few lines.

Useful functions

COMPARISON — DESIRE AND WISHES — DISAGREEMENT TO CRITICISM — REFUSAL — REPROACH.

Useful vocabulary

4. PEOPLE, THEIR WAYS AND CHARACTERS — 5. EMOTIONS — 6. ACTIVITIES OF THE MIND AND COMMUNICATION — 7. FEELINGS AND APPRECIATION — 8. JUDGEMENTS AND EVALUATION.

A few guidelines

1

→ ***"...he would never go by his garden without leaning..."*** (Gr: **9**, § 9)

Imagine Little Hans' and Hugh the Miller's daily activities, using the following pattern:

Every day, Hans would get up at five, he would...
Every day, Hugh would...

2

→ ***"...if Little Hans came up here, he might get envious, he might ask me to..."*** (Gr: **9**, §§ 3, 11)

Using the same pattern as the one in the example from the text, imagine all the things Little Hans might do or ask if he came up to the Miller's house.

3

→ ***"Real friends should have everything in common... / ...people should be left alone and not be bothered... / ...they should not be confused."*** (Gr: **9**, § 8)

Try to find as many morals to this tale as you can, using *should* or *shouldn't.* A few examples:

Real friends should help each other when times are hard.
A poor man shouldn't be left alone in winter.

4

→ ***"...he might ask me to let him have some flour on credit..."*** (Gr: **19**, § 3)

Try to think of all the things Little Hans usually lets people do and all the things Hugh the Miller won't let people do. Use the following pattern:

Little Hans usually lets his friends pick his flowers, he usually lets them...
Hugh the Miller won't let people come into his house, he won't let them...

5

→ ***"...without leaning over the wall... / ...felt very proud of having... / There is no good in my going... / ...what is the use of sending you to school."*** (Gr: **20**, § 3)

→ ***"...no garden so lovely as his. / ...the most devoted friend of all... / ...nothing gave him greater pleasure than to listen... / ...the Miller's youngest son... / I am his best friend..."*** (Gr: **7**)

→ ***"...the Miller used to say..."*** (Gr: **8**, § 2c)

→ ***"...all by himself..."*** (Gr: **5,** §§ 3)

→ ***"...a great many friends... / ...never gave anything... / ...a hundred sacks... / ...six cows... / ...nothing gave him... / ...all the wonderful things... / ...he had no fruit... / ...he suffered a good deal... / ...without any supper... / ...a few dried pears or some hard nuts... / There is no good... / ...half my porridge... / You seem not to learn anything. / ...would spoil anybody's nature. / ...led into any temptations. / ...to let him have some flour..."*** (Gr: **2 - 5,** § 7)

FOLLOW-UP WORK

1. Oral or written work: An experiment in human behaviour

First, look at this cartoon very carefully. You will then:

1) Tell the story, describing what you can see, the various characters' actions and reactions, their probable motives and feelings.

2) Imagine what each character is thinking of or wondering about in each picture. (They should speak for themselves, using *direct* speech.)

3) Find a moral to this story. Would you say that this story is only fiction or could it correspond to situations in real life? What is criticized through this cartoon?

Useful functions

CONDITION AND HYPOTHESIS — DISLIKING — INCAPACITY — REFUSAL — REGRET.

Useful vocabulary

4. PEOPLE, THEIR WAYS AND CHARACTERS — 8. JUDGEMENTS AND EVALUATION — 9. SOCIAL ATTITUDES — 12. TOWNS, SMALL AND LARGE.

"Are you all right, Mister? Is there anything I can do?"

"Young man, you're the only one who bothered to stop! I'm a millionaire and I'm going to give you five thousand dollars!"

2. Oral or written work: Help!

Either collectively in groups or individually, describe these two pictures and, keeping in mind his ideas and values, imagine what Hugh the Miller would tell his wife and children if he was faced with these situations. You should also, of course, imagine the wife's and the youngest son's reactions.

Useful functions

ADVICE — CAUSE — CONSEQUENCE — DISAGREEMENT TO CRITICISM — REPROACH.

Useful vocabulary

4. PEOPLE, THEIR WAYS AND CHARACTERS — 5. EMOTIONS — 8. JUDGEMENTS AND EVALUATION — 11. HUMAN COMMUNITIES.

3. Written work: Ten years later

Hugh the Miller is in deep trouble. His mill can no longer compete with the new modern electric mills. He even finds it difficult to provide food and clothing for his family. His sons are out of work too. But Little Hans' garden has developed beautifully. Hans now manages a market garden with greenhouses and many workers. The Miller decides to write Hans a letter asking for help.

Imagine what he will write about, his arguments, hopes, possible regrets and wishes. Hans will of course answer his letter. You should invent Hans' answer as well. Do not forget to write out the letters using the proper form with the right salutation and ending.

Useful functions

ADVICE — INCAPACITY — CAUSE — CONDITION AND HYPOTHESIS — DESIRE AND WISHES — PROPOSING — REQUESTS.

Useful vocabulary

4. PEOPLE, THEIR WAYS AND CHARACTERS — 5. EMOTIONS — 6. ACTIVITIES OF THE MIND AND COMMUNICATION — 7. FEELINGS AND APPRECIATION — 8. JUDGEMENTS AND EVALUATION — 9. SOCIAL ATTITUDES.

4. Translation

1 - Il menait une vie très régulière : tous les matins, il se levait à 6 heures. Puis il prenait son petit déjeuner à 7 heures et partait au travail.
2 - A quoi bon avoir beaucoup d'amis si on ne les voit jamais ?
3 - On ne devrait pas la laisser toute seule dans sa grande maison.
4 - Il se pourrait que j'aille la voir.
5 - Jadis, c'était mon meilleur ami et j'étais fier de travailler avec lui. Rien ne me procurait plus de plaisir. Mais c'est fini maintenant : son égoïsme a tout gâché...
6 - Je ne te laisserai pas partir sans rien dire.
7 - Tu sembles n'avoir rien compris... Tu pourrais au moins m'écouter !

2. Baba Fule

The writer, a black student in Malawi (Eastern Africa), has decided to write the life story of Baba Fule, a very old man living in a remote village. He is now interviewing him.

'This young man wants to write a book about me,' Baba Fule excitedly told his wife. The folds[1] on her face extended, indicating that she was smiling or doing something of the kind.

'Are you at school?' Baba Fule asked me.

'es, I am,' I replied.

'What standard[2] are you doing?' he asked. Telling him that I was in my third year at the university would not mean much to him, so I told him that I was doing Standard Fifteen.

'Standard Fifteen. Ma, ma, ma, the children of these days. Standard Fifteen. Ma, ma, ma.'

'What is Standard Fifteen?' his wife asked.

'As many as the fingers on your hands and the toes of one foot,' he explained, smiling, showing his partially-filled gums[3].

'Has he more standards than Josiah and Aleck?' his wife enquired.

'Yes, Josiah and Aleck have twelve standards.' Baba Fule told me who Josiah and Aleck were. They were his grandchildren. He had eleven children, three of whom had died while they were still young. The eight were still alive and were gifted with[4] big families as he had been.

'If I count all my grandchildren, they reach sixty-nine, and some of these have children of their own,' he said, smiling contentedly.

'Where do they all live?' I asked.

1. fold: *ride*
2. standard: *niveau*
3. gums: *gencives*
4. to be gifted with: *avoir le bonheur de posséder*

'They live in towns. If they all came back, this village would be too small to accommodate[5] them. But they all come here from time to time. I live with two of my great grandchildren here, a boy and a girl.'

'You've been blessed[6],' I said.

'Oh, yes, very much. Everything we eat and wear comes from our children and grandchildren. All we do is sit down, basking in the sun[7], waiting for the day.' He then boasted[8] of the cars some of his children and grandchildren had.

'The world has changed,' he said. 'In my youth[9] there were no cars, only bicycles, and even then only the very rich could afford[10] them. In fact, only the Azungu[11] possessed them. But these days, even children have bicycles and as for cars, even women drive them! In my youth many children did not go to school. Anybody who reached Standard Three was considered very educated. But these days, you get almost every child in school. You know, small children this high,' he indicated with his stick, 'are doing Standard Three. I finished my Standard Two at your age.' He paused, smiling at me. I was fascinated.

'If it were possible, would you exchange your life of those days for the life of these days?' I asked.

'The life these days is easier and more comfortable. But still I would not exchange the life I had.'

'Why?'

'There are many reasons. As boys, we had more fun and adventure in our days than the children of these days. You see, all that the children do these days is go to school from an early age and be stuffed[12] with books in foreign languages and mostly about foreign ways so that they lose their own things. Indeed[13], now things seem to have no direction, no purpose[14]. You see, in the old days, a man of my age and my family would have left this village long ago and founded his own village and would have been chief. But today, my wife and I are left alone to look after ourselves. I don't complain[15] about my children. They help me. I have some friends who are not in such a fortunate position. However, I still feel something is wrong. It's like a basket-weaver[16] exchanging his best baskets for a bag of maize only to find out that it's full of sand[17].' Baba Fule went on telling me about his youth with deliberate emphasis to show how superior it was to our youth. I was too absorbed with the conversation to realize that I had not begun my interview...

5. to accommodate: *loger*
6. to bless: *bénir*
7. to bask in the sun: *se dorer au soleil*
8. to boast: *se vanter*
9. youth: *jeunesse*
10. I can afford: *je peux me permettre*
11. the Azungu: *les Blancs*
12. to stuff: *farcir*
13. indeed: *en fait*
14. purpose: *but*
15. to complain: *se plaindre*
16. basket-weaver: *vannier*
17. sand: *sable*

Paul ZELEZA, *The Soldier without an Ear*, © Heinemann Educational Books.

MAIN TOPICS

1 Who are the main characters? Where and when does the story take place? Sum up the text in just a few words.

2 What do we learn about Baba Fule's life today? How old is he? Where does he live? What resources does he have? What are his activities? What do we learn about his family (relationships and feelings)?

3 What are the narrator's feelings and attitudes towards Baba Fule throughout the passage? Why? What about Baba Fule's feelings and attitudes towards the narrator? Why?

4 What are Baba Fule's views on education? In his opinion, what are the positive and negative aspects of education? Do you agree with him? Why?

5 What does Baba Fule think about the influence of foreign cultures on children? Do you agree with him or not? Why?

6 Baba Fule contrasts the present and the past: What advantages and drawbacks does he see in each? Why wouldn't he exchange his *"life of those days for the life of these days"?* Do you agree with his attitude or not? Why?

7 Try to discuss the various problems raised by this text:
- the loneliness of old people;
- the role of old people in Third World countries and in Western countries;
- the consequences of the rural exodus on family relationships.

Useful functions

ADMIRATION — COMPARISON — CONCESSION — CONTRAST AND CONTRADICTION — PAST.

Useful vocabulary

6. ACTIVITIES OF THE MIND AND COMMUNICATION — 7. FEELINGS AND APPRECIATION — 8. JUDGEMENTS AND EVALUATION — 11. HUMAN COMMUNITIES — 13. DEVELOPED AND DEVELOPING COUNTRIES — 14. EDUCATION AND SCIENCES.

A few guidelines

1

→ ***"As many as the fingers on your hands ... / Has he more standards than Josiah and Aleck? / The life these days is easier and more comfortable. / ... we had more fun and adventure than the children of these days."*** (Gr: **7,** § 1)

Using as many comparatives as you can, help Baba Fule compare the present with the past. You may find the following grid useful. We have only given a few adjectives on this grid, but remember that you can compare with **nouns** *(They had more time ...),* with **verbs** *(They worked less ...)* or with **adverbs** (*They talked more often* ...).

	Past	Present
Life	hard, tiring, pleasant, ...	comfortable, hectic, easy, ...
Towns	small, dirty, ...	big, polluted, noisy, ...
Children at school	few, happy, lucky, carefree, manual, ...	numerous, well-educated, miserable, intellectual, ...
Children and parents	helpful, close, grateful, considerate, severe, ...	busy, selfish, rich, free, lenient, ...
etc.		

2

→ ***"You've been blessed ... / Anybody who reached Standard Three was considered very educated. / I was fascinated. / ... all the children do these days is go to school and be stuffed with books ... / ... my wife and I are left alone ... / I was too absorbed with the conversation ..."*** (Gr: **14,** §§ 1, 2)

Use the passive to describe a child's life at school.

Hints: teach foreign languages, maths, history, ...
give good (or bad) marks, give homework, ...
reward, congratulate, ...
tell off, punish, keep in, ...

3

→ ***"... a man of my age would have left his village and would have been chief."*** (Gr: **9,** § 11b)

Use the above pattern to imagine what Baba Fule's life would have been like if things had been different.

Hints: have more children, more power, live outdoors, hunt, build his own house, etc.

4

→ ***"Baba Fule told me who Josiah and Aleck were."***
→ ***"He had eleven children, three of whom had died ..."*** (Gr: **13,** §§ 1, 2, 3)
→ ***"If it were possible, would you exchange your life ..."*** (Gr: **9,** § 11)
→ ***"... all the children do these days is go to school ..."*** (Gr: **19,** § 4)

FOLLOW-UP WORK

1. Oral or written work: Pictures through the ages

After looking carefully at this comic strip, try to:

1) Describe it in detail: Who? Where? When? What? What is the main character looking at in each picture? Why?

2) Compare this woman's life to that of Baba Fule. What are the similarities and the differences?

3) What are your feelings when looking at these pictures? Do they reflect reality or are they a caricature? Is the message optimistic or pessimistic? Why?

Useful functions

CAUSE — COMPARISON — DESIRE AND WISHES — DURATION — OBLIGATION.

Useful vocabulary

3. THE BODY AND ITS ACTIVITIES — 5. EMOTIONS — 7. FEELINGS AND APPRECIATION — 8. JUDGEMENTS AND EVALUATION — 11. HUMAN COMMUNITIES.

Posy SIMMONS, *Cosmopolitan*, Sept. 83.

2. Oral or written work: The man without an ear

Let us imagine that Baba Fule tells the young man one of his adventures when he was young: One day, he lost one of his ears ...

Finish the story, giving as many details as you can: Who was he with? Was he alone? What time of the year was it? What was the weather like? What was he doing? Why? What happened? How did it happen? Why? What did people say? How did they react? etc.

Useful functions

CAUSE — INTENTION — PURPOSE — REPORTING — SURPRISE.

Useful vocabulary

1. LIGHT, SOUNDS AND THE SENSES — 2. LANDSCAPES — 3. THE BODY AND ITS ACTIVITIES — 5. EMOTIONS.

3. Written work: The life story of Baba Fule

As you know from the introduction to the text *Baba Fule,* the writer is a student who intends to write the life story of Baba Fule. What will the first page of this biography look like? Write this page in the first person (250 to 350 words).

Hints: There are several possible ways of beginning a story like this. You can:
— Give the reasons for your choice of Baba Fule.
— Start right in the middle of a dialogue between Baba Fule and yourself, and then write a flashback to explain where you both are, what you are doing, why, etc.
— Start the story on the road to Baba Fule's village and explain why you are on this road.
— Start on the day the book is published.

Useful functions

They will depend on the way you decide to start the story, but you will probably need: ADMIRATION — CAUSE — INTENTION — PURPOSE — REPORTING.

Useful vocabulary

Here again, it will depend on your choice of a beginning ... Among the many possible chapters: 1. LIGHT, SOUNDS AND THE SENSES — 2. LANDSCAPES — 3. THE BODY AND ITS ACTIVITIES — 4. PEOPLE, THEIR WAYS AND CHARACTERS — 5. EMOTIONS — 7. FEELINGS AND APPRECIATION.

4. Translation

1 - Dis-moi ce que tu lis et je te dirai qui tu es.
2 - Partir en vacances maintenant serait bien sûr très agréable, mais ce serait beaucoup trop cher.
3 - Il continua à parler de ses enfants.
4 - Baba Fule me dit qu'il avait onze enfants, dont huit étaient encore vivants, et qu'eux-mêmes avaient autant d'enfants que lui.
5 - Autrefois, je ne pouvais pas me permettre d'acheter une bicyclette! Aujourd'hui, j'ai trois Rolls...
6 - Si cela avait été possible, est-ce que tu aurais quitté le village?
7 - Je l'aime encore beaucoup, mais je suis seule et je dois d'abord m'occuper de moi.
8 - De nos jours, n'importe qui peut aller à l'école.
9 - Je n'ai jamais vu un aussi mauvais film.
10 - Tout ce que j'achète est fabriqué à Hong Kong.

3. Dead letter

Laverty stepped through[1] the open French windows[2] and crossed the carpet silently until he stood behind the gray-haired man working at the desk. "Hello, Congressman[3]." he said.

Congressman Quinn turned his head and then rose shakily[4] as he saw the revolver Laverty was pointing at him. "Laverty," he said. "Don't be a fool."

Laverty grinned[5]. "I told you I'd do this someday. I've waited four years. It's safe[6] now."

"You won't get away with it[7], Laverty. I left a letter, a letter to be delivered in case I'm ever killed."

Laverty laughed. "You're lying, Quinn. You couldn't have written such a letter without incriminating yourself by telling my motive. Why, you wouldn't want me tried[8] and convicted[9]—because the truth would come out, and it would blacken your name forever."

1. to step through: *passer par*
2. French window: *porte-fenêtre*
3. Congressman (U.S.): *député (= membre du Congrès)*
4. shakily: *en tremblant*
5. to grin: *sourire*
6. safe: *sans risques*
7. You won't get away with it (pop.): *Vous ne vous en tirerez pas comme ça*
8. to try: *juger*
9. to convict: *condamner*

Laverty pulled the trigger[10] six times.

He went back to his car, drove over a bridge to rid[11] himself of the murder weapon[12], then home to his apartment and to bed.

He slept peacefully until his doorbell rang. He slipped on a bathrobe, went to the door and opened it.

His heart stood still[13], and stayed that way.

The man who had rung Laverty's doorbell had been surprised and shocked, but he had done the right thing. He had stepped over Laverty's body into the apartment and had used the phone there to call police emergency[14]. And he had waited.

Now, Laverty having been pronounced dead by the emergency squad[15], the man was being questioned by a lieutenant of police.

"Your name?" the lieutenant asked.

"Babcock. Henry Babcock. I had a letter to deliver to Mr. Laverty. This letter."

The lieutenant took it, hesitated a moment, and then opened and unfolded[16] it. "Why, it's just a blank sheet of paper."

"I don't know about that, Lieutenant. My boss, Congressman Quinn, gave me that letter a long time ago. My orders were to deliver it to Laverty right away if anything unusual ever happened to Congressman Quinn. So when I heard on the radio—"

"Yes, I know. He was found murdered late this evening. What kind of work did you do for him?"

"Well, it was secret, but I don't suppose the secret matters now. I used to take his place for unimportant speeches and meetings he wanted to avoid[17]. You see, Lieutenant, I'm his double."

Fredric BROWN, *Nightmares and Geezenstacks*, (1961),

10. trigger: *gachette*
11. to rid oneself of (rid, rid): *se débarrasser de*
12. weapon: *arme*
13. to stand still (stood, stood): *s'immobiliser*
14. police emergency: *police secours*
15. emergency squad: *brigade d'urgence*
16. to unfold: *déplier*
17. to avoid: *éviter*

MAIN TOPICS

1 Who are the various characters? Try to sum up the story very briefly. Where does the story take place (several places)? When does the story take place?

2 Congressman Quinn: What can you imagine about his life? What can you guess about his character as seen in the story?

3 Laverty: Who is he (job, life, etc.)? Try to guess the reasons for his revenge. What are / were his relationships with Quinn? What can be imagined about Quinn's and Laverty's pasts?

4 Henry Babcock: Who is he? What part does he play in the story? In Quinn's life?

5 What are *your* feelings at the end of the story? Is it a moral or an immoral ending?

6 Fredric Brown and suspense: What is suspense? How does the writer create it? Does it work on the reader? How?

Useful functions

DESIRE AND WISHES — PAST — PROBABILITY — REPROACH.

Useful vocabulary

4. PEOPLE, THEIR WAYS AND CHARACTERS — 5. EMOTIONS — 8. JUDGEMENTS AND EVALUATION.

A few guidelines

1

→ ***"Laverty stepped ... / The man who had rung ..."*** (Gr: **8,** § 2a - **11,** § 6)

Using the preterite and the pluperfect, and with the help of the text, imagine Henry Babcock's testimony to the police. You must give as many details as you can about the reasons why Babcock went to Laverty's, what he did, what he saw, what he did when he found the body, why, etc.

When I heard on the radio that Congressman Quinn ...

2

→ ***"I told you I'd do this someday."*** (Gr: **17,** § 3 - **8,** § 3e)

Now, here is the second part of Henry Babcock's testimony ... Babcock, who has an extraordinary memory, remembers the exact circumstances in which he got the letter. It was a phone call from Quinn ...

QUINN: *Babcock? Quinn speaking ...*

BABCOCK: *Oh! Hello, Mr. Quinn. How are you? I ...*

QUINN: *I have no time to lose, Babcock. I want you to listen carefully. I'm going to send you a letter. You'll probably get it in a couple of hours because I'll have it brought to you by a speed cop ...*

BABCOCK: *But what ...*

QUINN: *I asked you to listen, didn't I? When you receive this letter, I don't want you to open it. You must keep it in a safe place. If anything unusual ever happens to me, I want you to deliver this letter personally, I repeat personally, to Mr. Laverty, 24 Prospect Street ...*

BABCOCK: *Sorry to interrupt, Mr. Quinn, sir, but I don't know where Prospect Street is ... You see, I'm new in Washington D.C., and ...*

QUINN: *Come on, Babcock! You'll have to find it! That's part of your job! Anyway, it'll be easy, it's near Georgetown University.*

BABCOCK: *All right, Mr. Quinn ... But what do you mean by "anything unusual"? You don't mean ...*

QUINN: *"Anything unusual" means if I ever have an accident, or if I die in strange circumstances, or anything like that ... Don't try to find out more than you need to, Babcock. That'll be all.*

BABCOCK: *All right, sir. Am I to call you when I receive this letter?*

QUINN: *Yes. Call me as soon as you get it. So long, Babcock, and ... thank you ...*

BABCOCK: *Good bye, sir. And ... er ... I hope I'll never have to deliver this letter!*

Babcock remembers this telephone conversation perfectly and repeats it to the police.

One day, I received a phone call from Mr. Quinn. I asked him ... he told me that ... and that ...

3 → ***"I used to take his place ..."*** (Gr: **8,** § 2c)

Imagine all the things Babcock used to do for Congressman Quinn and will no longer do because of his boss's death.

I used to take his place for unimportant speeches.
I used to replace him at meetings he wanted to avoid.
I used to ...

4 → ***"... in case I'm ever killed. / ... having been pronounced dead ... / ... was being questioned ... / He was found murdered ..."*** (Gr: **14,** §§ 1, 2)

→ ***"You couldn't have written such a letter ..."*** (Gr: **9,** § 11)

→ ***"... without incriminating ... / ... by telling ..."*** (Gr: **20,** § 3)

→ ***"... you wouldn't want me tried and convicted ..."*** (Gr: **19,** § 1 - **14,** § 6)

FOLLOW-UP WORK

1. Translation

1 - Lorsque je venais ici, il y avait des arbres partout. Maintenant, il y a des gratte-ciel.
2 - Ils n'auraient pas pu entrer dans la maison sans qu'on les voie.
3 - Je t'ai dit hier que je lui parlerais, et je le ferai.
4 - Si jamais tu voyais quoi que ce soit d'anormal, téléphone-moi.
5 - Je ne voudrais pas qu'il soit condamné sans être entendu auparavant.
6 - On l'a trouvé assassiné.

2. Written work: Congressman Quinn's last letter

Let us suppose that Quinn actually left a real letter, a kind of last will to be opened after his death if ever he died in strange circumstances. In this letter, Quinn decided to tell the whole truth about his past, his relationship with Laverty, why Laverty wanted to kill him, etc. Try to write this letter ...

Useful functions

DETERMINATION — INCAPACITY — OBLIGATION — PAST — REGRET.

Useful vocabulary

4. PEOPLE, THEIR WAYS AND CHARACTERS — 5. EMOTIONS — 7. FEELINGS AND APPRECIATION — 8. JUDGEMENTS AND EVALUATION — 9. SOCIAL ATTITUDES.

3. Written or oral work: A newspaper article

After they found Congressman Quinn's dead body, the police gave a short press conference to tell the journalists about the crime and its circumstances (remember that they know nothing about Laverty's part in the crime). You were a journalist at this press conference and you have to write a short article on the event.

Hints: Do not forget to give a few details about Quinn himself, his life and political career. You should also try to imagine some of the reasons why he was murdered.

This activity might well take the form of an interview with the Chief of the Police. In that case, it will be oral work which you will have to prepare in groups.

Useful functions

PAST — PROBABILITY — REGRET — REPROACH — SURPRISE.

Useful vocabulary

5. EMOTIONS — 7. FEELINGS AND APPRECIATION — 8. JUDGEMENTS AND EVALUATION.

4. Written or oral work: A strange story

For this activity, you can work either in groups or individually.

After looking at the picture very carefully, imagine a complete story which will cover the following points:

— Where does the scene take place?
— Who are the two characters?
— What are they doing?
— What is the link between the characters?
— What are the objects on the table and what will they be used for?
— What happened just before this scene?
— What will happen just after this scene?
— What title could be given to this story?

You should also describe and analyse the artist's use of light and darkness, perspective, etc.

Last (but not least), try to guess what this picture was originally intended for.

Useful functions

COMPARISON — CONTRAST AND CONTRADICTION — GETTING S.O. TO DO S.THING — INTENTION — PROBABILITY.

Useful vocabulary

1. LIGHT, SOUNDS AND THE SENSES — 3. THE BODY AND ITS ACTIVITIES — 4. PEOPLE, THEIR WAYS AND CHARACTERS — 7. FEELINGS AND APPRECIATION — 8. JUDGEMENTS AND EVALUATION.

5. Written or oral work: Do-it-yourself detective story

In groups, collectively or individually, make up your own detective story. Look at the 8 pictures, you will find all the classic ingredients. Now, you just have to mix these ingredients to your taste... The only rule: you must use all the elements which are given in the pictures.

Hints: Here are a few words you might need: clue: *indice* — confidence trickster: *escroc* — forgery: *faux* — greed: *convoitise* — smash and grab: *cambriolage (en brisant une devanture).*

Useful functions

CAPACITY — CAUSE — DESIRE AND WISHES — GETTING S.O. TO DO S.THING — INCAPACITY — INTENTION — PURPOSE — QUANTITY.

Useful vocabulary

1. LIGHT, SOUNDS AND THE SENSES — 3. THE BODY AND ITS ACTIVITIES — 4. PEOPLE, THEIR WAYS AND CHARACTERS — 5. EMOTIONS — 12. TOWNS, SMALL AND LARGE.

1

2

3

4

5

6

7

8

4. Escaping poverty

My mother only had an eighthgrade[1] education and was working as a domestic when she died at age 59, but she believed the system could work, even for blacks, if you prepared yourself. “Play by the rules,” she would say.

It was sound[2] advice, though I had my doubts at times in the ’60s when I was going through high school and college. We had no real role models for professional life.

The most I hoped for then was to be an electrician, but I discovered in high school that unions[3] offered few openings to blacks. So I dared[4] to dream about college. My mother supported me, but she was realistic: “Where will the money come from?”

Money was always a problem in our house. We didn’t live in misery, but there were some bad days, especially during my early childhood when we were on public assistance.

Toward the end of the month, money would run out. In winter, that might mean that my mother couldn’t afford to buy the 5-pound bags of coal for the furnace[5] of our row house[6]. I can remember an instance[7] when three of us youngsters shared[8] a single potato.

Toys were often things we made ourselves, and we would spend hours playing in the woods near the project[9] or at a nearby dump[10].

I got through college and law school[11] by seeking[12] loans[13] and scholarships[14].

But I also worked—continuously—at many jobs. I started my freshman year[15] at Delaware State[16] working at the Chrysler

1. eighth grade (U.S.): *troisième*
2. sound: *judicieux*
3. union: *syndicat*
4. to dare: *oser*
5. furnace: *poêle*
6. row house: *pavillon jumelé*
7. an instance when: *dans ce contexte, une fois où* (instance: *exemple*)
8. to share: *partager*
9. project: *cité*
10. dump: *décharge*
11. law school: *faculté de droit*
12. to seek (sought, sought): *chercher*
13. loan. *prêt*
14. scholarship: *bourse*
15. freshman year (U.S.): *première année d’étude*
16. Delaware State (University): *Université du Delaware*

17. plant: *usine*
18. shift: *dans ce contexte, temps de travail*
19. besides: *en plus*
20. to apply: *poser sa candidature*
21. to hitchhike: *faire de l'auto-stop*
22. bar: *barreau*
23. attorney: *avoué*
24. practice: *clientèle*
25. school board: *bureau scolaire (chargé de l'administration des écoles publiques d'une ville)*
26. to hire: *engager*
27. tough: *dur*

plant[17] in Newark, Del. When my shift[18] was over at midnight or later, I'd drive—half asleep—to Dover for early-morning classes.

I had plenty of encouragement along the way. Besides[19] my mother, there was a Delaware State professor, who happened to be white. He convinced me that a law career was possible and assisted me in applying[20] to Rutgers University Law School.

Law school was harder than I ever thought, and the people I met there were different from those I grew up with. There were kids who had spent summers in Europe or hitchhiking[21] around the country.

But I survived. In 1973, another lawyer and I became the first blacks to be admitted to the Delaware bar[22] since 1959. I started my law firm in 1981—one of only a half-dozen black attorneys[23] in the entire state with their own practice[24].

Now, I have more than I ever dreamed of. I earn a very comfortable living, own a nine-room house in a nice neighborhood and three cars. My twin boys have a life that is Disneyland compared with my childhood.

Yet I still feel at home visiting the old neighborhood. I serve on the school board[25] there, have represented the poor and hired[26] them to work in my law office.

Things have changed in the project, though. I see far more drugs, crime and vandalism—and less respect for adults and teachers.

Poor kids now have a tougher[27] time than I did. Those well-paying auto jobs are gone, and many youngsters won't work in fast-food places, though I don't know why. The money would give them some independence.

George E. EVANS, in *U.S. News & World Report*, March 26, 1984.

MAIN TOPICS

1 The story of George E. Evans: Sum up what you learn about his childhood, his student years, his life today.

2 George E. Evans' mother: What sort of woman was she? What part did she play in his life?

3 *"We had no real role models for professional life."*... What does this mean? What does it reveal about a young Black's life in the 1960's in the U.S.A.?

4 What can you imagine about George E. Evans' character? Why did he choose this particular job?

5 With the help of the text, compare a young Black's life in the 1960's and today. What has changed? Why?

6 George E. Evans' experience: Would you say it is exceptional or typical? Why?

7 What do you know about the origin of George E. Evans' problems in particular and of the Black problem in the U.S.A. in general? What do you know of the Blacks' struggles in the 1950's, the 1960's and today? Are there the same problems in France or are they different? How? Why?

Useful functions

CAPACITY — COMPARISON — DESIRE AND WISHES — INCAPACITY — OBLIGATION.

Useful vocabulary

4. PEOPLE, THEIR WAYS AND CHARACTERS — 7. FEELINGS AND APPRECIATION — 8. JUDGEMENTS AND EVALUATION — 9. SOCIAL ATTITUDES — 11. HUMAN COMMUNITIES.

A few guidelines

1

→ ***" ... she would say. / ... money would run out. / ... we would spend hours ... / ... I'd drive ...".*** (Gr: **9,** § 9)

With the help of the text and using *your* own imagination, try to guess a few more things which happened regularly during George E. Evans' youth and student years. Complete the following sentences, adding as many things as you can think of, and using the following pattern:

When there was no money in the house, we would eat only potatoes, we would ..., my mother would ...

Hints: We didn't have toys, so we ...
At the nearby dump, we ...
In winter, we ...
When I was both a student and a car worker, I ...
When I was at Rutgers University Law School, I ...

2

→ ***"We had no real role models ... / ... unions offered few openings ... / ... I worked at many jobs. / I had plenty of encouragement ..."*** (Gr: **2,** §§ 1d, 2)

Before doing the following exercise, you must remember that:

- **no** / **not any** = pas de :

  We had no real role models.
  We didn't have any role models.

- **(very) few** / **(very) little** = (très) peu de :

  Unions offered few openings.
  There was little work for Blacks.

- **many** / **plenty of** = beaucoup de / plein de :

  I worked at many jobs.
  I had plenty of encouragement.

Now, describe George E. Evans' youth and that of his children, using the following pattern:

George's mother had very little money. George had no toys, he ...
George's children have no problems, they have plenty of food, they ...

3

→ ***"Law school was harder than I ever thought ... / I have more than I ever dreamed of. / I see far more drugs, less respect ... / Poor kids have a tougher time than I did."*** (Gr: **7,** § 1)

Using *more, -er* and *less* as often as possible, compare:

George E. Evans' youth and that of his children.
Black teenagers today and in the 1960's.
Black and white students at Rutgers University Law School.
The life of George E. Evans' mother and that of his wife.
Black and white teenagers today.
Your youth and that of George E. Evans.

4

→ ***" ... she believed the system could work ..."*** (Gr: **17,** § 3 - **8,** § 3e)

→ ***" ... there were some bad days ... / The money would give them some independence."*** (Gr: **2,** § 1d)

→ ***" ... we would spend hours playing in the woods ..."*** (Gr: **9,** § 9 - **20,** § 3)

→ ***"I got through college by seeking loans ..."*** (Gr: **20,** § 3)

→ ***"... the people I met there were different from those I grew up with."*** (Gr: **13,** §§ 1, 5)

→ ***"Yet I still feel at home ..."***

1. Translation

1 - Je croyais pouvoir obtenir du travail très facilement, mais je me trompais ; c'était beaucoup plus difficile que ce que j'avais pensé.
2 - Je ne peux pas me permettre d'acheter une nouvelle voiture ; j'ai trop peu d'argent.
3 - Quand elle était plus jeune, elle avait si peu d'amis qu'elle passait des journées entières à jouer toute seule dans sa chambre.
4 - Ces gens sont-ils vraiment tellement différents de ceux avec qui tu sors habituellement ?
5 - Je persiste à croire que ce n'est pas en restant chez toi que tu trouveras des amis.

2. Written work: A letter of application

When he applied to Rutgers University Law School, George E. Evans had to write a letter of application in which he had to tell everything about himself, his studies, his motives, etc. Write this letter and try to be as convincing as possible. Remember that you are a Black in the late 1960's and that there were very few Blacks admitted into Universities ...

Useful functions

CAPACITY — CONDITION AND HYPOTHESIS — DESIRE AND WISHES — INTENTION — PURPOSE — REQUESTS.

Useful vocabulary

7. FEELINGS AND APPRECIATION — 8. JUDGEMENTS AND EVALUATION — 9. SOCIAL ATTITUDES — 11. HUMAN COMMUNITIES — 14. EDUCATION AND SCIENCES.

3. Written or oral work: Mother and son

How will George announce to his mother that he has passed the final exam at Rutgers University Law School and will become the first Black *"to be admitted to the Delaware bar since 1959"?*

There are several possible ways of doing this. Among others:

1) You can imagine and write both George's letter to his mother and her answer.

2) You can imagine a telephone conversation between George and his mother just after the results of the exam.

3) You can imagine George's visit to his mother in her miserable row house to bring her the good news.

Useful functions

ADMIRATION — ADVICE — FUTURE — INTENTION — SURPRISE.

Useful vocabulary

3. PEOPLE, THEIR WAYS AND CHARACTERS — 5. EMOTIONS — 7. FEELINGS AND APPRECIATION — 8. JUDGEMENTS AND EVALUATION.

4. Written or oral work: ***"I have represented the poor ..."***

In this photograph, you can see Mr. X... and his family. For six years now, he has been living in this miserable shack. Although he has repeatedly and desperately applied for an apartment in a project run by Town Hall, he has still received no answer. As a last resort, he calls George E. Evans for help. You can work along several possible lines:

1) Imagine the kind of letter that Mr. X... would write to George E. Evans to ask him for legal help.

2) Imagine that Mr. X... has called at George E. Evans' office. What kind of conversation would they have?

3) Imagine what George E. Evans could say to the official in charge of the projects run by Town Hall, to convince him (or her) to give or allocate an apartment to Mr. X...

Hints: Before starting any of these activities, you should first establish Mr. X...'s identity card: name, age, job (if any), professional position, salary (if any), family status, etc.

Useful functions

ADVICE — INCAPACITY — REFUSAL — REPROACH — REQUESTS.

Useful vocabulary

1. LIGHT, SOUNDS AND THE SENSES — 4. PEOPLE, THEIR WAYS AND CHARACTERS — 8. JUDGEMENTS AND EVALUATION — 9. SOCIAL ATTITUDES — 12. TOWNS, SMALL AND LARGE.

UNIT 4

1. “Your attention please …”

A sudden silence hit the Earth. For a while nothing happened.

The great ships hung motionless in the sky, over every nation on Earth. Motionless they hung, huge[1], heavy, steady[2] in the sky, a blasphemy against nature. Many people went straight into shock as their minds tried to encompass[3] what they were looking at.

And still nothing happened.

Then there was a slight whisper[4], a sudden spacious whisper of open ambient sound. But there was no concert, no music, no fanfare, just a simple message. *‘People of Earth, your attention please,’* a voice said, *‘this is Prostetnic Vogon Jeltz of the Galactic Hyperspace Planning Council. As you will no doubt be aware*[5]*, the plans for development of the outlying*[6] *regions of the Galaxy require the building of a hyperspatial express route through your star system, and regrettably your planet is one of those scheduled*[7] *for demolition. The process will take slightly less than two of your Earth minutes. Thank you.’*

1. huge: *énorme*
2. steady: *stable*
3. to encompass: *dans ce contexte, saisir*
4. slight whisper: *léger murmure*
5. to be aware: *être au courant*
6. outlying: *extérieur*
7. to schedule: *programmer, prévoir*

8. PA = Public Address: *(système de) sonorisation*
9. to settle on: *s'emparer de*
10. gathered: *assemblé*
11. to sprout: *surgir*
12. to flee (fled, fled): *s'enfuir*
13. chart: *tableau*
14. to be on display: *être exposé*
15. to lodge a complaint: *porter plainte*
16. to make a fuss: *faire des histoires*
17. to drift off: *s'évanouir*
18. hatchway: *écoutille*
19. to man: *faire fonctionner*
20. to plead: *plaider*
21. on behalf of: *au nom de*
22. to slam: *claquer*
23. for Heaven's sake: *pour l'amour du ciel*
24. to bother: *se soucier*
25. that's your own lookout: *cela ne regarde que vous*
26. beam: *rayon*
27. ghastly: *épouvantable*

The PA[8] died away.

Uncomprehending terror settled on[9] the watching people of Earth. The terror moved slowly through the gathered[10] crowds. Panic sprouted[11] again, desperate fleeing[12] panic, but there was nowhere to flee to.

Observing this, the Vogons turned on their PA again. It said:

'There's no point in acting all surprised about it. All the planning charts[13] and demolition orders have been on display[14] in your local planning department in Alpha Centauri for fifty of your Earth years, so you've had plenty of time to lodge any formal complaint[15] and it's far too late to start making a fuss[16] about it now.'

The PA fell silent again and its echo drifted off[17] across the land. The huge ships turned slowly in the sky with easy power. On the underside of each a hatchway[18] opened, an empty black square.

By this time somebody somewhere must have manned[19] a radio transmitter, located a wavelength and broadcast a message back to the Vogon ships, to plead[20] on behalf of[21] the planet. Nobody ever heard what they said, they only heard the reply. The PA slammed[22] back into life again. The voice was annoyed. It said:

'What do you mean you've never been to Alpha Centauri? For heaven's sake[23] mankind, it's only four light years away you know. I'm sorry, but if you can't be bothered[24] to take an interest in local affairs that's your own lookout[25]. Energize the demolition beams[26].'

Light poured out of the hatchways.

'I don't know,' said the voice on the PA, *'apathetic bloody planet, I've no sympathy at all.'* It cut off.

There was a terrible ghastly[27] silence.

There was a terrible ghastly noise.

There was a terrible ghastly silence...

Douglas ADAMS, *The Hitchhiker's Guide to the Galaxy* (1979),

MAIN TOPICS

1 When and where does this story take place? Who are the main characters? Try to sum up this text in a few words.

2 The Vogons: What can you guess about them? Try to imagine their physical appearance, clothes, ships, way of life, social and political system.

3 What are the Vogons' feelings and attitudes towards the people of the Earth throughout the story? How can they be explained?

4 Draw a parallel between the Vogons' language and words and the reactions of the people of the Earth. Where is the irony?

5 The people of the Earth: What are their various feelings and reactions? Are they the same throughout the whole story? Why?

6 Would you say that such a story is purely fictional or is it somehow plausible? Imagine in what circumstances it could occur. How would you feel and react?

Useful functions

COMPARISON — CONTRAST AND CONTRADICTION — INCAPACITY — INTENTION — OBLIGATION — PROBABILITY.

Useful vocabulary

1. LIGHT, SOUNDS AND THE SENSES — 4. PEOPLE, THEIR WAYS AND CHARACTERS — 5. EMOTIONS — 7. FEELINGS AND APPRECIATION.

A few guidelines

1 → ***"... as their minds tried to encompass what they were looking at."*** (Gr: **8,** §§ 2a, 2 b)

In the following summary of the text, put each verb in brackets either into the simple past *(their minds tried)* or the progressive past *(they were looking at).*

The people *(walk)* in the streets when they *(see)* spaceships hanging in the sky. First, they *(try)* to understand what *(happen),* but suddenly, as they *(watch)* the ships, they *(hear)* a voice telling them that they would be destroyed. At the beginning, they *(not - grasp)* what the voice *(talk)* about, but when they *(understand),* they *(start)* running in all directions ...

2 → ***"... somebody somewhere must have manned a radio transmitter ..."*** (Gr: **9,** § 5)

Try to imagine the Vogons' probable scientific achievements up to now. Use the following pattern:

The Vogons must have explored several planets.
They must have ...

3 → ***"The charts have been on display for fifty years ... / ... you've had plenty of time ... / ... you've never been to Alpha Centauri?"*** (Gr: **11,** §§ 2, 4)

Are we as advanced as the Vogons?... Draw up a list of Man's main scientific achievements in this century. Use the following pattern:

Men have walked on the Moon.
They have launched several space shuttles.
They have eliminated smallpox, etc.

4 → ***"... nothing happened ... / ... over every nation ... / ... there was no concert ... / ... there was nowhere to flee to. / There's no point in acting ... / ... to lodge any formal complaint ... / ... somebody somewhere must have manned ... / Nobody ever heard ... / ... I've no sympathy at all."*** (Gr: **2,** §§ 1d, 3 - **5,** § 7)

Using *every, some, any, no* and their compounds *(-body, -where, -thing),* fill in the blanks in the following dialogue between Captain Krats and Lieutenant Nehoc, two Vogons. This dialogue takes place just after the destruction of the Earth.

KRATS: *I think we've destroyed ____. Look at your screen, Nehoc. Does it show ____ life on the Earth? Can you see ____ ____?*

NEHOC: *Let me see ... No ... The scanner says there's ____ life remaining on what was the Earth. Anyway, Captain, I don't see how ____ could have escaped! They had ____ to go!*

KRATS: *That's right. A very inferior race ... They had ____ spaceships, ____ rockets. They couldn't possibly go ____. ____ could have saved them.*

NEHOC: *Anyhow, even if there were ____ human beings still alive, they wouldn't survive long!*

KRATS: *True! The Earth has burst into millions of meteorites and ____ one of these meteorites is now flying out into space.*

NEHOC: *Captain ...*

KRATS: *Yes, Nehoc? What is it?*

NEHOC: *Has ____ told you ... I mean, does ____ know if we still have ____ planets to destroy for the express route?*

KRATS: *I can't tell you ____, Nehoc. It'll depend on the Council's decision. Why are you asking?*

NEHOC: *Well, you see ... I'm a bit puzzled. When I joined the Galactic Navy, ____ twenty years ago, ____ told me I'd have to destroy whole planets ... And I feel that ...*

KRATS: *Your feelings are of ____ importance, Lieutenant Nehoc! You are to obey ____ order given by the Council! Is that clear, Lieutenant?*

NEHOC: *Yes, Captain.*

KRATS: *Have you got ____ to add, Lieutenant?*

NEHOC: *No, Captain.*

KRATS: *Very well, Nehoc. I'm glad to see you're more reasonable. Would you like ____ Schproontz? I took a bottle with me when we left. It'll cheer you up ...*

FOLLOW-UP WORK

1. Translation

1 - Il n'y avait personne dans les rues : tout le monde était rentré chez soi.
2 - Il y a maintenant plus de vingt ans qu'il habite aux États-Unis, depuis 1962 très exactement.
3 - Est-ce que quelqu'un a vu ma pipe? ... Personne? ... Quelqu'un a bien dû la voir quelque part!
4 - Quand il a commencé son discours, j'ai essayé de comprendre de quoi il parlait. Je me suis vite rendu compte que ce qu'il disait ne signifiait rien du tout!

2. Written work: *"Somebody must have manned a radio transmitter"*

Imagine the dialogue between this "somebody" and the Vogon ship. You should first imagine this "somebody"'s identity card: Who? Job? Country? How he / she managed to contact the ship, etc. You will then have him/her ask all the possible questions someone might ask in such circumstances, and the Vogons' answers, of course.

Useful functions

INTENTION — OBLIGATION — REFUSAL — REPROACH — REQUESTS — SURPRISE.

Useful vocabulary

7. FEELINGS AND APPRECIATION.

3. Oral or written work: Life on Nibrov

Before doing anything, look at the picture very carefully.

These people are on Nibrov, a small planet not far from Vogon. Either collectively, in groups or individually,

1) Describe the two Nibrovians in the picture, their clothes, their environment, what they may be doing and why. What is the function of each element of the environment?

2) Imagine what life is like on Nibrov. What sort of civilisation is it? What is their way of life? What are their resources? What are their values? What is their political, social and economic system? Why have they been spared by Vogon?

3) Imagine a short dialogue between the two Nibrovians (who speak very good English!).

Useful functions

COMPARISON — CONTRAST AND CONTRADICTION — GETTING S.O. TO DO S.THING — PROBABILITY — QUANTITY.

Useful vocabulary

2. LANDSCAPES — 3. THE BODY AND ITS ACTIVITIES — 4. PEOPLE, THEIR WAYS AND CHARACTERS — 9. SOCIAL ATTITUDES — 11. HUMAN COMMUNITIES.

2. Those were the days ...

Ralph Whitlock is having a chat with the ghost of his great-grandfather. The writer is complaining that very young children understand computers and technology better than he does.

"When I was a boy," my great-grandfather reminisced[1], "my parents sent me to a dame's school[2]. My father used to pay twopence a week for my schooling, and often enough he had a job to find that. So I didn't have many years at school. About four, I think, though of course I missed a lot of time, helping with haymaking[3], harvest[4] and so on, in summer. The dame concentrated on the basics. When I left, when I was about eleven, I could read, write, spell and do adding, subtracting, multiplying and dividing sums, and that was about all. How long do they spend at school now?"

"Oh, they start when they're four or five and carry on[5] till they're sixteen, as a rule[6]—sometimes a good deal longer if they go in for further education[7]."

"Well, there you are! I had four years at school; my children had about seven, and now your lot have eleven or twelve or a bit more. No wonder they're better educated and make you feel inadequate."

I pondered[8] this. "They can't spell," I told him sadly, thinking of some of the mistakes in the latest letter from one of my grandchildren now living overseas."

"Well, some people never can seem to learn spelling," said my great-grandfather, philosophically. "Are they good at sums?"

"No."

"I used to be quite good at sums," he reminisced. "I could do any ordinary multiplication and division in my head."

"Well, they can't. They don't even know their tables. They have pocket calculators even to do simple addition sums."

"Pocket calculators?"

"Another device[9] to make things easy for them. All they have to do is to press the right buttons and the correct answer appears."

1. to reminisce: *raconter (ses souvenirs)*
2. dame's school: *cours privé (pour enfants pauvres).*
3. haymaking: *les foins*
4. harvest: *récolte*
5. to carry on: *continuer*
6. as a rule: *en règle générale*
7. further education: *études supérieures*
8. to ponder: *méditer (sur)*
9. device: *appareil*

My great-grandfather was in a tolerant mood[10]. "Well, if they have to learn about these computers, which even you don't understand, I dare say[11] they need all the time and short cuts[12] they can get. After all, there must be some wonderful careers open to them after eleven or twelve years of that sort of education."

"For some of them," I agreed, "but half of them can't get jobs at all."

"Well, then, see how well they are equipped for leisure[13]," said this optimistic old-timer. "In the winter evenings there was nothing much to do, out on the farm where we lived, so I read all the classics, like Dickens and Scott and Thackeray, and I learned to play the old harmonium, and I taught myself shorthand[14]. I was pretty good at figures[15], so they made me secretary of the Pig Club and then Parish Clerk[16], and I was chairman of the local Liberal Party, which was strong about here in those days. Not bad for a man who had less than four years at school, eh? But I could have done with some of the opportunities these youngsters get nowadays. I did have to spend most of my life ploughing[17] fields and mucking out pigs[18] and mowing[19] grass and milking cows and castrating lambs and pressing cider under this here old appletree, after all. I wish I had had more time for other things. And I reckon[20] I would have mastered those computers, even if you can't!"

Ralph WHITLOCK, in *The Guardian*, February 19, 1984.

10. mood: *humeur*
11. I dare say: *j'imagine*
12. short cut: *raccourci*
13. leisure: *loisirs*
14. shorthand: *sténo(graphie)*
15. figure: *chiffre*
16. Parish Clerk: *clerc de paroisse (= secrétaire de mairie)*
17. to plough: *labourer*
18. to muck out pigs: *nettoyer la porcherie*
19. to mow (mowed, mown): *faucher*
20. to reckon: *penser, croire*

MAIN TOPICS

1 Draw the great-grandfather's portrait: What sort of man was he? What do we learn about his life and various activities? What does/did he believe in?

2 How far can we say that the great-grandfather was a self-made man?

3 Education in the past and nowadays: With the help of the text (and your own knowledge), compare education in the past and now. Number of years spent at school? Curriculum? Goals? Pupil-teacher relationships? The pupils' achievements? What are the great-grandfather's views on education in the past and today? What does the writer think of today's education? Is it a success or a failure? Why?

4 Would you say that this text is optimistic, pessimistic or realistic? Why?

Useful functions

CAPACITY — COMPARISON — CONCESSION — CONTRAST AND CONTRADICTION — INCAPACITY.

Useful vocabulary

4. PEOPLE, THEIR WAYS AND CHARACTERS — 6. ACTIVITIES OF THE MIND AND COMMUNICATION — 8. JUDGEMENTS AND EVALUATION — 14. EDUCATION AND SCIENCES.

A few guidelines

1 → ***"... I could read, write, spell ... / They can't spell. / I could do any multiplication ... / ... they can't. / ... half of them can't get jobs ..."*** (Gr: **9,** § 1)

Use the same pattern as the one in the example to compare what the great-grandfather could do in the past with what children can't do nowadays.

2 → ***"I wish I had had more time for other things."*** (Gr: **8,** § 2d - **11,** § 6)

The writer's great-grandfather had a very hard life. Try to imagine all his regrets, using the following pattern:

I wish my father had been richer.
I wish the dame's school had not been so expensive.
I wish ...

Hints: go to another school, go to university, have rich parents, be born in the XXth century, not live on a farm, learn foreign languages, ...

3

→ ***"... I could have done with some of the opportunities ... / ... I would have mastered those computers ..."*** (Gr: **9,** § 11b)

Imagine all the things the writer's great-grandfather would/could have done if he had been born in 1950. Use the following pattern:

He would have had a wonderful career.
He could have gone to university.
He ...

Hints: find a good job, be a great mathematician / a famous scientist / a computer expert, go up the social ladder, (not) live in a farm, (not) plough fields / muck out pigs / milk cows, have opportunities, earn a lot of money, meet interesting people, ...

4

→ ***"My father used to pay twopence ... / I used to be quite good ..."*** (Gr: **8,** § 2c)

Compare education a century ago and education today. You will contrast them by using *whereas* or *while*, according to the following pattern:

A century ago, most children used to leave school at an early age whereas today they can't leave school before they are sixteen.
A century ago, girls did not use to receive further education while today there is no difference between girls and boys.
A century ago, ...

5

→ ***"No wonder they make you feel inadequate."*** (Gr: **19,** § 1)
→ ***"All they have to do is to press the right buttons ..."*** (Gr: **10,** § 2b - **19,** § 4)
→ ***"Well, if they have to learn about these computers ..."*** (Gr: **10,** § 2b)
→ ***"... there must be some wonderful careers ..."*** (Gr: **9,** § 5)
→ ***"... these computers, which even you don't understand ... / ... they need all the time they can get ... / ... I was chairman of the Liberal Party, which was strong ... / Not bad for a man who had ... / ... some of the opportunities these youngsters get ..."*** (Gr: **13,** §§ 1, 2, 3)

FOLLOW-UP WORK

1. Translation

1 - Si mes parents avaient été plus riches, j'aurais pu quitter la ferme et je serais allé à Oxford ou Cambridge pour y étudier.
2 - J'aurais aimé avoir assez d'argent pour m'acheter une calculatrice de poche.
3 - Elle est si intelligente que lorsqu'elle parle, elle me donne l'impression que je suis stupide.
4 - Si tu dois vraiment acheter un ordinateur, prends-en un qui ne soit pas trop cher. Après tout, il doit bien y en avoir un sur le marché.
5 - Il y a vingt-cinq ans, j'étais très bon en calcul alors qu'aujourd'hui je ne sais même pas faire une addition sans ma calculatrice ...
6 - Au début du siècle, plus de la moitié des enfants ne savaient ni lire ni écrire.

2. Oral or written work: A visit to town

Let us imagine that the writer and his great-grandfather go for a walk in town. The great-grandfather asks a lot of questions about what he sees (dish-washers, video-recorders, T.V. sets, etc.). His great-grandson explains what they are. The (optimistic) great-grandfather immediately sees all the advantages of these machines whereas the (pessimistic) writer points out their drawbacks and society's failure to solve important problems. Imagine the dialogue ...

Useful functions

ADMIRATION — CAPACITY — COMPARISON — INCAPACITY — PAST — PURPOSE — SURPRISE.

Useful vocabulary

7. FEELINGS AND APPRECIATION.

3. Oral or written work: Times are changing

After looking carefully at this ad,

1) Describe it in detail: Who are these people? How old are they? Where is it situated? What are they talking about?

2) Imagine a conversation between the two characters. What is the old man advising the boy to do? Why? How does the boy react?

Useful functions

ADVICE — CAPACITY — OBLIGATION — PAST — PROBABILITY.

Useful vocabulary

3. THE BODY AND ITS ACTIVITIES — 6. ACTIVITIES OF THE MIND AND COMMUNICATION — 14. EDUCATION AND SCIENCES.

© Saudi American Bank.

4. Oral or written work: Lucky him!

After looking carefully at this ad,

1) Describe it in detail. Who are these people? Where are they? What are they doing?

2) Compare both men and their desks. What does this ad suggest? What is its aim? Who is its target?

3) Imagine you are the man on the right. What would you think or say? What would you decide? Why?

4) Imagine a short dialogue between the two men.

Useful functions

COMPARISON — CONTRAST AND CONTRADICTION — DESIRE AND WISHES — INCAPACITY — INTENTION.

Useful vocabulary

3. THE BODY AND ITS ACTIVITIES — 4. PEOPLE, THEIR WAYS AND CHARACTERS.

© Agfa Gewaert.

3. In search of[1] mother

For most of my life, I knew very little of my biological parents. They were an 18-year-old couple whose brief marriage was torn apart[2] by World War II. They lasted[3] just six months together after the young GI returned home, long enough for my birth mother to get pregnant[4]. She decided to give up[5] the baby—me—while she was still pregnant.

Naturally, I was always curious about them, especially my mother. I remember how I felt as a teenager when I looked at my birth certificate for the first time and saw my birth name. It really blew me away[6].

Not that I considered myself the least bit deprived[7]. I never felt like a secondhand[8] child. In fact, I always thought that people who go out and adopt a child give something very special. No biological parent could have loved me more than my adoptive parents have.

Still, after I got married and became pregnant, I found myself with an overwhelming[9] desire to contact my natural mother. I felt a need to complete the circle of my life.

My birth mother was getting older—if indeed[10] she was still alive—and if I wanted to find her, I'd better do it quickly. More than anything, I wanted to look her in the eye and say, "It's all right. You

1. in search of: *à la recherche de*
2. to tear apart (tore, torn): *briser*
3. to last: *rester*
4. pregnant: *enceinte*
5. to give up (gave, given): *abandonner*
6. it blew me away (to blow, blew, blown): *ça m'a soufflée*
7. to deprive: *déposséder*
8. secondhand: *d'occasion*
9. overwhelming: *irrésistible*
10. if indeed: *pour autant que*

11. to be reluctant: *rechigner*

12. to threaten: *menacer*

13. to swear (swore, sworn): *jurer*

14. expectations: *espérances*

15. to raise (U.S.) = to bring up (G.B.): *élever*

16. quest: *recherche*

17. root: *racine*

did the right thing. I'm happy. I've had wonderful parents. I understand your sacrifice."

Mom—that is, my adoptive mother—was reluctant[11] at first and didn't want to help. Even though we have a very close relationship, especially since Dad died, she felt threatened[12], perhaps a little afraid of losing me.

I talked to Mom again and again, both on visits and during long phone conversations. One day, I really opened my heart to her. "Mom, this is really important to my life," I pleaded. "Won't you help? Please?"

She agreed to "think about it." But it wasn't long before I got her return call from Illinois. "I'll do this for you," was what she said. I swear[13], that's the greatest act of courage and love my mother has ever done for me. I believe it cost her a great deal emotionally to do it.

My birth mother had moved many times. She had remarried, had children and was now a professor in California.

Mom gave me her name and phone number and told me: "She's waiting to hear from you. But don't have any expectations[14] about how it is going to be. I don't know how she's going to react."

It was an incredible phone call. We both cried. She told me all that happened in her life. It was a very sad story of a young girl who had tried to do everything right. But how was she going to raise[15] a child with no father and no family support?

Even though my quest[16] is over, I may yet become a part of another one because one of my sons, Daniel, is adopted. It won't be so easy for him to find his biological parents; he was abandoned at birth at an orphanage in India. Right now, he is not interested in his Indian background—he likes to think he looks like Michael Jackson. But one day, he may want to go back to search his roots[17]. If that time comes, we'll help in any way we can.

Carolyn DELEVITT, in *U.S. News and World Report*, June 25, 1984.

MAIN TOPICS

1 Who are the main characters? Where and when does the story take place? What do we learn about Carolyn's origins?

2 Why did Carolyn want to contact her birth mother? Try to analyse her probable feelings towards her birth mother at that time. What can we guess about her hopes and fears?

3 Try to analyse the relationships between Carolyn and her adoptive mother. What did her adoptive mother fear?

4 What do we learn about Carolyn's first phone call to her birth mother? What can we guess about its consequences?

5 Find and imagine the various reasons why Carolyn's birth mother gave up her baby. What are *your* feelings about it? Was she right or wrong? Why? Can she be forgiven or not? Why?

6 What is the narrator determined to do now? Why?

7 Adoption ... Should adoptive parents tell their children they have been adopted? Why? Why is adoption such a difficult question? What are the different problems linked to adoption, for the parents and for the children?

Useful functions

CAUSE — COMPARISON — DESIRE AND WISHES — INCAPACITY.

Useful vocabulary

4. PEOPLE, THEIR WAYS AND CHARACTERS — 5. EMOTIONS — 6. ACTIVITIES OF THE MIND AND COMMUNICATION — 7. FEELINGS AND APPRECIATION — 11. HUMAN COMMUNITIES.

A few guidelines

1

→ ***"No biological parents could have loved me more ..."*** (Gr: **9,** §§ 1, 11)

A. Use the same pattern as the one in the example to imagine what Carolyn's adoptive mother could have done to prevent her daughter from knowing her birth mother.

She could have destroyed Carolyn's birth certificate.
She could have ...

B. Carolyn eventually forgave her birth mother. But she could have blamed her for many things. Use the following pattern to imagine what she could have blamed her for:

She could have blamed her for giving her up.
She could have blamed her for ...

2

→ ***"... I'd better do it quickly."*** (Gr: **10,** § 1b)

Carolyn has talked to a friend about her intention of trying to find her biological mother. Try to imagine how this friend could advise Carolyn on what to do and what not to do. Use the following pattern. (It would be interesting to imagine Carolyn's reactions and the friend's reasons as well.)

FRIEND: *You'd better tell your mother about your intentions.*
CAROLYN: *Why?*
FRIEND: *Because ...*

3

→ ***If ... had/hadn't + past participle ... would have + past participle*** (Gr: **9,** § 11)

Try to imagine how Carolyn would have felt and what she would have done if her adoptive mother had not given her her birth mother's address. Use the following pattern:

If she hadn't given her the address, Carolyn would have tried to find it alone, she would have ...

4

→ ***Fear ... might V*** (Gr: **9,** § 3)

It is fairly easy to understand why Carolyn's mother *"was reluctant at first"* when her adoptive daughter asked her to give her the address... Try to imagine her fears, using the following pattern:

She feared Carolyn might forget her.
She feared Carolyn might ...

5

→ ***"It won't be easy for him to find his biological parents ..."*** (Gr: **18,** § 3b)

Make as many sentences as you can, using the various elements in the following columns. You will not necessarily use *all* the elements and some elements might well be used several times. It would be interesting to justify your sentence briefly.

It was It wasn't It is It isn't It will be It won't be	difficult easy possible impossible important painful necessary	for	Carolyn Carolyn's birth mother Carolyn's adoptive mother Carolyn's son an adopted child	to not to	find his/her parents. talk to her daughter/son. know who she/he is. tell her child the truth. help her son/daughter in his/her quest. get on well with his/her birth parents. get on well with her mother. forget her/his origins. compare his/her birth parents with his/her adoptive parents.

6

→ ***"... I knew very little of ... / ... both on visits and during long phone conversations. / ... it cost her a great deal ... / My mother had moved many times. / We both cried. / She told me all that happened..."*** (Gr: **2,** §§ 2, 3)

→ ***"... long enough for my mother to get pregnant."***

→ ***"... while she was still pregnant ... / ... if she was still alive ..."***

→ ***"... that's the greatest act of courage my mother has ever done for me."*** (Gr: **11,** § 3b)

→ ***"... I may become a part of another one ... / ... he may want to go back ..."*** (Gr: **9,** § 3)

FOLLOW-UP WORK

1. Translation

1 - Je n'aurais jamais pu faire cet exercice si tu ne m'avais pas aidé.
2 - Ta voiture se fait vieille ; tu ferais mieux de la montrer à un mécanicien.
3 - Si tu m'avais dit qu'elle était encore à Londres, je lui aurais téléphoné.
4 - Je suis heureux que tu sois là ; j'avais peur que tu manques ton train.
5 - C'est le plus beau cadeau que j'ai jamais reçu.
6 - Je sais que c'est très important pour toi d'avoir tous tes amis autour de toi le jour de ton anniversaire, mais ça ne me sera pas facile de venir. J'ai très peu de temps. Il se peut que je vienne, mais je ne resterai pas longtemps.
7 - Nous ne sommes pas restés assez longtemps en Angleterre pour que ma mère perde son accent français.

2. Oral or written work: Giving up Carolyn

When Carolyn's natural mother decided to give up her baby, she may have gone to an institution where she had to explain why she was giving Carolyn to them. Imagine the dialogue between Carolyn's natural mother and the person in charge of this institution.

Hints: You should try to introduce in your dialogue:
— The mother's identity card.
— Her reasons for giving up her baby.
— The reactions of the person she is speaking to.
— The consequences of the mother's decision.
— What will become of Carolyn, etc.

Useful functions

ADVICE — CAUSE — CONDITION AND HYPOTHESIS — DESIRE AND WISHES — INCAPACITY — PROHIBITION — REGRET.

Useful vocabulary

5. EMOTIONS — 7. FEELINGS AND APPRECIATION — 8. JUDGEMENTS AND EVALUATION — 9. SOCIAL ATTITUDES — 11. HUMAN COMMUNITIES.

3. Oral or written work: Who am I?

"I remember how I felt as a teenager when I looked at my birth certificate for the first time ..." When she discovered that her birth name was different from that of her parents, Carolyn probably went to see her father and mother to ask them why their names were different. How did her parents react? How did they tell her the truth about her birth? How did Carolyn react?... Imagine their conversation ...

Useful functions

CAUSE — INCAPACITY — OBLIGATION — PROBABILITY — REFUSAL — REGRET — REPROACH — SURPRISE.

Useful vocabulary

4. PEOPLE, THEIR WAYS AND CHARACTERS — 5. EMOTIONS — 7. FEELINGS AND APPRECIATION — 8. JUDGEMENTS AND EVALUATION — 9. SOCIAL ATTITUDES.

4. Written work: From mother to mother

Let us imagine that several years after she had given up her baby, Carolyn's mother, then a professor in California, desperately wanted to know her child. She wrote a letter to Carolyn's adoptive mother, asking her if she could see her daughter from time to time. Of course, Carolyn's adoptive mother answered that letter. Write these two letters ...

Useful functions

CONDITION AND HYPOTHESIS — DESIRE AND WISHES — DISAGREEMENT TO CRITICISM — FUTURE — PROHIBITION — PROPOSING — REFUSAL — REGRET — REPROACH — REQUESTS.

Useful vocabulary

4. PEOPLE, THEIR WAYS AND CHARACTERS — 7. FEELINGS AND APPRECIATION — 8. JUDGEMENTS AND EVALUATION.

5. Oral or written work: "Hello, Mom? It's Carolyn ..."

"It was an incredible phone call ..." Imagine this first phone call between the mother and the daughter. You should show how embarrassed they both are at the beginning and how happy they are at the end. The mother should also try to justify herself.

Useful functions

CAUSE — INCAPACITY — OBLIGATION — PAST — REGRET — REQUESTS — SURPRISE.

Useful vocabulary

5. EMOTIONS — 7. FEELINGS AND APPRECIATION — 8. JUDGEMENTS AND EVALUATION.

4. Sisters and brothers

We were downstairs one evening after supper. Both Tom and Mother were already asleep. Sue told Julie and me that she had had the 'weirdest'[1] conversation with Tom. Sue waited for one of us to prompt[2] her.

'What did he say then?' I said wearily[3] after half a minute had gone by. Sue giggled[4].

'He told me not to tell anyone.'

'You'd better not then,' Julie said, but Sue went on, 'He came into my room and said, "What's it like being a girl?" and I said, "It's nice, why?" And he said he was *tired* of being a boy and he wanted to be a girl now. And I said, "But you can't be a girl if you're a boy," and he said, "Yes I can. If I want to, I can." So then I said, "Why do you want to be a girl?" And he said, "Because you don't get hit when you're a girl." And I told him you do sometimes, but he said, "No you don't, no you don't." So then I said, "How can you be a girl when everyone knows you're a boy?" and he said, "I'll wear a dress and make my hair like yours and go in the girls' entrance." So I said he couldn't do that, and he said yes he could, and then he said he wanted to anyway, he wants ...'

1. weird: *bizarre*
2. to prompt: *inciter à parler*
3. wearily: *d'une voix lasse*
4. to giggle: *glousser*

5. frock: *robe*

6. bloody (pop.): *vachement*

7. was gathering and shaping her anger: *laissait monter sa colère*

8. to mutter: *marmonner*

9. daft (pop.): *borné*

10. to take a deep breath (took, taken): *respirer à fond*

11. inches from: *à quelques centimètres de*

12. ugh!: *pouah!, beûûûrk!*

13. to collapse: *s'écrouler*

Sue and Julie were laughing so much now that it was not possible for Sue to continue her story. I did not even smile. I was horrified and fascinated.

'Poor little thing,' Julie was saying. 'We should let him be a girl if he wants to.' Sue was delighted. She clapped her hands together. 'He'd look so beautiful in one of my old frocks[5]. That sweet little face.' They looked at each other and laughed. There was a strange excitement in the air.

'He'd look bloody[6] idiotic,' I said suddenly.

'Yes?' Julie said coolly. 'Why do you think that?'

'You know he would ...' There was a pause; Julie was gathering and shaping her anger[7].

'Making him look stupid,' I muttered[8] when I sensed I should be silent, 'just so you can have a laugh.'

Julie spoke quietly. 'You think girls look idiotic, daft[9], stupid ...'

'No,' I said indignantly.

'You think it's humiliating to look like a girl, because you think it's humiliating to *be* a girl.'

'It would be for Tom, to look like a girl.' Julie took a deep breath[10] and her voice dropped to a murmur.

'Girls can wear jeans and cut their hair short and wear shirts and boots because it's okay to be a boy, for girls it's like promotion. But for a boy to look like a girl is degrading, according to you, because secretly you believe that being a girl is degrading. Why else would you think it's humiliating for Tom to wear a frock?'

'Because it is,' I said determinedly.

'But why?' Julie and Sue called together, and before I could think of anything Julie said, 'If I wore your trousers to school tomorrow and you wore my skirt we'd soon see who had the worse time. Everyone would point at you and laugh.' Here Julie pointed across the table, her fingers inches from[11] my nose.

'Look at him! He looks just like ... ugh![12] ... a *girl*!'

'And look at her,' Sue was pointing at Julie, 'she looks rather ... *clever* in those trousers.' My two sisters laughed so hard they collapsed[13] in each other's arms.

Ian McEWAN, *The Cement Garden*, (1978),

MAIN TOPICS

1 How many characters are involved? Who are they? When and where does the scene take place? Sum up the story briefly.

2 The conversation with Tom: Who spoke to him? When did it happen? Guess Tom's motives. What may have happened at school? At home? What solution did he find? What were his sister's reactions? How would other people react? What are Tom's views of the boys' world? And of the feminine world? True or false?

3 What is the narrator's reaction to Sue's report? Guess his reasons. Compare Tom and the narrator (age, experiences, maturity, etc.). Sum up Julie's reproaches and accusations. What is the narrator's answer?

4 What is the role of clothes, hairstyle and fashion in sex identification? In the past? Today?

5 Try to find out why some things are considered "for boys" and others "for girls": toys, jobs, attitudes, qualities and defects, hopes and expectations, career and ambition, family life, leadership in family life, in love life, in politics, etc.

Useful functions

CAPACITY — CAUSE — COMPARISON — CONDITION AND HYPOTHESIS — DISLIKING — OBLIGATION — REGRET.

Useful vocabulary

4. PEOPLE, THEIR WAYS AND CHARACTERS — 5. EMOTIONS — 6. ACTIVITIES OF THE MIND AND COMMUNICATION — 7. FEELINGS AND APPRECIATION — 8. JUDGEMENTS AND EVALUATION — 9. SOCIAL ATTITUDES — 11. HUMAN COMMUNITIES.

A few guidelines

1

→ ***"... he was tired of being a boy ..."*** (Gr: **20,** § 3d)

Use the same structure as the one in the example above and imagine Tom's dislikes. You should try to use the following expressions: *I hate ..., I can't stand ..., I can't bear ..., I dislike ..., I don't like ..., I resent ... .*

I'm tired of fighting with boys.
I hate having to wear trousers.
I can't stand ...

2

→ ***"You'd better not then ... / We should let him be a girl ... / ... I sensed I should be silent ..."*** (Gr: **10,** § 1b - **9,** § 8)

Imagine that Tom is criticized by his friends who think he should behave like a real boy. What could they tell him? Use the following pattern.

You should play Star Wars, you should ..., you shouldn't ...
You'd better not play with dolls, you'd better not ..., you'd better ...

3

→ ***"He'd look so beautiful ... / He'd look idiotic ... / You know he would ... / It would be for Tom ... / If I wore your trousers ... we'd soon see ... / Everyone would point out at you ..."*** (Gr: **9,** § 11)

Imagine what would happen (at home, in the streets, at school) if Ian (the narrator) decided to go to school wearing his sister's dress ...

4

→ ***"Both Tom and Mother ..."*** (Gr: **2,** § 3b)

→ ***"... Tom and Mother were already asleep."***

→ ***"Sue waited for one of us to prompt her."*** (Gr: **18,** § 3c)

→ ***"What's it like being a girl?"*** (Gr: **20,** § 3)

→ ***"Their looked at each other ... / ... they collapsed in each other's arms.*** (Gr: **5,** § 4)

→ ***"... it was not possible for Sue to continue her story. / ... you think it's humiliating for Tom to wear a frock?"*** (Gr: **18,** § 3b)

FOLLOW-UP WORK

1. Translation

1 - Il m'est impossible de le voir avant le mois prochain.
2 - Quel effet ça te fait d'être millionnaire?
3 - J'en ai assez de vivre dans une grande ville. Si j'habitais à la campagne, je verrais des animaux, je me promènerais dans les bois, je me sentirais mieux...
4 - Ils s'aimaient tellement qu'ils ne pouvaient vivre l'un sans l'autre.
5 - Il m'a dit qu'il ne pouvait pas aller au cinéma avec nous et que de toute façon, il avait horreur de sortir le soir.
6 - Tu ferais mieux de ne pas conduire par ce temps. Tu devrais prendre le train.
7 - A: Où sont les enfants? B: Ils sont tous les deux en train de travailler. A: Déjà au travail!
8 - J'attends que tu me dises la vérité... Tu ferais mieux de te dépêcher.

2. Oral or written work: The family circus

First, look at this cartoon very carefully. You will then:

1) Describe what you see, the various characters' actions, their probable feelings.

2) Explain what each character is dreaming of in each picture. They speak for themselves, so you should use *direct* speech.

3) Try to analyse how the pictures are related to the title: "The family circus". In your opinion, are these pictures still valid today? Would you agree with the implied criticism of the cartoonist?

© Minneapolis Tribune, March 82.

Useful functions

CAPACITY — DESIRE AND WISHES — CONDITION AND HYPOTHESIS — REGRET.

Useful vocabulary

4. PEOPLE, THEIR WAYS AND CHARACTERS — 5. EMOTIONS — 6. ACTIVITIES OF THE MIND AND COMMUNICATION — 7. FEELINGS AND APPRECIATION.

3. Oral or written work: Sisters and brothers?

After looking at these three pictures, try to compare them in order to understand what each one represents. You should try to answer the following questions: Who? Physical appearance? Style of songs? When? Audience? Message? etc.

Useful functions

COMPARISON — CONTRAST AND CONTRADICTION — DISLIKING — GETTING S.O. TO DO S.THING — LIKING.

Useful vocabulary

1. LIGHT, SOUNDS AND THE SENSES — 3. THE BODY AND ITS ACTIVITIES — 4. PEOPLE, THEIR WAYS AND CHARACTERS — 5. EMOTIONS — 7. FEELINGS AND APPRECIATION — 16. THE MEDIA.

2

1

3

UNIT 5

1. The Canterville ghost

The Otises, an American family, are travelling in Britain and have just rented a manor which is said to be haunted by the ghost of Sir Simon de Canterville.

The day had been warm and sunny; and, in the cool of the evening, the whole family went out for a drive. They did not return home till nine o'clock, when they had a light[1] supper. The conversation in no way turned upon ghosts. The subjects discussed

1. light: *léger*

were merely such as form the ordinary conversation of cultured Americans of the better class, such as the immense superiority of Miss Fanny Davenport over Sarah Bernhardt as an actress; the importance of Boston in the development of the world-soul[2]; and the sweetness of the New York accent as compared to the London drawl[3]. No mention at all was made of the supernatural, nor was Sir Simon de Canterville alluded to in any way. At eleven o'clock the family retired, and by half past all the lights were out. Some time after, Mr Otis was awakened by a curious noise in the corridor, outside his room. It sounded like the clank[4] of metal, and seemed to be coming nearer every moment. He got up at once, struck a match, and looked at the time. It was exactly one o'clock. He was quite calm, and felt his pulse, which was not at all feverish[5]. The strange noise still continued, and with it he heard distinctly the sound of footsteps. He put on his slippers, took a small oblong phial[6] out of his dressing-case, and opened the door. Right in front of him he saw, in the wan[7] moonlight, an old man of terrible aspect. His eyes were as red as burning coals[8]; long grey hair fell over his shoulders in matted coils[9]; his garments[10], which were of antique cut, were soiled and ragged[11], and from his wrists and ankles hung heavy manacles[12] and rusty[13] gyves[14].

'My dear sir,' said Mr Otis, 'I really must insist on your oiling those chains, and have brought you for that purpose a small bottle of the Tammany Rising Sun Lubricator. It is said to be completely efficacious upon one application, and there are several testimonials[15] to that effect on the wrapper[16]. I shall leave it here for you by the bedroom candles, and will be happy to supply you with more should you require it.' With these words he laid the bottle down on a marble table, and, closing his door, retired to rest.

For a moment the Canterville ghost stood quite motionless in natural indignation; then, dashing the bottle violently upon the polished floor, he fled down the corridor, uttering hollow groans[17], and emitting a ghastly[18] green light. Just, however, as he reached the top of the great oak[19] staircase, a door was flung open[20], two little white-robed figures appeared, and a large pillow whizzed[21] past his head! There was evidently no time to be lost, so, hastily adopting the Fourth Dimension of Space as a means of[22] escape, he vanished[23] through the wainscoting[24], and the house became quite quiet.

Oscar WILDE, *The Canterville Ghost* (1887).

2. soul: *âme*
3. drawl: *accent traînant*
4. clank: *cliquetis*
5. feverish: *fiévreux*
6. phial: *flacon*
7. wan: *blafard*
8. burning coals: *braises*
9. matted coils: boucles entremêlées
10. garments (lit.): *vêtements*
11. soiled and ragged: *souillé et en lambeaux*
12. manacles: *menottes*
13. rusty: *rouillé*
14. gyves (lit.): *chaînes*
15. testimonial: *témoignage*
16. wrapper: *emballage*
17. hollow groans: *grognements caverneux*
18. ghastly: *spectral*
19. oak: *chêne*
20. to fling open (flung, flung): *ouvrir brusquement*
21. to whizz: *siffler*
22. a means of: *un moyen de*
23. to vanish: *disparaître*
24. wainscoting: *lambris*

MAIN TOPICS

1 Who are the various characters? When and where does the story take place? Try to sum up the main facts of the story.

2 Describe and analyse the Otises' attitude towards the ghost. What can you imagine about their reasons for not being afraid?

3 The ghost... Describe him and imagine his past life. Why is he a ghost? What may he have done? Why must he haunt the manor?

4 Try to imagine the ghost's feelings towards the Otises.

5 The Otises... What do we learn about them? Who are they? What can you guess about their life, their social background, their characters, the reasons why they are in England?

6 What is Oscar Wilde's attitude towards the Otises?

7 List all the elements which are traditional in a ghost story (setting, atmosphere, etc.) and the elements which differ. What is the effect on the reader? What was Oscar Wilde's goal when writing this story?

Useful functions

COMPARISON — GETTING S.O. TO DO S.THING — INCAPACITY — INTENTION — PAST — PROBABILITY.

Useful vocabulary

1. LIGHT, SOUNDS AND THE SENSES — 3. THE BODY AND ITS ACTIVITIES — 4. PEOPLE, THEIR WAYS AND CHARACTERS — 5. EMOTIONS.

A few guidelines

1 → ***"The subjects discussed... / No mention was made of... / ... was alluded to... / ... was awakened... / ... were soiled... / ... was flung open ... / There was no time to be lost..."*** (Gr: **14**)

Use the passive to describe what happened to the Otises and the ghost that night.

Hints: You could build your sentences around the following verbs: wake up, disturb, hear, see, ask, give, throw, break, surprise, scare, astonish, disappoint, etc.

2 → ***"... a manor which is said to be haunted... / It is said to be efficacious..."***

Use the above pattern to imagine what was said about the Otises in the village, before their arrival. There were rumours about the husband, the wife, the daughter and the two sons.

Mr. Otis was said to be quite rich.
He was said to... / not to...

3 → ***"... I really must insist on your oiling those chains..."*** (Gr: **20**, § 3)

What else could Mr. Otis say to the ghost?

I insist on your being silent,...

4 → ***Prepositions and verbal particles*** (Gr: **12**)

After the incident, the ghost went back to his room. Look at this map of the manor and describe what he did to get there. You should use as many of the following prepositions and verbal particles as you can.

Hints: go, turn, run,...
up, from, to, into, back, in, out of, through, down, near, by.

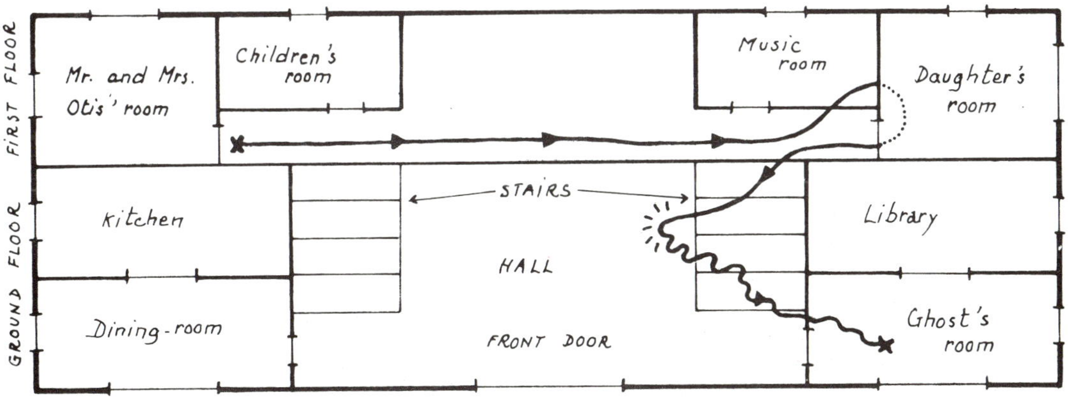

5

→ *"The Otises have just rented a manor... / I have brought you a small bottle..."* (Gr: **11,** §§ 1, 2, 3c)

→ *"... the whole family went out..."* (Gr: **2,** § 3c)

→ *"... which is said... / ... which was not at all feverish. / ... which were of antique cut..."* (Gr: **13,** §§ 1, 2, 3)

→ *"His eyes were as red as burning coals..."* (Gr: **7,** § 1c)

→ *"... two little white-robed figures..."*

FOLLOW-UP WORK

1. Translation

1 - Je viens de faire un rêve curieux.
2 - On dit de lui que c'est un des hommes les plus riches du monde.
3 - Toute la famille était là. On aborda de nombreux sujets, mais on ne fit aucune allusion à la guerre.
4 - Je n'insiste pas pour qu'il vienne tout de suite ; je sais qu'il ne le fera pas.
5 - Tu devrais aller te laver les mains : elles sont noires comme du charbon.
6 - Je viens de louer une maison qui te plaira certainement.
7 - C'est un beau bébé aux yeux bleus et aux cheveux noirs.

2. Written work: Simon de Canterville's memoirs

Let us imagine that one day Simon de Canterville decides to write his memoirs... What will they be like?

Hints: Try to imagine an answer to the following questions:
— Did he kill anyone? Why? How?
— How did he die? Why?
— When did it happen? How many centuries ago? Where?
— Why does he still haunt the manor?
— What is he looking for? When will he stop?
— What sort of life does he lead? How many people has he scared so far? How? How did they react?
— What does he complain about and what does he wish?

P.S.: The same activity might well take the form of an interview. In that case, it could be oral work either in groups or collectively. You will have to imagine the circumstances of the interview: Mr. Otis? A journalist? When? Where? Why? How?

Useful functions

CAUSE — COMPLAINING — DESIRE AND WISHES — DISLIKING — GETTING S.O. TO DO S. THING — LIKING — REGRET — REPROACH.

Useful vocabulary

1. LIGHT, SOUNDS AND THE SENSES — 3. THE BODY AND ITS ACTIVITIES — 4. PEOPLE, THEIR WAYS AND CHARACTERS — 5. EMOTIONS.

3. Oral or written work: The ghost makes plans

Once he is back in his bedroom, the ghost starts thinking... He has never been so humiliated in his long life and must get his revenge. How can he retaliate (= *riposter*)? What tricks will he play on the Otises to scare them and make them go away? Imagine his thoughts and plans...

Useful functions

CAPACITY — CONDITION AND HYPOTHESIS — DESIRE AND WISHES — FUTURE — GETTING S.O. TO DO S. THING — INTENTION — OBLIGATION.

Useful vocabulary

1. LIGHT, SOUNDS AND THE SENSES — 3. THE BODY AND ITS ACTIVITIES — 5. EMOTIONS.

4. Written or oral work: Another end to the story

Try to rewrite the story differently... Imagine it is a traditional ghost story. The characters should be very surprised, scared and panic-stricken. The ghost should be diabolical; you could insist on his happiness on seeing the Otises so frightened.

You could also imagine another end to the story: the Otises could be so fed up that they would all meet, have a long discussion about the ghost and decide to...

Useful functions

ADVICE — AGREEMENT — CONDITION AND HYPOTHESIS — DETERMINATION — DISAGREEMENT — GETTING S.O. TO DO S. THING — INCAPACITY — OBLIGATION — REFUSAL.

Useful vocabulary

1. LIGHT, SOUNDS AND THE SENSES — 3. THE BODY AND ITS ACTIVITIES — 5. EMOTIONS — 6. ACTIVITIES OF THE MIND AND COMMUNICATION — 7. FEELINGS AND APPRECIATION.

2. A speech from the Head[1]

'As far as I can see there's been no advance at all in discipline, decency, manners or morals. And do you know how I know this? Well, I'll tell you. Because I still have to use this every day.'

He brought the stick[2] round from behind his back for the boys to have a look at.

'It's fantastic isn't it, that in this day and age, in this superscientific, all-things-bright-and-splendiferous[3] age, that the only way of running this school efficiently is by the rule[4] of the cane. But why? There should be no need for it now. You lot have got it on a plate[5].

'I can understand why we had to use it back in the 'twenties and 'thirties. Those were hard times; they bred[6] hard people, and it needed hard measures to deal with[7] them. But those times bred people with qualities totally lacking[8] in you people today. They bred people with respect for a start. We knew where we stood in those

1. Head = Headmaster: *Proviseur*
2. stick: *baguette*
3. splendiferous: *merveilleux*
4. ... is by the rule of: *...est de se servir de* (rule: *règle*)
5. you've got it on a plate: *vous avez tout sur un plateau*
6. to breed (bred, bred): *engendrer*
7. to deal with (dealt, dealt): *venir à bout de*
8. lacking: *absent*

9. to chat: *bavarder*
10. thrashing: *correction*
11. honk: *coup de klaxon*
12. greasy: *gominé*
13. wheel: *volant*
14. to quote: *citer*
15. to shoot off (shot, shot): *se précipiter*
16. guts: *tripes*
17. backbone: *énergie (= colonne vertébrale)*
18. to commend you: *dont vous puissiez être fiers*
19. nothing whatsoever (= whatever): *absolument rien*
20. fodder: *pâture*
21. to wink: *cligner de l'œil*
22. to frown: *froncer les sourcils*
23. for want of: *faute de*

days, and even today a man will often stop me in the street and say "Hello Mr Gryce, remember me?" And we'll pass the time of day and chat[9], and he'll laugh about the thrashings[10] I gave him.

'But what do I get from you lot? A honk[11] from a greasy[12] youth behind the wheel[13] of some big second-hand car. Or an obscene remark from a gang—after they've passed me.

'They took it then, but not now, not in this day of the common man, when every boy quotes[14] his rights, and shoots off[15] home for his father as soon as I look at him... No guts[16]... No backbone[17]... you've nothing to commend[18] you whatsoever[19]. You're just fodder[20] for the mass media!'

The boys winked[21] at each other.

'I don't know. I just don't know.'

He turned round slowly. The boys met him with serious expressions, frowning[22] and compressing their lips as though they were trying their hardest to solve his problems.

'So for want of[23] a better solution I continue using the cane, knowing full well that you'll be back time and time again for some more...'

Barry HINES, *Kes* (1968), © Barry Hines.

MAIN TOPICS

1 Who is the main character? What is he doing? Where do you think the scene takes place? What can we guess about the reasons for the Head's speech? Who are the other characters?

2 Use the text and your imagination to draw the Head's portrait. Age? Physical appearance? Character? Values? Educational methods?

3 How do the pupils react to this speech? What can we suppose about their feelings?

4 The Head compares pupil-teacher relationships in the past and in the present: What does he say and feel about each period? Do you agree with him? Why? What differences can *you* find between education in the past and today? Methods, pupil-teacher relationships, goals, pupil-school relationships, curriculum, etc.? Would *you* have liked to be a pupil 50 or 60 years ago? Why?

5 *"You're just fodder for the mass media!":* What does the Head mean? Is it true or not? Give examples of children being "fodder for the mass media" (on TV, in the news, books, advertising, music, etc.). What are the media's goals? Why is this a new phenomenon?

6 Caning and thrashing... How does the Head justify corporal punishment? Do you agree with him? Try to list as many positive and negative aspects of corporal punishment as you can think of (for the pupils, the teachers, education in general, society at large, etc.). Would *you* be in favour of some sort of corporal punishment? Why? Do you think discipline at school should be stricter than it is today? Why?

Useful functions

COMPARISON — GETTING S.O. TO DO S. THING — OBLIGATION — PAST — PROBABILITY — PROHIBITION — REGRET — REPROACH.

Useful vocabulary

4. PEOPLE, THEIR WAYS AND CHARACTERS — 7. FEELINGS AND APPRECIATION — 8. JUDGEMENTS AND EVALUATION — 14. EDUCATION AND SCIENCES — 16. THE MEDIA.

A few guidelines

1 → ***no longer / not... any longer*** (Gr: **16,** § 4)

Draw up a list of some changes in French education over the last century. Use both *no longer* and *not... any longer* for each sentence, according to the following pattern. (You could also give your opinion about these various changes, stating whether you find them positive or negative.)

The teachers no longer thrash the pupils.
The teachers don't thrash the pupils any longer.

Hints: (leave) school at a very early age, (be) kept in after the lessons, (have) term exams, (be) afraid of asking questions, boys and girls (be) taught in different schools, boys (wear) ties at school, (bully) the new pupils, (be) given books on prize day, etc.

2

→ ***"Because I still have to use this every day."***

Imagine what the Head could reproach the pupils with, using the following pattern:

Although I asked you to work, you still don't.
Although I asked you not to smoke in the toilets, you still do.

Hints: respect your teachers, learn your lessons, do your homework, bully the young ones, stop throwing pellets at Mr. Garfield, play with the fire extinguishers, stop littering the classrooms, throw orange peel in the yard, stick chewing gum under the chairs and tables, carve obscenities on the tables, use the staff toilets, etc.

3

→ ***"... there's been no advance.../There should be no need.../... the wheel of some big car.../No guts... No backbone... you've nothing to commend you.../... you'll be back for some more..."*** (Gr: **2,** §§ 1d, 1e - **5,** § 7)

Using *some, any, no* and their compounds *(-body/-one, -thing, -where),* complete the following dialogue between two pupils.

SIMON (coming out of the Head's office and holding back his tears): *Blimey! The thrashing he gave me! I'd never...*

PETER (passing by): *What's the matter, mate? ____ wrong?*

SIMON: *It's the Head... He caught ____ of us smoking in the toilets... ____ heard him coming. He pounced on me like ____ big cat on a mouse!*

PETER: *Wasn't there ____ on the lookout outside?*

SIMON: *Course there was! But he didn't see ____ ! The Head tiptoed behind the toilets without making ____ noise, and there he was, leaving us ____ time to rush away... We were cornered, there was ____ to go!*

PETER: *How come you were the only one to get caught? Didn't he get ____ of the others?*

SIMON: *I was the one with the fag in my mouth!*

PETER: *What d'you mean?*

SIMON: *We were sharing one! The others didn't have ____ in their mouths. That's why he couldn't say ____ !*

PETER: *And so he gave you a caning...*

SIMON: *Yeah... And a good one, too...*

PETER: *In my sister's school, they don't cane____ anymore. The Headmistress says there will ____ longer be ____ corporal punishment in her school. Says she's against it.*

SIMON: *They are lucky!*

PETER: *Yeah... She says ____ child is stupid enough not to listen to reason. That's what she says.*

SIMON: *What about the kids?*

PETER: *They're all right. Of course, ____ teachers are stricter than others, but on the whole, they've got ____ problems with them.*

SIMON: *You know what? There are times I wish I were a girl...*

4

→ ***"... there's been no advance.../There should be no need..."***

→ ***"He brought the stick round from behind for the boys to have a look at."*** (Gr: **18,** § 3e)

→ ***"... the only way of running this school..."*** (Gr: **20,** § 3)

→ ***"The boys winked at each other."*** (Gr: **5,** §§ 2, 4)

→ ***"... compressing their lips as though they were trying..."*** (Gr: **8,** § 2d)

1. Translation

1 - Il n'y avait personne dans la pièce.
2 - Il me regarde comme si j'étais un monstre.
3 - Il a sorti sa nouvelle voiture pour que tout le monde l'admire.
4 - Est-ce que tu habites toujours à Chicago?
5 - Non. Je n'aime plus cette ville. Je préfère New York, mais j'ai encore beaucoup d'amis à Chicago.
6 - Tu veux encore du thé?
7 - Qu'est-ce que vous faites là! Il ne devrait y avoir personne dans cette salle de classe!
8 - Ils se regardèrent un long moment, se sourirent et coururent l'un vers l'autre.
9 - Une bonne correction... C'est ce que tu veux? C'est la seule façon de te faire travailler?

2. Written or oral work: A nonsensical school

In the small village of Tongue-in-Cheek, there is a very strange school... Just look at the school rules which are posted on the bulletin board in the hall.

THE TEN GOLDEN RULES OF TONGUE-IN-CHEEK SCHOOL

1 - Pupils are not allowed to leave the classroom during a lesson unless they have to go on an important date with a girlfriend.
2 - It is forbidden to smoke during a lesson, but pupils may offer their teachers a cigar if they happen to have a good Havana.
3 - Pupils must not invite teachers to a cheap fast food restaurant. The only invitations which will be accepted by a teacher will have to be to a luxury inn in a high-class area.
4 - Pupils are expected to know their lessons. If they do not, they will not be permitted to enter the classroom before they have given their teacher a huge home-made pudding.
5 - Pupils must be happy at school and must show everyone they are. Every morning, for five minutes, all the pupils will be required to sing nice love songs.
6 - Any pupil who cannot sing or does not trust his singing abilities will be forbidden to sing. Of course, this pupil will not be allowed to leave the classroom while the others are singing.
7 - At the end of the school year, pupils may not leave school before they have rewarded their teachers with at least one "Thank you so much, Dear Mr. X... or Mrs. Y..., you are the best teacher I have ever had or will ever have". (They can show their gratitude differently: cf. Rule 4.)
8 - Work is a serious matter and pupils have to be serious. Every pupil will be required to be serious for five minutes every day, from 9.30 to 9.35. After 9.35, he may become normal again.
9 - Eating in class is prohibited unless there is enough for everyone to have a share (including a double share for the teacher).
10 - Pupils are permitted to ignore these rules but if so, they will be severely punished (sitting in the front row for a whole year, eating one of the frogs from the school pond, etc.)

After you have read these rules,

1) List all the structures expressing *obligation, permission* and *prohibition.*

2) Add a few rules to the list, keeping in mind that this is a nonsensical school...

3) Imagine the school rules of a very strict (and normal) school, using as many of the above expressions as you can.

A few hints: be late, bring pets into class, smoke on the school premises, leave school before 4 o'clock, speak rudely to the teachers, talk during the lessons, etc.

3. Written work: Two letters...

This is the first day at school. Mr. Faraday, a young inexperienced biology teacher, is giving his first lesson to the fifth-formers, a lesson during which quite a few unexpected things happen...

Imagine and write two letters written by two different people about this lesson.

1) The first letter will be written by Mr. Faraday to his parents.

2) The second letter will be written by a pupil to one of his friends.

Hints: The same events will appear in both letters, but of course, from two different points of view: how Mr. Faraday introduced himself, the pupils' reactions and feelings, the teacher's attitude, etc.

Useful functions

DISLIKING — GETTING S.O. TO DO S. THING — INTENTION — LIKING — REQUESTS.

Useful vocabulary

3. THE BODY AND ITS ACTIVITIES — 4. PEOPLE, THEIR WAYS AND CHARACTERS — 5. EMOTIONS — 6. ACTIVITIES OF THE MIND AND COMMUNICATION — 7. FEELINGS AND APPRECIATION.

4. Written or oral work: A speech from the Head

Just for once, imagine you are the Head of a school for boys and girls from 12 to 18. It is the beginning of the year and you have to deliver a speech in front of all the pupils, teachers and staff. What will your speech be like?...

Hints: Among many possible topics, you could deal with the following ones: last year's achievements, discipline problems, the exams, the pupils' future, the various extra-curricular activities in the school, the pupils' behaviour in and out of school, the need to keep the school tidy, pupil-teacher relationships, etc.

Useful functions

ADVICE — DESIRE AND WISHES — DISLIKING — GETTING S.O. TO DO S. THING — INTENTION — LIKING — OBLIGATION — PROHIBITION — PURPOSE — REGRET — REQUESTS.

Useful vocabulary

3. THE BODY AND ITS ACTIVITIES — 4. PEOPLE, THEIR WAYS AND CHARACTERS — 6. ACTIVITIES OF THE MIND AND COMMUNICATION — 7. FEELINGS AND APPRECIATION — 8. JUDGEMENTS AND EVALUATION — 9. SOCIAL ATTITUDES — 14. EDUCATION AND SCIENCES.

3. What we are

Teenagers, of course, dress outrageously[1]. They listen to pop music, take drugs and break the law[2]. People not given to these habits may fail[3] to see the value of this most pure and well beloved lifestyle, or they may even start whining[4] about haircuts, national service and life in "their day".

Clothes and haircuts are traditional bones of contention[5] between generations. This clash was never fiercer[6] than when boys and girls started dyeing[7] their hair bright colours. Many teenagers take massive care over their appearance. ("You'd never guess it to look at them", we hear you gaily say). This is a good thing. Anyone who remembers being treated like an idiot for half his or her waking hours, for no better reason than being at a difficult age, will understand the sweet satisfaction of a secret language, a private land into which no parent or policeman will ever intrude[8].

There is such an abundance of music for youth available[9] today that it is wrong to lump[10] it all together under the heading[11] of "pop music". Whatever you want you can get it: sweet sounds for lovers; tribal rhythms made for feet; sad songs for sensitive[12] people. Music like rockabilly and soul, heavy metal and jazz funk, rock and reggae. The nation shakes[13] beneath a thousand separate rhythms, from clubs and pubs, parties and town halls[14]. The question "Has any of this music lasting[15] merit?" is surely missing the point[16]. We like it.

There's no doubt that a lot of teenage fun involves[17] breaking the law. Some laws plead[18] to be broken, for example that law which forbids a 17-year-old mother of two to accompany her 18-year-old husband into an X-rated film[19]. Also forbidden to the underage are smoking, drinking, driving, retiring to night clubs, and making love—all of which make life sweet and mysterious. As to

1. outrageously: *avec extravagance*
2. to break the law (broke, broken): *enfreindre la loi*
3. to fail (to): *ne pas arriver (à)*
4. to whine (about): *se lamenter (sur)*
5. bone of contention: *pomme de discorde*
6. fierce: *violent*
7. to dye: *teindre*
8. to intrude (into): *s'immiscer (dans)*
9. available: *disponible*
10. to lump: *réunir*
11. heading: *rubrique*
12. sensitive: *sensible*
13. to shake (shook, shaken): *vibrer*
14. town hall: *ici, salle des fêtes* (town hall: *mairie*)
15. lasting: *durable*
16. to miss the point: *être hors de propos*
17. to involve: *impliquer*
18. to plead (to): *ici, demander (à)* (to plead: *plaider*)
19. X-rated film: *film interdit aux moins de 18 ans*

20. agony: *angoisse*
21. alive and thriving: *bel et bien vivace*
22. pimples: *boutons*
23. freckles: *taches de rousseur*
24. patronage: *condescendance*

violent crime, there are just as many vicious teenagers per hundred as there are vicious adults.

This might all seem a little enthusiastic... Have no fear, teenage agony[20] is alive and thriving[21]; we still suffer from pimples[22], freckles[23], patronage[24], and frustration. But from where we stand, today's teenagers are more lively, bright, colourful, and energetic than any before them.

John HONDERICH & Ben ROGALY, in *The Guardian*, September 22, 1981.

MAIN TOPICS

1 Where is this passage taken from? Who wrote it? When? What can we guess about the two boys (social background, lives, studies, etc.) and the reasons why they wrote this article?

2 What is John and Ben's definition of a teenager? Do you agree with this definition or not? Why? What is *your* definition of a teenager (i.e. yourself)?

3 How do adults react to teenagers? Sum up their reproaches. Do you agree with them? How can their attitude be explained?

4 What do teenagers reproach adults with? Do you agree? Why?

5 According to John and Ben, how important is music in a teenager's life? What part does it play? Is it *your* idea of music?

6 List all the examples John and Ben give of law-breaking activities. According to them, what accounts for this attitude? Can you think of other possible explanations (social, economic, psychological)?

7 In conclusion... If you had been asked to, would *you* have written such an article to define what teenagers are or are not? What would *you* have written about? What would *you* have insisted upon?

Useful functions

CAUSE — DISLIKING — LIKING — PROHIBITION — REPROACH.

Useful vocabulary

4. PEOPLE, THEIR WAYS AND CHARACTERS — 7. FEELINGS AND APPRECIATION — 8. JUDGEMENTS AND EVALUATION — 9. SOCIAL ATTITUDES — 15. THE ARTS — 16. THE MEDIA.

A few guidelines

1

→ ***"Anyone who remembers being treated.../Some laws plead to be broken.../Also forbidden to the underage are smoking..."*** (Gr: **14,** §§ 1, 2)

Using the verbs *permit, allow, forbid, prohibit,* compare teenagers' lives today and in the past (60 or 70 years ago). Use the following pattern:

In the past, teenagers used to be forbidden to smoke whereas today they are allowed to smoke almost anywhere.
In the past,...

Hints: drinks, films, discos, parties, going out, boyfriends, girlfriends, holidays, school, car, motorbike, travels, etc.

P.S.: As you do this exercise, it would be interesting to discuss the positive and negative aspects of this evolution.

2

→ ***"Anyone who remembers being treated..."*** (Gr: **20,** § 3d)

What do some teenagers *resent* in adults' attitudes towards them? Give a few examples, using the following pattern:

They resent being treated like idiots.
They resent...

Hints: look down upon, ignore, misunderstand, patronise, forbid, criticise, reject, label, ask, order, ...

3

→ *... reproach s.o. with/for + V-ing - ... blame s.o. for + V-ing* (Gr: **20,** § 3d)

A. What do adults reproach teenagers with/for (blame teenagers for)? You may find a few useful hints in the following grid:

Clothes	messy, dirty, scruffy,... look, wear, buy,...
Hair	long, dirty, unkempt,... cut, shave, wash, dye,...
Music	loud, worthless, monotonous, savage,... listen to, play, love,...
Manners	rude, impolite, disrespectful,... smoke, drink, take drugs, drive,...
Language	vulgar, illiterate, cheeky,... answer back, argue,...
Character	promiscuous, disobedient, lazy, selfish, boisterous, aggressive,... work, learn, loaf about,...

B. What do teenagers often reproach adults for/with (blame adults for)?

Hints: square, conformist, intolerant, narrow-minded, boring, unimaginative, strict, aloof, patronising, condescending,...
judge, generalize, reject, despise, help, understand, ...

P.S.: In both exercises (A and B), do not forget to give a few explanations to justify and illustrate what you say.

4

→ ***"Whatever you want you can get it..."***

Using *whatever, wherever, whenever, whoever,* imagine a teenager's dreams. Use the following pattern:

I wish I could do whatever I wanted...
If only I could see whatever film I liked...

P.S.: Only *whatever* can be used both as a pronoun (i.e. alone) or as an adjective (i.e. with a noun). *Wherever, whenever and whoever* can only be used as pronouns.

5

→ ***"People may fail to see.../... they may start whining.../This might seem a little enthusiastic..."*** (Gr: **9,** § 3)

→ ***"... they start whining about haircuts.../... boys and girls started dyeing their hair.../... for no better reason than being.../... teenage fun involves breaking the law.../Also forbidden to the underage are smoking, drinking, driving, retiring to night clubs and making love..."*** (Gr: **20,** §§ 3, 4)

→ ***"This clash was never fiercer than when.../... for no better reason than being.../... there are just as many vicious teenagers as there are vicious adults./... today's teenagers are more lively than any before them."*** (Gr: **7,** §§ 1a, 3)

→ ***"You'd never guess it to look at them."***

→ ***"... a private land into which.../... that law which forbids.../... all of which make life..."*** (Gr: **13,** §§ 1, 2, 3, 5)

→ ***"... no parent will ever intrude..."*** (Gr: **11,** § 3b)

→ ***"There is such an abundance of music that it is wrong..."***

FOLLOW-UP WORK

1. Translation

1 - J'ai commencé à conduire quand j'avais 17 ans.

2 - Il a une si belle voiture que beaucoup de gens sont jaloux.

3 - Quand tu auras 18 ans, tu feras tout ce qui te plaira avec qui tu voudras.

4 - A l'entendre, on ne devinerait jamais qu'il est étranger.

5 - Personne ne m'a jamais comprise!

6 - J'irai peut-être au cinéma ce soir, je ne sais pas.
7 - Je suis allé aux États-Unis l'année dernière et maintenant, je parle anglais beaucoup mieux qu'avant.
8 - En Angleterre, on interdit aux mineurs de boire au pub.
9 - Si tu manges autant de chocolats, tu vas sûrement être malade !
10 - Les parents reprochent aux jeunes d'aujourd'hui de trop regarder la télévision.
11 - Regarde le ciel : il se pourrait qu'il pleuve.
12 - Ça ne me plaît pas du tout d'être traité comme un enfant.

2. Oral or written work: We are not a sub-species...

First, read the following article by Lois McNAY in *The Guardian*, September 22, 1981.

Now that you have read this article,

1) Try to find out what Lois reproaches adults with, and why.

2) Explain what Lois means when she says that the word teenager will never disappear *"as a lot of people would stop making a lot of money"*.

3) Compare what Lois says about adults and teenagers to what was said by John and Ben in *What we are.* You may find it useful to fill in a comparative chart of the following kind:

	John and Ben	Lois
Teenagers as seen by adults		
Adults as seen by teenagers		
What teenagers like and want		
What teenagers resent		
General tone of the article		

Useful functions

CAUSE — COMPARISON — CONTRAST AND CONTRADICTION — DESIRE AND WISHES — DISLIKING — LIKING — REFUSAL — REPROACH.

Useful vocabulary

4. PEOPLE, THEIR WAYS AND CHARACTERS — 7. FEELINGS AND APPRECIATION — 8. JUDGEMENTS AND EVALUATION — 9. SOCIAL ATTITUDES — 16. THE MEDIA.

The worst thing about being a teenager is the word "teenager". Being a teenager doesn't feel any different to being a normal person. The word teenager prevents some people from treating adolescents as young adults; in their eyes we become a kind of sub-species[1].

For a short time I was a waitress in a restaurant. The average[2] age of the staff[3] was 19, that of the clientele about 40. We, the staff, used to watch amused and slightly disgusted as overweight[4] middle-aged swingers[5], who in the light of day would claim[6] that discos were a load[7] of teenage nonsense, jerked violently around to the latest hits—as they say. If, in the eyes of adults, "teenage culture" is such a contemptible[8] thing, why, given the opportunity, do they throw themselves into it with so much enthusiasm and a lot less style?

I may be cynical, but I think it is partly due to jealousy. Some adults patronise teenagers because they are envious of their youth and because the respect they don't get from their peers[9] they demand from their juniors.

It always seems like sour grapes[10] to me, when I say something predictable[11] like "I won't get married," and adults smile knowingly[12] and say equally as predictably "you'll soon change." Whether they believe I'll change or not, doesn't matter. What they don't like is that I'm indirectly criticising their way of life. Also I'm enjoying a freedom of opinion and expression which they never had. What their "you'll soon change" actually means is: "shut up you stupid girl, you don't know what you're talking about. We know best." I don't think you would find such narrow-mindedness in an adolescent.

I would like the word "teenager" to be banned, but I suppose that will never happen, as a lot of people would stop making a lot of money.

Vocabulary: 1. sub-species: *sous-espèce* — **2.** average: *moyen* — **3.** staff: *personnel* — **4.** overweight: *trop gros* — **5.** swinger: *frimeur* — **6.** to claim: *déclarer* — **7.** load: *tas* — **8.** contemptible: *méprisable* — **9.** peer: *égal (pair)* — **10.** sour grapes: *dépit (= raisins amers)* — **11.** predictable: *prévisible* — **12.** knowingly: *d'un air entendu.*

3. Written or oral work: The generation gap?

After looking carefully at these two pictures,

1) Describe each picture in detail: characters, setting, probable place, probable time, colours, activities, ages, etc.

2) Try to answer these questions about the girls in each picture:

— What is their social background?

— What type of education did they receive?

— What do they believe in? What are their hopes?

— What are their hobbies?

— What sorts of relationships do they have with their parents and with other young people (male or female)?

— What can we guess about their future? (Marriage? Children? Attitude to men? Job? etc.).

Once again, you may find it useful to draw a comparative chart of the following kind:

	Picture 1	Picture 2
Characters		
Setting		
Place		
etc.		

Useful functions

COMPARISON — CONTRAST AND CONTRADICTION — DISLIKING — LIKING — PROBABILITY.

Useful vocabulary

3. THE BODY AND ITS ACTIVITIES — 4. PEOPLE, THEIR WAYS AND CHARACTERS — 7. FEELINGS AND APPRECIATION — 8. JUDGEMENTS AND EVALUATION — 9. SOCIAL ATTITUDES — 11. HUMAN COMMUNITIES.

4. Porgie

Porgie was in the front-room, flipping[1] the pages of his schoolbooks and looking studious. His uncle settled down[2] in his easy-chair[3], opened his paper, and lit his pipe. He reached out to put the charred[4] match in the ashtray[5], and as usual the ashtray wasn't there.

'Damn that woman', he muttered[6] to himself and raised his voice: 'Porgie.'

'Yes, Uncle Veryl?'

1. to flip: *feuilleter*
2. to settle down: *s'installer*
3. easy-chair: *fauteuil*
4. to char: *carboniser*
5. ashtray: *cendrier*
6. to mutter: *marmonner*

'Bring me an ashtray from the kitchen, will you please? Your aunt has them all out there again.'

'Sure thing,' said Porgie and shut his eyes. He thought of the kitchen until a picture of it was crystal-clear in his mind. The beaten copper[7] ashtray was sitting beside the sink where his aunt had left it after she had washed it out. He squinted[8] the little eye inside his head, stared hard at the copper bowl, and whispered[9]:

'Ashtray fly,
Follow eye.'

Simultaneously he lifted[10] it with his mind. The ashtray quivered[11] and rose slowly into the air.

Keeping it firmly suspended, Porgie quickly visualized the kitchen door and the hallway and drifted it through[12].

'Porgie!' came his uncle's angry voice.

Porgie jumped, and there was a crash in the hallway outside as the bowl was suddenly released[13] and crashed to the floor.

'How many times have I told you not to levitate around the house? If it's too much work to go out to the kitchen, tell me, and I'll do it myself.'

'I was just practising', mumbled[14] Porgie defensively.

'Well, practise outside. You've got the walls all scratched[15] up from banging things against them. You know you shouldn't fool around with telekinesis outside sight range[16] until you've mastered full visualization. Now go and get me that ashtray.'

Crestfallen[17], Porgie went out the door into the hall. When he saw where the ashtray had fallen, he gave a silent whistle[18]. Instead of coming down the centre of the hall, it had been three feet off course and heading directly for the hall table when he let it fall. In another second, it would have smashed into his aunt's precious black alabaster[19] vase.

'Here it is, Uncle', he said, taking it into the front room. 'I'm sorry.'

His uncle looked at his unhappy face, sighed[20], and reached out and tousled[21] his head affectionately.

Theodore COGSWELL, *The Wall around the World*, © 1953, Piramide Pub.

7. beaten copper: *cuivre martelé*
8. to squint: *cligner*
9. to whisper: *murmurer*
10. to lift: *soulever*
11. to quiver: *frémir*
12. to drift through: *faire passer*
13. to release: *libérer*
14. to mumble: *marmonner*
15. to scratch: *érafler*
16. sight range: *champ de vision*
17. crestfallen: *déconfit*
18. to give a whistle (gave, given): *siffler*
19. alabaster: *albâtre*
20. to sigh: *soupirer*
21. to tousle: *ébouriffer*

MAIN TOPICS

1 Who are the main characters? Where does the story take place? Does the story take place in the past, the present or the future? Why? What are Porgie's powers and what does he do with them? Sum up the story in a few words.

2 Porgie's uncle: What are his reactions to Porgie's powers? What can be deduced about Uncle Veryl's own powers?

3 What are the relationships between Porgie, his uncle and his aunt? How can these relationships be explained? What is the aunt's role in the family?

4 What about Porgie's parents? Where are they? Why aren't they mentioned in the story? What can you imagine about them?

5 Children and the supernatural... Find examples of children having a privileged or special relationship with the unknown (in films, books, comics, etc.). Why is it such a successful topic in the media? (Cf. *Poltergeist, The Omen, The Exorcist, Gremlins, E.T.*, etc.). Why do the media choose children and not adults? What do these children represent?

6 Porgie's powers... Do *we* have such powers, but which are unexploited? What do you know about such phenomena as telepathy, spiritism, premonitory dreams, people with the evil eye, witchcraft, etc.? Do you believe in these phenomena? Why? Describe and analyse people's attitudes towards these phenomena in the past and today.

7 What would *you* do if you had Porgie's powers?...

Useful functions

CAPACITY — CONDITION AND HYPOTHESIS — GETTING S.O. TO DO S. THING — PAST — PROBABILITY.

Useful vocabulary

1. LIGHT, SOUNDS AND THE SENSES — 3. THE BODY AND ITS ACTIVITIES — 4. PEOPLE, THEIR WAYS AND CHARACTERS — 5. EMOTIONS — 10. RELIGION AND OTHER BELIEFS — 16. THE MEDIA.

A few guidelines

1

→ ***... make someone / something + V...*** (Gr: **19**, § 1)

Imagine some of Porgie's powers, using the following pattern:

He can make ashtrays fly from one room to another.
He can make...

2

→ ***"Porgie was in the front-room.../His uncle settled down in his easy-chair, opened his paper, and lit his pipe, etc./... where his aunt had left it after she had washed it out./When he saw where the ashtray had fallen.../... it had been three feet off course..."*** (Gr: **8**, § 2a - **11**, § 6)

Put each verb in brackets either into the preterite or the pluperfect.

Last night, as Porgie *(be)* quietly reading his book in the front-room, he suddenly *(hear)* a strange noise in his bedroom. He *(be)* quite surprised for he *(know)* there *(be)* nobody up there—his uncle and aunt *(go)* out for the evening to see some friends. Furthermore, he *(be)* sure that he *(shut)* the door when going downstairs. He *(rush)* upstairs, *(knock)* down the vase that his aunt carefully *(place)* on a stool, *(swing)* the bedroom door open and... *(see)* Jennifer, his aunt's beloved Siamese cat, helplessly drifting about in the room and mewing her head off! All of a sudden, Porgie *(remember)* that he completely *(forget)* to release Jennifer... A few hours before he *(practise)* with the cat: he *(lift)* her two yards above the ground and *(leave)* her there, forgetting to release her on leaving his room! How lucky he *(be)* that Uncle Veryl *(go)* out that night! He *(can)* just hear him: "Porgie! How many times have I told you not to practise with Jennifer! You'll drive her crazy!"...

3

→ ***"Bring me an ashtray, will you?"*** (Gr: **9**, § 10)
→ ***"If it's too much work..."*** (Gr: **2**, § 2b)
→ ***"... you shouldn't fool around..."*** (Gr: **9**, § 8)
→ ***"Instead of coming down..."*** (Gr: **20**, § 3d)
→ ***"... when he let it fall."*** (Gr: **19**, § 3)
→ ***"In another second, it would have smashed into his aunt's vase."*** (Gr: **9**, § 11b)

FOLLOW-UP WORK

1. Translation

1 - Quand tu es allé dans le salon il y a deux minutes, est-ce que tu as vu le cendrier que j'avais laissé près de mon fauteuil ?
2 - Tu devrais étudier ta grammaire anglaise au lieu de regarder la télévision !
3 - Si ce n'est pas trop te demander, arrête de fumer la pipe près du bébé, veux-tu ? Tu vas le faire tousser (= *to cough*).
4 - Je t'avais demandé de ne pas soulever ce vase tout seul ! Il est beaucoup trop lourd et tu aurais pu le laisser tomber !
5 - Si tu me l'avais demandé, je l'aurais fait moi-même au lieu de le faire faire par quelqu'un d'autre.

Useful functions

COMPLAINING — CONDITION AND HYPOTHESIS — DESIRE AND WISHES — DISLIKING — DURATION — EMPHASIS — GETTING S. O. TO DO S. THING — INCAPACITY — INTENTION — REPROACH — REQUESTS.

Useful vocabulary

1. LIGHT, SOUNDS AND THE SENSES — 3. THE BODY AND ITS ACTIVITIES — 4. PEOPLE, THEIR WAYS AND CHARACTERS — 5. EMOTIONS — 7. FEELINGS AND APPRECIATION — 8. JUDGEMENTS AND EVALUATION.

2. Oral or written work: Porgie's revenge →

You should first look at the pictures very carefully.

One day, Porgie went to these places and had problems with the people there. So, he decided to get his revenge by using his powers...

Either in groups, individually or collectively, study each picture and try to:
1) Find out where and when the scene takes place.
2) Guess why Porgie went to these places and what problems he had with the people there.
3) Describe how he got his own back (= his revenge).
4) Describe in detail the various consequences of Porgie's revenge.
5) Describe and imagine the people's feelings and reactions. (You should have them express themselves as far as possible in *direct* speech.)

Useful functions

CAUSE — DESIRE AND WISHES — GETTING S.O. TO DO S. THING — PROBABILITY — PROHIBITION — REFUSAL — REPORTING — SURPRISE.

Useful vocabulary

1. LIGHT, SOUNDS AND THE SENSES — 3. THE BODY AND ITS ACTIVITIES — 5. EMOTIONS.

3. Oral or written work: A conversation between two neighbours

For some time now, Uncle Veryl's next door neighbours have heard and seen strange things happening in or around his house... Imagine the kind of conversation they could have.

You should first imagine the neighbours' identity cards: name, sex, age, occupation, character, etc.

Hints: The same activity could also be a letter written by one of the neighbours to the local authorities. In this letter, he/she will complain about his/her neighbours, Uncle Veryl and Porgie.

UNIT 6

1. Maths demon-stration

Henry Blodgett looked at his wrist watch[1] and saw that it was two o'clock in the morning. In despair, he slammed[2] shut the textbook he'd been studying and let his head sink[3] onto his arms on the table in front of him. He knew he'd never pass that examination tomorrow; the more he studied geometry the less he understood it. Mathematics in general had always been difficult for him and now he was finding that geometry was impossible for him to learn.

And if he flunked[4] it, he was through with[5] college; he'd flunked three other courses in his first two years and another failure this year would, under college rules[6], cause automatic expulsion.

1. wrist watch: *montre bracelet*
2. to slam: *claquer*
3. (he) let his head sink: *il enfouit sa tête*
4. to flunk (pop.): *se faire recaler*
5. to be through with (pop.): *en avoir fini avec*
6. rule: *règlement*

He wanted that college degree badly too, since it was indispensable for the career he'd chosen and worked toward. Only a miracle could save him now.

He sat up suddenly as an idea struck him. Why not try magic? The occult had always interested him. He had books on it and he'd often read the simple instructions on how to conjure up[7] a demon and make it obey his will[8]. Up to now, he'd always figured[9] that it was a bit risky and so had never actually tried it. But this was an emergency[10] and might be worth[11] the slight[12] risk. Only through black magic could he suddenly become an expert in a subject that had always been difficult for him.

From the shelf he quickly took out his best book on black magic, found the right page and refreshed his memory on the few simple things he had to do.

Enthusiastically, he cleared the floor by pushing the furniture against the walls. He drew the pentagram[13] figure on the carpet with chalk and stepped inside it. He then said the incantations.

The demon was considerably more horrible than he had anticipated. But he mustered[14] his courage and started to explain his dilemma.

"I've always been poor at geometry," he began...

"You're telling *me*,"[15] said the demon gleefully[16].

Smiling flames, it came for him across the chalk lines of the useless hexagram[17] Henry had drawn by mistake instead of the protecting pentagram.

Fredric BROWN, *Honeymoon in Hell* (1958), © Agence littéraire Renault-Lenclud.

7. to conjure up: *faire apparaître*
8. will: *volonté*
9. to figure: *s'imaginer*
10. emergency: *urgence*
11. to be worth: *valoir*
12. slight: *faible*
13. pentagram: *pentagone*
14. to muster: *rassembler*
15. you're telling me: *à qui le dis-tu !*
16. gleefully: *joyeusement*
17. hexagram: *hexagone*

MAIN TOPICS

1 Sum up the story briefly in your own words:
— Who is the main character? Draw his portrait (probable age, character, likes and dislikes, etc.).
— What is his main problem? Why?
— How does he want to solve this problem? What does he hope?
— Why hadn't he tried black magic before?
— How does he conjure up the demon?
— Draw the demon's portrait.
— What happens at the end of the story?

2 Look in an encyclopaedia and find out what is said about *Faust*. Sum up your findings and compare the story of Dr. Faust to that of Henry Blodgett. What are the main similarities and differences?

3 Describe and analyse Henry's feelings in the first three paragraphs. Why is he so desperate? What does it reveal about the importance of college and a career in Henry's life? What career?

4 Henry and black magic... What are the risks? Are there always risks in using black magic? What kind of risks? Why? Can you find examples of the use of black magic in books you have read or films you have seen? Didn't Henry have other means of succeeding? What means? Why didn't he choose them? Would *you* be ready to use black magic to succeed? Why?

5 The end of the story... How is Henry punished? What can we guess about what happens afterwards? Do we pity Henry or not? Why? Why is the end humorous? Try to find another end to the story, supposing Henry had *not* made that stupid mistake...

Useful functions

CAPACITY — CONDITION AND HYPOTHESIS — DESIRE AND WISHES — GETTING S. O. TO DO S. THING — INCAPACITY — PROBABILITY.

Useful vocabulary

4. PEOPLE, THEIR WAYS AND CHARACTERS — 7. FEELINGS AND APPRECIATION — 8. JUDGEMENTS AND EVALUATION — 10. RELIGION AND OTHER BELIEFS.

A few guidelines

1

→ ***"... he slammed shut the textbook he'd been studying.../Mathematics had always been difficult.../... he'd flunked three other courses..."*** (Gr: **8,** § 2a - **11,** § 6)

A. Find 8 other verbs in the pluperfect in the text.

B. The following dialogue is an imaginary conversation between two demons, Mephy and Harpy (the one who got Henry Blodgett). Choose either the preterite or the pluperfect for each verb in brackets.

MEPHY: Harpy, my dear fiend! Long time no see! *(you - have)* a nice day?
HARPY: Oh, hello, Mephy! Yes, gorgeous. Our Master will surely be satisfied.
MEPHY: Someone *(call)* you?
HARPY: Yes, a young idiot... As he *(read)* lots of books on black magic, he *(think)* he *(can)* call me without any harm coming to him... How foolish of him!
MEPHY: These youngsters today... I'll be blessed! But tell me the whole story... How *(it - happen)?*
HARPY: Well, I *(be)* in my den, quietly preparing a few snakes for breakfast, when suddenly I *(hear)* incantation N° 39. It *(go)* like this: "Abracadabra - Lucifer and Belzebuth - Astaroth and..."
MEPHY: Yes, I know, I know... The usual stuff... Carry on with your story.
HARPY: Well, I *(stop)* stirring my snakes at once. I *(be)* all excited. I *(not - be called)* with incantation N° 39 for quite a long time and this *(get)* me into a lot of trouble. Our Master just *(tell)* me the day before that it *(be)* high time I *(make)* myself useful and that so far I *(be)* more interested in starring in American horror movies and video clips than...
MEPHY: All right, all right... What about the young idiot?
HARPY: Well, he *(want)* me to help him with his maths. He already *(flunk)* a few courses because of geometry and...
MEPHY: And you *(help)* him, of course, *(do - not)* you?
HARPY: You bet I *(help)* him! He *(draw)* a hexagram instead of a pentagram! Can you imagine that! A hexagram!
MEPHY: Poor devil... What *(you - do)* with him?
HARPY: Well... Guess what I'm having for breakfast tomorrow, instead of the usual snakes...

2

→ ***"... and make it obey his will."*** (Gr: **19,** § 1)

Suppose Henry Blodgett had *not* drawn a useless hexagram but a useful pentagram... Imagine what he could have made the demon do, not only with regard to college but also other matters. For instance,

He could have made it teach him maths in a few minutes.
He could have made it give his maths teacher a heart attack.
He could have made it...

3

→ ***"... geometry was impossible for him to learn."*** (Gr: **18,** § 3b)

Use the following grid to make as many sentences as you can, keeping in mind that you are expected to
1) respect the logic of the text;
2) justify your sentences whenever you can.

It was	easy difficult possible impossible usual unusual risky	for	Henry the demon	to	conjure up a demon. draw a pentagram. understand geometry. help Henry. use black magic. make mistakes. have a scientific job. appear at any time. earn a lot of money.

4

→ ***"... he let his head sink onto his arms..."*** (Gr: **19,** § 3)

→ ***"He knew he'd never pass that examination..."*** (Gr: **8,** § 3e)

→ ***"... the more he studied geometry the less he understood it."*** (Gr: **7,** § 1d)

→ ***"Only a miracle could save him.../Only through black magic could he become an expert..."***

→ ***"... he cleared the floor by pushing..."*** (Gr: **20,** § 3d)

FOLLOW-UP WORK

1. Translation

1 - Je savais bien que tu ne pourrais pas résister !

2 - Plus j'apprends l'anglais, plus je suis heureux et plus j'aime l'apprendre.

3 - Il le savait bien : ce ne serait qu'en travaillant beaucoup qu'il pourrait réussir ses examens.

4 - Je suis désolé, mais il me sera impossible de vous voir demain.

5 - Ne laisse pas ton frère conduire ta mobylette. Il est trop jeune.

6 - Il trouva enfin le livre qu'il cherchait depuis plus d'une heure.

7 - Tu aurais pu lui faire se laver les mains avant de le mettre au lit !

2. Written or oral work: Once upon a time...

In *Maths demon-stration,* the hero puts magic to bad use and will pay for it. But what happens to a hero (in this case a Prince Charming) who makes good use of magic?...

Look at the pictures carefully: you will find all the main ingredients of a fairy tale, but the captions have been removed. Either in groups, collectively or individually, imagine how to use the pictures (in the order you wish) to create a fairy tale. It's up to you...

Hints: You might need the following words: *lance:* lance — *lutin:* goblin — *talisman:* talisman — *fée:* fairy — *baguette magique:* magic wand — *élixir:* elixir — *grenouille (ou crapaud?):* frog (or toad?) — *enchanteur:* enchanter — *épée:* sword — *sorcière:* witch — *chaudron:* cauldron — *géant:* giant — *trésor:* treasure.

Useful functions

CAPACITY — DESIRE AND WISHES — GETTING S. O. TO DO S. THING — PURPOSE — REPORTING.

Useful vocabulary

1. LIGHT, SOUNDS AND THE SENSES — 2. LANDSCAPES — 3. THE BODY AND ITS ACTIVITIES — 4. PEOPLE, THEIR WAYS AND CHARACTERS — 5. EMOTIONS.

1

2

3

4

POUTCH
POUTCH
RON
ZZZ
POUTCH

1. sin: *faute (= péché)*

2. Adam's sin[1]

1737... Elizabeth Larsson, the only survivor of an expedition through the South African wilderness, has been rescued by Adam, a black runaway slave. He has decided to take her back to the Cape. One day, she notices horrible scars[2] on his back...

2. scar: *cicatrice*

'What happened to your back?'

'Your people put the cat o' nine tails[3] to it.' He remains with his back to her, while he adds with subdued[4] fury: 'But what about it? It's nothing. It happens every day.'

'Is that why you ran away?'

'I raised[5] my hand against my master,' he says bluntly[6].

'One doesn't do that sort of thing without any reason.'

'My reasons are my own.'

'If that's what you think, you needn't answer my question.'

'All right,' he says, choking[7]. 'I'll tell you if you want to know.'

She looks round, with a defensive gesture; but now he won't be stopped.

'You wanted to know, didn't you?' he says harshly[8]. 'So I'll tell you, Madam! I raised my hand against my master because sooner or later one reaches a point where one has got to say no. I was his *mantoor*[9], I had to supervise everything. I even had to punish the other slaves when he ordered it. He had a bad heart, a thrashing[10] would tire him out[11] too much, so he only watched. I never wanted to. Not my own people. But I was a slave, I had no voice against him.' He is quiet for a moment, breathing[12] heavily. 'And then my old grandmother died of cold because I wasn't allowed to deliver her firewood[13]. My mother wanted to go to the funeral, but the Baas[14] refused, he needed her for pruning[15] in the vineyard[16]. So she went off on her own to put away[17] the old woman. And when she came back, the next day, she went into the vineyard as if nothing had happened. Singing.'

He looks past her, into the night.

'And then?' she asks, when he doesn't go on.

'He had her taken to the backyard[18], to the post[19]. And he gave me the sjambok[20] and told me to flog[21] her.

'It can't be true, Adam!'

'It is the truth,' he says, looking at her as if he wants to scorch[22] her with his eyes. And she stares[23] back, unable to look away. 'I pleaded[24] with him. He refused to listen. I kept on. He grabbed[25] a piece of wood—I was working there, making a table, and he grabbed one of the stinkwood[26] legs—and hit me in the face with it. I wrenched[27] it from him. And I only stopped beating him when he was lying on the ground.'

'And afterwards?'

'Nothing.'

'They punished you and then you escaped?'

'What else could I do? I didn't choose the wilderness because I wanted to. I simply had to. And by now I've learned to stay alive, to survive like an animal. But I'm not an animal. I'm a human being. And I want to live with people again. So I must go back some day:

3. cat o'nine tails: *chat à neuf queues (fouet)*
4. to subdue: *contenir*
5. to raise: *lever*
6. bluntly: *d'un ton brusque*
7. choking: *d'une voix étranglée* (to choke: *s'étrangler*)
8. harshly: *durement*
9. mantoor (Afrikaans): *régisseur*
10. thrashing: *correction*
11. to tire out: *épuiser*
12. to breathe: *respirer*
13. firewood: *bois de chauffage*
14. Baas (Afrikaans): *patron*
15. to prune: *élaguer*
16. vineyard: *vignoble*
17. to put away (put, put): *enterrer*
18. backyard: *arrière-cour*
19. post: *poteau*
20. sjambok (Afrikaans): *fouet, cravache*
21. to flog: *fouetter*
22. to scorch: *brûler*
23. to stare: *fixer*
24. to plead: *supplier*
25. to grab: *saisir*
26. stinkwood: *bois (de laurier)*
27. to wrench: *arracher*

not crawling[28] like a runaway dog, but walking on my own two feet, straight[29], with nothing to be ashamed of.'

She bows[30] her head.

'How can it ever happen?' she asks.

'It can happen if I take you back to the Cape. Not only to the sea, but all the way, home. Back to the Cape and its Mountain. You can explain to them. If you tell them I brought you back, if you will tell them I saved your life, if you demand my freedom, they'll give it. You can buy me my freedom. No one else can. I am in your hands.'

André BRINK, *An Instant in the Wind* (1976), W.H. Allen and Co Ltd.

28. to crawl: *ramper*
29. straight: *droit*
30. to bow: *incliner*

MAIN TOPICS

1 Who are the characters in this story? Where and when does it take place? Try to sum up the story in a few words.

2 Adam's life: Could you draw his portrait (status, age, probable education, living and working conditions in the past and now, etc.)? List all the elements you learn about his relatives. What may have happened to the others? Why?

3 The incident: Explain Adam's job and his relationship to the Baas and the other slaves. What did Adam's position entail? Explain the decision of Adam's mother. Guess the Baas' reaction to this disobedience and Adam's feelings towards his grandmother and his mother.

4 Adam's choice: What were Adam's duties as a slave? As a son? How did he resolve this dilemma? What were the consequences of his action in 18th century Cape Town? Explain Adam's decision to escape.

5 Elizabeth Larsson: What do you know about her past life? How does she react to Adam's story? Explain her attitude towards Adam. Who is the rescued and who the rescuer? Find the reasons why they need each other so much.

6 A white woman and a black slave: Guess what their relationship would probably have been in 1737 in the white settlements. Why and how could they change in the wilderness? Finally, guess how the white settlers in the Cape might react to Elizabeth's plea for Adam's liberty.

Useful functions

CAUSE — CONSEQUENCE — GETTING S.O. TO DO S.THING — INCAPACITY — PROHIBITION — REFUSAL — REPROACH.

Useful vocabulary

4. PEOPLE, THEIR WAYS AND CHARACTERS — 5. EMOTIONS — 6. ACTIVITIES OF THE MIND AND COMMUNICATION — 7. FEELINGS AND APPRECIATION — 8. JUDGEMENTS AND EVALUATION — 9. SOCIAL ATTITUDES — 11. HUMAN COMMUNITIES.

A few guidelines

1

→ ... ***would*** + ***V***... (Gr: **9,** § 9)

Using *would* (= regular actions or activities in the past), imagine the white settlers' lives in the Cape in the 1730s. The following grid will provide you with some elements.

They would	often never always occasionally usually	punish the slaves. trade with Holland. explore the interior. treat the slaves humanely. travel to Europe.

Now, it is your turn to find examples...

2 → ***"... I've learned to stay alive..."*** (Gr: **11,** §§ 1, 2, 5)

Using the present perfect (= *parfait*), guess what Adam and Elizabeth have done or been doing so far in the wilderness.

Elizabeth has learned how to find food.
Adam has been hunting.
They have...

3 → ***"... you needn't answer my question."*** (Gr: **10,** § 1c)

It goes without saying that Elizabeth's needs in the African wilderness are quite different from what they were at home in the Cape. Try to think of all the things she needn't have or do.

She needn't wear fashionable dresses.
She needn't...

4 → ***"... he told me to flog her."*** (Gr: **18,** §§ 3a, 4b)

In the Cape, Elizabeth probably had slaves to work in the kitchen, the bedrooms, the garden and the fields. Imagine all the things she would tell them to do or not to do.

She would tell them to clean the rooms.
She would tell them not to go out at night.
She would tell them...

5 → ***"He had her taken to the backyard..."*** (Gr: **14,** § 6)

In André Brink's novel, we learn that Adam, although he was his master's *mantoor,* would often stand up to him (= refuse to obey his orders). Consequently, the Baas would often have to threaten him. Imagine his threats, using the following pattern:

If you don't..., I'll have you...

6 → ***"... I had to supervise everything. I even had to punish the other slaves.../I simply had to./... I wasn't allowed to deliver her firewood."*** (Gr: **10,** §§ 2a, 2d)

In 18th century South Africa, slaves' lives were ruled by black codes which explained in detail what the slaves had to do, were allowed and not allowed to do. Guess what those rules were, using the following patterns:

Slaves had to obey their masters.
They were not allowed to disobey their masters' orders.
They...

7 → ***"And I only stopped beating him..."*** (Gr: **20,** § 3d)

Adam probably hopes that one day black people will no longer be kept as slaves. Imagine his hopes, using the following pattern:

When I am free, I will stop working for a master.
When I am free, I will stop...

8 → ***"... he won't be stopped."*** (Gr: **9,** § 6)

→ ***"I never wanted to./... because I wanted to. I simply had to./No one else can."*** (Gr: **18,** § 2b)

→ ***"... he needed her for pruning..."*** (Gr: **20,** § 3d)

→ ***"... she went into the vineyard as if nothing had happened./... as if he wants to scorch her...***

→ ***"... if you will tell them..."*** (Gr: **9,** § 6)

FOLLOW-UP WORK

1. Oral or written work: On board the *Marie-Caroline*...

1

2

3

4

F. BOURGEON, *Les passagers du vent*, T. 5, éd. Glénat.

After looking at the pictures, try to imagine a story based on them. You can work individually, collectively or in groups along the following lines:

— What may have happened to these slaves *before* they ended up on the *Marie-Caroline?* How/where/when/by whom were they caught?

— Imagine their feelings on board the *Marie-Caroline.*

— Who is punished? How? Why? Why has she been placed just above her companions? Imagine their feelings.

— Describe the sailors who are watching the scene. What can you guess about their feelings? Do you think they agree or disagree with the punishment? Why?

— Who is the girl in the last picture? What is she doing on board the ship? How does she react to the flogging? Why? Imagine her relationship with the girl who is being flogged.

— What can you guess about the fate of these slaves once they reach the West Indies?

Useful functions

AGREEMENT — CAUSE — DISAGREEMENT — DISLIKING — GETTING S. O. TO DO S. THING — INCAPACITY — LIKING — PROBABILITY — PROHIBITION.

Useful vocabulary

1. LIGHT, SOUNDS AND THE SENSES — 3. THE BODY AND ITS ACTIVITIES — 4. PEOPLE, THEIR WAYS AND CHARACTERS — 5. EMOTIONS — 7. FEELINGS AND APPRECIATION.

2. Oral or written work: Two conversations

The death of Adam's master and the way Adam managed to escape the Cape police soon became a daily subject of conversation among the white and black communities. Their opinions differed of course. So did their conversations.

Either collectively, in groups or individually, imagine the slaves' and then the masters' conversations. In both conversations you should keep the following points in mind:

— The settings may well be different: fields, the slaves' quarters, the Baas' home, etc.

— The identity cards of the people talking may help you: origins, family links, probable education, values, job, status in the community, motives for being and staying in the Cape, probable future, etc.

— The subject of their conversations may be interpreted differently: reasons for Adam's actions, master's reactions, death of the grandmother, family relationships among the slaves, the means of escape, the probable refuge, etc.

— The consequences of the incident may seem different to the slaves and the masters: rebellion/freedom, hopes/fears, approval/reproach, satisfaction/horror, etc.

Naturally, before starting you may feel you need to know some more about the history of South Africa in the 18th century. Dictionaries or encyclopaedias may provide the necessary information.

Useful functions

ADMIRATION — CAUSE — CONDITION AND HYPOTHESIS — GETTING S. O. TO DO S. THING — INCAPACITY — INTENTION — PROBABILITY — REPROACH.

Useful vocabulary

4. PEOPLE, THEIR WAYS AND CHARACTERS — 5. EMOTIONS — 6. ACTIVITIES OF THE MIND AND COMMUNICATION — 8. JUDGEMENTS AND EVALUATION — 11. HUMAN COMMUNITIES.

3. Oral or written work: Adam's trial

"You can explain to them. If you tell them I brought you back, if you will tell them I saved your life, if you demand my freedom, they'll give it." This was Adam's bargain. After a long journey trekking through the interior, Adam and Elizabeth are back in the Cape. Elizabeth's plea for Adam's freedom led them both to court. Imagine the trial and the verdict.

Either collectively, in groups or individually, you could organize this trial around the following tips:

— The trial could start with Elizabeth's account of her life with Adam in the wilderness (facts, discovery of the truth, trek back to the Cape, Adam's qualities, etc.) and Adam's account of his past actions.

— The witnesses may be the slaves who witnessed Adam's actions in the past and the murder of his Baas. They may also be some white people who knew Adam when he was younger, or knew his family. Their testimony may help either the defence or the prosecution.

— The prosecution will do all they can to show how guilty Adam is. A clergyman may (or may not) choose to provide the prosecution (or the defence) with supplementary arguments.

— Finally, the judge will have a discussion with the members of the jury on whether Adam is guilty or not. Then he will have to decide upon the appropriate punishment.

Remember that a man's life depends on the fairness and seriousness of this trial.

Useful functions

ADVICE — CAPACITY — DISLIKING — DISAGREEMENT TO CRITICISM — INTENTION — OBLIGATION — PROHIBITION — REFUSAL — REPROACH.

Useful vocabulary

4. PEOPLE, THEIR WAYS AND CHARACTERS — 5. EMOTIONS — 7. FEELINGS AND APPRECIATION — 9. SOCIAL ATTITUDES.

4. Translation

1 - Tôt ou tard, il faudra que tu obéisses aux ordres de ton maître.
2 - Elle s'est conduite comme si nous avions été des étrangers.
3 - Je sais qu'il t'a dit d'arriver tôt, mais tu n'as pas besoin d'être là-bas avant 9 heures.
4 - Il refuse qu'on l'aide. Maintenant, si tu veux essayer de lui parler...
5 - Il avait besoin de moi pour punir les esclaves.
6 - Ça fait très longtemps que je chasse en Afrique.
7 - Quand je serai très riche, j'arrêterai de travailler et je me ferai construire une maison au bord de la mer.
8 - Je voulais souvent aller au cinéma alors que lui ne voulait jamais.
9 - Tous les mois, nous allions voir nos cousins.

3. The creature

A party of students from Takon, a big city on Venus, are visiting a sort of zoo in which recent discoveries made in the Valley of Dur are exhibited. They come to a small cage occupied by a curious creature...

The creature raised its head and looked at them from sullen[1] eyes. Its mouth opened but instead of the expected bellow[2] there came from it a stream[3] of clattering gibberish[4] which it accompanied with curious motions of its forelimbs[5].

The interest of some of the class was at last aroused[6]. The young Sadul, for instance, was far more intrigued by it than he had been by those monsters with the poly-syllabic names. He drew closer[7] to the bars, observing it intently.

The creature's eyes met his own and held them. More queer[8] jabber[9] issued from its mouth. It advanced to the front of the cage, coming quite near to him. Sadul held his ground[10]—it did not look dangerous. With one foot it smoothed[11] the soil of the floor, then squatted down[12] to scrabble[13] in the dirt.

'What's it doing?' asked someone.

'Probably scratching for something to eat,' suggested another.

Sadul continued to watch with interest. When the guide moved the party on he contrived[14] to remain behind unnoticed.

After a while the creature rose to its feet again and extended one paw[15] towards the ground. It had scrawled[16] a series of queer lines in the dust. They made neither pattern[17] nor picture. They did not seem to mean anything. Yet there was something regular about them.

Sadul looked blankly[18] at them and then back to the face of the creature. It made a quick movement towards the scrawls. Sadul continued to stare blankly. It advanced, smoothed out the ground once more with its foot and began to scrabble again. Sadul

1. sullen: *morne*
2. bellow: *beuglement*
3. stream: *flot*
4. clattering gibberish: *charabia assourdissant*
5. forelimbs: *pattes avant*
6. to arouse: *éveiller*
7. to draw closer (drew, drawn): *s'approcher*
8. queer: *étrange*
9. jabber: *bredouillis*
10. to hold one's ground (held, held): *ne pas bouger*
11. to smooth: *aplanir*
12. to squat down: *s'accroupir*
13. to scrabble: *gratter*
14. to contrive (to): *s'arranger (pour)*
15. paw: *patte*
16. to scrawl: *gribouiller*
17. pattern: *dessin*
18. blankly: *sans comprendre*

wondered whether or not he should move on. He ought, he knew, to have kept together with the rest. Magon might be nasty[19] about it. Well, he'd stay just long enough to see what the creature was doing this time.

It stood back and pointed again. Sadul was amazed[20]. In the dirt was a drawing of a Takonian such as himself. The creature was pointing first to himself and then back to the drawing.

Sadul grew excited. He had made a discovery? What was this creature which could draw? He had never heard of such a thing. His first impulse was to run after the rest and tell them. But he hesitated and curiosity got the better of him.

Rather doubtfully, he opened the bag at his side and drew out his writing tablet and stylus. The creature excitedly thrust[21] both paws through the bars for them and sat down, scratching experimentally with the wrong end of the stylus. Sadul corrected it, then leaned close to the bars, watching over its shoulder.

First the creature made a round mark in the middle of the tablet, then it pointed up. Sadul looked up at the ceiling, but quite failed[22] to see anything remarkable there. The creature shook its head impatiently. About the mark it drew a circle with a small spot[23] on the circumference—outside that another circle with a similar spot, then a third. Still Sadul could see no meaning.

Beside the spot on the second circle the creature drew a small sketch[24] of a Takonian. Beside the spot on the third, a creature, itself. Sadul followed intently. It was trying very hard to convey something but for the life of him[25] he could not see what it was.

19. to be nasty: *se mettre en colère*

20. to be amazed: *être ébahi*

21. to thrust (thrust, thrust): *tendre*

22. to fail (to): *ne pas parvenir (à)*

23. spot: *point*

24. sketch: *dessin*

25. for the life of him he could not…: *il n'arrivait absolument pas à…*

Again a paw pointed up at the light globe, then the forelimbs were held wide apart[26].

The light—an enormous light!

Suddenly Sadul got it—the sun—the sun and the planets! He nearly choked[27] with excitement. Reaching between the bars, he grabbed[28] his tablet and ran off up the corridor in search of his party. The man in the cage watched him go and as Sadul's shouts diminished in the distance he smiled his first smile for a very long time.

John WYNDHAM, *The Man from Beyond* (1934), © D. Higham Associates Ltd.

26. wide apart: *largement écarté*
27. to choke: *s'étrangler*
28. to grab: *saisir*

MAIN TOPICS

1 Who are the characters? Where and when does the story take place? Try to sum it up as briefly as you can.

2 The visit to the zoo: Guess the reasons why the students visited this zoo. Imagine what they had to do (take notes, analyse, report, etc.). Define the students' and the guide's views of this creature and the other creatures.

3 Sadul: Guess what he expected from the creature. Find what puzzled him in the creature's behaviour (language, eyes, actions, etc.). List and compare the elements referring to the animal and human worlds. Try to find out what the creature wanted Sadul to understand. Would you say that Sadul is different from the other students? How? Why?

4 The first drawing: Why did the creature choose to draw? What did it draw? Where? Explain Sadul's feelings at that moment. Imagine the creature's feelings and thoughts too.

5 The second drawing: Why did Sadul offer the creature his tablet? What might it imply for the creature? Following the writer's description, try to draw what the creature drew on the tablet. (A dictionary may help you name and locate each planet.) What does this drawing imply as far as the creature's scientific knowledge is concerned? Can it still be called a creature? Why?

6 Describe and explain Sadul's reactions in the end. What will he try to do next? What about the creature's reactions?

7 The writer's techniques: How is suspense created? How are the characters' feelings described? Have you ever read stories similar to this one? Could you tell them briefly and compare them to John Wyndham's?

Useful functions

CAPACITY — CONDITION AND HYPOTHESIS — DESIRE AND WISHES — GETTING S. O. TO DO S. THING — INCAPACITY — PROBABILITY.

Useful vocabulary

3. THE BODY AND ITS ACTIVITIES — 4. PEOPLE, THEIR WAYS AND CHARACTERS — 5. EMOTIONS — 6. ACTIVITIES OF THE MIND AND COMMUNICATION — 8. JUDGEMENTS AND EVALUATION — 9. SOCIAL ATTITUDES.

A few guidelines

1

→ ***Prepositions and verbal particles*** (Gr: **12**)

Translate the following sentences from the text into French and state each time whether the elements in ***bold letters*** are prepositions or verbal particles.

— *The creature... looked **at** them **from** sullen eyes.*
— *... there came **from** it a stream...*
— *He drew closer **to** the bars...*
— *It advanced **to** the front of the cage, coming quite near **to** him.*
— *... it squatted **down** to scrabble **in** the dirt.*
— *When the guide moved the party **on**...*
— *... the creature rose **to** its feet...*
— *Sadul looked blankly **at** them and then **back to** the face of the creature.*

— *It advanced, smoothed* ***out*** *the ground once more...*
— *... he should move* ***on.***
— *It stood* ***back*** *and pointed again.*
— *The creature was pointing first* ***to*** *himself and then* ***back to*** *the drawing.*
— *His first impulse was to run* ***after*** *the rest...*
— *... he drew* ***out*** *his writing tablet...*
— *The creature excitedly thrust both paws* ***through*** *the bars* ***for*** *them and sat* ***down...***
— *Sadul... leaned close* ***to*** *the bars, watching* ***over*** *its shoulder.*
— *... it pointed* ***up.*** *Sadul looked* ***up at*** *the ceiling...*
— *Again a paw pointed* ***up at*** *the light globe...*
— *He nearly choked* ***with*** *excitement.*
— *Reaching* ***between*** *the bars... and ran* ***off up*** *the corridor in search of his party.*

2

→ ***... expect somebody to + V.../... want somebody to + V ...*** (Gr: **18,** §§ 3a, 4b)

Re-tell the whole story, using the following patterns, according to your needs:

Sadul didn't expect the creature to speak a language.
The creature wanted Sadul to understand he was different.

3

→ ***may/must + have + past participle*** (Gr: **9,** §§ 3, 5)

A: Imagine what may have happened to the creature before he was imprisoned by the Takonians. Use the two following patterns:

He may have met a Takonian spaceship near his planet.
He may have been kidnapped by Takonian explorers.

Hints: lose his way, beat the enemy, crash his plane, be a spy, etc.

B: Imagine what the creature must have felt in the cage, using the following pattern:

He must have been lonely.
He must have looked for help.

Hints: be hungry, dream of his planet, fight his way out of the cage, etc.

4

→ ***"The man in the cage watched him go..."*** (Gr: **19,** § 2)

Using such verbs as *watch, see, hear,* imagine or describe all the things which Sadul watched, saw or heard the creature do.

Hints: scrabble in the dirt, speak, draw, explain, etc.

5

→ ***"The young Sadul was far more intrigued by it than he had been by those monsters.../He drew closer.../More queer jabber.../... curiosity got the better of him."*** (Gr: **7,** §§ 1a, 3)

Using as many comparatives and superlatives as you can, imagine how Sadul would compare the creature to the "poly-syllabic" monsters in his zoology paper, or if you like, in an article for the Takonian Express.

6

→ ***"... a sort of zoo in which recent discoveries are exhibited.../... a stream of clattering gibberish which it accompanied.../What was this creature which could draw?"*** (Gr: **13,** §§ 1, 2, 3, 5)

→ ***"The interest of some of the class.../... asked someone./... probably scratching for something to eat.../They did not seem to mean anything. Yet there was something regular.../... quite failed to see anything remarkable.../... Sadul could see no meaning./... trying very hard to convey something..."*** (Gr: **2,** § 1d - **5,** § 7)

→ ***"They made neither pattern nor picture."*** (Gr: **16,** § 4)

→ ***"... a drawing of a Takonian such as himself./He had never heard of such a thing."***

→ ***"The creature thrust both paws..."*** (Gr: **2,** § 3b)

FOLLOW-UP WORK

1. Translation

1 - Sa mère veut qu'il travaille, mais personne ne s'attend à ce qu'il réussisse la première année.

2 - Il sortit de la pièce sans regarder personne.

3 - Je les ai vus sortir du cinéma et entrer dans un pub.

4 - Il a dû oublier que nous devions nous voir à 11 heures.

5 - Je n'ai jamais vu une telle voiture ! Il a dû l'acheter après avoir trop bu !

6 - A: Où sont les enfants ? B: Ils sont sortis tous les deux.

7 - Elle ne parlait ni anglais ni espagnol.

8 - Il vivait dans une maison qui était très vieille et dans laquelle il n'y avait ni électricité ni eau courante.

9 - Je ne comprends rien à ce problème... Penses-tu que le prof a pu faire une erreur ?

10 - C'est beaucoup plus difficile que ce à quoi je m'attendais.

2. Oral or written work: Let's talk

Sadul and the creature got to know each other so well that the creature learned the Takonian language and even went to live with Sadul's family. They often talked about Takon and the Earth, the creature's planet.

Either individually in groups or collectively, imagine the conversation between the creature, Sadul and the Takonian family. The following points may be of some help:

1) First, you could introduce the various characters, stating for each one his age, sex, job, education, and attitude towards the creature (fear, suspicion, liking, interest, etc.).

2) Secondly, you could imagine the questions which the Takonians might ask about the Earth. The creature would naturally answer them to provide the family with a vivid image of his planet and home country.

3) Thirdly, you may imagine the questions which the creature might ask the Takonians about *their* planet.

Some of the following topics may prove useful in making up the various questions or answers: social classes on both planets, politics, forms of government, education, scientific developments and discoveries, military projects, leisure and entertainment, travel, ecology and environment, war and peace, etc. You will probably find many other topics.

Useful functions

CAPACITY — COMPARISON — CONDITION AND HYPOTHESIS — OBLIGATION — PERMISSION — QUANTITY — REGRET.

Useful vocabulary

10. RELIGION AND OTHER BELIEFS — 11. HUMAN COMMUNITIES — 12. TOWNS, SMALL AND LARGE — 14. EDUCATION AND SCIENCES — 15. THE ARTS — 16. THE MEDIA.

3. Oral and written work: Dangers on Venus

Sadul has discovered that Magon (his teacher) and other Takonian scientists intend to kill the creature to examine "it" more closely. Sadul then decides to tell the creature that his life is in danger on Venus and advises him to escape as quickly as he can. But the creature needs Sadul to find a way off Venus and he would like Sadul to follow him back to the Earth.

1) Imagine the conversation between Sadul and the creature, who tries to convince Sadul to steal a spaceship, leave Venus, and find refuge on the Earth.

2) Sadul should write a "good-bye" letter to his family to explain why he felt he had to leave with the creature.

P.S.: Sadul may be hard to convince so the creature's arguments in favour of escaping to the Earth should be *very* convincing. He could tell Sadul of all the good things he would discover on this planet.

Useful functions

ADVICE — CAPACITY — DESIRE AND WISHES — DISLIKING — OBLIGATION — PROPOSING — PURPOSE — REGRET — REQUESTS.

Useful vocabulary

2. LANDSCAPES — 4. PEOPLE, THEIR WAYS AND CHARACTERS — 5. EMOTIONS — 7. FEELINGS AND APPRECIATION.

1

2

3

4

© J.-C. MÉZIÈRES et P. CHRISTIN, *Valérian*: extraits de *L'empire des mille planètes*, *La cité des eaux mouvantes*, *Les oiseaux du maître*, éd. Dargaud.

4. Oral and written work: Do-it-yourself sci-fi story

The pictures (p. 106) are all yours. The elements you need to write your own science fiction story are there. You will find heroes and villains, means of transport, planets, cities and monsters. If you need other elements, you may either draw them or describe them or do both. Now it's up to you!

Useful functions

CAPACITY — CAUSE — CONDITION AND HYPOTHESIS — GETTING S. O. TO DO S. THING — INCAPACITY .

Useful vocabulary

2. LANDSCAPES — 3. THE BODY AND ITS ACTIVITIES — 4. PEOPLE, THEIR WAYS AND CHARACTERS.

4. Four days in the life of Adrian Mole

Monday March 2nd

My mother has just come into my room and said she had something awful[1] to tell me. I sat up in bed and put a dead serious expression on my face just in case she'd got six months to live or she'd been caught shoplifting[2] or something. She fiddled[3] with the curtains, dropped cigarette ash all over my Concorde model and started mumbling[4] on about 'adult relationships' and 'life being complicated' and how she must 'find herself'. She said she was fond of me. Fond!!! And would hate to hurt me. And then she said that for some women marriage was like being in prison. Then she went out.

Marriage is nothing like being in prison! Women are let out every day to go to the shops and stuff[5], and quite a lot go to work. I think my mother is being a bit melodramatic.

Sunday March 8th

My mother has gone to a woman's workshop[6] on assertiveness training[7]. Men aren't allowed. I asked my father what 'assertiveness training' is. He said 'God knows, but whatever it is, it's bad news for me'.

We had boil-in-the-bag cod[8] in butter sauce and oven-cooked[9] chips for Sunday dinner, followed by tinned[10] peaches and Dream-topping[11]. My father opened a bottle of white wine and let me have some. We watched a film on television, then my mother came home and started bossing us around[12]. She said, 'The worm has

1. awful: *affreux*
2. to shoplift: *voler à l'étalage*
3. to fiddle: *tripoter*
4. to mumble: *marmonner*
5. and stuff: *et compagnie*
6. workshop: *atelier, séminaire*
7. assertiveness training: *dans ce contexte, épanouissement de la personnalité*
8. boil-in-the-bag cod: *cabillaud au bain-marie (en sachet)*
9. oven-cooked: *cuit au four*
10. tinned: *en conserve*
11. Dream topping: *crème dessert*
12. to boss s.o. around: *mener qqn à la baguette*

turned'[13], and 'Things are going to be different around here', and things like that. Then she went into the kitchen and started making a chart[14] dividing all the housework into three. I pointed out to her that I already had a paper round[15] to do, an old age pensioner[16] to look after and a dog to feed, as well as my school work, but she didn't listen, she put the chart on the wall and said 'We start tomorrow'.

13. the worm has turned (pop.): *ras-le-bol de se faire marcher dessus*
14. chart: *tableau*
15. paper round: *distribution des journaux*
16. old age pensioner: *retraité*

Monday March 9th

Cleaned toilet, washed basin[17] and bath before doing my paper round. Set table, served dinner, washed up. Put burnt saucepans[18] in to soak[19]. Got washing out of machine; everything blue, including white underwear[20] and handkerchiefs[21]. Hung washing on clothes-horse[22]. Fed dog. Cleaned shoes. Did homework. Took dog for a walk, had bath. Cleaned bath. Made three cups of tea. Washed cups up. Went to bed. Just my luck to have an assertive mother!

17. basin: *lavabo*
18. saucepan: *casserole*
19. to soak: *tremper*
20. underwear: *sous-vêtements*
21. handkerchief: *mouchoir*
22. clothes-horse: *séchoir*

Tuesday March 10th

Why couldn't I have been born Prince Edward and Prince Edward been born Adrian Mole? I am treated like a serf.

Sue TOWNSEND, *The Secret Diary of Adrian Mole, Aged 13¾* (1982),

MAIN TOPICS

1 Who are the main characters? Where and when does this story take place? Find the structure of this text and sum it up in a few words.

2 What do we learn about Adrian's mother? What sort of woman is she? Draw her portrait, imagining her physical appearance, the sort of education she had, her daily life before March 8th, her likes and dislikes, etc.

3 Analyse her attitude when talking to her son and husband. What can you say about Adrian's reactions?

4 What accounts for the mother's decision? Who or what may have influenced her? What can you guess about her relationships with her husband? What does she reproach her husband with?

5 Try to analyse the relationships between the father and the son before and after March 8th. Are they similar or different? Why?

6 What are the various consequences of the mother's rebellion?

7 Women's Lib... Is it still a burning issue today or has it become an out-dated question? Why?

8 Try to list all the elements in the text which could be dramatic, and for each of them, try to find out what makes them humorous.

Useful functions

CAUSE — COMPARISON — DESIRE AND WISHES — DISLIKING — GETTING S.O. TO DO S. THING — OBLIGATION — PROBABILITY.

Useful vocabulary

4. PEOPLE, THEIR WAYS AND CHARACTERS — 6. ACTIVITIES OF THE MIND AND COMMUNICATION — 7. FEELINGS AND APPRECIATION — 8. JUDGEMENTS AND EVALUATION — 9. SOCIAL ATTITUDES.

A few guidelines

1

→ ***... can't stand + V-ing*** (Gr: **20,** § 3d)

You can well imagine why Adrian's mother went to *"a woman's workshop on assertiveness training"*. Try to guess what she thought before going to the first meeting. Use the following pattern:

I can't stand doing all the housework,...

2

→ ***... make s.o. + V*** (Gr: **19,** § 1)

As soon as the mother came back home, what did she make her husband and her son do? Use the following pattern:

She made her son do the washing-up,...

3

→ ***"My mother has just come..."*** (Gr: **11,** § 3c)

→ ***"My mother said she had something.../She said she was fond of me.../(She said she) would hate.../... she said that marriage was like.../I pointed out that I had a paper round..."*** (Gr: **17,** §§ 1, 3, 4)

→ ***"... in case she'd got six months to live or she'd been caught shoplifting..."*** (Gr: **11,** § 6)

→ ***"... started mumbling.../... started bossing us around.../... started making a chart..."*** (Gr: **20,** § 3d)

→ ***"... marriage was like being in prison./I'm treated like a serf."*** (Gr: **12,** § 3)

→ ***"... my mother is being a bit melodramatic."*** (Gr: **8,** § 1b)

→ ***"... let me have some."*** (Gr: **19,** § 3)

→ ***"... before doing my paper round."*** (Gr: **20,** § 3)

→ ***"Why couldn't I have been born..."*** (Gr: **9,** § 1)

4

→ ***... used to + V*** (Gr: **8,** § 2c)

A few months later, Adrian's mother compares what she used to be and to do in the past with what she is and does now. You may find the following grid useful. We have only given a few adjectives and verbs, but remember that you can compare with **nouns** *(I used to have fewer friends...)* or with **adverbs** *(I go out more often...).*

	Past	Now
Time - table	hectic,...	peaceful,...
Activities - in the house - in the garden - for her son - for her husband	 wash the dishes,... mow the lawn,... make the bed,... darn his socks,...	
Leisure or hobbies	watch television,...	enjoy, go,...
Mood	grumpy, frustrated,...	cool, happy,...
Health	exhausted, run-down, out-of-sorts, listless,...	fit, energetic,...

5

→ ***I wish + modal preterite or pluperfect*** (Gr: **8,** § 2d - **11,** § 6)

Now, Adrian and his father never stop working... Imagine their regrets, using either of the following patterns:

I wish I had time to watch TV.
I wish she had never gone to that workshop.
I wish...

FOLLOW-UP WORK

1. Translation

1 - Je viens de faire la vaisselle et je vais faire mes devoirs.

2 - Mon fils commence à parler.

3 - Maman a dit que tu devais mettre la table avant d'aller promener le chien.

4 - Mes parents m'ont laissé boire du champagne pour mon anniversaire.

5 - Tu fais vraiment l'idiot. Arrête !

6 - Je viens de lui envoyer de l'argent, au cas où il aurait déjà tout dépensé.

7 - Tu aurais pu faire les courses.

8 - Le fils est comme le père ; ils ne comprennent pas ce qui se passe.

9 - Je regrette qu'il ne soit pas venu pour Noël.

10 - Je ne supporte plus de vivre dans cette maison.

11 - Jadis, mon mari m'achetait des fleurs chaque dimanche.

12 - Mon professeur nous fait trop travailler...

2. Oral work: Women of the world, unite!

Either in groups or individually, try to imagine the first meeting of the feminist group mentioned in the text. Each member should have an identity card (name, age, place of birth, married since..., number of children, level of education, job?,...). Five or six liberated women could lead the debate and advise the others. The other women could talk about their husbands, their family lives, ask questions; then they could all define a strategy.

Useful functions

ADVICE — AGREEMENT TO APPRECIATION — CONDITION AND HYPOTHESIS — CONSEQUENCE — OBLIGATION.

Useful vocabulary

4. PEOPLE, THEIR WAYS AND CHARACTERS — 6. ACTIVITIES OF THE MIND AND COMMUNICATION — 7. FEELINGS AND APPRECIATION — 8. JUDGEMENTS AND EVALUATION — 9. SOCIAL ATTITUDES.

1

3. Oral or written work: A few women

Either collectively in groups or individually, describe these pictures and compare these women's ages, heights, clothes, attitudes, settings; try to imagine their likes, dislikes, their moral values, etc.

Then, analyse what image of women each of them reflects. Finally, do you think these roles are compatible or not?

Useful functions

CAUSE — COMPARISON — CONTRAST AND CONTRADICTION — PAST — PROBABILITY.

Useful vocabulary

3. THE BODY AND ITS ACTIVITIES — 4. PEOPLE, THEIR WAYS AND CHARACTERS — 7. FEELINGS AND APPRECIATION — 8. HUMAN COMMUNITIES.

2 3 4 5

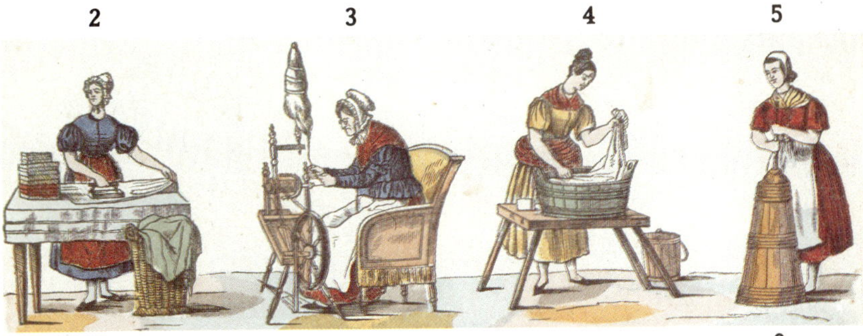

6 7 8 9

10 11 12

4. Oral or written work: Free at last!

First, look at this comic strip very carefully. You will then:

1) Describe what you can see, the main character's attitudes, his probable feelings and reactions.

2) Imagine you are this man, what would you say or think in each picture? You can also try to make the wife, the boss, the children speak.

3) Compare this man's life to that of Adrian Mole's mother. What are the similarities and differences?

4) What is Sempé's message in this story? Would you say that it reflects reality or that it is a caricature? Is the message optimistic or pessimistic?

Useful functions

COMPARISON — DESIRE AND WISHES — DISLIKING — INCAPACITY — OBLIGATION.

Useful vocabulary

4. PEOPLE, THEIR WAYS AND CHARACTERS — 5. EMOTIONS — 7. FEELINGS AND APPRECIATION — 9. SOCIAL ATTITUDES.

SEMPÉ, *Sauve qui peut,* © Christiane Charillon.

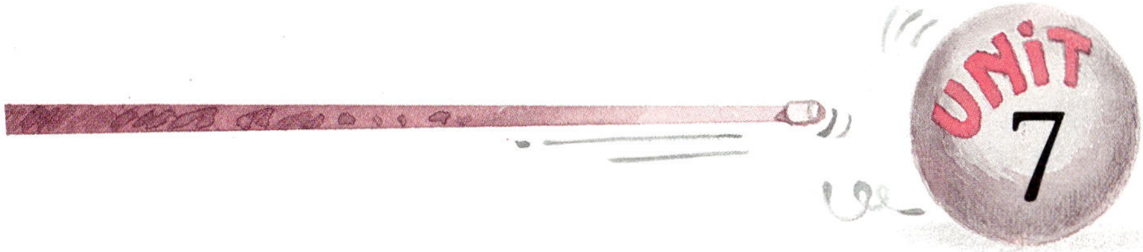

1. Michael and the piccanins[1]

Michael, a 12 year old white boy, lives in a South African city. He has recently met two poor African children in the street near his house and has given them some bread, a torch and a few presents. Since then, the children have spent hours every day at Michael's door, waiting.

Michael was a lonely child. He had neither brothers nor sisters; both his parents worked during the day, and he had made few friends at school. But he was not by any means[2] unhappy in his loneliness. He was used to it, in the first place; and then, because he was lonely, he was all the better[3] able to indulge himself in[4] his own fantasies. He played for hours, by himself, games of his own inventions—games of war, of exploration, of seafaring[5], of scientific invention, of crime, of espionage, of living in a house beneath or above his real one. It was not long before the two African children, who were now accosting him regularly, appeared in some of his games, for their weakness[6], poverty and dependence gave Michael ample scope[7] to display[8] in fantasy his kindness, generosity, courage and decisiveness. Sometimes in his games Michael saved the boy's life, and was thanked for it in broken English. Sometimes he saved the girl's, and then she humbly begged his pardon for having caused him so much trouble. Sometimes he was just too late to save the life of either, though[9] he tried his best, and then there were affecting scenes of farewell[10].

But in real life, Michael did not play with the children at all: they were too dirty, too ragged[11], too strange, too persistent[12]. Their persistence eventually drove Dora to tell Michael's mother about them; and his mother did her duty by telling Michael that on no account[13] should he play with the children, nor should he give them anything of value.

"Play with them!" Michael laughed at the idea. And apart from bread and the torch, he had given them nothing but a few old toys, a singlet[14] or two, a pair of old canvas shoes[15]. No one could begrudge[16] them those gifts. And the truth was that Michael's mother begrudged the piccanins neither the old toys and clothes nor the bread. What she was anxious to do was simply to prevent her son from playing with the piccanins, fearing that he would pick up

1. piccanin = picaninny (pop.): *enfant noir (très péjoratif)*
2. not by any means (*ou* by no means): *pas du tout, pas le moins du monde*
3. all the better: *d'autant mieux, d'autant plus*
4. to indulge (oneself) in: *s'adonner à*
5. seafaring: *voyages sur les océans*
6. weakness: *faiblesse*
7. ample scope: *dans ce contexte, de nombreuses occasions*
8. to display: *montrer*
9. though (*ou* although): *bien que, quoique*
10. farewell: *adieu(x)*
11. ragged: *dépenaillé*
12. persistent: *obstiné*
13. on no account: *en aucun cas*
14. singlet: *maillot de corps*
15. canvas shoes: *chaussures en toile*
16. to begrudge s.o. s.thing: *reprocher qqch à qqn*

17. Kaffir: *Cafre (Noir d'Afrique australe) (péjoratif)*
18. let alone: *encore moins*

germs, bad language, and "kaffir[17] ways" generally from them, if he did. Hearing both from Michael and Dora that he did not play with them at all, and that he had never even asked them into the backyard, let alone[18] the house, Michael's mother was satisfied.

Dan JACOBSON, *Beggar My Neighbour,* © La Nouvelle Agence.

MAIN TOPICS

1 Who are the main characters? Where and when does the story take place? Sum up the text in just a few words.

2 Draw Michael's portrait: age, character, likes and dislikes, education, etc.

3 Describe and analyse Michael's feelings and attitudes towards the black children. What is paradoxical in his behaviour? What are the various influences that make him behave as he does? Would you say that Michael is a likeable character or not? Why? If *you* were Michael, how would *you* behave? Why?

4 Dora: Who is she? What can we guess about her role in the family? How can you account for her attitude towards the black children? What does her attitude reveal about social and racial relationships in South Africa?

5 Michael's mother: Describe and try to explain her attitude and feelings towards the black children. What do you think of the reasons she gives to prevent Michael from playing with them?

6 The black children: Imagine how they live: parents, family life, everyday life, living conditions, hopes, frustrations, etc. How can you account for their attitude towards Michael? What does their attitude reveal about the situation of the Blacks in South Africa?

7 Look in a dictionary or an encyclopaedia: What do you learn about South Africa, its political regime, its social and economic situation, etc.? How could you explain the survival of such a régime in Africa? Are there any possible solutions to the problem of Apartheid?

8 *Michael and the piccanins:* What do you think the writer's goal was when writing this story? Would you say it is a pessimistic or an optimistic story? Why? Try to imagine how this story could continue.

Useful functions

COMPARISON — DESIRE AND WISHES — DISLIKING — INCAPACITY — LIKING — OBLIGATION — PERMISSION.

Useful vocabulary

4. PEOPLE, THEIR WAYS AND CHARACTERS — 5. EMOTIONS — 7. FEELINGS AND APPRECIATION — 8. JUDGEMENTS AND EVALUATION — 9. SOCIAL ATTITUDES — 11. HUMAN COMMUNITIES — 13. DEVELOPED AND DEVELOPING COUNTRIES.

A few guidelines

1 → ***"He had neither brothers nor sisters; both his parents worked... / ... he had made few friends... / ... too late to save the life of either... / ... nothing but a few old toys... / ... Michael's mother begrudged the piccanins neither the old toys nor the bread."*** (Gr: **16,** § 4 - **2,** §§ 1c, 2a, 3b)

A. Compare Michael's life to that of the two children, using the following pattern:

The black children had neither nice clothes nor nice shoes, whereas Michael had both nice clothes and nice shoes.

Hints: You can compare: their toys, their houses, their friends, their parents' jobs, what they usually eat, what they do and where they go on holiday, etc.

B. Using *few / little* and *nothing but a few / nothing but a little,* imagine what the black children generally have. For example,

They have few clothes. They have nothing to eat but a little food once a day.

2 → ***"... he had made few friends... / ... he had given them nothing... / ... he had never asked them into the backyard..."*** (Gr: **11,** § 6)

Imagine what Dora said to Michael's mother about the black children and imagine how Michael justified what he had done. Use the following pattern:

Dora told Michael's mother that he had spoken to the children, but Michael said that he had just exchanged a few words with them and given them a toy or two.

3 → ***"He was used to it..."*** (Gr: **20,** § 3)

Compare Michael and the black children, using the following pattern:

Michael was used to having three meals a day, whereas the black children were used to eating once every two or three days.

4 → ***"... the two African children, who were now accosting him regularly, appeared..."*** (Gr: **13**)

Here are a few simple sentences. Try to give some more information about the people by adding to each sentence one or several clauses introduced by a relative pronom *(who, whom, which* or *whose).* Example:

A: *The children were waiting at Michael's door.*
B: *The children, who had not eaten for two days, were waiting at Michael's door.*
A: *Michael talked to the children.*
B: *Michael, whose mother was out shopping, talked to the children.*

A: The black children were admiring Michael's house. **B:**...
A: The black children loved Michael's toys. **B:**...
A: Dora saw Michael give the children a few toys. **B:**...
A: Dora told Michael's mother about what she had seen. **B:**...
A: Michael's mother was very angry. **B:**...
A: Michael justified what he had done. **B:**...
A: Michael's mother was satisfied. **B:**...
A: Michael's toys were old. **B:**...
A: The black children realized how poor they were. **B:**...
A: Michael's house was the biggest in the neighbourhood. **B:**...

Now, *you* find a few simple sentences and ask the other pupils to add a clause introduced by a relative pronoun.

5 → ***"... telling Michael that on no account should he play with the children, nor should he give them anything of value."*** (Gr: **15,** § 7b)

Use the same structure as above to imagine a few pieces of advice Michael's mother gave her son. Remember that you must invert subject and auxiliary in the sentence which follows, in order to give more emphasis to your sentence. For example,

Michael's mother told Dora that on no account should she allow Michael to talk to the black children. She told him that on no account should he play with black children.

6 → ***"... she was anxious to prevent her son from playing with the piccanins..."*** (Gr: **20,** § 3) ***"... fearing that he would pick up germs..."***

What else did Michael's mother want to prevent her son from doing and why? Use the following pattern:

She wanted to prevent him from talking to black children, because she was afraid/feared he would learn rude words.

7 → ***"... he was all the better able..."***

→ ***"He played for hours, by himself..."*** (Gr: **5,** § 3b)

→ ***"... She begged his pardon for having caused... / ... his mother did her duty by telling..."*** (Gr: **20,** § 3)

FOLLOW-UP WORK

1. Translation

1 - Je suis désolé, je ne suis pas habitué à boire tant...
2 - Elle a essayé de m'empêcher de conduire car elle avait peur que quelque chose m'arrive.
3 - Il m'a dit que je ne pouvais en aucun cas espérer trouver du travail dans cette compagnie.
4 - Il était toujours tout seul car il n'avait ni amis ni ennemis.
5 - Très peu de gens l'avaient aidée, et il ne lui restait rien qu'un peu d'argent pour finir le mois.
6 - Il m'a remercié de lui avoir prêté ma voiture.
7 - Son professeur, qu'il admirait beaucoup et dont les plaisanteries faisaient toujours rire les élèves, avait fait ses études en Afrique du Sud.
8 - Il m'est d'autant plus difficile de t'aider que ce n'est pas en te prêtant un peu d'argent que je résoudrai tes problèmes.

2. Oral or written work: The piccanins' parents

Here are the black children's parents. After looking at the picture very carefully,

1) Describe the father and the mother, their clothes, their environment, the "house" they live in.

2) What can you imagine about their everyday life, their means of subsistence, their jobs (if any)?

3) Look at their faces once again. What can you guess about their feelings? Can you see a difference between the husband's expression and that of the wife? Imagine their thoughts at this very moment.

© Caroline Binch.

4) Imagine a dialogue between the husband and the wife. They talk about their problems, the difficulties they have to survive, their children's future, etc.

Useful function

COMPARISON — COMPLAINING — DESIRE AND WISHES — INCAPACITY — REGRET.

Useful vocabulary

2. LANDSCAPES — 3. THE BODY AND ITS ACTIVITIES — 4. PEOPLE, THEIR WAYS AND CHARACTERS — 9. SOCIAL ATTITUDES — 11. HUMAN

3. Oral or witten work: A dialogue between Dora, Michael and his mother

"Their persistence eventually drove Dora to tell Michael's mother about them..." Imagine the dialogue that followed between Dora, Michael and his mother, in *direct speech.* You will have to use what is said in the text (from *"Their persistence..."* to the end) but above all you must use your own imagination to create as lively a dialogue as possible.

Useful functions

CONDITION AND HYPOTHESIS — DISAGREEMENT TO CRITICISM — DISLIKING — ORDERS — PROHIBITION — REPORTING — REPROACH.

Useful vocabulary

4. PEOPLE, THEIR WAYS AND CHARACTERS — 7. FEELINGS AND APPRECIATION — 9. SOCIAL ATTITUDES — 11. HUMAN COMMUNITIES.

2. The chief

After their plane was shot down[1], a group of schoolboys found themselves scattered[2] on a desert island. One of them, Ralph, first met a fat boy nicknamed Piggy. Then, on Piggy's advice, he called the others by blowing a conch[3]. All the other boys arrived, including a school choir[4] and its head, Jack Merridew.

1. to shoot down (*shot, shot*): *abattre*
2. to scatter: *éparpiller*
3. conch: *conque*
4. choir: *chœur*

Merridew turned to Ralph.

"Aren't there any grown-ups[5]?"

"No."

Merridew sat down on a trunk and looked round the circle.

"Then we'll have to look after ourselves."

Secure on the other side of Ralph, Piggy spoke timidly.

"That's why Ralph made a meeting. So as we can decide what to do. We've heard names. That's Johnny. Those two—they're twins, Sam'n Eric. Which is Eric—? You? No—you're Sam——"

"I'm Sam——"

"'n I'm Eric."

"We'd better all have names," said Ralph, "so I'm Ralph."

"We got most names," said Piggy. "Got'em just now."

"Kid's names," said Merridew. "Why should I be Jack? I'm Merridew."

Ralph turned to him quickly. This was the voice of one who knew his own mind[6].

"Then," went on Piggy, "that boy—I forget——"

"You're talking too much," said Jack Merridew. "Shut up, Fatty."

Laughter arose.

"He's not Fatty," cried Ralph, "his real name's Piggy!"

"Piggy!"

"Piggy!"

"Oh, Piggy!"

A storm of laughter arose and even the tiniest[7] child joined in.

5. grown-up: *adulte*
6. to know one's own mind (knew, known): *savoir ce que l'on veut*
7. tiny: *petit*

For the moment the boys were a closed circuit of sympathy with Piggy outside: he went very pink, bowed[8] his head and cleaned his glasses again.

Jack spoke.

"We've got to decide about being rescued."

There was a buzz[9]. One of the small boys, Henry, said that he wanted to go home.

"Shut up," said Ralph absently. He lifted the conch. "Seems to me we ought to have a chief to decide things."

"A chief! A chief!"

"I ought to be chief," said Jack with simple arrogance, "because I'm chapter chorister[10] and head boy[11]. I can sing C sharp[12]."

Another buzz.

"Well then," said Jack, "I——"

He hesitated. The dark boy, Roger, stirred[13] at last and spoke up.

"Let's have a vote."

"Yes!"

"Vote for a chief!"

"Let's vote——"

This toy of voting was almost as pleasing as the conch. Jack started to protest but the clamour changed from the general wish for a chief to an election by acclaim[14] of Ralph himself. None of the boys could have found good reason for this; what intelligence had been shown was traceable to[15] Piggy while the most obvious leader was Jack. But there was a stillness[16] about Ralph as he sat that marked him out: there was his size, and attractive appearance; and most obscurely, yet most powerfully, there was the conch. The being that had blown that, had sat waiting for them on the platform with the delicate thing balanced on his knees, was set apart.

"Him with the shell."

"Ralph! Ralph!"

"Let him be chief with the trumpet-thing."

Ralph raised a hand for silence.

"All right. Who wants Jack for chief?"

With dreary[17] obedience the choir raised their hands.

"Who wants me?"

Every hand outside the choir except Piggy's was raised immediately. Then Piggy, too, raised his hand grudgingly[18] into the air.

Ralph counted.

"I'm chief then."

The circle of boys broke into applause. Even the choir applauded; and the freckles[19] on Jack's face disappeared under a blush[20] of mortification. He started up[21], then changed his mind and sat down again while the air rang. Ralph looked at him, eager[22] to offer something.

"The choir belongs to you, of course."

"They could be the army——"

"Or hunters——"

"They could be——"

The suffusion[23] drained away[24] from Jack's face. Ralph waved[25] again for silence.

8. to bow: *baisser*
9. buzz: *brouhaha*
10. chapter chorister: *choriste à la maîtrise de la cathédrale*
11. head boy: *soliste*
12. C sharp: *do dièse*
13. to stir: *bouger*
14. election by acclaim: *élection par ovation*
15. traceable to: *dû à*
16. stillness: *calme*
17. dreary: *morne*
18. grudgingly: *à contre-cœur*
19. freckles: *taches de rousseur*
20. blush: *rouge*
21. to start up: *se lever d'un bond*
22. eager: *avide*
23. suffusion: *rougeur*
24. to drain away: *disparaître*
25. to wave: *agiter la main*

"Jack's in charge of the choir. They can be—what do you want them to be?"

"Hunters."

Jack and Ralph smiled at each other with shy liking.

William GOLDING, *Lord of the Flies* (1954), Faber and Faber Publishers.

MAIN TOPICS

1 Who are the main characters in this story? Where and when could the scene have taken place? Find the structure of the text and give each part a title.

2 Could you sum up the children's situation? Imagine what they no longer have, and what they need to survive on the island. What would you say are the potential dangers for their lives, and for their small community? What are the positive aspects of their misadventure?

The children: Piggy: list all the things you know about him (language, manners, ideas, etc.). What sort of a schoolboy was he? Why and how did he organize the first meeting? How do the others react towards him? Why?

— Ralph: list all the things you know about him. Why was he elected? What could the conch represent for him? Could you guess what his qualities and shortcomings as a leader may be?

— Jack: list all the things you know about him. Imagine his past life. How would you account for his attitude towards the other children? What could this imply for their future on the island? Why wasn't he elected? Why did he make hunters out of choir boys? What could this change of roles be symbolic of?

— Describe and analyse the relationships between the three main characters. Which one do *you* find the most (the least) likeable? Why?

3 You have probably read or seen stories dealing with people lost on a desert island. Try to remember some of them and re-tell them.

Useful functions

CAPACITY — COMPARISON — GETTING S.O. TO DO S.THING — INTENTION — OBLIGATION — PROBABILITY.

Useful vocabulary

4. PEOPLE, THEIR WAYS AND CHARACTERS — 5. EMOTIONS — 6. ACTIVITIES OF THE MIND AND COMMUNICATION — 7. FEELINGS AND APPRECIATION — 8. JUDGEMENTS AND EVALUATION — 9. SOCIAL ATTITUDES.

A few guidelines

1

→ ***Prepositions and verbal particles*** (Gr: **2**)

Translate the following sentences from the text into French and state each time whether the elements in ***bold letters*** are prepositions or verbal particles.

— *After their plane was shot **down,** a group of schoolboys found themselves scattered **on** a desert island.*
— *Merridew sat **down on** a trunk and looked **round** the circle.*
— *"Then we'll have to look **after** ourselves."*
— *Ralph turned **to** him quickly.*
— *"Then", went **on** Piggy...*
— *"Shut **up,** Fatty."*
— *A storm of laughter arose and even the tiniest child joined **in.***
— *... Roger, stirred at last and spoke **up**.*
— *But there was a stillness about Ralph as he sat that marked him **out**...*
— *Ralph raised the hand **for** silence.*
— *Piggy... raised his hand grudgingly **into** the air.*
— *The circle of boys broke **into** applause.*
— *... the freckles **on** Jack's face disappeared **under** a blush of mortification.*
— *He started **up,**... and sat **down** again...*
— *The suffusion drained **away from** Jack's face. Ralph waved again **for** silence.*
— *Jack and Ralph smiled **at** each other...*

2

→ ***"... We ought to have a chief... / I ought to be chief..."*** (Gr: **9,** § 8)

Imagine what qualities a chief should have to lead the children properly, and what he should do for the community. You can use either *should* or *ought to.*

He should be courageous, he shouldn't be weak, he ought to organize the children's lives, etc.

3

→ ***"Let's have a vote. / Let's vote... / Let him be chief..."*** (Gr: **19,** § 3) ***"They could be the army... / They can be..."*** (Gr: **9**) ***"We'd better all have names..."*** (Gr: **10,** § 1b) ***"... we'll have to look after ourselves. / We' ve got to decide..."*** (Gr: **10,** § 2b)

Imagine a dialogue between the boys and Ralph, once he has been elected. The boys will suggest several activities *("Let's..., we could..., we can...");* Ralph will suggest a better solution *("We'd better...,")* and explain why *("We have to..., we' ve got to...").* For example:

Boy: *Let's swim in the sea!*
Ralph: *No, we'd better gather some wood. We' ve got to build a fire.*

4

→ ***"... he called the others by blowing a conch."*** (Gr: **20,** § 3b)

Imagine how the children could solve their problems. Use the following pattern:

They could try to be rescued by building a fire on a hill, they could... by...

5

→ ***"... to look after ourselves. / ... an election of Ralph himself."*** (Gr: **5,** § 3)

→ ***"So as we can decide what to do. / ... the voice of one who knew his own mind. / The being that had blown..."*** (Gr: **13,** §§ 2, 3, 6)

→ ***"Which is Eric? / Who wants Jack for chief? / Who wants me? / ... what do you want them to be?"*** (Gr: **15,** § 4)

→ ***"... he wanted to go home. / ... what do you want them to be?"*** (Gr: **18,** §§ 2b, 3a)

→ ***"None of the boys could have found good reason for this..."*** (Gr: **9,** § 11b)

FOLLOW-UP WORK

1. Translation

1 - Qui de vous deux veut que je l'aide ?
2 - On ferait mieux de trouver un moyen de quitter cette île... Essayons de penser à ce que nous pourrions faire...
3 - On devrait voter pour élire un chef.
4 - Il faudra que tu te souviennes que tu dois m'apporter ton livre sur Robinson Crusoë.
5 - Merci de ton aide : nous n'aurions jamais pu faire ça nous-mêmes.
6 - Tu pourrais avoir une réponse plus rapide en lui téléphonant, non ?

2. Oral or written work: A desert island quiz

There is a very popular programme on Radio 4 called: "Desert island discs." A well-known person is asked to imagine what he/she would take if he/she were stranded on a desert island. He/she is allowed to bring 5 books, 5 records and 5 other items of his/her choice. It is assumed that he/she would already have all the things essential to life (food, shelter, clothes, weapons, etc.).

Either in groups, individually or collectively, imagine what *you* would take on to your island. You should of course justify your choice and explain what sort of life you would try to lead on your island.

P.S.: Remember that the 5 items that you take with you are only *luxuries.* The bare essentials are provided on this very special island.

Useful functions

CAPACITY — CONDITION AND HYPOTHESIS — DESIRE AND WISHES — DISLIKING — INCAPACITY — LIKING — OBLIGATION — QUANTITY.

Useful vocabulary

2. LANDSCAPES — 3. THE BODY AND ITS ACTIVITIES — 7. FEELINGS AND APPRECIATION — 8. JUDGEMENTS AND EVALUATION.

3. Oral or written work: Piggy's diary

The boy called Piggy kept a diary, because he found an exercise-book in the remains of the plane which crashed on the island. You should imagine what Piggy wrote about his experiences on the day Ralph was elected and also explain what he would have done if *he* had been elected, or what he thinks should be done now.

Useful functions

CAPACITY — COMPARISON — CONDITION AND HYPOTHESIS — DESIRE AND WISHES — DISAGREEMENT TO CRITICISM — PROBABILITY — REGRET.

Useful vocabulary

4. PEOPLE, THEIR WAYS AND CHARACTERS — 5. EMOTIONS — 6. ACTIVITIES OF THE MIND AND COMMUNICATION — 7. FEELINGS AND APPRECIATION — 9. SOCIAL ATTITUDES — 11. HUMAN COMMUNITIES.

4. Oral or written work: Scenes from *Lord of the Flies*

Here are some pictures from Peter Brook's film: *Lord of the Flies.* You should first look at these pictures carefully. You will then:

1) Describe each picture, explaining what the children are doing, when, where and why.

2) Guess what the children's ideas and feelings are in each picture.

3) Imagine what happened between the pictures and why.

Useful functions

COMPARISON — CONTRAST AND CONTRADICTION — GETTING S.O. TO DO S.THING — INTENTION — PROBABILITY.

Useful vocabulary

1. LIGHT, SOUNDS AND THE SENSES — 2. LANDSCAPES — 3. THE BODY AND ITS ACTIVITIES — 5. EMOTIONS — 7. FEELINGS AND APPRECIATION.

3. Why I am doing it

Victor Zorza, the writer, is a famous journalist from "The Guardian" who one day decided to live in a small village in India and to write about the people there.

So many readers have asked why I gave up[1] my political column to settle[2] in a Himalayan village and what my life here is like, that I have to break my silence. It isn't what some of them think. I am not doing penance[3]. Aren't you bored, some of them ask; lonely? I have no time to be either. It's a good life, exciting and rewarding[4]—for the most part.

I still get up at half past four, in the dark, when the drummer[5] sounds the reveille. I still climb[6] the distant peak which has become my toilet and return for breakfast at about seven. But I no longer mind when neighbours come into my hut uninvited and stare[7] at me while I eat, or write, or read. Now that the novelty has worn off[8], they bring visitors from nearby villages.

They find my eating habits peculiar, because knife, fork and spoon are a needless encumbrance: it can all be done more cleanly and tastefully with your fingers. Writing is a mysterious procedure to them but they know that it conveys my impressions of village life to readers in other lands.

After breakfast I work on my notes and then follow the villagers to the fields. The walk, up hill and down dale[9], can take several hours. By then the sun is high. They rest in the shade[10]

1. to give up (gave, given): *abandonner*
2. to settle: *s'installer*
3. to do penance (for one's sins): *faire pénitence (pour ses péchés)*
4. rewarding: *plein de joie*
5. drummer: *tambour(rite bouddhiste)*
6. to climb: *gravir*
7. to stare: *regarder fixement*
8. to wear off (wore, worn): *se dissiper*
9. dale: *vallée*
10. shade: *ombre*

and we talk until the heat subsides[11]. When they resume work, I return to the village where old men, no longer fit for backbreaking toil[12], look after the children. They answer a stranger's questions more readily than younger folk, who are often too tired when they return from the fields towards the evening.

That's the time for my main meal—a heaped[13] plateful of rice, topped by a lentil gravy[14], garnished with fried vegetables when available[15].

The simple food tastes good after a day in the open. I don't miss the meat. I have some cans of corned beef and sardines, but these are my iron[16] rations. And so to bed, between eight and nine, to sleep untroubled, more soundly[17] than I have slept for years. A humdrum[18] existence? Don't you believe it!

The excitement comes from sharing[19] in the unending drama of village life, from unravelling[20] its mysteries, learning to understand new values—and to respect them. At first the villagers' ways of thinking seemed to me simple or naive and sometimes just misguided. Now I know how wise[21] some of them are, saner[22] and more wholesome[23] than our own ways.

Yet no one who has read these columns could accuse me of idealising the villagers' life—indeed, I have often been reproached for painting it in black colours, particularly by Indians who know richer, happier villages. There are 500,000 villages in India and I don't claim[24] that mine is typical. But I decided to write my village column because it had gradually dawned[25] on me that three-quarters of the world's people live in conditions of rural poverty that are not understood by the rest of us.

Victor ZORZA, *Village Voice* (1983), Guardian Publications Ltd.

11. to subside: *diminuer*
12. toil: *labeur (pénible)*
13. heaped: *bien rempli* (heap: *tas*)
14. lentil gravy: *purée de lentilles*
15. when available: *quand on en trouve*
16. iron: *fer*
17. soundly: *profondément*
18. humdrum: *monotone*
19. to share: *partager*
20. to unravel: *éclaircir*
21. wise: *sage*
22. sane: *sensé*
23. wholesome: *sain*
24. to claim: *prétendre*
25. it had dawned on me: *je m'étais rendu compte*

MAIN TOPICS

1 Who is the main character? What is his job? Where does he live now? Can you draw Victor Zorza's portrait: age, personality, tastes, ideas, etc.? What can you imagine about his life before?

2 What are the writer's various reasons for settling in this Indian village? What sort of difficulties did he probably have to overcome to adapt to his new life?

3 What do we learn about his life today? What are his resources? What are his activities? What do we learn about his relationships with and his feelings towards the villagers? What has he gained from his new experience? Are there any negative aspects?

4 What are the villagers' attitudes towards the journalist? How can you account for their behaviour?

5 What sort of articles do you think he writes? What are they about? What does he mean by: *"...no one could accuse me of idealising the villagers' life."*? What does he particularly insist on? Why?

6 Try to discuss the various problems raised by this text:

— The role of old people in this Indian village, and, more generally, in developing and developed countries.

— The role of journalists and their influence on their readers.

7 On the whole, what do *you* think about Victor Zorza's choice to live in an Indian village? Are you tempted by such a life-style? Why?

Useful functions

CAPACITY — CAUSE — COMPARISON — LIKING — PROBABILITY — PURPOSE.

Useful vocabulary

3. THE BODY AND ITS ACTIVITIES — 4. PEOPLE, THEIR WAYS AND CHARACTERS — 6. ACTIVITIES OF THE MIND AND COMMUNICATION — 7. FEELINGS AND APPRECIATION — 8. JUDGEMENTS AND EVALUATION — 9. SOCIAL ATTITUDES — 16. THE MEDIA.

A few guidelines

1

→ ***Used to*** + ***V*** (Gr: **8,** § 2c) — ***Since*** + ***Present perfect*** (Gr: **11,** §§ 4, 5)

Compare the way Victor Zorza used to live in England and the way he lives now in his Himalayan village. Use the following patterns:

He used to sleep very little, but since he settled there he has always slept soundly.
He used to live in a big house, but since he settled there he has been living in a small house.

2

→ ***"... more cleanly / ... more tastefully... / ... more readily than... / ... younger folk... / ... more soundly than... / ... saner... / ... more wholesome... / ... richer and happier..."*** (Gr: **7,** § 1)

Using as many comparatives as you can, help Victor Zorza compare his life in England and his life in India. We have only given a few adjectives in the grid below, but remember that you can compare with **nouns** *(He had more comfort),* with **verbs** *(He eats less)* or with **adverbs** *(He sees his neighbours more often).*

	England	India
Life	hectic, tiring, comfortable, cosy, artificial, ...	peaceful, slow, simple, sane, ...
Fitness	exhausted, fat, ...	slim, fit, strong, ...
Standard of living	high, ...	low, ...
Community life	anonymous, indifferent, selfish, ...	close, friendly, helpful, ...
etc.		

3

→ ***Enjoy*** + ***V-ing*** (Gr: **20,** § 3d)

With the help of the text, try to think of all the things Victor Zorza enjoys doing in this Indian village. Use the following pattern:

He enjoys getting up early in the morning.
He enjoys...

4

→ ***"So many readers have asked... that..."*** (Gr: **2,** § 2b)
→ ***"... what my life here is like..."***
→ ***"... I have to break my silence."*** (Gr: **10,** § 2b)
→ ***"Aren't you bored..."*** (Gr: **16,** § 5)
→ ***"I still get up... / I still climb..."***
→ ***"... I no longer mind... / ... no longer fit..."*** (Gr: **16,** § 4)
→ ***"... while I eat..."***
→ ***"... we talk until..."***
→ ***"... from sharing... / ... from unravelling its mysteries..."*** (Gr: **20,** § 3d)
→ ***"... the villagers' ways... / ... the villagers' life..."*** (Gr: **3,** §§ 1, 2)
→ ***"... no one who has read..."*** (Gr: **5,** § 7 - **13,** §§ 2, 3)
→ ***"... could accuse me of idealising..."*** (Gr: **9,** § 1 - **20,** § 3d)
→ ***"... I have often been reproached for painting..."*** (Gr: **14,** § 3 - **20,** § 3d)
→ ***"... I don't claim that mine is..."*** (Gr: **5,** § 5)

FOLLOW-UP WORK

1. Translation

1 - Il est cinq heures du soir, tu travailles depuis ce matin, n'es-tu pas fatigué ?
2 - Beaucoup de gens regardent la télévision pendant qu'ils mangent.
3 - Achète un lave-vaisselle, ta vaisselle sera faite plus rapidement qu'à la main.
4 - Mon père ne fume plus, car fumer est dangereux pour la santé.
5 - Regarde cette chaise, ses pieds *(= legs)* sont cassés.
6 - Il a bu tant de champagne et mangé tant de chocolats qu'il doit aller chez le docteur aujourd'hui.
7 - Comment se sont passées tes vacances ?
8 - Qui pourrait me dire quelle est la capitale de l'Australie ? Personne ? Quelle honte !
9 - On a souvent reproché à mon frère d'être trop naïf.
10 - Voilà ton manteau. Où est le mien?
11 - En Angleterre, plusieurs journaux accusent le gouvernement d'être indifférent aux problèmes des mineurs.
12 - Attendons jusqu'à ce que la pluie s'arrête.
13 - J'aime encore me lever tôt le matin.
14 - Quand j'étais jeune, j'allais voir ma grand-mère tous les dimanches.

2. Oral or written work: A conversation with old villagers

Let us imagine that one day some of the old villagers start asking Zorza questions about his life in England, and more generally about the way people live in the West. The old villagers could ask about various subjects: the climate, people's activities, the economic and political system, family relationships, the role of women, etc. You will have to imagine the old men's questions, Zorza's answers and the reactions they provoke.

Useful functions

CAUSE — FREQUENCY — GIVING ONE'S OPINION — QUANTITY — SURPRISE.

Useful vocabulary

1. FEELINGS AND APPRECIATION — 8. JUDGEMENTS AND EVALUATION — 11. HUMAN COMMUNITIES.

3. Oral and written work: A broken life

> There was a good chance that Kedu's broken leg would be mended and his broken life put together again if he could be persuaded to leave the village for a while. The hospital was in town, only a day's journey away. But instead of responding to this idea, with the enthusiasm I had expected, he said glumly that he would have to consult his wife. Then he began to avoid me...
>
> Victor ZORZA, *Village Voice* (1982), Guardian Publications Ltd.

Here is the beginning of an article by Victor Zorza. Read it carefully. Then,

1) Try to imagine the conversation between Victor Zorza and Kedu: Zorza tries to persuade Kedu to go to hospital, and offers to help him; Kedu refuses and tells him why. Think of all the consequences this decision might have on Kedu's life...

2) Write an article on Kedu, after the manner of Victor Zorza.

Useful functions

ADVICE — DISAGREEMENT TO CRITICISM — INCAPACITY — PROBABILITY — PROPOSING — REFUSAL.

Useful vocabulary

3. THE BODY AND ITS ACTIVITIES — 6. ACTIVITIES OF THE MIND AND COMMUNICATION — 7. FEELINGS AND APPRECIATION — 8. JUDGEMENTS AND EVALUATION.

1. tribe: *tribu*

4. The tribes[1] of Britain

2. sizeable: *assez important*
3. web: *tissu*
4. leather: *cuir (vêtements)*
5. closely: *de près*
6. accuracy: *précision*
7. Britons: *Anglais*
8. to belong: *appartenir; ici: (en) faire partie*
9. rate: *taux*
10. to be likely to: *être susceptible de*
11. on the dole: *au chômage (*dole: *allocation chômage)*
12. postwar: *d'après guerre*
13. renewal: *rénovation*
14. featureless: *ici, sans âme*
15. youths: *jeunes*

The British, in particular a sizeable[2] percentage of the population, have regrouped into a complex and curious web[3] of alternative cultures, the tribes of Britain.

The ornamentation of the new tribes is shocking. Says Punk Singer Nick Reynolds: "The clothes we wear are not normal. Dirty leather[4], chains, tattoos. Tribes used to paint themselves to frighten the enemy away and survive. That's what we're doing. And the chains? They say it's a free country, but we might as well be in chains."

Not even the police, who follow tribal movements as closely[5] as sociologists do, can say with accuracy[6] how many Britons[7] belong[8]. But the numbers are probably in the hundreds of thousands. Unemployment in Britain is currently 13.3%, yet for the 7.5 million Britons between the ages of 16 and 24, the rate[9] is 16%. It is these dispossessed young people who are most likely to[10] identify with a tribe. The continuing stagnation of the British economy has convinced many of the jobless young that they will never have a place in the working world and that they are facing a life on the dole[11]. At the same time, postwar[12] urban renewal[13] has left many British cities and towns sterile and featureless[14]. Those environments have helped produce a generation of alienated youths[15] who have turned to tribalism to give their lives meaning.

Working-class teenagers are especially attracted to the tribes. For them, Britain's age-old class system poses a formidable barrier. Says Author Peter York, an expert on the new tribes: "What they are saying about the future is that there is no future. Britain marching into the past is what this is all about. We now have a terribly divided and fragmented nation."

© Ronald Searle, 1976.

Such tribalism is by no means[16] restricted to Britain. Nowhere, however, are the youth tribes as extensive and cynical as they are in Britain. "The postwar governments promised kids[17] power and control over their lives," says Sociologist Paul Corrigan of North London's Polytechnic College. "These promises were taken seriously. Now young people feel let down[18]. They don't want a palace but they do want what the state[19] promised them: a job and some control over their lives." And nowhere else do tribe members work out[20] their hostilities and frustrations with so much flamboyance.

From *Time*, October 24, 1983.

16. by no means: *en aucun cas*
17. kid: *gosse*
18. to let down (let, let): *trahir, laisser tomber*
19. state: *état*
20. to work out: *ici, se défouler de*

MAIN TOPICS

1 Who is attracted to the tribes? How many people are concerned? What do we learn about their age, their social origins? What do they look like? What are the similarities and differences with regard to the past?

2 Find and analyse the following elements in the article:
— The reasons why young people belong to tribes (economic, social, psychological).
— What they find in tribes.
— Their feelings and attitudes towards adults and society in general.

3 Is it a widespread phenomenon? Does tribalism exist in France? Where else? Give examples.

Useful functions

CAUSE — CONSEQUENCE — DESIRE AND WISHES — INCAPACITY — PURPOSE.

Useful vocabulary

3. THE BODY AND ITS ACTIVITIES — 7. FEELINGS AND APPRECIATION — 9. SOCIAL ATTITUDES — 11. HUMAN COMMUNITIES — 12. TOWNS, SMALL AND LARGE.

A few guidelines

1

→ ***"Tribes used to paint themselves to frighten the enemy away and survive... / ... have turned to tribalism to give their lives meaning."*** (Gr: **18,** § 3e)

Try to analyse why young people turn to tribalism, and why they dress and behave outrageously. Before doing the following exercise, you must differentiate these two structures:

They dress outrageously in order to shock their parents.
They dress outrageously so that people will notice their hopelessness.

Hints: tell, show, express, realize, demonstrate, scare, mock, protest, see, etc.

2

→ ***They thought they would*** + ***V*** (Gr: **17,** § 3)

In the text, we are told that *"the postwar governments promised kids power and control over their lives... These promises were taken seriously."* Try to imagine what the governments promised them, and what these young people thought they would do, have, get, find, etc.

3

→ ***"Tribes used to paint themselves..."*** (Gr: **8,** § 2c)

→ ***"... we might as well be in chains."***

→ ***"... the police, who follow..."*** (Gr: **13,** §§ 2, 3)

→ ***"... as closely as sociologists do... / ... as extensive as they are..."*** (Gr: **7,** § 1c)

→ ***"... these young people... / Those environments... / ... what this is all about... / These promises..."*** (Gr: **1,** § 2 - **5,** § 6)

→ ***"... there is no future. / Nowhere are the youths... / ... some control over their lives. / ... nowhere else do tribe members..."*** (Gr: **2,** § 1d - **5,** § 7)

→ ***"Such tribalism..."***

1. Translation

1 - Regarde ces fleurs sur la table.
2 - Jadis, les femmes faisaient elles-mêmes leur pain.
3 - Regarde ces oiseaux sur le toit.
4 - La police, qui cherchait le petit garçon, ne le trouva nulle part.
5 - Les jeunes d'aujourd'hui ne sont pas aussi polis que jadis.
6 - Je n'ai jamais rien entendu de tel !
7 - On trouve tout ce que l'on veut chez Harrods ! Tu ne trouveras nulle part ailleurs un aussi beau magasin.
8 - Pourquoi as-tu besoin d'argent? Pour t'acheter une moto ?
9 - Nous sommes partis à la campagne pour que notre fils cesse de tousser.
10 - Il n'y a pas de lait dans le frigidaire.
11 - S'ils s'aiment, autant qu'ils se marient, non ?
12 - Il pensait qu'il trouverait un bon métier en Amérique.
13 - Il fut incapable de finir à temps.

2. Oral or written work: You are what you wear

Before starting anything, look at these three pictures very carefully. Either in groups, collectively or individually:

1) Describe these people, their clothes, their ornaments, what they are doing, their environment, etc.

2) Try to imagine and compare their way of life, their likes, their dislikes, the type of music they listen to, their activities, what they do in their free time, what they believe in, the relationships they have with their parents. You could use a grid with the following entries: age, clothes, hair-cut, activities, schooling, likes, dislikes, music, relationships with adults, fears, hopes, etc.

Useful functions

COMPARISON — CONTRAST AND CONTRADICTION — DISLIKING — LIKING — PROBABILITY.

Useful vocabulary

3. THE BODY AND ITS ACTIVITIES — 4. PEOPLE, THEIR WAYS AND CHARACTERS — 7. FEELINGS AND APPRECIATION — 9. SOCIAL ATTITUDES — 15. THE ARTS.

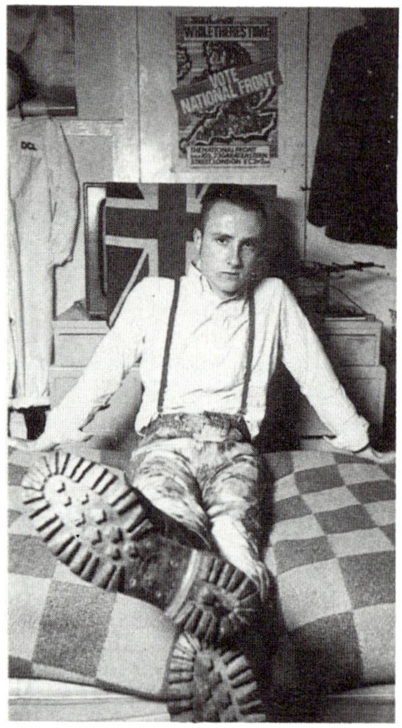

2

© *Time*, October 24, 1983.

3

© *The Sunday Times Magazine*, November 1, 1981.

1

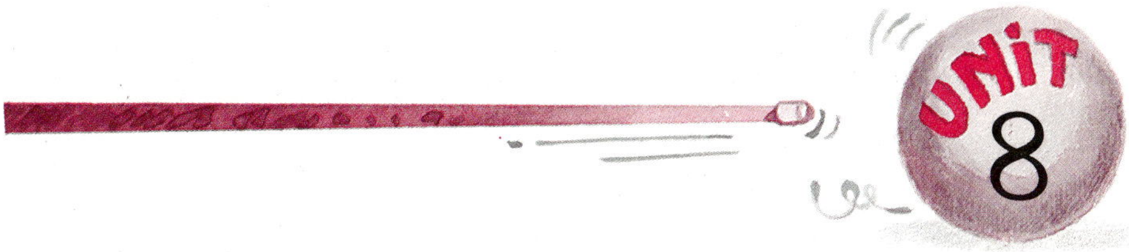

1. The new masters

The XXIst century... America has long since been destroyed by a nuclear war. The President of the United States has sent Jerry as an emissary to the Indians to ask for their help.

At the entrance to a large, expensively decorated tent, the Indian stood aside and casually[1] indicated that Jerry should enter.

It was dim[2] inside, but the illumination was rich enough to take Jerry's breath away[3]. Oil lamps! Three of them! These people lived well.

A century ago, before the whole world had gone smash[4] in the last big war, his people had owned plenty of oil lamps themselves. Better than oil lamps, perhaps, if one could believe the stories the engineers told around the evening fires. Such stories were pleasant to hear, but they were glories of the distant past.

The Indians, whose tribal organization had been the first to adjust to the new conditions, in the all-important present, the Indians had the granaries[5], the Indians had the oil lamps. And the Indians...

There were two nervous white men serving food to the group squatting[6] on the floor. An old man, the chief, with a carved[7], chunky[8] body. Three warriors[9], one of them surprisingly young for council[10]. And a middle-aged Negro, wearing the same bound-on rags[11] as Jerry, except that they looked a little newer, a little cleaner.

Jerry bowed low[12] before the chief, spreading his arms apart[13], palms[14] down.

"I come from New York, from our chief," he mumbled[15]. "I come with a message of importance and many gifts."

"Eat with us," the old man said. "Then you will give us your gifts and your message."

Gratefully, Jerry squatted on the ground a short distance from them. He was hungry, and among the fruit in the bowls he had seen something that must be an orange. He had heard so many arguments about what oranges tasted like!

After a while, the old man said, "I am Chief Three Hydrogen Bombs. This"—pointing to the young man—"is my son, Makes Much Radiation. And this"—pointing to the middle-aged Negro—"is a sort of compatriot of yours."

1. casually: *d'un air désinvolte*
2. dim: *sombre*
3. to take s.o.'s breath away (took, taken): *couper le souffle à qqn*
4. to go smash (went, gone): *s'écrouler*
5. granary: *grenier (à céréales)*
6. squatting: *accroupi*
7. carved: *bien fait*
8. chunky: *trapu*
9. warrior: *guerrier*
10. council: *conseil (= réunion)*
11. bound-on rags: *haillons rapiécés*
12. to bow low: *s'incliner très bas*
13. to spread apart (spread, spread): *écarter largement*
14. palm: *paume*
15. to mumble: *marmonner*

16. to raise: *lever*
17. to go down under (went, gone): *tomber aux mains de*
18. nod: *signe de tête*
19. to till the soil: *labourer la terre*
20. tithe: *dîme (1/10ᵉ des récoltes)*
21. to shift one's shoulders back and forth: *rouler les épaules*
22. to flex: *tendre*
23. to growl: *grogner*
24. sharply: *sévèrement*
25. to raise hell: *faire la foire*
26. to glare: *jeter un regard furieux*

At Jerry's questioning look, and the chief's raised[16] finger of permission, the Negro explained. "Sylvester Thomas. Ambassador to the Sioux from the Confederate States of America."

"The Confederacy? She's still alive? We heard ten years ago—"

"The Confederacy is very much alive, sir. The Western Confederacy that is, with its capital at Jackson, Mississippi. The Eastern Confederacy, the one centred at Richmond, Virginia, did go down under[17] the Seminole. We have been more fortunate. The Arapahoe, the Cheyenne, and"—with a nod[18] to the chief—"especially the Sioux, if I may say so, sir, have been very kind to us. They allow us to live in peace, so long as we till the soil[19] quietly and pay our tithes[20]."

Makes Much Radiations shifted his shoulders back and forth[21] and flexed[22] his arm muscles. "All this talk," he growled[23]. "Paleface talk. Makes me tired."

"Mr Thomas is not a paleface," his father told him sharply[24]. "Show respect! He's our guest and an accredited ambassador—you're not to use a word like paleface in his presence!"

"A-ah!" said Makes Much Radiation impatiently. "As far as I'm concerned, the only good palefaces are dead. And that's that." He thought a bit. "Except their women. Paleface women are fun when you're a long way from home and feel like raising a little hell[25]."

Chief Three Hydrogen Bombs glared[26] his son into silence.

William TENN, *Eastward Ho!*, © 1958 by Mercury Press, Inc.

MAIN TOPICS

1 Sum up the story in just a few words: When and where does it take place? Who are the main characters? What is the general situation?

2 Jerry: Guess the various reasons why he was sent as an emissary. What can we imagine about him: age, physical appearance, qualities, etc.? Describe and analyse his attitude towards the Indians. What can we guess about his probable feelings, hopes and fears?

3 Imagine the situation of the other people in America: living conditions, environment, political, social and economic system. What is the

role of the President of the United States? What can we imagine about the events which caused such a situation?

4 The Indians: Describe their material situation. How and why did they survive? Explain the title: *"The new masters."* What can we guess about the Indians' achievements?

5 The chief and his son: Why such names? Describe and analyse the chief's attitude and probable feelings towards Jerry and Sylvester. Why is his son's attitude so different? What can we guess about Makes Much Radiation's feelings towards Sylvester, Jerry and palefaces in general?

6 The writer's goal: Would you say this story is tragic or comic? Why? What does the writer try to prove? Does he fear anything? What are his hopes?

7 The reader's reactions: Fear? Laughter? Disbelief? Would you say this story is purely fictional or could it come true? If there were a nuclear holocaust, who would survive? Where? How? Why?

Useful functions

CAPACITY — COMPARISON — INCAPACITY — PAST — PROBABILITY.

Useful vocabulary

3. THE BODY AND ITS ACTIVITIES — 4. PEOPLE, THEIR WAYS AND CHARACTERS — 9. SOCIAL ATTITUDES — 11. HUMAN COMMUNITIES.

A few guidelines

1

→ ***"Better than oil lamps... / ... a little newer, a little cleaner... / We have been more fortunate."*** (Gr: **7,** § 2)

Compare, according to what you can deduce or imagine, the Indians' living conditions with those of the Whites. Remember that you can compare with **adjectives** (1), **adverbs** (2), **nouns** (3) or **verbs** (4).

(1) *The Indians are richer.*
(2) *The Whites eat less often.*
(3) *The Indians have more land.*
(4) *The Whites suffer more.*

Hints: You can compare their clothes, food, the organisation of the communities, the relationships with other communities, political systems, etc.

2

→ ***"... before the whole world had gone smash... / ... his people had owned... / The Indians had been the first... / ... he had seen something... / He had heard so many arguments..."*** (Gr: **8,** §§ 2a, 2b - **11,** § 6)

There are two verbs in brackets in each of the following sentences. Choose the preterite for one of the two verbs and the pluperfect for the other. Use the progressive form (Be + V-ing) whenever possible. For example:

Jerry (walk) for hours when he (see) the Indian camp.

→ *Jerry had been walking for hours when he saw the Indian camp.*

— Jerry *(try)* to remember what the President *(tell)* him three days before.
— Jerry *(check)* that he *(not-forget)* the gifts he was to give to the chief.
— As he *(expect),* the Indian warrior outside the tent *(tell)* him to enter.
— When he *(see)* the oil lamps, Jerry remembered the stories he *(hear)* long ago.
— Two men *(serve)* food to the Indians who *(gather)* around the chief.
— Jerry *(tell)* the chief that the President *(send)* him to ask for help.
— In a bowl, there *(be)* some fruit which Jerry *(never-see)* in his life.
— The chief *(introduce)* the young man who *(stand)* at his side ever since Jerry's arrival.
— Jerry *(think)* that the Confederacy *(be destroyed)* ten years before.

3

→ ***"... you're not to use a word..."*** (Gr: **10,** § 2c)

Imagine that Jerry has come to ask the Indians to allow a group of white people to settle on their territory. The chief agrees, but on certain conditions. Imagine as many conditions as you can, using the following pattern:

You're not to approach the camp without permission.
You are to give us one tenth of your crops.
You are... You are not...

4

→ ***"America has long since been destroyed... / The President has sent Jerry... / We have been more fortunate... / ... the Sioux have been very kind to us."*** (Gr: **11**)

→ ***"... the illumination was rich enough to take..."***

→ ***"... Jerry's breath... / ... Jerry's questioning look... / ... the chief's raised finger..."*** (Gr: **3,** §§ 1, 2)

→ ***"The Indians, whose tribal organization..."*** (Gr: **13,** § 4)

→ ***"... something that must be an orange."*** (Gr: **9,** § 5)

→ ***"We heard ten years ago..."*** (Gr: **8,** § 2a - **11,** § 1)

FOLLOW-UP WORK

1. Translation

1 - Le fils du chef regarda les cadeaux de Jerry d'un air furieux.

2 - Tu ne dois pas te servir de cette voiture sans la permission de ton père.

3 - Cela faisait des heures que Jerry cherchait le camp indien lorsque soudain il aperçut la fumée d'un feu de bois.

4 - Les Indiens mangeaient de la meilleure nourriture que les Blancs et souffraient donc moins.

5 - Les Blancs n'étaient pas assez forts pour lutter contre les Indiens.

6 - Le Président des États-Unis, dont la capitale était maintenant New York, avait envoyé Jerry auprès des Indiens.

7 - Ça fait longtemps que nos récoltes sont bonnes.

8 - Il y a plus d'un siècle, les Blancs étaient riches et puissants.

9 - Regarde cette fumée ; ça doit être le camp !

2. Oral or written work: Jerry and the President

Imagine the meeting which preceded Jerry's mission to the Indians: the President summons Jerry, explains the various problems the Whites are faced with, the many solutions which have been proposed, his choice of the Indians, his reasons, etc. Jerry should mention the possible dangers, suggest other solutions, point out the probable consequences of the President's choice, etc.

Hints: Before starting the dialogue, you should describe the setting and the characters' physical appearance. You can add other characters if you wish.

Useful functions

ADVICE — CAPACITY — CONDITION AND HYPOTHESIS — DISAGREEMENT TO CRITICISM — INCAPACITY — OBLIGATION — PROBABILITY.

Useful vocabulary

4. PEOPLE, THEIR WAYS AND CHARACTERS — 8. JUDGEMENTS AND EVALUATION — 9. SOCIAL ATTITUDES — 11. HUMAN COMMUNITIES.

3. Oral or written work: The immortals

After looking at the picture very carefully, try to:

1) Describe the setting, the characters, their feelings and actions, in as much detail as possible.

2) Build a story around this picture: Where does the scene take place? When? Who are the characters? What are their relationships? What

are they doing? Why? What happened before this picture? What may happen after?

3) Guess Susan Calvin's aim when drawing this picture. Is it an optimistic or a pessimistic picture? Why? Why did she call it "the immortals"? Do you agree with this title? Why? Could you suggest other titles?

4) Imagine why this picture has been associated with the text "The new masters".

Useful functions

CAPACITY — GETTING S.O. TO DO S.THING — INTENTION — PROBABILITY — PURPOSE.

Useful vocabulary

1. LIGHT, SOUNDS AND THE SENSES — 3. THE BODY AND ITS ACTIVITIES — 5. EMOTIONS — 7. FEELINGS AND APPRECIATION.

4. Written or oral work: A man called horse

You may have seen *"A man called horse"* at the cinema or on T.V. Look at the picture and try to remember (or imagine) what happened before this episode. What will happen next?

After telling the story, try to imagine how this man himself would have written about his adventures among the Indians. You can choose to write his diary or an article in a magazine.

Useful functions

ADMIRATION — COMPARISON — GETTING S.O. TO DO S.THING — INCAPACITY — OBLIGATION — PROHIBITION — REPORTING.

Useful vocabulary

3. THE BODY AND ITS ACTIVITIES — 4. PEOPLE, THEIR WAYS AND CHARACTERS — 8. JUDGEMENTS AND EVALUATION — 9. SOCIAL ATTITUDES — 11. HUMAN COMMUNITIES.

2. Starting off on the right foot

Billy Casper, 14, is having an interview with the Employment Officer at school.

"Now then, Casper, what kind of job had you in mind?"

He shunted[1] the record cards[2] to one side, and replaced them with a blank form[3], lined and sectioned[4] for the relevant[5] information. CASPER, WILLIAM, in red on the top line. He copied age, address and other details from the record card, then changed pens and looked up.

"Well?"

"I don't know, I haven't thought about it right."

"Well you should be thinking about it. You want to start off on the right foot, don't you?"

"I suppose so."

"You haven't looked round for anything yet then?"

"No, not yet."

"Well what would you like to do? What are you good at?"

He consulted Billy's record card again.

"Offices held... Aptitudes and Abilities... right then... would you like to work in an office? Or would you prefer manual work?"

"What's that, manual work?"

"It means working with your hands, for example, building, farming, engineering. Jobs like that, as opposed to pen pushing jobs[6]."

1. to shunt: *pousser*
2. record card: *fiche*
3. blank form: *formulaire vierge*
4. lined and sectioned: *avec les lignes et les rubriques*
5. relevant: *utile*
6. pen pushing job: *travail de rond-de-cuir*

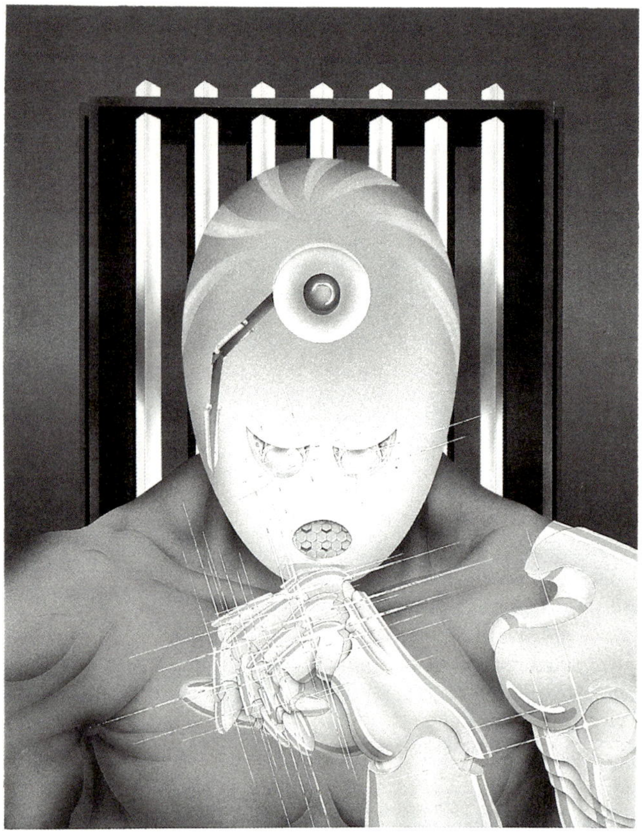

"I'd be all right working in an office, wouldn't I? But I've a job to[7] read and write."

The Employment Officer printed[8] MANUAL on the form, then raised his pen hand as though he was going to print it again on the top of his head. Billy was staring[9] straight past him out of the window.

"Have you thought about entering a trade[10] as an apprentice? You know, as an electrician, or a bricklayer[11] or something like that. Of course the money isn't too good while you're serving your apprenticeship. You may find that lads[12] of your own age who take dead end jobs[13] will be earning far more than you; but in those jobs there's no satisfaction or security, and if you do stick it out[14] you'll find it well worth your while[15]. And whatever happens, at least you'll always have a trade at your finger tips[16] won't you?...

"Well, what do you think about it? And as you've already said you feel better working with your hands, perhaps this would be your best bet[17]. Of course this would mean attending[18] Technical College and studying for various examinations, but nowadays most employers encourage their lads to take advantage of these facilities, and allow them time off[19] to attend, usually one day a week. On the other hand, if your firm wouldn't allow you time off in the day, and you were still keen to[20] study, then you'd have to attend classes in your own time. Some lads do it. And they'll all tell you that it's worth it in the end... Had you considered continuing your education in any form after leaving?... I say, are you listening, lad?"

"Yes."

7. to have a job to do s.thing: *avoir du mal à faire qqch*
8. to print: *écrire en caractères d'imprimerie*
9. to stare: *regarder fixement*
10. trade: *métier*
11. bricklayer: *maçon*
12. lad: *gars*
13. dead end job: *métier sans avenir.*
14. to stick it out (stuck, stuck): *tenir bon jusqu'au bout*
15. (it is) worth your while: *ça en vaut la peine*
16. finger tips: *bout des doigts*
17. best bet: *meilleure chance*
18. to attend: *assister (aux cours)*
19. time off: *congé, temps libre*
20. keen to: *désireux de*

"You don't look as though you are to me. I haven't got all day you know, I've other lads to see before four o'clock."

He looked down at Billy's form again.

"Now then, where were we? Oh, yes. Well if nothing I've mentioned already appeals[21] to you, and if you can stand a hard day's graft[22], and you don't mind getting dirty, then there are good opportunities in mining..."

"I'm not goin' down t'pit[23]".

"Conditions have improved tremendously..."

"I wouldn't be seen dead down t'pit[24]."

"Well what do you want to do then? There doesn't seem to be a job in England to suit[25] you."

Barry HINES, *Kes* (1968), © Barry Hines.

21. to appeal: *séduire*
22. graft (pop.): *dur boulot*
23. t'pit: *l'puits*
24. I wouldn't be seen dead down t'pit: *pour rien au monde j'irais au fond du puits*
25. to suit: *convenir*

MAIN TOPICS

1 Who are the characters in this story? Guess when and where the scene takes place. Find out how many parts there are in this passage and give each part a title. Sum them up briefly.

2 The Employment Officer: List all the things you know about him. Try to explain what his job consists in doing. Could you imagine how he has spent the day before seeing Billy?

3 Billy Casper: Could you draw his psychological portrait? What can we guess about his social milieu? Imagine his parents' jobs. Could you guess what sort of a pupil he has been? (You should justify your answers.) What would he like to do in the future? Imagine his reasons. What does he refuse to do? Why? What would *your* reaction be?

4 Billy and the Officer: How different are Billy's wishes from the Officer's advice and suggestions? How does Billy react to this difference? What does it reveal about the Officer's ideas? What does it reveal about Billy's personality?

5 After reading this passage and with the help of your own experience, how would you define the role of schooling and education in the search for jobs, in the past and today?

Useful functions

CAPACITY — CONDITION AND HYPOTHESIS — DESIRE AND WISHES — DISAGREEMENT TO CRITICISM — INCAPACITY — REFUSAL.

Useful vocabulary

4. PEOPLE, THEIR WAYS AND CHARACTERS — 6. ACTIVITIES OF THE MIND AND COMMUNICATION — 7. FEELINGS AND APPRECIATION — 8. JUDGEMENTS AND EVALUATION — 14. EDUCATION AND SCIENCES.

A few guidelines

1 → ***"... I haven't thought about it... / You haven't looked round for anything yet then? / Have you thought about... / ... as you've already said... / Conditions have improved..."*** (Gr: **11**, §§ 2, 3)

Although he is fourteen, Billy himself says that he has "a job to read and write"... Can you imagine the various reasons why he is not a very bright pupil? Use the following pattern:

He has missed school too often.
He hasn't worked hard enough.
He...

2 → ***"... what would you like to do? / ... would you like to work... / ... would you prefer... / I'd be all right... / ... this would be your best bet. / ... this would mean... / ...if your firm wouldn't allow you time off in the day, and you were still keen to study, then you'd have to attend..."*** (Gr: **9**, § 11b)

Try to imagine Billy's life if he eventually decided to work "down t'pit." Use the following pattern:

If he worked down the mine, Billy would have a hard job.
If he were a miner, Billy would run many risks.
If...

3

→ ***"It means working with your hands... / Have you thought about entering... / ... this would mean attending Technical College... / Had you considered continuing your education after leaving? / ... you don't mind getting dirty..."*** (Gr: **20,** § 3)

A. If Billy decided to go to college to improve his job prospects, it would mean many changes in his life. Imagine these changes, using the following pattern:

It would mean working until late at the night.
It would mean...

B. Imagine that Billy has a friend, Jeff, who would like to be a miner. Imagine all the things Jeff would not mind doing. Use the following pattern:

Jeff wouldn't mind being a miner.
Jeff wouldn't mind...

Hints: You can use quite a few elements from exercise 2!

4

→ ***"You want to start off on the right foot, don't you? / I'd be all right working in an office, wouldn't I? / ... you'll always have a trade, won't you?"*** (Gr: **15,** § 5b)

Here are a few sentences from the text. Add a "tag" whenever possible.

— What kind of job had you in mind?
— You should be thinking about it.
— You haven't looked around for anything yet then?
— What would you like to do?
— Would you like to work in an office?
— Perhaps this would be your best bet.
— You don't look as though you are to me.
— Conditions have improved tremendously.
— What do you want to do then?
— There doesn't seem to be a job in England to suit you.

5

→ ***"... you should be thinking about it. / ... while you're serving... / ... lads of your age will be earning... / ... are you listening, lad? / I'm not goin' down t'pit."*** (Gr: **20,** § 1 - **8,** § 3d)

→ ***"... you'll find it well worth your while. / ... they'll tell you that it's worth it..."*** (Gr: **20,** § 3d)

FOLLOW-UP WORK

1. Translation

1 - Ça fait longtemps que je cherche du travail.
2 - Est-ce que tu as déjà envisagé de quitter l'Angleterre?
3 - Ça ne te gênerait pas de travailler tard le soir, n'est-ce pas?
4 - Si tu allais la voir, elle serait contente.
5 - Est-ce que tu aimerais être mineur?
6 - Tu devrais être en train de travailler au lieu de regarder la télévision!
7 - Tu verras que ça vaut la peine de travailler dur.
8 - Tu m'écoutes, n'est-ce pas?
9 - Ça ne me gêne pas de travailler à la mine, mais cela veut dire se lever très tôt le matin...
10 - Pendant que tu liras le journal, j'irai faire les courses.

2. Oral or written work: Applying for a job

Before starting anything, read the following ads which appeared in the *Bexley Daily Herald* (February 1, 1985):

SHOP ASSISTANT
wanted for Pullen Hardware, Ltd.
Sense of advertising and good selling technique. Exp. pref. Good job prospects (£6000 p.a.) Contact: Mrs. Pebble, (Tel: Crayford 29124) 36, Peyton Place. Bexley, Kent.

BARMAID/BARMAN
needed in busy pub. Part-time only. No exp. required.
Apply: Mr. Walker, (Tel: Crayford 16124) 59, Upton Terrace. Bexley, Kent.

SHOP ASSISTANT needed. Temp. work for Xmas period (Golding Garments, Ltd.). No exp. needed. Must dress well. Attractive wages. Tel: Albany 75317 or write: 22, Bel Air Av. Bexleyheath, Kent.

TEMP. WORKERS reqd. for summer season in busy hotel. Part-time only. £60. p.w. Write: Mrs. Fletcher, Greenfield Hotel, Highview Rise, Bexley, Kent. or phone: Crayford 35018.

Useful functions

AGREEMENT TO APPRECIATION — CAPACITY — CONDITION AND HYPOTHESIS — DESIRE AND WISHES — LIKING — PROPOSING.

Useful vocabulary

3. THE BODY AND ITS ACTIVITIES — 4. PEOPLE, THEIR WAYS AND CHARACTERS — 9. SOCIAL ATTITUDES — 14. EDUCATION AND SCIENCES.

Now, apply for one of these jobs. You can either write or phone.

3. Oral or written work: What went wrong?

The following interview did not quite go as Peter wished it had... Try to find out what went wrong. Justify your opinion and advise Peter on how he should have behaved.

1

→

© *The Helpline Team.*

3. Computers and education

Even among educators who worry about too much tilt[1] to technology, there is growing agreement that a computer is a powerful motivator of a school-age child. Students with access to a micro spend more time studying and solving problems. Those who write at their keyboards[2] compose more freely and revise their work more thoroughly[3]. “It's not just a matter of number crunching[4],” argues Arden Bement, a vice president of T. R. W. “It's a new way of thinking. The kids who don't get indoctrinated to computers by seventh grade[5] are not going to develop the same proficiency[6].” Says Andrew Molnar, computer education specialist at the National Science Foundation: “Power is not distributed evenly[7] now, and computers will broaden[8] that gap[9].”

Other observers disagree, seeing instead a potential educational leveling device[10]. “In the long run[11], all God's children will have computers,” says Computer Consultant[12] Charles Lecht. “Students who used to fail because they could not master geometry the first time around will be able to turn to the computer for

1. tilt: *penchant*
2. keyboard: *clavier*
3. thoroughly: *à fond*
4. number crunching: *maniement de chiffres*
5. by seventh grade (U.S.): *avant la 6e*
6. proficiency: *compétence*
7. evenly: *de façon égale*
8. to broaden: *élargir*
9. gap: *fossé*
10. educational leveling device: *moyen de démocratiser l'enseignement*
11. in the long run: *à long terme*
12. consultant: *expert conseil*

relief[13]. The machines will emerge as great equalizers." But the majority in the field[14] worry about the near-term specter[15] of the rich taking control of the technology while the poor play video games.

Steven Jobs, the 27-year-old chairman[16] of Apple Computer, had proposed donating a free computer to every school in the country, provided[17] Congress[18] grant[19] manufacturers the same tax break[20] that would be available[21] if they gave the equipment to a university. The companies that took advantage of the law would then have been able to do a public service, while also building future markets.

But Jobs is now backing off[22], unhappy with various limitations in the version of the tax break that has passed[23] the House and is awaiting Senate action. If he were to get the bill[24] he wants, the delivery of thousands of free machines would help to even out[25] the inequities. "Computers will be taught in most schools eventually," says Jobs. "But that's five to ten years from now. The question is, why wait?"

From *Time*, November 15, 1982.

13. relief: *aide*
14. field: *domaine*
15. near-term specter: *spectre à court terme*
16. chairman: P.D.G.
17. provided: *à la condition que*
18. Congress (U.S.): *Chambre des représentants + Sénat*
19. to grant: *accorder*
20. tax break: *diminution d'impôts*
21. ... available: *dont ils bénéficieraient*
22. to back off: *faire machine arrière*
23. to pass: *être voté*
24. bill: *proposition de loi*
25. to even out: *gommer*

MAIN TOPICS

1 After a first reading, try to sum up this article in just a few words. Then, after a second reading, select the key-words or key-expressions of each paragraph. Could you give a short definition of these words, using your *own* language? Choose one of the examples given by the journalist for each key-word and explain it.

2 Computers at school: Have *you* already used computers at school? Where, when and how many times a week? Did you find it useful or not? Why? Say when, where and how computers could be used in *your* school, either by teachers or by students. What subjects would you choose to study with computers? Why? Are there subjects you could *not* study with computers? Which ones? Why? Finally, do you think computers could replace teachers in the classroom? What would the advantages and disadvantages be?

3 Computers against inequality: Using your own experience, say when and how schoolchildren can have access to computers. Could age be important in learning about computers? Why? Imagine the advantages of having a computer available at home *and* at school for a child. Now, according to this article, what are the dangers of having no computer, either at home *or* at school? What consequences could it have on students' career choices, on their diplomas, job opportunities, job qualifications, social status, etc.? Could you imagine a way of compensating for those inequalities?

4 Rich versus poor: *"Power is not distributed evenly now."* Could you find examples of this in your own society? How would you account for these inequalities? According to the article, who might control the technology? How? What about the poor?

5 Steven Jobs: Try to establish his identity card (with the help of a dictionary or an encyclopaedia), giving his age, place of birth, education, university degrees, probable ambitions as a student, etc. Find out as much as you can on the firm he created (name, location, size, etc.). Why could he be called a modern hero?

6 Steven Jobs' offer: Try to sum up Jobs' intentions. Why didn't it work? What would have been the advantages of this offer for schools? And for Apple Computer? Guess Jobs' feelings towards Congress. Could you sum up the pros and cons of such offers for schools? In your opinion, what role should business play in the school system? Justify your opinion.

Useful functions

ADVICE — CAPACITY — CONDITION AND HYPOTHESIS — FUTURE — INCAPACITY — INTENTION — REGRET — REPROACH.

Useful vocabulary

6. ACTIVITIES OF THE MIND AND COMMUNICATION — 8. JUDGEMENTS AND EVALUATION — 11. HUMAN COMMUNITIES.

A few guidelines

1

→ ***"Students with access to a micro spend more time studying and solving problems."*** (Gr: **20,** § 3d)

First, try to imagine what children, students, teachers and parents spent their time doing a hundred years ago. Then, try to compare the past with the present using the following pattern:

A hundred years ago students used to spend their time studying classics, whereas now they spend their time working on computers.

2

→ ***Relative clauses*** (Gr: **13,** §§ 2, 3, 4)

Before doing the following exercise, you must compare these two relative clauses:

The man whom you see over there is my uncle.
My uncle, whom you see over there, is eighty.

In the first example the relative clause is *restrictive,* whereas in the second example the relative clause is *non-restrictive.*

A. Pick out at least five restrictive clauses in this text.

B. Transform these sentences, using the following pattern:

Some students failed their exams.
→ *The students who hadn't worked enough failed their exams.*
Some companies will go bankrupt.
→ *The companies which do not invest enough will go bankrupt.*

Some students got very good marks.
Some people were sunburnt.
Some children can't get up on Monday mornings.
Some children often go to the dentist's.
Some businessmen make profits.
Some students were kept in after school.
Some people are overweight.
Some people are lucky.

3

→ ***"... would be available if they gave... / ... if he were... would help..."*** (Gr: **9,** § 11b)

Using the following pattern, try to imagine what would change in your school if it had more money.

If we had more money, we would have a swimming-pool.
Now, let's dream: If...

4

→ ***"... too much tilt..."*** (Gr: **2,** § 2b)
→ ***"... more freely, more thoroughly..."*** (Gr: **7,** § 1a)
→ ***"It's a new way of thinking."*** (Gr: **20,** § 3)
→ ***"The kids are not going to develop..."*** (Gr: **8,** § 3b)
→ ***"... could not master... / ... will be able to... / ... would have been able to..."*** (Gr: **9,** § 1 - **10,** § 2a)
→ ***"Computers will be taught in most schools..."*** (Gr: **14,** §§ 1, 2, 4)

FOLLOW-UP WORK

1. Translation

1 - J'en ai assez ! Mon mari passe trop de temps à travailler sur l'ordinateur.
2 - Quand j'étais jeune, j'allais faire du ski tous les hivers.
3 - Si j'étais riche, j'achèterais un yacht.
4 - Si j'avais eu un bon professeur de chinois, j'aurais pu parler le chinois couramment (= *fluently*).
5 - Bientôt les enfants recevront leur enseignement à domicile. Ils auront tous des ordinateurs dans leur chambre.
6 - Nos voisins vont acheter l'appartement qu'ils ont visité aujourd'hui.

7 - J'ai trouvé un nouveau moyen d'apprendre l'anglais plus rapidement. Je pars aux États-Unis pour un an.
8 - Ceux qui ont un magnétoscope pourront enregistrer le film d'Hitchcock. Quelle chance !

2. Oral or written work: Father and son →

Either individually, collectively, or in groups, analyse this cartoon. You should note:
1) What each character is doing.
2) Who the father and son may be (age, probable education, social milieu, probable likes and dislikes, probable tastes in clothes, music, books, hobbies, etc.).
3) What they expect from each other.
4) What they probably feel towards each other.

Finally would you agree with Plantu's vision of the generation gap? Would you say that the children of the 1980s are better suited to modern life than their parents are? Justify your opinion.

Useful functions

ADVICE — CAPACITY — COMPARISON — DESIRE AND WISHES — REPROACH — REQUEST.

Useful vocabulary

5. EMOTIONS — 6. ACTIVITIES OF THE MIND AND COMMUNICATION — 7. FEELINGS AND APPRECIATION — 8. JUDGEMENTS AND EVALUATION — 9. SOCIAL ATTITUDES — 14. EDUCATION AND SCIENCES.

Le Monde, Dossiers et documents, *La société française en mouvement*, 1981.

3. Oral or written work: Man and technology through the ages

Either collectively, in groups or individually, try to:
1) Find the elements which are common to all the pictures.
2) Describe each picture in detail, dating each one and explaining who discovered what (don't forget to look up names and inventions in a dictionary or an encyclopaedia).
3) Comment on man's role and relation to technology in the first five pictures.
4) Comment on the last picture: imagine what happened, and guess who is missing and why.

You could also imagine the characters' feelings in each picture, the fifth one included!

Plantu's cartoon is provocative. Would you agree with his view of our life and future? Would you say he gives us a realistic, pessimistic, or stereotyped vision of our future? Justify your opinion.

Useful functions

ADMIRATION — CAPACITY — COMPARISON — DURATION — INTENTION — REGRET.

Useful vocabulary

3. THE BODY AND ITS ACTIVITIES — 4. PEOPLE, THEIR WAYS AND CHARACTERS — 5. EMOTIONS — 11. HUMAN COMMUNITIES — 12. TOWNS, SMALL AND LARGE.

4. Sweet fifteen

1. wild: *sauvage*
2. clean crazy: *complètement fou*
3. to yell: *hurler*
4. superfluity: *trop plein*
5. vlei (South African word): *cuvette*
6. crimson: *pourpre*
7. leaping strides: *grandes foulées*
8. crisp: *vif*
9. ankle: *cheville*
10. tangled: *emmêlé*
11. to clear: *sauter au-dessus*
12. duiker = diverbuck: *petite antilope*
13. to leap (leapt, leapt): *bondir*
14. dash: *course*
15. waist: *taille*
16. he was breathing hoarsely: *son souffle était rauque*
17. to poise: *se tenir en équilibre*
18. stretches: *étendues*
19. to gleam: *miroiter*
20. stooping: *penché*
21. wonderingly: *avec émerveillement*
22. to swell (swelled, swollen): *grandir*
23. marbles: *billes*
24. sultry: *étouffant*
25. brisk: *vivifiant*

He began to run, not carefully, as he had before, but madly, like a wild[1] thing. He was clean crazy[2], yelling[3] mad with the joy of living and a superfluity[4] of youth. He rushed down the vlei[5] under a tumult of crimson[6] and gold, while all the birds of the world sang about him. He ran in great leaping strides[7], and shouted as he ran, feeling his body rise into the crisp[8] rushing air and fall back surely on to sure feet; and thought briefly, not believing that such a thing could happen to him, that he could break his ankle[9] any moment, in this thick tangled[10] grass. He cleared[11] bushes like a duiker[12], leaped[13] over rocks; and finally came to a dead stop at a place where the ground fell abruptly away below him to the river. It had been a two-mile-long dash[14] through waist-high[15] growth, and he was breathing hoarsely[16] and could no longer sing. But he poised[17] on a rock and looked down at stretches[18] of water that gleamed[19] through stooping[20] trees, and thought suddenly, I am fifteen! Fifteen! The words came new to him; so that he kept repeating them wonderingly[21], with swelling[22] excitement; and he felt the years of his life with his hands, as if he were counting marbles[23], each one hard and separate and compact, each one a wonderful shining thing. That was what he was: fifteen years of this rich soil, and this slow-moving water, and air that smelt like a challenge whether it was warm and sultry[24] at noon, or as brisk[25] as cold water, like it was now.

There was nothing he couldn't do, nothing! A vision came to him, as he stood there, like when a child hears the word "eternity" and tries to understand it, and time takes possession of the mind. He felt his life ahead of him as a great and wonderful thing, something that was his; and he said aloud, with the blood rising to his head: All the great men of the world have been as I am now, and there is nothing I can't become, nothing I can't do; there is no country in the world I cannot make part of myself, if I choose. I contain the world. I can make of it what I want. If I choose, I can change everything that is going to happen: it depends on me, and what I decide now.

Doris LESSING, *A Sunrise on the Veld* © 1951 by Doris Lessing, reprinted by permission of Jonathan Clowes Ltd.

MAIN TOPICS

1 Who is the main character? When and where does this story take place? What is the boy doing? Describe his itinerary as precisely as you can. (You may even draw it!)

2 Analyse the boy's feelings throughout the text. What are his feelings towards his natural environment? What are his reasons for being so happy? Try to guess what may have happened just before, which triggered off such a reaction.

3 Try to draw the boy's physical portrait and to describe his personality. What colour is he? What about his social origin? What do his parents do? What are his probable likes and dislikes, his activities, his hopes for the future, etc.?

4 How would you characterize the boy's emotional state? (Optimism, madness, narcissism, megalomania, etc.?) Why?

5 You are or you were fifteen not long ago: Have you had a similar experience? How do you view your own future? Are you as optimistic as the boy in the text? Why? Why not?

Useful functions

CAPACITY — DISAGREEMENT TO CRITICISM — FUTURE — INTENTION — PROBABILITY.

Useful vocabulary

2. LANDSCAPES — 3. THE BODY AND ITS ACTIVITIES — 5. EMOTIONS — 6. ACTIVITIES OF THE MIND AND COMMUNICATION.

A few guidelines

1

→ ***May have*** + ***V-past participle*** (Gr: **9,** § 3)

Try to guess what may have just happened to the young boy in the text. Use the following pattern:

He may have just passed an exam.
He may have...

2

→ ***All the*** + ***adj.-er / more adj.*** + ***as / because / since***

Why is this boy happier than he has ever been before? Answer this question using the following pattern:

He is all the happier because he knows he will be famous one day.

Hints: thrilled, excited, elated, eager, optimistic, self-confident, etc.
discover, learn, be sure of, be able to, realize, etc.

3

→ ***When/As soon as*** + ***Present***

What will this teenager do when he is an adult, as soon as he finishes school? Use the following pattern:

When he is older, he will have his own farm.
As soon as he finishes school, he will...

4

→ ***Feel like** + **V-ing / Look forward to** + **V-ing*** (Gr: **20,** § 3)

What does the boy now feel like doing, or look forward to doing, when he is of age? Use the following pattern:

He feels like travelling all over the world.
He looks forward to having his own car.
He...

5

→ ***"... not believing that such a thing could happen to him..."***
→ ***"It had been a two-mile-long dash..."*** (Gr: **3,** § 4)
→ ***"... and could no longer sing."*** (Gr: **16,** § 4)
→ ***"... he kept repeating..."*** (Gr: **20,** § 3d)
→ ***"... whether it was warm, or as brisk..."***

FOLLOW-UP WORK

1. Translation

From French

1 - Je n'aurais jamais pensé qu'une telle chose puisse m'arriver. Je suis amoureux!
2 - Il a l'air triste, il a peut-être reçu des mauvaises nouvelles de sa mère.
3 - Mon professeur d'anglais ne cesse de répéter qu'il faut que j'apprenne mes leçons, comme si je ne le savais pas déjà!
4 - J'irai en Irlande dès que j'aurai assez d'argent.
5 - Viens me voir quand tu voudras ; je resterai à la maison, qu'il soit deux heures du matin ou onze heures du soir.
6 - Je fus d'autant plus surprise de la voir dans la rue que je la croyais malade.
7 - A: J'ai envie de faire une promenade de quinze kilomètres dans la neige! B: Je ne te suivrai pas! Je ne peux plus marcher.

From English

1 - He began to run, not carefully *as* he had before, but madly, *like* a wild thing.
2 - He shouted *as* he ran.
3 - He felt the years of his life with his hands, *as if* he were counting marbles.
4 - This air smelt *like* a challenge whether it was warm and sultry at noon, or *as* brisk *as* cold water, *like* it was now.
5 - A vision came to him, *as* he stood there, *like* when a child hears the word "eternity."
6 - He felt his life *as* a great and a wonderful thing.
7 - All the great men of the world have been *as* I am now.

2. Oral or written work: An imaginary conversation

Imagine a dialogue between this young boy and a punk of the same age. If you have not studied *The tribes of Britain* (Unit 7, Text 4) in class, read it carefully first. Then try to draw a comparative chart; your dialogue could focus on the following points:
— Clothes, hairstyle, social position, likes and dislikes.
— Hopes for the future. Why? Why not?
— Fears for the future. Why? Why not?
— Attitudes towards the adult world and its values, etc.

Useful functions

CAPACITY — COMPARISON — CONTRAST AND CONTRADICTION — DISAGREEMENT TO CRITICISM — INCAPACITY.

Useful vocabulary

4. PEOPLE, THEIR WAYS AND CHARACTERS — 5. EMOTIONS — 7. FEELINGS AND APPRECIATION — 8. JUDGEMENTS AND EVALUATION — 9. SOCIAL ATTITUDES.

3. Written work: An essay on youth and money

"You can be young without money but you can't be old without it." A Cat on a Hot Tin Roof, 1955, Tennessee WILLIAMS.

1) Explain what Tennessee Williams meant when writing these lines.
2) Would you say that Tennessee Williams' views on youth are still valid today? If you think so, analyse the reasons and find examples to illustrate your views. If you don't, give instances showing that young people also need money to achieve their goals.

Useful functions

AGREEMENT TO APPRECIATION — CAPACITY — CAUSE — GIVING ONE'S OPINION — INCAPACITY.

Useful vocabulary

3. THE BODY AND ITS ACTIVITIES — 4. PEOPLE, THEIR WAYS AND CHARACTERS — 7. FEELINGS AND APPRECIATION — 8. JUDGEMENTS AND EVALUATION.

READ AND SPEAK

SUMMIT MEETING

A man, Adams, is standing on the ledge[1] of the 36th floor of a skyscraper. Several people have already tried to talk him into not jumping, but with no success up to now.

For a while no one came to the window. And then a policeman's head popped out, looking at him for a moment, rather cynically.

"Hey, fella," the policeman said.

Adams looked at him, studying his face. "What do you want?" he asked.

"They called me up from downstairs. Said there's a guy up here threatening to take a dive[2]. You're not really going to jump, are you?"

"Yes."

"What do you want to do that for?"

"It's my nature to do spectacular things."

"Hey, you got a sense of humor," the policeman said. He pushed his cap back on his head, sitting out on the window sill[3]. "I like that. Want a cigarette?"

"No", Adams said.

The policeman shook a cigarette loose from his pack and lighted it. He inhaled deeply, expelling the smoke out into the sunshine where the wind snapped it up. "It's sure a pretty day, you know?"

"A good day to die," Adams said, looking at him.

"You're pretty morbid, fella. You got a family?"

"No. Do you?"

"I've got a wife."

"Well, I have no one."

"That's too bad."

"Yes," Adams said. It wasn't so long ago that I did have a family, he thought. Only yesterday in fact. He had left the house in the morning to go to work and Karen had said good-bye to him at the door (not kissed him, like she used to do; theirs was a kissless marriage now, but she was still his wife, he still loved only her, then and forever, would never give her the divorce, remained firm about that even though she said she would leave him eventually[4]). And then he had come home at six o'clock and there was no wife any more, no love, nothing, only the empty bottle of sleeping pills and the note and the silent apartment... and Karen's body lying on the couch.

She had left the note on his pillow. It was written neatly, thoughtfully, explaining. Steve had told her he could not go away with her. Steve had deceived[5] her. (It was that open, that blunt and brusque; she could mention Steve like that and he would know—as he had known for months now. Once he had even seen them together in a neighborhood cabaret. There had been nothing surreptitious[6] about it on her part. She told him that their marriage was over, spoke freely of Steve to him.) He had gone out that night and walked the streets until after midnight, come back to the house and gone to sleep. He awoke that morning knowing immediately that his mind had been made up[7], that he was going to do this which he was now planning. He walked

1. ledge: *corniche* — **2.** to take a dive: *plonger* — **3.** window sill: *rebord de fenêtre* — **4.** eventually: *finalement* — **5.** to deceive: *tromper* — **6.** surreptitious: *caché* — **7.** to make up one's mind (made, made): *se décider*

ONE AFTERNOON IN A LARGE CITY

to this part of town and checked[8] into the hotel, asking for a room near the top...

The policeman reappeared. Adams knew he would. He had been more responsive to him than any of the others and so the policeman would try again.

"You know, Adams," the officer said, sitting out on the window sill again, casually[9], "in a way you're doing me a favor."

"How's that?"

"Well, normally I'd be down there directing traffic. But because of you I'm up here taking it easy."

"Is that so?"

"That's so."

"You might just as well be up here. That traffic isn't moving anyway."

The policeman laughed. "That's right," he said. "Those people down there," he said with a gesture, "are expecting you to jump. They're looking forward to it."

Adams looked at him. "Looking forward to it?"

"Sure. They've made up their minds that you're going to jump and they want to see it. You going to disappoint them?"

Adams looked down, his eyes sweeping over the blocks and blocks of clustered people.

8. to check into (a hotel): *arriver (= remplir sa fiche)* — 9. casually: *d'un air désinvolte*

"You can't hear them up here," the policeman said, "but they're yelling[10] for you to jump."

"Are they?"

"Uh-huh. They feel you owe[11] them that for making them stand around here all afternoon."

"They're like a pack of hungry wolves[12]," Adams said.

"That's right. Why give up your life just so they can have a thrill[13]?" The policeman watched Adams' face, thought he detected a flicker of uncertainty. "Come on in," he said in a low, cajoling voice. "The hell with all those people."

"Maybe you're right," Adams said.

"Sure."

Adams wavered[14], his back coming away from the wall for a moment, then he fell back, covering his eyes for a second.

"What's the matter?" the policeman asked.

"I guess I'm a bit dizzy[15]. Maybe you'd better give me a hand."

The policeman looked across the street, there were news photographers on the roof there, their cameras poised. It would make quite a picture for the morning papers.

"All right," the policeman said. "Hold on."

The crowd sent up a roar of thrill and terror when they saw the policeman climb out of the window and stand on the ledge, a few feet from the immobile man in the white shirt. They watched him edge along, carefully extending his hand.

Adams reached his hand toward the policeman's.

"I knew you would come up eventually," Adams said. "That's why I chose this place."

"What?" the policeman said, trying to maintain his balance on the narrow ledge.

"My name isn't Adams, Steve. Karen was my wife. Do you know that last night she..."

The terror spread over the policeman's face...

Donald HONIG, *Man with a problem* (1958)

10. to yell: *hurler* — **11.** to owe: *devoir* — **12.** wolf (plur: wolves): *loup* — **13.** thrill: *frisson* — **14.** to waver: *vaciller* — **15.** to be dizzy: *avoir le vertige.*

MAIN TOPICS

1 Who are the various characters? When does the story take place? Where does the story take place (there are several places)? Try to find the structure of this short story and give each part a title. How many endings can you imagine for this short story?

2 Adams: What do you learn about his character, his feelings towards Karen and Steve?

3 Steve: What can you imagine about his feelings and behaviour at work, with his family, with Karen?

4 Karen: What can you guess about her probable personality? What were her relationships with her husband, with her lover?

5 What can you say about the relationships between Adams and Steve throughout the short story? How do both characters' feelings and attitudes evolve?

6 Describe and analyse the public's feelings and reactions throughout the short story.

7 What are *your* feelings at the end of the story?

Useful functions

DESIRE AND WISHES — DISLIKING — GETTING S.O. TO DO S. THING — INTENTION — PURPOSE — REPROACH.

Useful vocabulary

3. THE BODY AND ITS ACTIVITIES — 4. PEOPLE, THEIR WAYS AND CHARACTERS — 5. EMOTIONS — 6. ACTIVITIES OF THE MIND AND COMMUNICATION — 7. FEELINGS AND APPRECIATION.

A few guidelines

1
→ ***"He had left the house... / ... Karen had said good-bye... / She had left the note... / Steve had told her... / Steve had deceived her... / etc."*** (Gr: **8,** § 2a - **11,** § 6)

Preterite or pluperfect? Put the verbs in brackets into the correct tense.

When Adams came back home that night, he *(discover)* that Karen *(commit)* suicide by taking an overdose of sleeping pills. He *(be)* all the more shocked because when he *(leave)* home in the morning, Karen *(say)* good-bye normally. Of course, he *(know)* for months that she *(have)* a lover—he *(see)* them in a cabaret—but suicide... No, he *(can)* not believe it. When he *(see)* Karen lying lifeless on the couch, in this house where they *(be)* so happy, he *(make)* up his mind. He *(decide)* to avenge her death by killing the man who *(cause)* it and who *(deceive)* her. He *(go)* out...

2
→ ***"... not kissed him, like she used to do..."*** (Gr: **8,** § 2c)

Imagine Karen and Adams' life before Karen met Steve. Use the following pattern:

Before Karen met Steve, they used to kiss each other good-bye, they used to love each other, they used to...

3
→ ***I want him to V...*** (Gr: **18,** § 2a)

Imagine Adams' thoughts while walking to the hotel. Use the following pattern:

I want him to die, I want him to see me face to face, I want him to...

Hints: come with me on the ledge, take risks, pay for Karen's death, be scared to death, ...

4
→ ***I'll make him V...*** (Gr: **19,** § 1)

Imagine Adams' intentions just before checking in. Use the following pattern:

I'll make him come up, I'll make him talk, I'll make him...

5
→ ***Blame someone for V-ing...*** (Gr: **20,** § 3)

What are Adams' reproaches to Karen and Steve? Use the following pattern:

Adams blames Karen for deceiving him, for...
Adams blames Steve for causing Karen's death, for...

6
→ ***"... she said she would leave him eventually..."*** (Gr: **17,** §§ 3, 4)
→ ***"Those people... are expecting you to jump."*** (Gr: **18,** § 2a)
→ ***"Maybe you'd better give me a hand."*** (Gr: **10,** § 1b)

FOLLOW-UP WORK

1. Written work: Karen's letter

"She had left the note on his pillow..." Write the letter Karen wrote to her husband before taking the sleeping pills. We can imagine that she told him about their life together and what it had become, her relationship with Steve and how he had deceived her, etc.

Useful functions

COMPARISON — CONDITION AND HYPOTHESIS — INCAPACITY — REGRET — REPROACH.

Useful vocabulary

4. PEOPLE, THEIR WAYS AND CHARACTERS — 5. EMOTIONS — 7. FEELINGS AND APPRECIATION.

2. Written or oral work: An article in the Press

With the help of the text, try to imagine what a journalist might have written about the story. You should mention the facts (characters' names, etc.) and also give a possible explanation of the events as seen by an outsider. You might also praise the policeman's heroic attitude.

You could also imagine that you are a radio or TV reporter witnessing what is happening on the ledge. In this case, you will not hear anything and will have to guess what the man and the policeman are saying, etc.

Useful functions

ADMIRATION — CAUSE — GETTING S.O TO DO S.THING — INCAPACITY — PROBABILITY.

Useful vocabulary

3. THE BODY AND ITS ACTIVITIES — 4. PEOPLE, THEIR WAYS AND CHARACTERS — 5. EMOTIONS — 6. ACTIVITIES OF THE MIND AND COMMUNICATION.

3. Oral work: Adams' trial

Let us imagine that Adams has pushed Steve off the ledge (it is one of the possible endings). He is accused of having killed Steve, and is tried in court. The trial will include the defence, the prosecution, a judge and several jurors, witnesses, etc. You will have to find all the possible arguments for and against put forward in this case and reach a verdict.

Hints: In order to make the trial sound more realistic, you could first imagine the various characters' identity cards: name, age, job, sex, what he/she was doing at the time of the tragedy, why, etc.

Useful functions

CAUSE — DESIRE AND WISHES — GETTING S.O TO DO S.THING — REPORTING — REPROACH.

Useful vocabulary

1. LIGHT, SOUNDS AND THE SENSES — 3. THE BODY AND ITS ACTIVITIES — 5. EMOTIONS — 7. FEELINGS AND APPRECIATION.

THE PEDESTRIAN

A man is walking alone at night in a big city. There is no one around.

He turned back on a side street, circling around toward his home. He was within a block of his destination when the lone[1] car turned a corner quite suddenly and flashed a fierce[2] white cone of light upon him. He stood entranced[3], not unlike[4] a night moth[5], stunned[6] by the illumination, and then drawn toward it.

A metallic voice called to him:

"Stand still[7]. Stay where you are! Don't move!"

He halted.

"Put up your hands!"

"But——" he said.

"Your hands up! Or we'll shoot!"

The police, of course, but what a rare, incredible thing; in a city of three million, there was only *one* police car left, wasn't that correct? Ever since a year ago, 2052, the election year, the force[8] had been cut down from three cars to one. Crime was ebbing[9]; there was no need now for the police, save for this one lone car wandering[10] and wandering the empty streets.

"Your name?" said the police car in a metallic whisper[11]. He couldn't see the men in it for the bright light in his eyes.

"Leonard Mead," he said.

"Speak up!"

"Leonard Mead!"

"Business or profession?"

"I guess you'd call me a writer."

"No profession," said the police car, as if talking to itself. The light held him fixed, like a museum specimen, needle[12] thrust through[13] chest[14].

"You might say that," said Mr. Mead. He hadn't written in years. Magazines and books didn't sell any more. Everything went on in the tomb-like houses at night now, he thought, continuing his fancy[15]. The tombs, ill-lit[16] by television light, where the people sat like the dead, the gray or multi-colored lights touching their faces, but never really touching them.

"No profession," said the phonograph voice, hissing[17]. "What are you doing out?"

1. lone: *solitaire* — **2.** fierce: *violent* — **3.** to entrance: *fasciner* — **4.** not unlike: *semblable à* — **5.** night moth: *papillon de nuit* — **6.** to stun: *paralyser* — **7.** to stand still (stood, stood): *rester immobile* — **8.** the force = the police force: *la police* — **9.** to ebb: *diminuer* — **10.** to wander: *errer* — **11.** whisper: *chuchotement* — **12.** needle: *épingle* — **13.** to thrust through (thrust, thrust): *transpercer* — **14.** chest: *poitrine* — **15.** fancy: *imagination* — **16.** ill-lit: *mal éclairé* — **17.** to hiss: *siffler*

"Walking," said Leonard Mead.

"Walking!"

"Just walking," he said simply, but his face felt cold.

"Walking, just walking, walking?"

"Yes, sir."

"Walking where? For what?"

"Walking for air. Walking to *see*."

"Your address!"

"Eleven South Saint James Street."

"And there is air *in* your house, you have an air *conditioner,* Mr. Mead?"

"Yes."

"And you have a viewing screen[18] in your house to see with?"

"No."

"No?" There was a crakling[19] quiet that in itself was an accusation.

"Are you married, Mr. Mead?"

"No."

"Not married," said the police voice behind the fiery[20] beam[21]. The moon was high and clear among the stars and the houses were gray and silent.

"Nobody wanted me," said Leonard Mead with a smile.

"Don't speak unless you're spoken to!"

Leonard Mead waited in the cold night.

"Just *walking,* Mr. Mead?"

"Yes."

"But you haven't explained for what purpose[22]."

"I explained; for air, and to see, and just to walk."

"Have you done this often?"

"Every night for years."

The police car sat in the center of the street with its radio throat faintly humming[23].

"Well, Mr. Mead," it said.

"Is that all?" he asked politely.

"Yes," said the voice. "Here." There was a sigh[24], a pop. The back door of the police car sprang wide[25]. "Get in."

"Wait a minute, I haven't done anything!"

"Get in."

"I protest!"

18. viewing screen: *écran* — **19.** crackling: *grésillant* — **20.** fiery: *aveuglant* — **21.** beam: *rayon* — **22.** purpose: *but* — **23.** to hum: *bourdonner* — **24.** sigh: *soupir* — **25.** to spring wide (sprang, sprung): *s'ouvrir brusquement*

"Mr. Mead."

He walked like a man suddenly drunk. As he passed the front window of the car he looked in. As he had expected, there was no one in the front seat, no one in the car at all.

"Get in."

He put his hand to the door and peered[26] into the back seat, which was a little cell, a little black jail with bars. It smelled of riveted steel. It smelled of harsh[27] antiseptic; it smelled too clean and hard and metallic. There was nothing soft there.

"Now if you had a wife to give you an alibi," said the iron voice. "But——"

"Where are you taking me?"

The car hesitated, or rather gave a faint whirring[28] click, as if information, somewhere, was dropping card by punch-slotted card[29] under electric eyes. "To the Psychiatric Center for Research on Regressive Tendencies."

He got in. The door shut with a soft thud[30]. The police car rolled through the night avenues, flashing its dim lights[31] ahead.

They passed one house on one street a moment later, one house in an entire city of houses that were dark, but this one particular house had all of its electric lights brightly lit, every window a loud yellow illumination, square and warm in the cool darkness.

"That's *my* house," said Leonard Mead.

No one answered him.

The car moved down the empty riverbed streets and off away, leaving the empty streets with the empty sidewalks, and no sound and no motion all the rest of the chill[32] November night.

Ray BRADBURY,
The Golden Apples of the Sun (1951),

26. to peer: *regarder (ici, avec inquiétude)* — **27.** harsh: *âcre* — **28.** whirring: *ronronnant* — **29.** punch-slotted card: *carte perforée* — **30.** thud: *bruit sourd* — **31.** dim lights (U.S.): *codes* — **32.** chill: *glacial.*

MAIN TOPICS

1 Who are the main characters in this story? Where and when does it take place? Try to sum up the whole story in just a few words.

2 Leonard Mead: List all the things you learn or can guess about him (job, education, family, age, etc.). What are his likes and dislikes? Explain what he was doing that night? Why?

3 The police force: When and how does Leonard Mead meet the car? Describe the police investigation. List all the unusual elements of Leonard Mead's arrest: mode of arrest, nature of the charge (= *accusation*), the car's "behaviour", what is inside the car, etc.

4 List the images which are associated with Leonard Mead when arrested, then list the images associated with the police car. What impressions are suggested? Now, list the images associated with the city. Would you enjoy living in that city? Why? In these images, what does Ray Bradbury suggest about Leonard Mead, the police and the city?

5 List all the elements in Leonard Mead's life which show he is different from other people.

6 Can you guess what will happen to Leonard? Imagine the purpose of the Psychiatric Center. Who else do they probably keep there? Why? How do they probably treat them? What can you guess about the probable results?

7 Judging from this story, can you guess what type of society Leonard Mead lives in? Would you say it is a purely fictional story or does it sometimes refer to actual situations? Why did Ray Bradbury write such a story? What were his aims behind the science-fiction setting? Is it an effective story? Why?

Useful functions

COMPARISON — DESIRE AND WISHES — DISLIKING — INCAPACITY — OBLIGATION — PROHIBITION — PURPOSE — REPORTING.

Useful vocabulary

1. LIGHT, SOUNDS AND THE SENSES — 3. THE BODY AND ITS ACTIVITIES — 4. PEOPLE, THEIR WAYS AND CHARACTERS — 6. EMOTIONS — 9. SOCIAL ATTITUDES — 11. HUMAN COMMUNITIES.

A few guidelines

1

→ ***Expect somebody to V*** (Gr: **18,** § 2a)

A. Imagine what the citizens of this city expect or do not expect the police to do, using the following pattern:

They expect the police to arrest dangerous people, ...
They don't expect the police to help them, ...

Hints: watch citizens, arrest delinquents, patrol the city, ...

B. Now imagine what the citizens of this city are or are not expected to do by the city authorities, using the following pattern:

People are expected to stay at home, ...
People are not expected to go out at night, ...

Hints: read novels, paint, watch T.V., obey the rules, ...

2

→ ***"He stood entranced, not unlike a night moth stunned by... and drawn... / ... the force had been cut down... / Don't speak unless you're spoken to!"*** (Gr: **14**)

Using the passive, re-tell as much as you can of what happened to Leonard Mead that night, from the beginning to the end. (You should try to do this exercise *without* looking at the text...)

He was stopped by the police car, ...

3

→ ***"Now if you had a wife to give you an alibi..."*** (Gr: **9,** § 11b)

Leonard Mead may well regret he did not get married... Use the following pattern to imagine what he would have done or said if he had been married.

If I had been married, my wife would have saved me, she...

Hints: tell lies, say that... go shopping, buy cigarettes, walk the dog, help a neighbour, ...

4

→ ***"Have you done this often? / But you haven't explained... / ... I haven't done anything!"*** (Gr: **11,** §§ 1, 2, 5)

The year is 2053... Try to figure out what the police have done or have been doing since 2052, using the following pattern:

The police have been looking for suspects, ...

Hints: patrol at night, investigate crimes, improve techniques, be more efficient, ...

5

→ ***"Ever since a year ago, ... the force had been cut down... / He hadn't written in years..."*** (Gr: **11,** § 6)

→ ***"He couldn't see the men in it..."*** (Gr: **9,** § 1)

→ ***"And you have a viewing screen in your house to see with?"*** (Gr: **13,** § 5)

FOLLOW-UP WORK

Oral or written work: The refuge outside the city

The door of the police cell was not properly locked and Leonard Mead has managed to get out and escape from the city. He knew that a gang of runaway men and women had also broken away from the city and had tried to organize a new life in an abandoned area, according to their own principles and values.

Leonard manages to get in touch with them and hopes that they will accept him. But the two leaders of the group want to check that Leonard is not a plant (= *taupe*). Imagine their investigation, thinking of all the questions which could embarrass Leonard and of the answers which could prove his innocence.

Hints: They may ask him questions about his past life and job, his reasons for escaping the city and joining them, his ideas and ideals, etc.

Useful functions

CAUSE — COMPARISON — DESIRE AND WISHES — CONDITION AND HYPOTHESIS — DETERMINATION — INCAPACITY — PROHIBITION — PROPOSING — REQUEST.

Useful vocabulary

4. PEOPLE, THEIR WAYS AND CHARACTERS — 5. EMOTIONS — 6. ACTIVITIES OF THE MIND AND COMMUNICATION — 7. FEELINGS AND APPRECIATION — 8. JUDGEMENTS AND EVALUATION — 9. SOCIAL ATTITUDES.

ABOMINABLE

Sir Chauncey Atherton waved a farewell[1] to the Sherpa guides who were to set up camp here and let him proceed alone. This was Abominable Snowman country, a few hundred miles north of Mount Everest, in the Himalayas. Abominable Snowmen were seen occasionally on Everest, on other Tibetan or Nepalese mountains, but Mount Oblimov, at the foot of which he was now leaving his native guides, was so thick with[2] them that not even the Sherpas would climb it, but would here await his return, if indeed he did. It took a brave man to pass this point. Sir Chauncey was a brave man.

Also, he was a connoisseur of women, which was why he was here and about to attempt, alone, not only a dangerous ascent but an even more dangerous rescue[3]. If Lola Gabraldi was still alive, an Abominable Snowman had her.

Sir Chauncey had never seen Lola Gabraldi, in the flesh[4]. He had, in fact, learned of her existence less than a month ago, when he had seen the one motion picture in which she had starred—and through which she had become suddenly fabulous, the most beautiful woman on Earth, the most glamorous[5] movie star Italy had ever produced, and Sir Chauncey could not understand how even Italy had produced her. In one picture she had replaced Bardot, Lolobrigida, and Ekberg as the image of feminine perfection in the minds of connoisseurs of women everywhere, and Sir Chauncey was the top connoisseur anywhere. The moment he had seen her on the screen he had known that he must know her in the flesh, or die trying.

But by that time Lola Gabraldi had vanished[6]. As a vacation after her first picture she had taken a trip to India and had joined a group of climbers about to make an assault on Mount Oblimov. The rest of the party had returned, Lola had not. One of then had testified[7] that he had seen her, at a distance too great for him to reach her in time, abducted[8], carried off screaming by a nine-foot-high hairy more-or-less manlike creature. An Abominable Snowman. The party had searched for[9] her for days before giving up and returning to civilization. Everyone agreed that there was no possible chance, now, of finding her alive.

Everyone except Sir Chauncey, who had immediately flown to India from England.

He struggled on[10], now high into the eternal snows. And in addition to mountain-climbing equipment he carried the heavy rifle[11] with which he had, only the year before, shot tigers in Bengal. If it could kill tigers, he reasoned, it could kill Snowmen.

Snow swirled[12] about him as he neared the cloud line. Suddenly, a dozen yards ahead of him which was as far as he could see, he caught a glimpse of[13] a monstrous not-quite-human figure. He raised his rifle and fired. The figure fell, and kept on falling; it had been on a ledge[14] over thousands of feet of nothingness.

And at the moment of the shot arms closed around Sir Chauncey from behind him. Thick, hairy arms. And then, as one hand held him easily, the other took the rifle from him and bent it into an L-shape as easily as though it had been a toothpick[15], and then tossed it away[16].

A voice spoke from a point about two feet above his head. "Be quiet, you will

---

1. to wave a farewell: *faire ses adieux (de la main)* — **2.** to be thick with: *abonder en* — **3.** rescue: *sauvetage* — **4.** in the flesh: *en chair et en os* (flesh: *chair*) — **5.** glamorous: *fascinante* — **6.** to vanish: *disparaître* — **7.** to testify: *témoigner* — **8.** to abduct: *enlever* — **9.** to search for s.o.: *rechercher qqn* — **10.** to struggle on: *grimper avec peine* — **11.** rifle: *fusil* — **12.** to swirl: *tourbillonner* — **13.** to catch a glimpse of: *apercevoir* — **14.** ledge: *corniche* — **15.** toothpick: *cure-dent* — **16.** to toss away: *jeter de côté*

not be harmed[17]." Sir Chauncey was a brave man, but a sort of squeak[18] was all the answer he could make, despite the seeming assurance of the words. He was held so tightly[19] against the creature behind him that he could not look upward and backward to see what its face was like.

"Let me explain," said the voice above and behind him. "We, whom you call Abominable Snowmen, are human, but transmuted. A great many centuries ago we were a tribe like the Sherpas. We chanced to discover a drug that let us change physically, let us adapt by increased size, hairiness, and other physiological changes to extreme cold and altitude, let us move up into the mountains, into country in which others cannot survive, except for the duration of brief climbing expeditions. Do you understand?"

"Y-y-yes," Sir Chauncey managed to say. He was beginning to feel a faint return of hope. Why would this creature be explaining these things to him, if it intended to kill him?

"Then I shall explain further. Our number is small, and we are diminishing. For that reason we occasionally capture, as I have captured you, a mountain climber. We give him the transmuting drug, he undergoes[20] the physiological changes and becomes one of us. By that means we keep our number, such as it is, relatively constant."

"B-but," Sir Chauncey stammered[21], "is that what happened to the woman I'm looking for, Lola Gabraldi? She is now eight feet tall and hairy and—"

"She *was.* You just killed her. One of our tribe had taken her as his mate[22]. We will take no revenge for your having killed her, but you must now, as it were[23], take her place."

"Take her place? But—I'm a *man.*"

"Thank God for that," said the voice above and behind him. He found himself turned around, held against a huge[24] hairy body, his face at the right level to be buried[25] between mountainous hairy breasts[26]. "Thank God for that—because I am an Abominable Snowwoman."

Sir Chauncey fainted[27] and was picked up and, as lightly[28] as though he were a toy dog[29], was carried away by his mate.

Fredric BROWN,
Nightmares and Geezenstacks (1961),

17. to harm s.o.: *faire du mal à qqn* — **18.** squeak: *couinement* — **19.** to hold tightly (held, held): *serrer fort* — **20.** to undergo (-went, -gone): *subir* — **21.** to stammer : *bégayer, bredouiller* — **22.** mate: *compagne, compagnon* — **23.** as it were: *en quelque sorte* — **24.** huge: *énorme* — **25.** to bury: *enfouir* — **26.** breasts: *seins* — **27.** to faint: *s'évanouir* — **28.** lightly: *légèrement* — **29.** toy dog: *chien en peluche*

MAIN TOPICS

1 Who are the characters? Where and when does the story take place? What sort of general atmosphere is created by Fredric Brown? Try to sum up the story briefly.

2 Sir Chauncey: Could you draw his portrait, including his age, probable education, social milieu, occupations in life, qualities and defects, likes and dislikes? Would you call him a true-to-life hero or a caricature? Justify your answer.

3 Sir Chauncey and women: Who were his dream women? And those of his life? What role did Lola play in his love life? Why? Sum up what happened to Lola and explain Sir Chauncey's reaction and decision.

4 The turning-point of the story: Explain what Sir Chauncey saw, thought and did in the snow. How and why does the second character in the story appear? What effect does it have on the reader? Could you compare Sir Chauncey to this second character (size, strength, intentions, etc.)?

5 From the Snowwoman's mouth: What did Sir Chauncey learn? Sum up what was revealed to him. What will happen to him? What effect do these revelations have on Sir Chauncey? And on *you?*

6 You probably know many stories, written in French, English, German or Spanish, etc. which described how a chivalrous nobleman tried to rescue a "damsel in distress". Would you say that Sir Chauncey's story is similar to or different from these stories? It might be useful to draw up a list of all the paradoxes in the story before giving your answer.

7 Tragedy or comedy? In this story what could be said to be tragic? How are these elements turned into comedy? What are the reader's feelings and impressions when he/she has finished reading?

Useful functions

COMPARISON — CONSEQUENCE — DESIRE AND WISHES — DETERMINATION — GETTING S.O. TO DO S. THING — INCAPACITY — INTENTION — PURPOSE — REGRET.

Useful vocabulary

4. PEOPLE, THEIR WAYS AND CHARACTERS — 5. EMOTIONS — 6. ACTIVITIES OF THE MIND AND COMMUNICATION — 7. FEELINGS AND APPRECIATION — 8. JUDGEMENTS AND EVALUATION — 11. HUMAN COMMUNITIES.

A few guidelines

1

→ ***"... guides who were to set up camp here and let him proceed alone."*** (Gr: **10,** § 2c)

Sir Chauncey's secretary is planning the program of their trip to India. Using the following pattern, find what they are to do.

I am/he is/we are to fly to India.

Hints: search for Lola, climb mountains, etc.

2

→ ***... intend to + V / ... want to + V /... want somebody to + V*** (Gr: **18,** §§ 1, 2a, 2b, 3a)

A. Lola Gabraldi went off to Mount Oblimov without telling anyone why she chose this of all places. Guess her reasons using either of the following patterns:

She intended to forget her films.
She wanted to seduce a mountain guide.

B. Once she had been caught by the Abominable Snowman, Lola was forced to do what her mate wanted her to. Using the following pattern, imagine what he wanted.

He wanted Lola to be his mate.

Hints: wash his hair, sing him to sleep, give him an heir, cook like his mother, etc.

3

→ ***"Abominable Snowmen were seen occasionally..."*** (Gr: **14,** §§ 1, 2, 3, 4)

A. Using the passive imagine all the things which happened or which will happen to Sir Chauncey. The following patterns may help you:

The Snowwoman caught him → He was caught by the Snowwoman.
She will take him to the village → He will be taken to the village.

Hints: give him the drug, teach him their language, show him how to survive, (not) hurt him, (not) beat him, etc.

B. There are 8 other passive forms in the story. Find them.

4

→ ***"Why would this creature be explaining those things to him, if it intended to kill him?"*** (Gr: **9,** § 11b)

One of the Sherpa guides who led Sir Chauncey to Mount Oblimov regretted having followed him. Using the following structure, imagine what he could have been thinking.

If I were in my village now, I would be playing with my children.

Hints: work in the fields, speak with my friends, sell my goods, etc.

5

→ ***... had + V (past participle)*** (Gr: **11,** § 6)

How many pluperfect verbs can you find in this story: 20? 21? 22? 23? 24? 25? You should be able to give the right answer in less than three minutes!

6

→ ***"... he was about to attempt... / ... climbers about to make..."*** (Gr: **8,** § 3c)

→ ***"... before giving up and returning... / ... there was no possible chance now, of finding her alive. / ... Kept on falling... / We will take no revenge for your having killed her..."*** (Gr: **20,** § 3)

→ ***"... as easily as though it had been a toothpick... / ... as though he were a toy dog..."*** (Gr: **11,** § 6 - **8,** § 2d)

FOLLOW-UP WORK

1. Written work: Sir Chauncey's diary

You remember how the Abominable Snow-woman told Sir Chauncey about a drug capable of transmuting humans. Well, he was actually given the drug and he discovered it had very slow effects on him. Like any self-respecting English gentleman, he kept his diary, writing about all the things that happened to him, his discoveries, his doubts, his regrets, etc. Imagine Sir Chauncey's diary from the day he was given the drug to a month later.

Useful functions

ADMIRATION — CAPACITY — COMPARISON — DESIRE AND WISHES — DISLIKING — GIVING ONE'S OPINION — OBLIGATION — PAST — PROHIBITION — REGRET.

Useful vocabulary

1. LIGHT, SOUNDS AND THE SENSES — 2. LANDSCAPES — 3. THE BODY AND ITS ACTIVITIES — 4. PEOPLE, THEIR WAYS AND CHARACTERS — 5. EMOTIONS — 6. ACTIVITIES OF THE MIND AND COMMUNICATION — 7. FEELINGS AND APPRECIATION — 8. JUDGEMENTS AND EVALUATION — 9. SOCIAL ATTITUDES.

2. Written or oral work: A speech at the Royal Academy of Science

The drug that was meant to transmute Sir Chauncey into an Abominable Snowman did not quite work on him. He remained a rather tall, beautifully hairy man, but that was all. Although he was very well treated, there was a deep longing in his heart for Mother England. One day he managed to get away and go back to London.

Thanks to his experiences in India, Sir Chauncey quickly became a member of the Royal Academy of Science, and the famous author of the well-known autobiography: "The Hairy Heir", published by the Royal Cheetah House Museum.

Imagine the speech he will deliver at the Royal Academy of Science about the life which apes, chimpanzees, baboons, gorillas, etc. have in England. Imagine his reproaches, violent accusations, his claims and demands, etc. He will naturally draw many forceful arguments from his life among the Snowpeople.

Useful functions

ADVICE — CAPACITY — COMPARISON — DESIRE AND WISHES — DISAGREEMENT TO CRITICISM — EMPHASIS — OBLIGATION — PROHIBITION — REGRET — REPROACH.

Useful vocabulary

4. PEOPLE, THEIR WAYS AND CHARACTERS — 5. EMOTIONS — 6. ACTIVITIES OF THE MIND AND COMMUNICATION — 7. FEELINGS AND APPRECIATION — 8. JUDGEMENTS AND EVALUATION — 9. SOCIAL ATTITUDES.

PRÉCIS GRAMMATICAL

1. LES DÉTERMINANTS

Un **déterminant** est **indispensable devant un nom** commun.On appelle **déterminants** les **articles,** les **démonstratifs** et les **possessifs.**

1. Les articles

Un nom peut être précédé de l'**article défini** THE *(**the** boy, **the** animal),* de l'**article défini** A(N) *(**a** concert, **an** evening)* ou bien d'un article qui n'est pas visible *(money, cars)* mais qui apporte des indications tout aussi utiles que les deux autres articles et qu'on appelle l'**article zéro** *(ø).*

a. L'article indéfini *a(n)*

Il précède toujours un **nom dénombrable singulier.**

*There is **a concert** tonight.*
*She has **an Indian friend.***

L'article A(N) est obligatoire :

— devant les **noms de métiers** au sens large (ce que les gens font dans la vie) :

*She is **an actress.***

— après les prépositions WITH et WITHOUT :

*He's riding **without a helmet.***

— devant les expressions de **temps** et de **mesure** :

*She gets **£2 an hour.***
*This perfume costs **£5 an ounce.***

b. L'article défini *the*

Il est l'équivalent de « le », « la », « les » et peut précéder des **noms singulier, pluriel, dénombrables** ou **indénombrables** :

The wine** is on **the table.
The boys** refused to do **the washing-up.

L'article THE est **obligatoire** quand le nom est suivi :

— d'un **complément de nom** introduit par OF, IN, ON, etc. :

***The price of that dress** was incredible!*

— d'une **relative** :

*I didn't see **the things which he bought!***

On emploie l'article THE chaque fois que tout le monde est certain de parler de la même chose ou de la même personne (dans une famille par exemple).

*Where's **the cat**?*
***The president** has just spoken on T.V.*

Attention ! On emploie parfois l'article THE devant des **noms propres** :

— les noms de **cours d'eau,** de **mers** *(**the** Pacific Ocean, **the** Thames).*

— mais on ne l'emploie pas devant les noms de **pays** *(France),* de **sommets** *(Mount Everest)* ou de **lacs** *(Lake Michigan).* (Quelques noms de pays au pluriel prennent l'article : ***the** U.S.A., **the** U.S.S.R., **the** Netherlands.)*

— ni devant les noms de **personnes,** même précédés d'un titre ou d'un grade *(Captain Nemo, Doctor Jekyll.)*

c. L'article zéro (symbole *ø*)

Il peut précéder des **dénombrables pluriel** ou des **indénombrables** (donc singulier). Il peut indiquer :

— une **quantité** ou un **nombre quelconque,** indéfini :

*There are **stamps** in the top-drawer.*
*There are **people** waiting.*
*I have just ordered **tea.***

— que l'on parle de quelque chose, ou des choses, des êtres, **en général** : c'est l'emploi **générique.**

People** are fond of **rock'n' roll.
***Concerts** are getting very expensive.*
(les gens, le rock, les concerts en général).

La présence d'un adjectif n'enlève pas le sens général : ***cars, fast cars.***

2. Les démonstratifs

Il y a deux démonstratifs, THIS et THAT (là où en français il n'y en a qu'un : « ce/cette »), qui s'accordent en nombre avec le nom :

***This ad** is interesting.*
***These ads** are interesting.*
***That man** looks dangerous.*
***Those men** look dangerous.*

Différence entre THIS et THAT : THIS désigne généralement ce qui est **proche,** THAT ce qui est plus **éloigné.**

— dans l'**espace** :

*Look at **this hole in my stocking!***
*Look at **that plane up there!***

— dans le **temps** :

*I am very busy **these days.*** (en ce moment)
*He was very happy in **those days.*** (à cette époque-là)

Note : Si l'on veut indiquer une notion **péjorative,** on utilise THAT :

***That girl** is horrible!*

3. Les possessifs

1re **remarque** :

***ma** moto, **mon** casque, **mes** bottes*
***my**— **my**— **my**—*

Les possessifs ne s'accordent pas en genre et nombre avec le nom qui suit.

2e **remarque** :

*Greg est dans **sa chambre.***
***Greg** is in **his** room.*

*Julie a pris **son manteau.***
***Julie** has taken **her** coat.*

On choisit le possessif en fonction du **genre de l'antécédent** : masculin, féminin, ou neutre (choses, animaux inconnus).

Cas particulier :

***Everyone** must leave **his** umbrella in the hall.*

On trouvera très souvent : ... ***their** umbrellas...*

Emploi de OWN. Le déterminant possessif peut-être **renforcé** par OWN :

*I can use **my own** racket.(ma propre...)*

EXERCICES

A. Pensez à tous les noms de matières que vous connaissez (le bois, le plastique, le verre, etc.) et puis regardez autour de vous et sur vous, et dites en quelle matière sont les objets qui vous entourent, vos vêtements... Dites aussi pourquoi vous aimez (ou vous n'aimez pas) cette matière.

Ex.: *This pencil case is made of plastic. I don't like plastic because it is not strong.* (ou : *I like plastic because it is cheap.)*

B. Voici une liste d'objets que vous devez acheter. A côté, divers noms de matières. Pour chaque objet, vous avez le choix entre deux matières (par exemple, pour une trousse : plastique ou cuir?). Proposez deux matières, et choisissez celle que vous préférez, en disant pourquoi.

Ex.: *For my pencil-case: leather or plastic? I prefer leather because it's stronger.*

tennis-shoes, t-shirt, pullover, coat, gloves, satchel, glasses, watch, pencil-case.	wood, plastic, canvas, silver, leather, gold, fur, wool, acrylic, glass, steel, cotton.

C. Donnez votre avis sur les métiers suivants, en fonction des salaires proposés.

Ex.: *nurse : £700/month.*
→ *I want to be a nurse: nurses get £700 a month.* (ou : *I don't want to be a nurse: nurses get only £700 a month.*)

1. baby-sitter: £6/evening. **2.** doctor: £30/hour. **3.** pilot: £2000/month. **4.** shop-assistant: £100/week. **5.** teacher: £300/month. **6.** film-star: £300 000/year.

Vous pouvez ensuite donner quelques avantages et inconvénients de ces métiers (ou d'autres métiers).
Ex.: *I don't want to be a nurse because nurses only see sick people.*

D. Mettre l'article *a, the* (ou pas d'article du tout) dans l'espace vide.

... first time I met Vishnu, I fell in ... love. It was at ... disco. He was wearing ... leather shirt without ... collar. We forgot all ... people who were dancing in ... room. We danced all ... evening, and I suddenly understood what... love meant. I know that ... beauty is not everything, but he was so beautiful! He was ... student at ... same school my brother went to. I was so excited I forgot ... drink he had offered me. It was ... time to go back home; ... last bus had gone, and ... taxis were too expensive, so we walked. When we arrived in ... street where I live, I suddenly panicked. I saw ... car outside my house: my father, ... Doctor Wilson, was there! I was afraid of him, and I knew he didn't like ... coloured boys. I could not tell him Vishnu was from ... India. I fled without ... word.

E. Thème.

1. Cette jeune fille a tout : la beauté, l'intelligence, le charme et l'argent ! **2.** Les vêtements sont toujours faits pour les gens grands ! **3.** Éteins la lumière dans le garage. **4.** L'huile est plus légère que l'eau. **5.** Qu'est-ce que c'est ? Du verre ou du cristal ? **6.** L'eau de cette rivière est glacée. **7.** Il ne peut pas travailler sans dictionnaire. **8.** Est-ce que le docteur est là ? **9.** Je suis allée aux U.S.A., en Californie : j'adore ce pays. **10.** Qu'est-ce que tu veux ? Du fromage ou des yaourts ? Les yaourts que j'ai achetés à la ferme, tu sais ?

2. EXPRESSION DE LA QUANTITÉ

Une quantité peut être considérée de deux façons :

— soit la quantité dépend de la façon dont le sujet la considère (par exemple, j'estime que j'ai **beaucoup** d'argent dans ma poche, 2 000 F, mais la même somme représente **très peu** d'argent pour un milliardaire) : c'est une **quantité subjective** : voir **1** et **2**.

— soit tout le monde peut décrire la même quantité (mesurer, peser, compter...) et être d'accord : c'est une **quantité objective** (**15** personnes, **350 g** de farine, **tous** les enfants) : voir **3** et **4**.

1. Quantité quelconque (pas très grande)

Pour décrire une quantité quelconque, imprécise, subjective, on peut utiliser :

a. *Several* (= plusieurs)

Il est toujours suivi d'un **dénombrable au pluriel** :

*I went to **several concerts** last month.*

b. *Enough* (= assez)

Il peut être suivi d'un **dénombrable au pluriel** ou d'un **indénombrable** :

*There were not **enough boys** to play football.*
*There is **enough room** for two cars.*

c. *A few* et *a little*

A FEW donne une idée de **nombre** et est suivi d'un **dénombrable au pluriel** :

*We have **a few friends** in the neigbourhood.* (quelques...)

A LITTLE donne une idée de **masse** et est suivi d'un **indénombrable** :

*Give me **a little time**!*

d. *Some* et *any*

Ils peuvent être suivis d'un **indénombrable** ou d'un **dénombrable au pluriel** :

*I bought **some pencils** and **some paper**.*

Ils expriment la même idée de quantité, mais on ne peut pas utiliser l'un ou l'autre indifféremment : cela dépend de la structure de la phrase (**affirmative, négative** ou **interrogative**) **quand** SOME **et** ANY **font partie du groupe nominal complément.**

On emploie toujours SOME dans les **compléments des phrases affirmatives** :

*There are **some bad boys** in that school.*
*I need **some help**.*

On emploie ANY dans les **compléments des phrases négatives** :

*They **don't need any milk**.*
*There are **not any tickets** left.*

La même idée *(**pas de...**)* peut être exprimée par NO, mot négatif qui remplace NOT + ANY :

*There are **no tickets** left.*

On emploie SOME ou ANY dans les **compléments des phrases interrogatives,** suivant le sens que l'on veut donner à la question. Il n'y a pas de règle absolue, il s'agit de **nuances** :

ANY pour exprimer une nuance de **doute.** On peut demander à quelqu'un qui ne joue pas au tennis :

*Have you got **any tennis-balls?***

Mais on ne doit pas dire à quelqu'un chez qui on est invité à dîner : **Have you got **any wine?*** Cela sous-entendrait que cette personne ne sait pas recevoir, et ne va servir que de l'eau !

SOME peut exprimer une **offre** (une offre est toujours positive) :

***Shall I bring you some** tea in bed?*

et s'emploie dans les questions commençant par WH-:

*Who could lend me **some** records?*

e. Autres emplois de *some* et *any*

Ils ont aussi un emploi **indéfini,** qui n'a rien à voir avec l'expression de la quantité vue au § **d** :

SOME s'emploie comme un **article indéfini,** suivi d'un **dénombrable au singulier** :

***Some day** my prince will come.*

Remarque : ***Some man*** est encore **plus indéfini** que ***a man.***

ANY s'emploie comme **indéfini** dans le sens de ***« n'importe quel... », « un quelconque... ».***

*I am free all week: I can come **any day.***

Attention ! Dans cet emploi indéfini de ANY, les règles vues au § **d** ne sont pas valables ; ANY peut être utilisé **quelle que soit la structure de la phrase** : dans l'exemple ci-dessus, ANY fait partie du **complément dans une phrase affirmative,** ce qui est impossible au § **d.** A cet égard, il est intéressant de comparer ces deux phrases :

*I don't want **any coffee,** thank you!* (je n'en veux pas ; emploi du § **d**)
*I don't want just **any coffee,** I want coffee from Columbia.* (pas n'importe lequel ; emploi du § e)

2. Petite et grande quantité

a. *Few* et *little*: petite quantité

FEW est suivi d'un **dénombrable pluriel** :

Few cinemas open before 2 p.m.

LITTLE est suivi d'un **indénombrable singulier** :

*Hurry up! There is **little time!***

Remarque : Il existe la même distinction en français entre ***peu*** et ***un peu*** et en anglais entre LITTLE/FEW et A LITTLE/A FEW. Dans : *There is **a little milk** for you (un peu de lait), **un peu*** est opposé à ***pas du tout (no milk).*** Tandis que dans la phrase : *There were **few people (peu de monde), peu*** est opposé à ***beaucoup (many).***

b. *A lot (lots), plenty, a good (great) deal, much, many:* grande quantité

A LOT (LOTS) est le plus utilisé car il peut être suivi de **noms dénombrables ou indénombrables** :

*There are **lots of cats** in the streets.*
*There are **a lot of cats** in the streets.*
*He has **a lot of patience.***
*There are **plenty of strangers.***
*She uses **a great deal of make-up.***

MANY, et surtout MUCH, sont devenus rares en dehors des phrases négatives. MANY est toujours suivi d'un **dénombrable pluriel** :

*There are not **many tigers** in the world.*

MUCH est toujours suivi d'un **indénombrable** :

*There is not **much money** in my bank-account.*

TOO MUCH et TOO MANY expriment l'**excès** *(trop de...)* :

*She wears **too much make-up.***
*She wears **too many jewels.***

TOO MUCH et VERY MUCH s'emploient aussi avec des **verbes** (mais pas MANY) :

*He sleeps **too much!***
*He doesn't work **very much.***

3. La totalité

a. *All, every, each*

Ils expriment la **totalité** d'un ensemble quelconque, **supérieur à deux.**

ALL s'emploie avec les **dénombrables** comme avec les **indénombrables** :

***All these records** are new.*
*He had to sell **all his furniture.***

ALL est toujours placé **avant le nom,** mais attention aux transformations suivantes, quand le nom est remplacé par un **pronom** :

*I sold **all my books.***
*I sold **all of them.***
*I sold **them all.***

Note : Absence de déterminant (contrairement au français) dans des expressions comme : ***all day, all night, all evening.***

EVERY s'emploie seulement devant un **dénombrable singulier** :

***Every boy** in the gang had a motorbike.*

EACH s'emploie comme EVERY, mais chaque fois que l'on veut insister sur les particularités individuelles :

***Each boy** wore a different helmet.*

b. *Both, either*

Ils expriment la **totalité d'un ensemble de deux** (deux jambes, deux yeux, deux roues pour un vélo, un mari et une femme, etc.).

BOTH peut être suivi d'un **nom pluriel** représentant l'ensemble :

*I had to pull with **both hands.***

ou des **deux éléments de l'ensemble,** chacun au singulier, dans une structure coordonnée :

***Both Nigel and Greg** came to the concert.*

Il peut être suivi d'un **déterminant** :

*I have met **both her** mother and **her** father.*

Il peut être associé à un **pronom** (comme ALL) :

*I know **both her brothers.***
*I know **both of them.***
*I know **them both.***

EITHER *(l'un ou l'autre)* et NEITHER *(ni l'un ni l'autre)* indiquent qu'il faut faire un **choix dans un ensemble de deux** :

*You can use **either racket.***
***Neither girl** wanted to dance with me.*

Remarque : NEITHER est un mot négatif ; il ne doit donc **pas** y avoir **d'autre négation** dans le groupe verbal.

EITHER et NEITHER peuvent être suivis d'un **complément en** OF :

*There are two assistants: **either of them** will help you.*
*There were two assistants: **neither of them** could speak English.*

Ils sont souvent employés dans des **structures coordonnées** :

***Either Greg or his brother** will call.*
*He has **neither a radio nor a record-player.***
Either we buy a T.V. set or we hire one.

c. *Whole*

Il exprime la **totalité** pour un **ensemble composé d'un seul élément.** WHOLE peut être un **adjectif épithète** :

*He has drunk a **whole bottle** of whisky.*

ou bien un **nom** :

*It's rather good, **on the whole.*** (dans l'ensemble)

4. Quantité précise et objective

a. Les mesures

Two metres, a pound, three miles, etc.
I can't buy ***two pounds*** *of caviar.*

b. Les numéraux

One, two, three, etc.

Attention ! Ne pas confondre le **numéral** ONE et l'**article indéfini** A(N) :
Give me ***a glass,*** *please.*
There is not ***one clean glass*** *in the kitchen!*

EXERCICES

A. Vous avez gagné un week-end de luxe à Londres, tous frais payés... A l'hôtel vous commandez votre repas qui vous sera servi sur un plateau.

1° Vous passez la commande, sans préciser les quantités. (Utilisez *some, the, a* et ø devant les noms proposés.)
chicken, caviar, sweet, chips, beer, packet of cigarettes, newspaper, coffee, bread, map of London.

2° Votre plateau arrive. Vous décrivez les quantités (pour les indénombrables) et les nombres (pour les dénombrables). Vous constatez également les absences !

B. Vos parents viennent de louer une maison. Vous vous renseignez sur cette maison que vous allez habiter et que vous n'avez pas encore vue. Complétez les questions.
Ex.: *... garden?*
→ *Is there a garden?*
... trees?
→ *Are there any trees?*

1. ... flowers? 2. ... cupboards in my room? 3. ... garage? 4. ... tennis-courts nearby? 5. ... room for my bike in the garage? 6. ... neighbours? 7. ... work to do in the house?

C. Complétez le dialogue suivant. Un mot correspond à chaque espace. (Utilisez au moins une dizaine de quantificateurs.)

A: Mummy, I want to make a "quiche" for my party. Do I need ... eggs?
B: Yes, there are ... in the fridge.
A: But, Mummy, there are only two! Is that ... for ten people?
B: No, it isn't. But there are ... eggs in the cupboard, too.
A: Do I need milk or cream?
B: You need ... milk and cream, darling.
A: Is there ... milk?
B: Yes, there is a ... bottle. You need ... cheese, too. There are ... kinds of cheese in the cupboard.
A: Can I put ... cheese in the "quiche"?
B: No, darling, put ... French cheese, it's better.
A: Can you give me ... butter, please?
B: Here you are! Don't use ... of it, we need ... for breakfast tomorrow morning!
A: Don't worry! There's a pound of butter, that's too ... for one "quiche"! Must I add ... salt?
B: No, it isn't necessary. There is ... salt in the cheese.
A: Which dish shall I use? There are two.
B: You can use ... dish. They are the same size.

D. Thème.

1. Il y avait un seul gâteau pour quinze personnes... On n'a pas beaucoup mangé. **2.** J'ai laissé la voiture au garage : ils ont changé les deux pneus qui étaient à plat. **3.** J'ai regardé le match en entier : ni Greg ni Nigel n'ont fait une seule faute. **4.** Chaque chanteur a un style particulier. **5.** Il y a beaucoup de restaurants indiens ici ; je les ai tous essayés. **6.** J'ai mis mon adresse sur chaque enveloppe. **7.** Tu as mis trop de lait et pas assez de café ! **8.** Tu as touché ces deux gâteaux, tu dois les manger tous les deux. **9.** Nous avons eu beaucoup de soleil. **10.** Est-ce qu'il y a des magasins ouverts le dimanche en Angleterre ?

3. LE GÉNITIF

Le **génitif** est un **complément de nom** placé **avant le nom** (alors qu'en français les compléments de nom sont toujours placés **après le nom**).

1. La marque du génitif : *'s*

La marque du génitif est 's. Cette marque **doit être prononcée** (selon la même règle que pour le s du pluriel) :

I like ***Nigel's house.***
Here is ***yesterday's paper.***
I prefer ***Liz's house.*** (prononcer /liziz/.)

Cas particulier : le pluriel :

*I saw your **neighbours' dog.***

Seul le s du pluriel est **écrit** et **prononcé.** Le génitif n'est marqué que par l'**apostrophe.**

Remarque : La marque du génitif s'écrit et se prononce normalement avec les pluriels irréguliers :

*Where are the **children's toys?***

2. Le génitif à la place du déterminant

Le génitif occupe la **même place que le déterminant, avant le nom** :

*I like **that house.***
*I like **Nigel's house.***

Attention ! Le complément génitif lui-même peut comporter un **déterminant** :

*It's **my father's** car (it's not my car!)*

3. Le génitif avec les noms de personnes, de pays, d'institutions

Le génitif est le plus souvent employé avec des noms de **personnes** et d'**animaux** (êtres animés). Mais les **pays**, les **villes**, les **clubs**, les **gouvernements**, les **écoles**, etc. représentent des personnes. On trouvera donc :

*I read about **the Queen's family, the Government's plan, London's weather, England's roads, schools' resources.***

Le génitif est **obligatoire** avec les **noms de personnes courts** (noms propres ou communs) :

*It's **Julie's turn.***
*It's **your sister's turn.***

Si le groupe nominal est **trop long**, on emploie un **complément en** OF :

*They found **the body of the old blond tramp.***

4. Le génitif dans les expressions de moment, de durée, de longueur

*This is **yesterday's newspaper!***
*It was **a three hours' concert.***
*It's only **a mile's walk.***

Mais on trouvera également :

*It's only **a one mile walk.***
*It was **a three hour concert.***

5. Le génitif elliptique

Dans certains cas, le **nom qui suit le génitif** peut être **supprimé** (il s'agit d'une **ellipse du nom**).

a. L'ellipse obligatoire

Pour **éviter la répétition du nom** :

*This t-shirt is nice, but I prefer **Julie's.*** (Le mot *t-shirt* n'est pas répété.)

Autre cas : *She is a friend of **Greg's.***

Note : Ici, une autre structure est possible, sans répétition du nom : *She is one **of Greg's friends.***

b. L'ellipse habituelle (sans être obligatoire)

Quand le nom qui suit le génitif est évident : ***school, house, shop, restaurant, church,*** etc. (noms de lieux).

(1) *We dined at **Alfredo's** (restaurant).*
(2) *We heard the bells of **St Paul's** (church).*
(3) *I met her at **the butcher's** (shop).*

Note : L'équivalent en français de ce génitif elliptique est souvent la préposition « chez », mais pas toujours. (Ici, en (1) et (3), mais pas en (2).)

6. Le génitif générique

Un groupe génitif commençant par l'article A(N) est appelé **génitif générique** : il indique une **catégorie d'objets ou de personnes.** Comparez :

(1) *He is not a postman; this is not **a postman's cap.***
(2) *Look! The baby is playing with **the postman's cap.***

En (1), c'est une **catégorie d'objets** : ***une casquette de facteur,*** opposée à une casquette de contrôleur, de gardien, etc.
En (2), ce n'est plus une catégorie, c'est un **objet en particulier** : *la casquette du facteur.*

Exemples de génitifs génériques : ***a butcher's knife, a policeman's helmet, a man's jacket, a doctor's secretary.***

7. Impossibilité d'utiliser le génitif

Dans les cas suivants, il est impossible d'utiliser le génitif. On utilise alors un **complément en** OF.

— avec les noms d'**objets matériels** :
The floor of the kitchen.
The handle of the case.

— avec les **noms suivis d'une relative** :
***The face of the man who was sitting next to us** seemed familiar.*

A. Remplacez le possessif par un génitif comme dans l'exemple :
Ex.: *I have seen his latest film.*
→ *I have seen Woody Allen's latest film.*

1. Can you give me their address? **2.** These pupils have written its newspaper. **3.** Do you know where her racket is? **4.** I have seen their cat. **5.** Its bells are very famous. **6.** My chair is on the right, next to her chair. **7.** His concerts are always fabulous. **8.** He introduced me to its members. **9.** Greg's hairstyle is nice, but her hairdo is nicer. **10.** Show me her car.

B. Le génitif générique. (voir § 6.)
Formez chaque fois que c'est possible un génitif générique à l'aide des noms qui vous sont proposés dans les deux colonnes.
Ex.: *postman/cap*
→ *This a postman's cap*

Note : Certains mots de la colonne 1 ne seront pas utilisés. Certains mots de la colonne 2 peuvent être utilisés plusieurs fois.

1	2
miner, butcher, judge, grocer, baker, cyclist, driver, hairdresser, tailor, footballer, sailor, architect, clown, policeman, guide.	table, scissors, knife, helmet, cap, oven, shoes, pull-over, lamp.

C. Thème.

1. La voix de la dame qui m'a répondu au téléphone était très agréable. **2.** La poignée de ma valise est cassée. **3.** C'est une opération de quatre heures. **4.** Le couteau du boucher est tombé par terre. **5.** Il a été élève de Mr Longman, pas de Mrs Longman. **6.** Ils se sont mariés à l'église St-Pierre, puis ils ont donné un grand dîner « chez Julien ». **7.** C'est un couteau ordinaire, ce n'est pas un couteau de boucher. **8.** Le nouveau recteur de l'Université de York est un homme très simple. **9.** La vie de cette jeune vendeuse est très fatigante. **10.** Il lit les livres de ses enfants.

4. LES NOMS COMPOSÉS

1. Le complément avant le nom, en position d'épithète

Nous avons vu (Fiche **3**, § 7) qu'il est impossible d'utiliser le génitif avec les noms d'objets matériels, et que l'on utilise alors un **complément en OF** :

The floor of the kitchen is wet.

Mais on peut aussi faire passer le **complément avant le nom,** en position d'**épithète** :

The kitchen floor is wet.

L'opération qui donne le résultat : **nom complément + nom** est extrêmement courante, en particulier pour les noms de **matières** qui se placent toujours **avant le nom** :

A leather case, a gold watch.

Beaucoup d'associations de ce type-là **(nom + nom),** très souvent employées, sont devenues des **noms composés,** qui figurent sous cette forme dans les dictionnaires *(a love story, a letter-box).*

2. Les noms composés. Définition

Un nom composé représente une **catégorie d'objets** (objets que l'on peut trouver dans le commerce, par exemple). Comparez :

(1) *a match-box* (nom composé)
(2) *a box of stamps*

En (1) il s'agit d'une *« boîte d'allumettes »,* catégorie d'objets que l'on peut trouver dans le commerce. En (2) il s'agit d'une *boîte quelconque,* dans laquelle on a rangé des timbres.

De même : *the week-end* (nom composé) est une catégorie reconnue de tous, tandis que *the end of the month* ne représente rien en particulier.

Opposition contenant/contenu. Comparez :

(1) *a coffee cup* (une tasse **à** café)
(2) *a cup of coffee* (une tasse **de** café)

En (1) : **nom composé** pour le **contenant,** qui est une **catégorie d'objets.**
En (2) : **complément en OF** pour le **contenu,** quantité de liquide qui pourrait aussi bien être servi dans un autre récipient : *a mug of coffee, a bowl of coffee, a tumbler of coffee.*

3. Forme des noms composés

Les deux éléments d'un nom composé sont séparés par un **tiret** *(a tooth-brush)* ou par un **intervalle** *(a fish fork)* ou bien encore réunis en **un seul mot** *(a bathroom).*

Le premier élément d'un nom composé est toujours au **singulier** : *a flower-bed.* (Attention ! En français : *« un parterre de fleurs ».)* Exception : *a sports-car.*

4. Noms composés de deux noms

a wine glass, a tea spoon, an oil stove, a sea bird, a windmill, a raincoat, a football ground, etc.

Remarque : Les noms composés correspondent généralement en français à des compléments en *de* ou *à*.

Cas particulier : on peut toujours associer le nom *man (girl, boy, woman)* à un autre nom, pour former un nom de **métier, d'occupation** :

a barman, a charwoman, a ticket man, a flower girl.

5. Noms composés d'un nom et d'une forme verbale

— **Nom + base verbale + suffixe -ER** :

a shop-keeper, a taxi-driver, a bottle-opener.

Ces noms composés indiquent l'**agent** (personne ou instrument qui fait l'action).

— **Base verbale + suffixe -ING + nom** :

a dining-room, a washing-machine, a swimming-pool.

Ces noms composés indiquent à quel **usage** servent les objets, les lieux.

EXERCICES

A. 1° Trouvez les noms composés qui correspondent à chacune des phrases suivantes.

Ex.: *This girl goes to school*
→ *This is a school-girl.*
This is to open bottles.
→ *This is a bottle-opener.*

1. I am looking for a room, to wait. **2.** Can you give me a brush for my hair? **3.** I need a fork to eat fish. **4.** I need a new handle for my door. **5.** She teaches in a school. **6.** The President is giving a conference for the press. **7.** This boy sells papers. **8.** He is a reporter, he works for the T.V. **9.** This knife is to cut paper. **10.** He is the manager in charge of the personnel.

2° Essayez maintenant l'exercice inverse, à l'aide des noms composés suivants :
a taxi-driver, a dress-maker, a sea-bird, a raincoat.

B. Le nom en position d'épithète.
Regardez autour de vous et décrivez les objets qui vous entourent en mentionnant en quelle matière ils sont faits.
Ex.: *a leather case.*

C. Opposition contenant/contenu.
Créez des noms composés à partir d'un nom de récipient et de plusieurs noms de contenu qui vous sont proposés.

Ex.: *bowl/salad, soup.*
→ *salad bowl, soup bowl*

1° Décrivez les catégories d'objets que vous pourriez reconnaître même vides (grâce à leur forme, à leur taille, à leurs caractéristiques.)
Ex.: *a salad-bowl* (un saladier ; nom composé).

2° Ces mêmes récipients peuvent être remplis d'un autre produit, d'autres objets, pour lesquels ils n'ont pas été conçus spécialement :
Ex.: *a bowl of soup* (complément en *of*).

Créez donc à partir des éléments donnés : 1° des noms composés, 2° des compléments en *of* :

bottle	beer, white spirit, milk, petrol, coke, scent, wine, hot water, paint.	bag	school, apples, tools, shoes, old papers, mail, potatoes, oranges.
glass	milk, wine, port, beer, coke, orange juice, champagne.	box	gloves, buttons, stamps, elastic bands, cigars, telephone, letters.

5. LES PRONOMS

Les pronoms remplacent les **groupes nominaux** pour éviter une répétition :

The man at the door said **he** wanted to see my father.

1. Pronoms personnels

		Fonction sujet	Fonction complément
sing.	1re personne	I	ME
	2e personne	YOU	YOU
	3e personne	HE / SHE / IT	HIM / HER / IT
plur.	1re personne	WE	US
	2e personne	YOU	YOU
	3e personne	THEY	THEM

Remarques :

- YOU sert au **singulier** comme au **pluriel.**
- 3e **personne du singulier** : on emploie :

— HE pour les personnes de sexe **masculin.**
— SHE pour les personnes de sexe **féminin.**
— HE ou SHE pour les **animaux familiers,** dont on connaît le sexe.
— IT pour les **animaux inconnus,** les **bébés,** et toutes les **choses inanimées.**

- Les **noms collectifs** sont remplacés par THEY ; des noms tels que ***family, police,*** représentent **plusieurs personnes** :

__The police__ say __they__ will soon arrest the man.

- Les **pronoms compléments** ne sont **jamais** placés **avant le groupe verbal** (contrairement au français) :

I gave him my address. (je lui ai donné...)
I'll think of it. (j'y penserai)

2. Pronom réfléchi ou pronom réciproque ?

En français le pronom ***se*** peut avoir un sens **réfléchi** ou un sens **réciproque,** qui correspondent en anglais à **deux** types de pronoms. Comparez :

(1) *Elle __se__ regarda dans la glace.*
(2) *Les danseurs doivent __se__ regarder dans un grand miroir quand ils s'entraînent.*
(3) *Les deux acteurs __se__ regardaient sans parler.*

En (1) et (2) une ou plusieurs personnes regardent **leur propre image** dans un miroir : c'est un sens **réfléchi.** En (3) chaque personne regarde l'**autre** : c'est une action **réciproque.** Deux types de pronoms en anglais :

— sens **réfléchi** : pronoms en -SELF.
— sens **réciproque** : EACH OTHER, ONE ANOTHER.

Attention ! Ne pas confondre avec les verbes toujours pronominaux ***(s'enfuir, se souvenir)*** où la forme pronominale n'a aucune signification. Dans ces cas-là, aucun pronom n'est nécessaire :

He fled. (il s'enfuit)
I remember. (je me souviens)

3. Pronoms en *-self*

MYSELF. YOURSELF. HIMSELF. HERSELF. ITSELF. ONESELF. OURSELVES. YOURSELVES. THEMSELVES.

Ces pronoms en -SELF ont **deux emplois** distincts :

— **réfléchi** (correspondant au sens réfléchi de *se*).
— **emphatique** (correspondant au français : ***moi-même, lui-même,*** pour insister sur la personne).

a. Pronoms en *-self* réfléchis

__She__ looked at __herself__ in the mirror.
__Dancers__ must look at __themselves__ in a big mirror when they practise.

Les **pronoms réfléchis** représentent toujours **la même personne que le sujet.**

Attention ! On n'emploie généralement pas de pronom réfléchi avec les verbes ***wash, dress, shave,*** etc. :

He __washed__ and __shaved__ quickly.

b. Pronoms en *-self* emphatiques

__The doctor__ answered the door __himself.__
I want to speak to __the director himself.__

Après la préposition BY, ces pronoms expriment l'**absence de toute autre personne** :

She was sitting all __by herself__ at a table.

4. Pronoms réciproques

Pour indiquer une action **réciproque** (voir § 2) on utilise indifféremment les pronoms composés EACH OTHER et ONE ANOTHER.

The two actors were looking at __each other__ without speaking.
They have always hated __one another.__

Attention ! Certains verbes sont eux-mêmes réciproques, et n'ont pas besoin de pronom : ***kiss, meet, fight, quarrel:*** *We have __met.__*

5. Pronoms possessifs

Les **pronoms possessifs** remplacent un **groupe nominal** contenant déjà un **déterminant possessif** :

That is not his motorbike, __his__ is red. (la sienne)
She says this book is __hers.__ (à elle, le sien)

Sing.	Plur.
MINE	OURS
YOURS	YOURS
HIS/HERS	THEIRS

Notez l'absence du pronom correspondant au déterminant ITS.

6. Pronoms démonstratifs

Ils ont la même forme que les déterminants vus fiche **1, § 2** : THIS et THAT au **singulier,** THESE et THOSE au **pluriel.** Tout ce qui a été dit de ces déterminants est valable pour les pronoms :

__That__ was not a very nice thing to say!
Let me tell you __this:__ I won't help him again!

Notez l'emploi de THIS dans les formules de **présentation** :

__This__ is Doctor Livingstone. (je vous présente...)

7. Pronoms indéfinis composés

	-ONE	-BODY	-THING	-WHERE
SOME	SOMEONE	SOMEBODY	SOMETHING	SOMEWHERE
ANY	ANYONE	ANYBODY	ANYTHING	ANYWHERE
NO	NO ONE	NOBODY	NOTHING	NOWHERE
EVERY	EVERYONE	EVERYBODY	EVERYTHING	EVERYWHERE

Note : Les formes en -**BODY** et -**ONE** SONT interchangeables.

Pour les différences entre les pronoms en ANY et SOME voir Fiche **2, § d.**

Tableau des significations

	-BODY /-ONE	-THING	-WHERE
SOME	quelqu'un	quelque chose	quelque part
ANY	(1) quelqu'un (2) n'importe qui	quelque chose n'importe quoi	quelque part n'importe où
NO	personne	rien	nulle part
EVERY	tout le monde	tout	partout

(1) *I didn't meet* ***anyone.***

(2) *You can invite* ***anyone,*** *I don't mind.*

Les pronoms indéfinis sont souvent associés à des **adjectifs.** L'adjectif est toujours placé **après le pronom, sans préposition.**

Something strange *happened.* (quelque chose d'étrange)

No one else *knew.* (personne d'autre)

L'adjectif est toujours **ELSE** après ces pronoms, jamais **OTHER.**

EXERCICES

A. Les pronoms indéfinis.
Trouvez une suite logique en utilisant un pronom indéfini.
Ex.: *I'd like to study Chinese or electronics.*
→ *All right, you can do anything you like.*

1. I'd like to go to Los Angeles or San Francisco. All right, ... **2.** I'd like to tell you. No, ... **3.** I'd like to invite Norman or Tina. All right, ... **4.** I'd like to take you to that restaurant. No, ... **5.** I'd like to introduce you to some friends. No, ... **6.** I'd like to buy a book or a record. No, ...

B. Les pronoms réfléchis.
Répondez aux questions en utilisant le verbe qui vous est proposé, et un pronom réfléchi chaque fois que c'est possible.
Ex.: *What's the matter? Do you need some sticking-plaster? Yes, ... (hurt)*
→ *Yes, I have hurt myself.*

1. You look sick. Have you seen your face? No, ... (look). **2.** Look! You are bleeding! Yes, ... (cut). **3.** Has she got a warm pull-over? Yes, ... (make). **4.** Is Daddy ready? No, ... (shave). **5.** Will they make this film in 3 months? Yes, ... (give). **6.** Are your hands clean? Yes, ... (wash). **7.** Has he got a computer? Yes, ... (buy). **8.** Do you know your own voice? No, ... (hear). **9.** There is paint on your clothes! Yes, ... (splash). **10.** Have you still got your cat? No, ... (run away).

C. Pronoms réfléchis et réciproques.
« Les gens ne devraient pas se battre... » « Les gens devraient se respecter... ». Donnez votre avis de cette façon-là en utilisant les verbes qui vous sont proposés (sens réfléchi ou réciproque).
Ex.: *People should love each other. People should not think only of themselves.*

Verbes : talk to, quarrel, hurt, wash more often, dress properly, envy, hate, fight, look in the mirror, take care of, help, understand, respect, be more... .

D. Thème.

1. Est-ce que Tina sait qu'il y a une boum samedi ? Oui, je le lui ai dit. **2.** Mon chien est très gentil, il porte mon journal. **3.** Est-ce que Nigel a son billet ? Oui, je le lui ai donné, et je lui ai donné l'adresse aussi. **4.** Quand ils étaient petits, ils ne s'aimaient pas, ils se disputaient tout le temps. **5.** La police n'a pas retrouvé le voleur qui s'est enfui. **6.** Quand je me suis vue à la T.V., je ne me suis pas reconnue. **7.** Ils ne se sont pas vus pendant les vacances. **8.** Quand elles se sont vues sur cette photo, elles ont ri. **9.** Tu te souviens de Mr Longman ? Il ne se rasait jamais en vacances. **10.** Veux-tu un sac comme celui de ton frère ? — Non, je préfère celui-là. — Mais ceux qui sont dans ce magasin sont trop chers. — Alors, je garde le mien, le vieux.

6. *ONE*

La forme ONE a trois emplois nettement différents : **numéral, pronom remplaçant le nom seul,** et **pronom indéfini.**

1. *One* numéral

On emploie ONE devant des **noms dénombrables** au **singulier** à la place de **A(N)** pour souligner le caractère **unique** de la chose ou de la personne :

There is not ***one*** *pianist like him.*

There is not ***one*** *clean glass in the kitchen.*

On emploie ONE dans les expressions de **temps** telles que : ***one*** *day,* ***one*** *night,* ***one*** *Sunday morning,* etc.

ONE peut s'employer **seul,** pour éviter la répétition du nom :

I need a bottle-opener, have you got ***one?***

Au **pluriel,** ONE doit être remplacé par TWO, SEVERAL, etc.

Can you lend me a pen? Yes, I have ***two.***

2. *One* remplaçant le nom seul

Le pronom ONE remplace le **nom seul,** pas un groupe :

*This **dress** is too small, here is a bigger **one.***

Comme un nom, ONE peut être précédé d'un **déterminant,** d'un **adjectif,** et suivi d'un **complément** ou d'une **relative :**

***The one that is in the window** is nicer.*

ONE remplace toujours un **nom dénombrable,** il peut donc être mis au **pluriel :**

*I have left my **friends** in Cambridge, now I must make new **ones.***

Attention ! On ne peut pas employer n'importe quel déterminant juste avant ONE : certains doivent être séparés de ONE par un **adjectif,** d'autres encore ne peuvent **pas du tout être suivis** de ONE. Dans le tableau suivant, quand l'adjectif est facultatif il est entre parenthèses, sinon il est obligatoire.

déterminant	adjectif	ONE
a	*new*	*one*
my	*old*	*one*
ø	*cheap*	*ones*
the	*(blue)*	*one*
that	*(big)*	*one*
these	———	———
Julie's	———	———

*I'll take Mother's **case,** you can take **Julie's.***
*These **shoes** are too big; are **those** smaller?*

On ne peut pas non plus employer ONE après un **quantificateur.** On efface le nom :

*I can lend you a helmet, I have **two.***

Comparez ONE **numéral** et ONE **pronom :**

*I have got **one*** (numéral) *record player, but it's a very old **one*** (pronom).

3. Quand remplacer le complément par *one ?*

Comparez :

*Did you wash **the car?** Yes, I washed **it.***
*Have you bought **a car?** Yes, I have bought **one.***
*Yes, I have bought a fast **one.***
*Have you got any **cigarettes?** Yes, I have some French **ones.***
*Yes, I have **some.***
*Have you seen **my cigarettes?** Yes, I have seen **them.***

IT et THEM remplacent des **groupes nominaux définis.** ONE, ONES remplacent des **noms** ou des **groupes nominaux indéfinis.**

4. *One* pronom indéfini

ONE est aussi un **pronom indéfini** qui remplace **tout le monde en général,** n'importe qui :

***One** needs a home to go back to.* (fonction sujet)
*This can always happen to **one.*** (fonction complément)

Cette valeur de ONE est un des emplois possibles du pronom français ***on*** (voir § **5.**)

ONE a aussi une forme en -SELF :

One** should never talk too much about **oneself.

5. Traduction du pronom français « on »

ONE pour les **généralités** (voir § **4**) :

***One** never knows.*

YOU remplace souvent ONE dans la langue familière :

***You** never know.* (on ne sait jamais)

WE si le locuteur fait partie du groupe de gens représentés par « on », THEY si le locuteur n'en fait pas partie :

Un Anglais dira :

*In England, **we** love animals.* (on adore...)

Un Français dira :

*In England, **they** drive on the left.* (on conduit...)

PEOPLE représente la **rumeur publique :**

***People** say he abandoned his children.* (on dit...)

SOMEONE représente **une seule personne :**

***Someone** knocked.* (on a frappé)

Le **passif** (voir Fiche **14**) :

*The strawberries **have been picked.*** (on a cueilli...)

EXERCICES

A. *One* remplaçant le nom seul.

Un choix vous est proposé. Dites ce que vous préférez en utilisant *one* ou *ones* (avec un adjectif, un complément, ou une relative).

Ex.: *This plant will grow fast, the other won't.*
→ *I prefer the one that won't grow fast.*

1. Trains to York: 6.30, 7.15, 8.00. **2.** This train stops at every station, that train does not. **3.** Pens cost 30 p, 50 p, 80 p. **4.** We have two kinds of leather jackets: with a zip and with buttons. **5.** These shoes come in three colours: brown, black, and red. **6.** We have two kinds of boots: you can see them in the window, and on the assistant! **7.** How do you want your hamburger? With or without cheese? **8.** This chair is folding, the other isn't.

B. Quand remplacer le complément par *one?* (voir §§ 2 et 3)

Répondez aux questions en remplaçant le complément par *one, ones, it,* etc. L'astérisque (*) devant certaines phrases indique que deux réponses différentes sont possibles. Donnez-les toutes les deux.

Ex.: **Are there any seats left? Yes, ...*

→ *Yes, there are some.*

→ *Yes, there are good ones.*

1. Did you see my new stereo? Yes, ... **2.** *Did you buy the two t-shirts? No, ... **3.** She never buys bus-tickets, does she? No, ... **4.** *Have you got my two records? Yes, ... **5.** Have you got Italian coffee? No, ... ***6.** Have you got strong cigarettes? No, ... but... **7.** Have you got a box of matches? No, ... ***8.** She has a leather jacket, doesn't she? Yes, ... **9.** She makes dresses, doesn't she? Yes, ... **10.** Have you got a blue shirt? Yes, ... **11.** Have you got any cartridges? Yes, ...

C. Thème. Traduction de « on ».

1. On ne peut jamais être sûr de rien. **2.** On a sonné. **3.** Alors, on y va? **4.** On construit un nouveau parking. **5.** Un Français : « En Angleterre, on boit beaucoup de café maintenant. » **6.** Un Anglais : « En Angleterre, on fait du vin aussi. » **7.** On dit que le tabac est plus dangereux que l'alcool. **8.** On n'est jamais trop prudent. **9.** On naît, on vit, on meurt sans avoir rien compris. **10.** Alors, on cherche la bagarre? **11.** On doit parler anglais en cours d'anglais. **12.** On peut dire ce que l'on veut, Paris est la plus belle ville du monde. **13.** On ira au bord de la mer. **14.** Dans les journaux, on dit que le Président est malade.

7. COMPARATIF. SUPERLATIF

Le **comparatif** et le **superlatif** servent à **comparer des éléments entre eux** : on peut comparer des êtres ou des choses pour une même **qualité,** par exemple : « cher ». Le nombre d'éléments qui entrent dans la comparaison peut varier :

Deux éléments :

La jupe est ***plus chère que*** *la robe.* (comparatif)
Les roses sont ***plus chères que*** *les iris.*

Un élément comparé à plusieurs :

Le grand paquet est ***moins cher que*** *les deux petits.* (comparatif)

Un élément comparé à tous les autres éléments de l'ensemble :

C'est ***le plus cher de tous.*** (superlatif)

1. Comparatif

La comparaison peut porter sur un **adjectif** *(il est* ***plus confortable****)*, sur un **adverbe** *(il va* ***moins vite****)*, sur une **quantité** *(il boit* ***plus de whisky****)* ou sur une **action** *(il* ***fume moins****)*.

a. Supériorité

Quand la comparaison porte sur un **nom** ou un **verbe,** elle est exprimée à l'aide de MORE :

He drinks ***more whisky.***
He ***works more.***

Quand la comparaison porte sur un **adjectif** ou un **adverbe,** la forme du comparatif dépend du nombre de syllabes :

— **3 syllabes et plus** : MORE.
— **1 syllabe** : suffixe -ER.
— **2 syllabes** : MORE pour la plupart des adjectifs et adverbes, -ER pour ceux ayant les mêmes terminaisons que *narrow, clever, happy, simple.*

I need a ***bigger*** *case.*
This camera is ***more expensive.***
This car is ***faster.***
He was ***happier.***
He is ***more pleasant.***

Ces phrases comparatives sont des phrases simples. On trouve aussi des phrases comparatives complexes, où le 2e terme de la comparaison est introduit par THAN :

He works ***more than before.***
He drinks ***more whisky than water.***
This car is ***faster than I thought.***

b. Infériorité

Dans tous les cas, le comparatif d'infériorité est exprimé à l'aide de LESS :

(1) *There was* ***less wind*** *yesterday.*
(2) *He* ***smokes less.***
(3) *My flat is* ***less large.***
(4) *These boots are* ***less expensive.***

Remarque : Le comparatif d'infériorité est **rarement utilisé.** On préfère un comparatif de supériorité chaque fois que c'est possible. Dans les cas (3) et (4), on dira plutôt :

(3) *My flat is* ***smaller.***
(4) *These boots are* ***cheaper.***

Phrases complexes : le 2e terme de la comparaison est introduit par THAN :

It was ***less difficult than I expected.***

c. Égalité

Avec les **adjectifs** et les **adverbes,** le comparatif **d'égalité** est exprimé par AS :

It is not ***as interesting as*** *I thought.*

Avec les **noms** et les **verbes,** il faut ajouter MANY ou MUCH après AS :

He doesn't make ***as much money as*** *his brother.*

He carried ***as many cases as*** *he could.*
He works ***as much as*** *the director.*

d. Autres structures comparatives

MORE AND MORE, -ER AND -ER, expriment l'**accroissement** :

She is becoming ***more and more arrogant.***
It is getting ***darker and darker.***

THE MORE ... THE MORE, THE -ER ... THE -ER expriment un **rapport entre deux accroissements** :

The faster *he drove,* ***the happier*** *he was.*

HAD/WOULD RATHER exprime une **préférence** à l'intérieur d'une comparaison :

I'd rather *read the book* ***than*** *see the film.*

e. Les adjectifs de comparaison : *same, other*

L'adjectif SAME **(même)** évoque une idée d'**égalité,** et fonctionne donc comme le comparatif d'égalité (AS introduit le 2ᵉ terme de la comparaison).

He got the ***same*** *job* ***as*** *his brother.*

L'adjectif OTHER **(autre)** évoque une idée de **différence,** et fonctionne donc comme les comparatifs qui expriment l'inégalité : comparatifs de supériorité et d'infériorité (THAN introduit le 2ᵉ terme de la comparaison) :

Would you like ***another*** *drink* ***than*** *Sherry?*

2. Superlatif

Le **superlatif** sert à comparer un élément à **tous les autres de l'ensemble.** Il porte le plus souvent sur un **adjectif,** et on retrouve la même distinction que pour le comparatif de supériorité entre adjectifs « longs » et « courts ».

— Adjectifs « longs » : MOST.
It's ***the most beautiful*** *car.*

— Adjectifs « courts » : suffixe -EST :
She is ***the nicest*** *person.*

Les **compléments du superlatif** peuvent avoir diverses formes :

She is ***the most patient*** *person* ***that*** *I have ever met.*
It is ***the highest*** *tower* ***in*** *town.*
It is ***the nicest*** *house* ***of*** *all.*
That is ***the biggest*** *rock* ***on*** *the beach.*

Remarque : En français le complément est toujours introduit par ***de,*** alors qu'en anglais la préposition peut varier (OF, ON, IN.)

Attention ! On ne peut pas employer le superlatif pour comparer deux éléments : on est obligé d'utiliser le comparatif. Comparer :

He is ***the tallest*** *of the* ***4*** *children* (+ de 2 éléments).
He is ***the taller*** *of the* ***2*** *boys.* (2 éléments)

(en français dans les deux cas : « le plus grand... »)

Autres emplois de MOST (à part sa valeur de superlatif) :

— devant un **adjectif,** MOST est aussi un adverbe proche de VERY (qui intensifie encore plus que VERY) :

It is ***very kind*** *of you.*
It is ***most kind*** *of you!*

— devant un **groupe nominal,** MOST indique ***« la plupart » :***

Most people *don't know anything about history.*
He writes ***most of his books*** *in English.*

3. Comparatifs et superlatifs irréguliers

	Comparatif	Superlatif
GOOD WELL	BETTER	BEST
BAD	WORSE	WORST
FAR	FURTHER	FURTHEST

Cas particulier :

OLD → ELDER/ELDEST, seulement dans les **relations familiales,** et seulement en **position épithète** :

He is my ***elder brother.***
épithète
Greg is ***older*** *than Nigel.*
attribut

EXERCICES

A. Le comparatif de supériorité est plus courant que le comparatif d'infériorité. Donnez de chaque phrase une autre version, plus courante :
Ex.: *It's less short → It's longer.*

1. It's less big. **2.** It's less new. **3.** It's less cheap. **4.** It's less clean. **5.** It's less bad. **6.** It's less unpleasant. **7.** It's less long. **8.** It's less near. **9.** It's less slow. **10.** It's less narrow. **11.** It's less easy. **12.** It's less good.

B. Vous proposez à un ami d'utiliser quelque chose qui fonctionne mieux, sur le modèle :

Ex.: *scissors → Take these scissors, they cut better.*
Attention : mentionnez pour chaque chose sa caractéristique principale, en fonction de son utilité.

Liste : glue, pen, knife, washing powder, aspirin, electric knife, walkman, motorbike, cartridges.

C. 1° Vous êtes avec des amis dans une boîte de nuit qui ne vous plaît pas. Vous proposez d'aller ailleurs en disant pourquoi l'autre est mieux :

Ex.: *Let's go to the "Nashville" where there are less people,* etc.

1. too many people. **2.** bad music. **3.** expensive drinks. **4.** too much smoke. **5.** too small dancing-floors. **6.** too hot. **7.** old videos.

2° Établissez le même type de comparaison entre deux stations de ski. vous proposez d'aller dans une autre station pour les prochaines vacances. Imaginez ce qui fait qu'une station de ski est mieux qu'une autre. Quelques éléments vous sont suggérés, vous pouvez en trouver d'autres : *people, snow, sun, wind, hotels, tracks, cold, discotheques, altitude,* etc.

D. Ces trois personnes (un médecin, une lycéenne, une employée de banque) vont bientôt changer de situation, et de lieu de travail : la lycéenne devient étudiante, le médecin va abandonner son cabinet pour travailler à l'hôpital, et l'employée va changer d'agence bancaire. Comparez les deux situations de chaque personne, en utilisant toutes les formes possibles de comparatif.

Ex.: *cashier*

supermarket	*cinema*
10 a.m. / 6 p.m. *free time: week-ends*	*4 p.m. / 12 p.m.* *free time: mornings*

→ *She will work later in the cinema, but she will have more free time.*

bank clerk	
now	next month
salary: £1300 39 hours / week up at 6 a.m. drive: 45 mn Oxford Street: 1 mile	salary: £900 28 hours / week up at 8 a.m. drive: 10 mn Oxford Street: 1/2 mile

doctor	
private surgery	hospital
8 a.m. / 9 p.m. pause: 1 hour patients: 20 / day £2000 / month holidays: 4 weeks/year	9 a.m. / 5 p.m. pause: 2 hours patients: 30 / day £1400 / month holidays: 5 weeks/year + week-ends

student	
school	university
re-opening: Sept. 10th classes: 28 h / week homework: + + subjects: 10	re-opening: Nov. 2nd classes: 12 h / week homework: + + + + + subjects: 2

E. Répondez comme dans l'exemple en utilisant un superlatif (changez d'adjectif à chaque phrase).

Ex.: *Did you like that record? / No, ...*

→ *No, it's the worst record I have ever heard.*

1. Did you like that book? Yes, ... **2.** Did you like that milkshake? No, ... **3.** Did you like that cake? Yes, ... **4.** Did that film make you laugh? Yes, ... **5.** Was that bus fast? No, ... **6.** Did the cat scratch you? No, ... **7.** Did you manage to do that exercice? No, ... **8.** Did the dog try to bite you? Yes, ...

F. Thème.

1. Les gens sont de plus en plus agressifs. **2.** Plus je vieillis, plus je me rends compte que les gens sont égoïstes. **3.** J'aimerais mieux lui écrire plutôt que lui téléphoner. **4.** J'aime de plus en plus la musique classique. **5.** Il a la même voiture que moi, mais la sienne est plus vieille. **6.** Mon mal de tête allait de plus en plus mal, et je n'avais plus d'aspirine. **7.** J'aimerais mieux écouter une autre radio que la B.B.C. **8.** « Lucy » est la plus vieille femme de la planète : elle a 3 500 000 ans. **9.** Qu'est-ce qui est le plus difficile ? Peindre ou dessiner ? **10.** La plupart des invités sont partis.

8. LES TEMPS

Nous distinguerons 3 temps : **présent, passé** et **futur.** La **marque du temps** est toujours présente dans le groupe verbal ; elle est **obligatoire.** Elle est portée par le **verbe** s'il est seul *(he worked hard yesterday)* ou par l'**auxiliaire** dès qu'il y en a un *(he'll work hard tomorrow).*

Nous n'étudierons dans cette fiche que les phrases affirmatives ; les questions et les phrases négatives feront l'objet de fiches ultérieures. (Cf. Fiches **15** et **16**).

1. Le présent

Il faut bien distinguer le **présent simple** du **présent progressif.** Comparez :

*He always **watches** the Tuesday movie.* (présent simple)

*He **is watching** the Tuesday movie now.* (présent progressif)

a. Présent simple

Il exprime des **états**, des **actions habituelles**, des **généralités**. La marque du temps est portée par le verbe ; elle n'est visible qu'à la 3e personne du singulier (s ou -ES) et aux autres personnes elle se confond avec la base verbale.

*You **look** tired.*
*She **works** in London.*
*It **rains** a lot in England.*
*He **goes** fishing every Saturday.*

b. Présent progressif

Il décrit une **action en cours de déroulement**, non achevée au moment dont on parle. Le présent progressif est l'association du présent et de la forme progressive BE + -ING. La marque du temps est portée par l'auxiliaire BE.

*Hush! The baby **is sleeping.***
*In that photo, they **are dancing.***

• Avec quels verbes peut-on utiliser la forme progressive ?

La forme BE + -ING s'emploie surtout avec des **verbes d'actions**, mais également

— avec BE pour indiquer un **comportement** (et non un état). Comparez :

*He **is** a very arrogant young man.* (état)
*You **are being** very arrogant, young man!* (comportement)

— avec HAVE dans sa valeur de **verbe** (= prendre) et non d'auxiliaire. Comparez :

*She **has** finished lunch.* (auxiliaire)
*She **is having** lunch.* (verbe)

— avec THINK lorsqu'il est équivalent de *« réfléchir »*.

*I **am thinking** about the future.*

Mais la forme progressive est **impossible** avec THINK lorsqu'il exprime une **opinion**.

*I **think** he is very nice.*

• Incompatibilités

Certains verbes sont absolument **incompatibles avec la forme progressive** : BELONG, KNOW, MEAN, MATTER. D'autres sont presque toujours incompatibles avec la forme progressive, dans leur emploi le plus courant : NEED, LIKE, LOVE, SEE, HEAR, COST. On les emploie donc le plus souvent au **présent simple**.

*This record **belongs** to my sister.*
*She **likes** rock music.*
*We **need** another car.*

Remarque : Les deux présents (simple et progressif) peuvent être associés à un **contexte futur**. (Cf. § 3 de cette fiche).

2. Le passé

Les **faits** et les **états du passé** sont décrits ou racontés au **prétérit**. Il faut bien distinguer le **prétérit simple** du **prétérit progressif**. Comparez :

*We **watched** a good film last night.* (prétérit simple)
*We **were watching** a good film when the lights **went out**.* (prétérit progressif + prétérit simple)

a. Prétérit simple

Il est le **temps du récit** (succession d'actions). La marque du temps est portée par le verbe lui-même.

— **verbes réguliers** : base verbale + suffixe -ED.

*We **danced** all night.*
*They **talked** a lot at the party.*

— **verbes irréguliers** : cf. la liste à la fin du livre.

*They **met** last night.*
*I **had** a bad dream.*
*She **was** happy.*

b. Prétérit progressif

Il indique qu'une action **était en cours** à un **moment donné du passé**. Le prétérit progressif est l'association du **prétérit** et de la **forme progressive** BE + -ING. La marque du temps est portée par l'auxiliaire BE.

*It **was snowing** when we arrived in Ottawa.*
*We **were playing** bridge when you phoned.*

Comparez ces deux phrases :

*I **did** the shopping, **made** a cake and **got** everything ready for the party.* (récit, succession d'actions au prétérit simple)
*I **was making** a cake when you **phoned.*** (l'action au prétérit progressif était en cours lorsque l'action au prétérit simple est intervenue)

c. Passé révolu : *Used to*

La forme figée USED TO (toujours utilisée au passé) indique une **opposition entre le passé et le présent** : ce qui était vrai dans le passé ne l'est plus dans le présent.

*I **used to** go to the cinema when I had no T.V.* (sous-entendu : maintenant, je n'y vais plus)
*There **used to** be a painting on that wall.* (maintenant, il n'y a plus rien)

Remarque : En français, cette notion de **passé révolu** est souvent traduite par *« **avant** »* dans la langue familière, et par *« **jadis** »* dans une langue plus relevée.

*We **used to have** breakfast in bed.*
***Avant (Jadis)**, nous **prenions** le petit-déjeuner au lit.*

d. Prétérit modal

Parfois, le prétérit n'**exprime pas des faits du passé**. Si l'on considère la phrase :

*If only I **had** a car,*

on se rend compte que le prétérit HAD n'exprime pas un fait passé. Ce type de prétérit exprime des **faits non réels** : faits **souhaités, soumis à condition,**

non encore réalisés. Cette valeur du prétérit est appelée **prétérit modal.**

*I wish I **had** a fast car!* (souhaité)
*If only I **knew** how to play the piano!* (souhaité)
*If you **brought** some records, we would dance.* (soumis à condition)
*Suppose I **bought** a Jaguar...* (non encore réalisé)
*It is time you **worked** seriously.* (non encore réalisé)

3. Le futur

Par définition, le futur n'est **pas encore réalisé.** Il dépend donc de la façon dont on le considère. Il y a plusieurs façons d'envisager un événement futur.

a. *Will*

L'auxiliaire modal WILL (et, exceptionnellement SHALL) suivi de la base verbale a, entre autres valeurs, une **valeur de futur.** (Pour les autres valeurs de WILL, cf. Fiche **9, §§ 5, 6, 10** et **11a**). On peut utiliser WILL à toutes les personnes ; peu de gens utilisent couramment SHALL. On dira couramment :

*I **will (I'll)** be thirty next week.*
*They **will (They'll)** arrive soon.*
*There **will** be a break at one o'clock.*

On dira beaucoup plus rarement :

*I **shall be** delighted to see you.*
*We **shall** invite you.*

b. *Be going to*

BE GOING TO exprime l'**intention du sujet,** ou bien la **prévision** (lorsque le sujet est non-animé).

*I **am going to** rent a car.* (intention)
*It's **going to** cost you a fortune.* (prévision)
*It's **going to** rain.* (prévision)

Remarque : La forme BE GOING TO, toujours suivie d'une base verbale, est parfois appelée à tort « futur proche ». En fait, l'action peut être envisagée **aussi bien dans un futur proche que dans un futur lointain.** L'important est d'indiquer l'**intention** du sujet.

I'm going to *take an aspirin.* (proche)
They are going to *build a new town in that area.* (lointain)

c. *Be about to*

BE ABOUT TO, suivi de la base verbale, exprime un **futur imminent.**

*The water **is about to** boil.*
*Careful! That tree **is about to** fall down.*

d. Le présent

Le **présent** peut exprimer un **événement futur** (cf. en français : ***Nous partons demain***). Mais dans ce cas un **complément circonstanciel futur** est **obligatoire.**

Le **présent simple** exprime un **programme,** un **horaire prévu.**

*The plane **takes off in four hours.*** (présent simple + complément circonstanciel futur)

Le **présent progressif** exprime l'**intention du sujet.**

I am leaving tomorrow. (présent progressif + complément circonstanciel futur)

e. Le futur dans le passé

WILL, BE GOING TO et BE ABOUT TO peuvent être mis au **prétérit :** à un certain moment du passé, l'action **était envisagée au futur** (concordance des temps). (Cf. Fiche **17**). Comparez :

Présent : *He **knows** he **will** arrive on time.*
Passé : *He **knew** he **would** arrive on time.*

Présent : *He **tells** us that he **is going to** buy a scooter.*
Passé : *He **told** us that he **was going to** buy a scooter.*

Présent : *I **suppose** that the plane **is about to** take off.*
Passé : *I **supposed** that the plane **was about to** take off.*

EXERCICES

A. Thème.

1. Regarde, il fait de grands gestes, mais je ne comprends pas ce qu'il veut dire. 2. Je n'entends pas, parle plus fort. 3. Tu crois qu'il travaille ? Je ne veux pas le déranger. 4. Il porte des lunettes, comme son père. 5. Mais sur cette photo, il ne porte pas de lunettes. 6. Mrs Kidgrave ? Elle prend un café dans le bureau du directeur, comme d'habitude. 7. En ce moment, j'ai besoin de silence. 8. Nous sommes allés dans la « boîte » après minuit, et nous n'avons pas payé. 9. Le chat entra, déposa la souris morte sur le tapis du salon, et repartit, fier de lui. 10. Je crois que je ne roulais pas à plus de 90 km/h, monsieur l'agent.

B. Le futur (voir § 3).

Suite à la phrase qui vous est donnée, exprimez un futur imminent, une intention, ou une prévision.
Attention : il peut aussi s'agir de futurs dans le passé.
Ex.: *She has asked for a telegram form. She ...*
→ *She is going to send a telegram.*

1. I have lost my father's car-keys. He ... 2. The match is nearly over: 15 sec—10 sec—the match ... 3. This board is not strong enough. I ... 4. He is taking all his books with him on holiday; he ... 5. When I last met him, he was spending his last days in that bank. He ... 6. He is tired of spending hours in traffic-jams; he ... 7. When the T.V. went

off, the President was opening his mouth and he ... **8.** The policewoman had just stopped near my car and she ...

C. Prétérit simple et progressif (voir § 2).
La conjonction *as* relie deux actions simultanées :
— s'il s'agit de deux actions ponctuelles (1), elles sont exprimées au prétérit simple;
— si l'une des deux actions était en cours quand l'autre est intervenue, on a le contraste prétérit simple/prétérit progressif (2) :
Ex.: (1) *As I stood up, I dropped my napkin.*
(2) *As I was reading in bed, I fell asleep.*

Les actions suivantes vous sont données dans le désordre au présent de narration. Reliez-les deux par deux grâce à la conjonction *as*, et choisissez le prétérit qui convient à chacune :

1. the toast jumps up/I press the button **2.** I help an old lady/someone steals my wallet **3.** I switch on the T.V./the President speaks **4.** I realise it's just a dream/I hold out a gun **5.** I put my key in the keyhole/the telephone rings **6.** I arrive/he dances with another girl **7.** I switch off the walkman/the telephone rings **8.** my favourite tennis champion wins/the rain start to fall **9.** the waiter comes and says: "Sorry, we're closing"/we read the menu outside **10.** he calls me on the phone/I write to him.

9. LA MODALITÉ ET LES MODAUX

Des phrases comme : *« J'ai acheté une voiture »*, ou *« Je suis en train de discuter avec le vendeur »*, expriment des **faits réels.** Ce sont des phrases factuelles, qui ne sont pas du domaine de la modalité. La **modalité** est le domaine des **faits non réels,** ou **non encore réalisés** ; c'est le domaine des faits **possibles, probables, nécessaires, souhaités,** etc. La modalité est le domaine de nuances telles que : *« Il **doit** acheter une voiture », « Il **pourrait** acheter une voiture », « Il **devrait** acheter une voiture », « Il achètera **peut-être** une voiture »*, etc.

Nous allons étudier les diverses notions exprimées par la modalité, à travers les divers **auxiliaires modaux,** qui ont chacun plusieurs **significations différentes** en fonction de la **forme de la phrase** (négative, interrogative), du **temps,** et du **contexte** immédiat.

Particularités des modaux :
— Un modal est **toujours suivi d'une base verbale.**
— Il ne peut y avoir qu'**un seul modal par groupe verbal.**
— Un modal **ne peut pas porter la marque de l'infinitif** (TO).

1. Possibilité, capacité

Le modal CAN exprime la **possibilité physique, intellectuelle, matérielle :**

*He **can** swim for hours.*
***Can** you remember that song?*
*They **can** pay for it.*

Dans les **phrases négatives,** CAN exprime l'**incapacité** : *He **can't** swim.*

Noter : En français CAN correspond souvent au verbe **« savoir »** : *Il **sait** / **ne sait pas** nager.*

Au **passé,** la capacité est exprimée par le modal COULD **(prétérit de** CAN) :

*He **could** read a lot when he worked in that bookshop.*

2. Obligation. Interdiction

Le modal MUST exprime l'**obligation** que ressent la personne qui parle (obligation morale, par exemple, mais pas seulement) :

*We **must** help these poor people.*
***Must** she stay with her mother?*
*I **must** go now, it's late.*

Dans les **phrases négatives,** MUST exprime l'**interdiction** :

*You **mustn't** step on the grass.*

3. Incertitude, éventualité

Le modal MAY exprime l'**incertitude** de celui qui parle :

*He **may** be at home, but I'm not sure.*
*He **may not** come.* (il se peut que...)

Le modal MIGHT **(forme passée** de MAY**)** exprime une **incertitude plus grande :**

*It **might** snow in January, though it seldom does.* (il se pourrait que...)

Attention ! Les adverbes de modalité **PERHAPS** et **MAYBE** ont le **même sens que** le modal MAY, mais la structure de la phrase est différente. Comparez :

***He may not** come.*
***Maybe he won't** come.*
***Perhaps he will** come.*

4. Autorisation, permission

Le modal MAY exprime les **autorisations,** surtout quand elles sont **officielles :**

***May** I take pictures?*
*Visitors **may** borrow a guide-book.*

Dans la **langue familière,** on utilise plutôt CAN pour exprimer les **autorisations :**

***Can** I borrow your pen?*
*You **can** use my phone if you like.*

5. Probabilité

Le modal MUST + BE exprime une **forte probabilité** :

(1) *No noise: he **must be** sleeping.*
*There **must be** a way out.*

Dans les **phrases négatives,** le modal CAN'T + BE exprime une **forte improbabilité** :

*He **can't be** at home, there's no light on.*
(2) *There **can't be** any mistakes, I have checked.*

Le modal SHOULD exprime une **probabilité moins forte** :

(3) *There **should** be a better solution.*
*It **should** not last long.*

Le modal WILL a aussi une valeur de **probabilité** :

(4) *A parcel? That **will** be from Aunt Agatha.*

Attention ! Les adverbes de modalité CERTAINLY *et* PROBABLY expriment aussi la **probabilité,** dans une structure de phrase différente :

(1) *He **is certainly** sleeping.*
(2) *There **certainly isn't** any mistake.*
(3) *There **is probably** a better solution.*
(4) *That **is probably** from Aunt Agatha.*

6. Bonne volonté, acceptation. Refus

Le modal WILL (en dehors de son sens futur vu Fiche **8,** § **3**) peut exprimer l'**acceptation** ou le **refus** :

*She **will** see you, I am sure!*
*No, I **won't** see anyone!* (je refuse de...)

7. Souhait

Le **souhait** peut être exprimé par les modaux WOULD et COULD **(conditionnel)** :

***I would like to** spend my holidays with him.*
***I wish he would** stop annoying me!*
***I wish he would not** stare at me like that!*
***I wish I could** stay longer!*

Le **souhait** peut aussi être exprimé par l'expression WOULD (HAD) **rather,** qui fonctionne comme un modal, **toujours suivie d'une base verbale** :

***I'd rather stay** at home tonight.*
***I'd rather not go** out.* (voir Fiche **10,** § **1b**)

8. Conseils. Reproches. Regrets

Le modal SHOULD exprime un **conseil,** une **suggestion,** dans un contexte présent :

*You **should** tell me the truth.*
*He **should not** smoke too much!*

Le modal SHOULD associé au **parfait** (SHOULD HAVE + **participe passé**) exprime un **regret,** un **reproche** :

*You **should have come,** it was fun!*
*He **should not have bought** that dog, it's dangerous.*

La forme OUGHT (TO) a exactement le **même sens que** SHOULD. Cette forme se comporte comme un **modal dans les questions et les phrases négatives,** mais est **toujours suivie de l'infinitif** :

*You **ought to speak** the truth.* (conseil)
*You **ought not to have waited** so long.* (reproche)
*There **ought to be** an interesting programme.* (probabilité : voir § **5**)

L'expression HAD BETTER exprime aussi **conseils** et **suggestions.** Elle est **suivie d'une base verbale,** comme un modal :

***You'd better stop** smoking!* (voir Fiche **10,** § **1b**)

9. Action répétée dans le passé. Tendance

Le modal WOULD exprime aussi la **répétition d'une action dans le passé** (1) et (2) (même si cette action n'est pas fréquente), ou une **tendance** (3).

(1) *He **would** often sleep after lunch.*
(2) *Once in a while, he **would** go to a concert.*
(3) *— I have forgotten the key.*
*— You **would!*** (il fallait s'y attendre, c'est bien toi)

10. Dans les questions : propositions, offres, requêtes polies

Le modal SHALL (suivi des pronoms I et WE) exprime une **offre,** une **proposition** :

***Shall I** carry your case?*
***Shall we** go to bed?*

Le modal WILL (suivi du pronom YOU) peut exprimer une **invitation,** une **demande** :

***Will you** have dinner with us?*
***Will you** help me, please?*

Les modaux WOULD et COULD expriment des **requêtes polies** (conditionnel de politesse) :

***Would you** accept to play for us?*
***Could you** open the window?*
***Would you** lend me your pen, please?*

11. Phrases conditionnelles

Les phrases conditionnelles sont des phrases qui contiennent une **condition,** introduite par IF :

a. Si on a le **futur** (WILL) dans la **principale,** on a le **présent dans la subordonnée** avec IF :

*If **we hurry,** we **will** see the beginning of the film.*

b. Si on a le **conditionnel** (WOULD, COULD) dans la **principale,** on a le **prétérit** (modal) dans la **subordonnée** avec IF.

*If **I knew** his number, I **would** call him.*
*You **could** become rich **if** you **worked** harder.*

c. Si les modaux WOULD et COULD sont associés au **parfait,** on a le **plus-que-parfait** dans la **principale** :

*If I **had known** his number, I **would have called** him.*
*You **could have become** rich **if** you **had worked** more.*

EXERCICES

A. Probabilité. Obligation. Impossibilité (voir §§ 1, 2, 5). *Can't* peut exprimer l'impossibilité *(he can't swim)* ou l'improbabilité au présent *(he can't be at home)* et au passé *(he can't have been at home yesterday). Must* peut exprimer l'obligation *(I must go)* ou la probabilité au présent *(he must be sleeping)* et au passé *(he must have been sleeping when I phoned).* Utilisez ces 6 notions pour compléter les phrases suivantes, à l'aide du verbe qui vous est donné au début de chaque phrase.
Ex.: *(be) This dirty book... mine, mine is new!*
→ *This dirty book can't be mine, mine is new!*

1. (be) This key is very small, it ... easy to lose. 2. (be) The light is still on in his room, he ... up. 3. (be) This jacket is so cheap, it ... real leather. 4. (open) You ... that door, it's all rusty. 5. (be) He doesn't know where the Eiffel Tower is, he ... a tourist. 6. (be) In this play, you ... a tourist, someone who has never been in this town before. 7. (be) He comes to work on a bike, he ... the director, he ... a clerk. 8. (open) He ... the door, he didn't have the key, I had it all the time! 9. (work) He ... for a living. 10. (be) He arrived in Ottawa in January, it ... very cold. 11. (be) I have some bad news to give you, you ... brave. 12. (joke) You're not serious, you ...!

B. Expression du souhait (voir § 7).
Exprimez vos souhaits de façon différente selon que vous pensez qu'ils sont réalisables ou non.
Ex.: non réalisables : *I wish I could stay longer (but I can't)./I wish he would stop annoying me (but he doesn't);* réalisables : *I would like to buy a new racket./I'd rather stay at home.*

1. Your favorite group are giving a concert next week, but your parents won't let you go. 2. You don't get on well with your sister (brother). 3. Your Granny is offering to give you for Christmas: a new tennis racket or a pair of leather boots. 4. You tell your parents you are going to take a baby-sitter's job to make some money. 5. You love horses, but you and your parents live in a town. 6. Your parents are planning to move, and they ask you your opinion. 7. You play tennis fairly well, but you think a few tennis lessons would do you good. You tell your parents. 8. There's an English test at 9 a.m. It's 8 a.m. and you know nothing.

C. Le conditionnel dans les phrases conditionnelles. Le conditionnel évoque l'irréel. Décrivez comment ce serait si...
Ex.: *imitation jewellery/real jewellery.*
→ *It is only imitation jewellery. If it were real jewellery, it would be more expensive, I would not have bought it, it would not be in this shop, etc.*

1. Clerk/director. 2. baby vulture/grown-up vulture. 3. imitation caviar/real caviar. 4. apprentice journalist/famous journalist. 5. « amateur »/professional thief. 6. street musician/concert-musician.

10. LA MODALITÉ SANS LES MODAUX : QUASI-MODAUX, FORMES À SENS MODAL

La modalité (voir définition Fiche 9) a déjà été étudiée à travers les **auxiliaires modaux** et aussi quelques **adverbes de modalité** (PROBABLY, MAYBE, PERHAPS, CERTAINLY. Voir Fiche 9, §§ 3 et 5). Nous allons maintenant étudier deux autres moyens d'exprimer la modalité : les **quasi-modaux,** et les **formes à sens modal.**

Les **quasi-modaux** sont, comme leur nom l'indique, « presque » des modaux : ils se **comportent partiellement comme des modaux.**

Les **formes à sens modal** ont chacune une des significations des modaux, mais ne se comportent pas comme eux, puisqu'elles sont **suivies d'un infinitif.**

1. Les quasi-modaux

Ce jeu de mots indique bien que les formes qui suivent ressemblent partiellement à des modaux : OUGHT (TO), HAD BETTER (RATHER), DARE, NEED.

a. *Ought (to)*

OUGHT (TO) est un **modal irrégulier** qui a la **même signification** que le modal SHOULD (voir Fiche 9, §§ 5 et 8).

Il occupe la **même place qu'un modal dans les phrases négatives et interrogatives** (mais on préfère toujours employer SHOULD à ces formes-là) :

*Ought you really **to** see a doctor?* (conseil)
*There **ought not to** be any problem.* (prob.)

Mais en même temps, il se comporte **différemment d'un modal** puisqu'il est **toujours suivi d'un infinitif** :

You ***ought not to be*** *here.*
You ***ought to be*** *ashamed of yourself.*

b. *Had better. Had / would rather*

Ces formes se comportent **comme des modaux** :
— elles sont **suivies d'une base verbale.**
— elles occupent la **même position que les modaux** dans les phrases

— **affirmatives** : ***You'd better*** *watch your step!*
Had / would you rather *go now?*

(**Attention !** Le sujet est placé **après** HAD / WOULD)

— **négatives** : *She* ***had / would rather not stay*** *alone in the old house.*

(**Attention à la place de la négation** : la négation ne porte pas sur **HAD / WOULD,** mais sur le **groupe verbal.**)

Signification de ces formes : voir Fiche **9**, §§ **7** et **8**.

c. *Dare et need*

Ils peuvent se comporter soit **comme des modaux,** soit **comme des verbes,** mais cela ne se fait pas au hasard. En principe, ils se comportent :

— comme des **modaux** dans les **phrases négatives et interrogatives** (position d'auxiliaire dans la phrase, et suivis d'une base verbale).
— comme des **verbes** dans les **phrases affirmatives.**

- ***Dare*** **(oser)**

Dans les **phrases interrogatives et négatives** (modal).

Au **présent** :

How ***dare you*** *speak to me like that?*
You ***daren't*** *go alone!*

Au **prétérit** :

He ***dared not*** *claim his money.*

Dans les phrases **affirmatives** (verbe + infinitif).
Attention ! L'emploi de **DARE** dans les phrases affirmatives est **rarissime,** on l'utilise presque toujours aux **deux autres formes** :

He ***dared to*** *insult a policeman!*

- ***Need***

Il exprime un **besoin,** une **nécessité.**

Dans les phrases **interrogatives** et **négatives** (modal) au **présent** :

Need you *drive so fast?*
You ***needn't*** *worry.* (voir § **2b**)

Attention ! NEED, contrairement à **DARE,** ne fonctionne **pas** comme un **modal** au **prétérit.** Pour exprimer une **nécessité au passé,** on utilise NEED associé au **parfait** :

You ***need not have cleaned*** *my room.*

Dans les phrases **affirmatives** (verbe + infinitif) :

I ***need to*** *learn how to type.*

Note : En cas de doute, on peut toujours employer NEED comme un **verbe,** sauf pour exprimer la **négation de l'obligation** qui est toujours NEEDN'T.

2. Les formes à sens modal

Elles sont appelées ainsi car chacune possède une des **significations des modaux.**

a. *Be able (to)*

Il exprime un des deux sens de CAN : la **capacité** (l'adjectif ABLE signifie « capable »). Cette forme peut être utilisée à **tous les temps** :

I ***will be able to*** *give you the answer next week.*
I'd like ***to be able to*** *get away.*
He ***was able to*** *open the door, he had a pass-key!*

Attention ! Au **prétérit,** COULD indiquerait une **nuance différente** :

He ***could*** *speak English, but he* ***didn't.***

Remarque : BE ABLE(TO) doit toujours avoir un **sujet animé.** Pour un **sujet inanimé,** on utilise CAN :

The milk ***can*** *be thrown away.*

b. *Have (to)*

Il exprime un des sens de MUST : l'**obligation** (« il faut que »). Mais il s'agit en fait d'une **nécessité extérieure,** due aux circonstances, et non pas d'une obligation ressentie par le sujet comme pour MUST.
Comparez :

I ***have to*** *see her before Christmas because I'll be abroad next year.*
I ***must*** *write to my grand mother for Christmas.*

Attention ! Dans les **phrases négatives, HAVE(TO)** n'a pas le même sens que MUST : MUSTN'T exprime l'**interdiction,** alors que **HAVE(TO) négatif** exprime l'**absence d'obligation,** la **liberté** de faire ou de ne pas faire l'action :

— **non-obligation** :

You ***don't have to*** *read the whole book for tomorrow.*

— **interdiction** :

You ***mustn't*** *read that book, it's not for children.*

Note : Ce sens de **HAVE(TO) négatif** peut aussi être exprimé par **NEEDN'T** (quasi-modal. Voir § **1c**).

You ***needn't*** *do the washing up, I'll do it.*

c. *Be (to)*

Le verbe BE **suivi de l'infinitif** exprime un des sens de MUST : une **obligation** exprimée avec force :

You ***are to*** *wait here until we come back!*
You ***are not to*** *tell anyone.*

Il peut aussi exprimer (comme le verbe « devoir ») un **futur de projet** :

We ***are to*** *meet them at the station at 8.*

d. *Be allowed (to)*

Il exprime un des sens de MAY : l'**autorisation**, la **permission** :

*Are we **allowed to** smoke here?*
*We **were not allowed to** go out.*
*You **will be allowed to** leave earlier.*

Attention ! Les formes vues en §§ **2a, 2b** et **2d** peuvent être **précédées d'un modal** (WILL par exemple), mais pas BE (TO).

EXERCICES

A. « Il faut » : Le verbe « falloir » exprime le plus souvent l'obligation (il faut, il faudra, etc.) mais aussi parfois un conseil (il faudrait). Traduisez le texte suivant en utilisant *have to* chaque fois que c'est possible (nécessité). Sinon, vous utiliserez le modal *must* (obligations : § 2) ou bien *should* (§ 8).

(Deux amis, Bert et Andy, à la sortie du lycée)
Bert : « Il faut que tu m'aides. Je voudrais inviter Julie à ma soirée d'anniversaire, mais il faut que tu le fasses pour moi, je n'ose pas le lui demander. Il faudra que je te la montre au lycée. Il ne faut pas que tu lui parles brusquement, il va falloir que tu sois très prudent, elle est très timide. Il faudrait que tu lui parles le plus vite possible, avant samedi. »
(Deux jours plus tard)
Andy : « C'est vrai, elle est très timide. Il a fallu que je sois très patient avec elle. J'ai même été obligé de lui offrir un verre. Ensuite, il a fallu que je la raccompagne chez elle. Il aurait fallu que je lui parle de toi à ce moment-là, mais j'ai oublié, mon vieux ! De toute façon, elle n'est pas libre samedi, elle sort avec moi ! »

B. *Had better* (voir § 1b).
Une amie veut aller en Italie. Vous avez déjà fait le voyage, vous lui donnez des conseils. N'oubliez pas de donner aussi des conseils à la forme négative.
Ex.: *I have to go to the bank to get some Italian "lire".*
→ *You'd better go during the lunch-break, it's less crowded.*

1. I'd like to go to Rome for the week-end. **2.** I may go in August. **3.** I will probably go by train. **4.** You are right, then, I'll go by plane. **5.** I'll have to take a taxi to the airport. **6.** I'd like to rent a car there. **7.** I'd like to go to Naples too.

C. *Dare. Need.* Traduire :
1. Tu n'as pas besoin de m'attendre, je peux prendre le bus. **2.** Il a osé monter sur la scène à la fin du concert pour embrasser le chanteur. **3.** A-t-il vraiment besoin d'être aussi grossier ? **4.** Est-il besoin de discuter ? **5.** Je n'ose pas entrer dans la salle pendant la conférence. **6.** J'ai besoin de me faire de nouveaux amis. **7.** Il avait besoin d'aide. **8.** Tu n'avais pas besoin d'arriver si tôt, j'aurais pu ouvrir le magasin toute seule.

D. Pour compléter les phrases suivantes, vous utiliserez les quatre formes à sens modal ou le modal *could* au temps qui convient (voir § 2) :
1. I would like to ... talk to people in the street, but I 'm too shy. **2.** There is an official meeting tomorrow, but you ... get in if you are not wearing a badge. **3.** He ... open a chemist's shop, because he didn't have a diploma. **4.** He ... give the right answer before the game was over and he won the 1st prize. **5.** He is very good at gymnastics, he ... become an acrobat if he didn't get dizzy so easily. **6.** He ... give the right answer, I am sure, but it was too late, the game was over. **7.** To be sure of getting in at Wimbledon, he ... book 6 months in advance. **8.** I have arranged everything: we ... pick them up in the car at 7.30, so that they ... take a taxi. **9.** I am sure that case ... hold all the clothes, we needn't have taken two!

11. LE PARFAIT

Le **parfait** a **deux** formes : une forme **présent** *(he has changed)* et une forme **passé** *(he had changed)* autrement appelée **« plus-que-parfait »**. Le plus-que-parfait pose peu de problèmes car il existe en français et s'emploie de la même façon. Nous étudierons le plus-que-parfait à la fin de cette fiche (voir § 6). Le **parfait présent** est, lui, une source d'erreur pour les Français, à cause de sa similitude de forme avec le passé composé (avoir + participe passé).

1. Parfait et passé composé. Parfait et prétérit

Le parfait et le passé composé ont la **même forme** (avoir + participe passé) mais des **emplois différents.** Le **passé composé** est employé comme un temps du **récit** *(« hier soir, j'**ai téléphoné** à Nigel, nous **avons parlé** pendant une heure, et j'**ai oublié** de faire mes devoirs »).* Il a détrôné le passé simple *(« nous **parlâmes** pendant une heure »)* dans la langue courante, et est devenu le temps le plus couramment employé pour **raconter les faits du passé.** En anglais, les **faits du passé** sont toujours racontés au **prétérit** (voir Fiche **8,** § **2a**). Le parfait ne peut pas jouer ce rôle-là. Il est donc **impossible** de trouver le parfait associé à des indications de **moment passé,** comme YESTERDAY ou LAST NIGHT, c'est le domaine du **prétérit** exclusivement :

*Last night, I **phoned** Nigel, we **talked** for an hour and I **forgot** to do my homework.*

Attention ! Sachez reconnaître les indications de moment passé sous les formes les plus diverses, et ne pas les employer avec le parfait, mais bien avec le prétérit :

*The British **won** the battle of Waterloo.*
*He **spent** his holiday in Brighton.*

2. Le parfait présent est un présent

Le parfait présent exprime une **relation entre le présent et le passé :** le passé **explique** le fait présent, le passé est évoqué non pas pour être raconté, mais seulement en **rapport avec le présent.** Par exemple, si je dis d'un enfant :

*He **has grown** a lot.*

Je ne raconte pas sa croissance dans le passé, mais je constate maintenant, au **présent :**

*He **is much taller** than last time.*

Ces deux dernières phrases sont **équivalentes.** Le **passé** n'est évoqué que pour **éclairer le présent.** Le lien présent-passé apparaît clairement dans des dialogues de ce type :

— *Where **is** the car?* (présent)
— *I **have left** it at the garage* (parfait), ***it is not** ready.* (présent)

Le parfait **justifie** ce que l'on dit au présent :

*What **have you done?** There is paint all over the floor.*
*I **have found** a key; whose is it?*

3. Adverbes couramment associés au parfait

a. *Now, tonight, today*

Le parfait présent peut être associé à des **adverbes présent** comme NOW et TONIGHT :

*I **have finished** packing **now,** we can go.*
*I **have drunk** too much **tonight,** I have a headache.*

b. *Already. Yet. Ever. Never*

Le parfait est souvent associé à des adverbes comme YET, ALREADY, EVER, NEVER, qui expriment aussi un lien passé-présent (est-ce que l'action a déjà été faite, au moment présent où l'on parle ?). Pour employer ces adverbes, la seule difficulté vient de la traduction du français ***« déjà »,*** dont il faut se méfier.

- ***Already***

ALREADY se traduit par ***« déjà »*** quelle que soit la forme de la phrase :

*I **have seen** that film **already,** let's try another channel.*
***Have you eaten already?** It's only 7.*
*They can't **have gone** to bed **already,** it's only 9.*

- ***Yet***

YET (dans la valeur temporelle) ne s'utilise que dans les phrases **interrogatives** et **négatives,** et se traduit de deux façons différentes :

Has he arrived yet? (déjà)
*He **hasn't arrived yet.*** (pas encore)

- ***Ever. Never.***

EVER et NEVER se traduisent par ***« jamais »*** quelle que soit la forme de la phrase. Ne pas oublier que ***« jamais »*** n'est pas automatiquement associé à un groupe verbal négatif : dans les phrases **affirmatives** et **interrogatives,** ***« jamais »*** indique que l'action a été **faite au moins une fois :**

*Avez-vous **jamais** été en U.R.S.S. ?*

et dans les phrases **négatives,** ***« jamais »*** indique que l'action n'a **pas été faite** (donc, même pas une fois) :

*Je n'ai **jamais** été en U.R.S.S.*

En anglais, NEVER correspond à ***« jamais »*** dans les phrases **négatives :**

*I **have never driven** a B.M.W.*

EVER correspond à ***« jamais »*** dans les autres phrases :

***Have you ever driven** a B.M.W.?*

Dans les phrases **affirmatives,** EVER est très souvent associé au **superlatif :**

*It's **the best** video I **have ever seen.*** (que j'aie jamais vue)

Attention ! Dans ce cas-là, ***« jamais »*** signifie « au moins une fois » et ne doit pas être confondu avec « déjà » (voir plus haut : ALREADY).

c. *Just*

Le parfait présent peut être associé à l'adverbe JUST, pour indiquer une **proximité encore plus grande avec le présent** (en français : « je viens de... », « ...à l'instant ») :

*I **have just spoken** to him on the phone.*
*I **have just** come back.*

4. *Since* et *for*

Pour indiquer qu'une **action commencée dans le passé se prolonge jusqu'au moment présent,** il n'y a pas en français un temps spécifique : on utilise le **présent,** et c'est la préposition ***« depuis »*** qui renvoie au passé :

(1) *Il **joue** dans cette équipe **depuis** 1984.*

(2) *Il **joue** dans cette équipe **depuis** plusieurs années.*

Remarque : La même préposition ***« depuis »*** peut : (1) renvoyer au **point de départ** de l'action *(1984)*, ou bien (2) insister sur la **durée** écoulée entre le moment où l'action a commencé dans le passé et le moment présent *(plusieurs années)*. Dans le 2ᵉ cas, on peut aussi utiliser ***« il y a... que... »***, mais pas dans le 1ᵉʳ.

*Il **y a** plusieurs années **qu'**il joue dans cette équipe.*

En anglais, on utilise le **parfait présent** dans les **deux cas**, mais associé à **deux prépositions différentes** :

— SINCE pour renvoyer au **point de départ de l'action** dans le passé :

*He **has played** in this team **since 1984.***

FOR pour insister sur la **durée écoulée depuis le début de l'action** :

*He **has played** in this team **for** several years.*

De même, avec les verbes ***« être »*** et ***« avoir »*** :

*He **has been** a good player **since the very beginning.***

*I **have had** a motorbike **for 2 weeks.***

Toutes ces phrases indiquent que l'action (l'état, la situation) commencée dans le passé **continue** jusqu'au moment présent.

Attention ! Comparez :

(1) *He **started** playing **in 1984** (then he had an accident and stopped).*

(2) *He **has played since 1984** (and he's still playing).*

Seule la phrase (2) est traduite en français par un **présent** et indique que l'action **continue** au moment présent.

- **Les compléments qui suivent *for* et *since***

— La préposition SINCE renvoie au **point de départ** de l'action, qui peut être indiqué sous diverses formes :

since 1984, since 6 o'clock, since they left, since last week, since the day when his father died, since the holidays, etc.

Attention ! « Point de départ de l'action » n'implique pas qu'il s'agisse d'un moment précis ; il peut être **vague** : ***since the 50's.*** Les expressions comme ***last year*** ou ***the holidays*** sont toujours considérées comme un **point de départ,** jamais comme une durée.

— La préposition FOR insiste sur la **durée** écoulée :

For 2 minutes, for years,for a long time, etc.

Attention ! FOR peut être **absent** dans l'expression de la durée écoulée : les groupes nominaux comprenant l'article THE suivi de noms tels que AFTERNOON, YEAR, DAY, NIGHT, WEEK, etc. ne peuvent être employés après FOR. Dans ces cas-là, la préposition FOR **disparaît,** au profit de l'expression : ALL DAY, ALL NIGHT, ALL AFTERNOON :

*He **has played** the piano **all afternoon.***

*He **has lived** here **all his life.***

- **Différence entre *for* et *since***

La préposition SINCE est toujours associée au **parfait,** car elle indique une relation passé-présent.

La préposition FOR exprime ***« pendant une durée de... ».*** Elle peut donc être associée au **présent,** au **futur,** au **passé,** indifféremment.

*The circus **is** here **for** 2 days.*

*They **will stay** with us **for** a week.*

*They **stayed for** a whole month.*

5. Le parfait et la forme progressive

Le **parfait** (HAVE + **participe passé)** peut être associé à la **forme progressive** (BE + ING), pour indiquer que l'action commencée dans le passé est **inachevée** au moment présent, ou vient à **peine de s'achever** :

*You are late, what **have you been doing?*** (A quoi avez-vous occupé votre temps jusqu'au moment où je vous pose cette question?)

Comparez : (1) *What **did you do?***

(2) *What **have you done?***

(3) *What **have you been doing?***

(1) Je pose une question concernant **exclusivement le passé,** je demande qu'on me raconte les faits passés, détachés du présent.

(2) Je pose une question concernant **le passé** seulement parce qu'il explique ce que je **constate au présent** (*« there is paint all over the floor"*. Voir § 2). C'est le lien **passé-présent** qui m'intéresse, les faits passés peuvent être terminés.

(3) Je pose une question concernant une **période de temps allant du passé jusqu'au moment présent,** l'action étant le plus souvent inachevée, ou s'achevant à peine.

Avec les prépositions SINCE et FOR, la forme progressive est souvent associée au parfait :

*They **have been arguing since** they came back.*

*They **have been arguing for** hours.*

Attention ! Certains verbes sont **incompatibles** avec la forme progressive (voir Fiche **8,** § **1b**).

*They **have known** each other **since** September.*

*He **has had** his driving-licence **for** a month.*

*This car **has been** here **for** ages.*

*She **has wanted** to become an actress **for** a long time.*

6. Le plus-que-parfait

Le **plus-que-parfait** s'emploie comme le parfait présent, mais avec un décalage : le **point de repère** n'est **plus le présent,** c'est un **point du passé,** et ce qui est évoqué au plus-que-parfait est **antérieur à ce point** :

*When I **arrived,** she **had prepared** everything.*

Le plus-que-parfait exprime les **mêmes significations que le parfait présent,** et peut être associé aux **mêmes adverbes et prépositions** (sauf bien sûr les adverbes de sens présent comme NOW et TODAY)

Le plus-que-parfait avec les adverbes NEVER, ALREADY, YET :

*He **had never been** to L.A. before the Olympic Games.*
*When I left this morning, the postman **had not come yet.***

Le plus-que-parfait avec l'adverbe JUST :

*I **had just hung up** when the telephone rang again.*

Le plus-que-parfait avec les prépositions SINCE et FOR :

*He **had had** his motorbike **for** one month when it was stolen.*
*He **had known** her **since** chilhood.*

Remarque : Dans ces deux dernières phrases, contrairement aux précédentes, le plus-que-parfait correspond en français à l'**imparfait** *(« il avait..., je le connaissais... »,* comme le parfait présent correspondait au présent (voir § **4**).

Le plus-que-parfait avec les expressions ***the day before, the week before.*** Ces expressions expriment un **décalage dans le passé** par rapport à ***yesterday,*** tout comme le plus-que-parfait. Ils sont donc compatibles :

*He **had changed** the aerial **the week before.***
*He **had gone** to Scotland **the year before.***

Le plus-que-parfait avec la **forme progressive** :

*When I arrived, I saw that she **had been crying.***

Remarque : Dans un plus-que-parfait, HAD peut aussi être un **prétérit modal** (voir Fiche **8,** § **2d**).

***If you had come,** you would have seen him.*
***If only I had met** him before.*
***I wish you had told** me.*

EXERCICES

A. **Complétez avec un verbe au parfait présent, au prétérit, ou au plus-que-parfait (il peut être nécessaire de déplacer l'adverbe donné) :**

1. Columbus ... America in 1492. **2.** Carl Lewis ... three gold medals at the L.A. Olympic Games. **3.** ... you ever ... a Russian film? **4.** I already ... the results when you phoned me. **5.** I ... to Ireland for my holidays. **6.** The driver ... when the policeman ... him to. **7.** I cannot remember when I last ... caviar. **8.** She ... just ..., if you run you'll catch her. **9.** I ... a black cat the day before my accident. **10.** When I arrived, he ... with that girl since the beginning of the party. **11.** Can you repeat that, please, I ... not ... **12.** They just ... their dog when they left on holiday.

B. **Trouvez une suite logique au parfait présent :**

1. I can't get into those jeans, I ... **2.** He is tired, he ... **3.** —Where is he?—He ... **4.** You cannot get into that famous restaurant if you ... **5.** Don't come in, I ... **6.** The dog is all out of breath, he ... **7.** I must go back home, I ... **8.** The ground is all wet, it ... **9.** Your hands are dirty, you ... **10.** He's got a black eye, he ...

C. **Thème.**

1. Tu ne trouves pas qu'elle a maigri ? **2.** J'ai regardé les J.O. à la T.V. **3.** Il a beaucoup maigri quand il a été malade. **4.** Il n'a jamais compris les femmes. **5.** A-t-il jamais aimé quelqu'un ? **6.** Il chantera pendant 3 heures sans interruption. **7.** Nous avons parlé des heures au téléphone. **8.** C'est vraiment l'homme le plus drôle que j'aie jamais rencontré. **9.** Depuis qu'il a neigé, il fait très froid. **10.** Il y a longtemps que je le connais. **11.** Il y a des années que je n'ai pas fumé. **12.** Il aime la musique depuis le jour où il a entendu ce merveilleux quatuor tchèque. **13.** Il chante depuis les années 60. **14.** Il doit être malade. Ça fait deux jours qu'il ne sort pas de sa chambre.

12. PRÉPOSITIONS ET PARTICULES VERBALES

Pour étudier les prépositions et les particules verbales, il faut s'intéresser à la **structure du groupe verbal** : comporte-t-il des compléments, et si oui, quelle forme ont-ils ?

1. Verbes intransitifs, transitifs, et prépositionnels

On peut classer les verbes en **4 catégories,** selon la présence ou l'absence de **compléments** du groupe verbal, et selon la **forme** et le **nombre** de ces compléments :

a. Les verbes **intransitifs** ne peuvent être suivis d'**aucun complément d'objet.**

b. Les verbes **transitifs** peuvent ou doivent être suivis d'un **complément direct.**

c. Les verbes **prépositionnels** sont suivis d'un **complément introduit par une préposition** (complément **prépositionnel**).

d. Les verbes à la fois **transitifs et prépositionnels** sont suivis de **deux compléments** : l'un **direct** et l'autre **prépositionnel.**

Il apparaît clairement que seuls les verbes des catégories **c** et **d** entreront dans l'étude des prépositions (voir § 2 de cette fiche).
Voyons rapidement les catégories **a** et **b**.

a. Verbes intransitifs

Les verbes **intransitifs** ne peuvent être suivis d'**aucun complément d'objet** :

He was trembling.
I am bleeding.

L'absence de complément d'objet est leur caractéristique, mais rien n'empêche bien entendu que ces verbes soient suivis d'un **complément circonstanciel** : *We slept **in the barn.*** (complément circonstanciel de lieu)

Attention ! Certains verbes sont **toujours intransitifs,** comme MATTER ***(It doesn't matter),*** SHINE, SNORE, TREMBLE. D'autres, au contraire, peuvent fonctionner dans les **deux catégories,** sans changer de sens pour autant, comme SMOKE ou DREAM.

*He doesn't **smoke.*** (intransitif)
*He prefers to **smoke a pipe.*** (transitif)
*He **was dreaming.*** (intransitif)
*He **was dreaming of a farm** in Wyoming.* (prépositionnel)

D'autres verbes **changent de sens** quand ils changent de **catégorie.** Comparez :

*This plant **is growing.*** (intr. : pousser, grandir)
*He **grows tomatoes** on his balcony.* (trans. : faire pousser)

Comparez : *The boys **were running.*** (intr. : courir)
*He **runs a shoe-factory.*** (trans. : diriger)

b. Verbes transitifs

Les verbes **transitifs** sont suivis d'un **complément direct,** qui peut être obligatoire ou non selon les verbes : il est **obligatoire** après des verbes comme TAKE, SHUT, LIKE, FIND :

*He **took a taxi.***
*They **found a nice camping-site.***

Il n'est **pas obligatoire** après des verbes comme EAT, DRINK, DRIVE, BREAK, SING, qui admettent deux structures : *He **drinks.***
*He never **drinks beer.***
*The glass **broke.***
*He **broke his watch.***

Attention ! Certains verbes transitifs sont source d'erreur pour les Français, car leurs équivalents en français sont des verbes prépositionnels. Il faut faire tout particulièrement attention à des verbes comme : ANSWER, ASK, DOUBT, ENTER, FORGIVE, RESEMBLE, etc.

*You didn't **answer my question.*** (répondre à...)
*He **entered the room** at the last minute.* (entrer dans...)
*She never **forgave her sister.*** (pardonner à...)

2. Verbes et prépositions

a. Verbes prépositionnels

Les verbes **prépositionnels** sont **toujours suivis d'un complément prépositionnel** (préposition + groupe nominal) :

*I **agree with you.***
*He **applied to the director** himself.*
*Everyone **had hoped for a quick recovery.***

Quelques verbes prépositionnels : BELONG (TO), CARE (ABOUT), COMPLAIN (ABOUT), LISTEN (TO), LOOK (AFTER), RELY (ON). Certains verbes admettent **deux prépositions différentes** suivant que le groupe nominal est une personne ou une chose : ***agree with** someone/**agree about** something. **Apply to** someone/**apply for** something.*

Attention ! Certains verbes prépositionnels sont source d'erreur pour les Français car leurs équivalents sont **transitifs** (et vice versa. Voir § **1b**). Ex.: WAIT (FOR), LOOK (AT). Autre source d'erreur possible : confondre un verbe prépositionnel avec un verbe à particule (voir § **4**).

b. Verbes transitifs et prépositionnels

Les verbes à la fois **transitifs et prépositionnels** admettent un **complément direct** et un **complément prépositionnel** (parfois même : deux compléments directs).

(1) *She wrote/a long letter/to her boy friend.*
(2) *He borrowed/a helmet/from his brother.*
(3) *I forgave/him/his carelessness.*

Ces 3 cas ne sont pas identiques, car dans les cas (2) et (3) cette structure est la **seule possible,** alors que dans le cas (1) une autre structure que celle-ci est possible.

Voyons les 3 cas l'un après l'autre :

(1) **Deux structures possibles** (dont une seule existe en français) ; les verbes du type GIVE : BRING TO, BUILD FOR, BUY FOR, LEND TO, PROMISE TO, SEND TO, SHOW TO, TEACH TO, TELL TO, etc.

She wrote/a long letter/to her boyfriend.
She wrote/her boyfriend/a long letter.

Seule la 1re structure existe en français, d'où la difficulté. Dans la 2e structure : le 2e complément est placé **avant** le 1er, et **la préposition disparaît.**

(2) **Une seule structure** (semblable au français) :

He borrowed/a helmet/from his brother.

Autres verbes du même type : ACCUSE OF, ADVISE ON, REMIND OF, COMPARE WITH, INVITE TO, etc.

(3) **Une seule structure** (très différente du français) :

I forgave/him/his carelessness.
It will cost/your parents/a lot of money.

Autres verbes du même type : CHARGE, REFUSE, ALLOW, etc.

Le 1er complément est **toujours un groupe nominal** évoquant une **personne,** alors qu'en français, le 1er complément est toujours un groupe nominal évoquant une chose, la personne se trouve en 2e position avec préposition ***(pardonner, refuser, faire payer... quelque chose à quelqu'un).***

3. Le choix de la préposition

Les prépositions sont trop nombreuses pour que nous puissions en donner la liste. La plupart des prépositions sont **simples** : AFTER, BETWEEN, UNTIL, WITH, etc. Mais il existe des **prépositions complexes** : BECAUSE OF, NEXT TO, IN FRONT OF, INSTEAD OF, AWAY FROM, etc.

Certains verbes et adjectifs commandent l'emploi d'**une** préposition, et d'aucune autre. Dans ce cas, le locuteur n'a pas le choix. **Verbes** : WAIT (FOR), LOOK (AT), THINK (OF, ABOUT), etc. **Adjectifs** : AFRAID (OF), KEEN (ON), etc.

Certaines expressions ont une **forme fixe** : ON PURPOSE, BY CHANCE, OUT OF ORDER, etc.

Quand le locuteur a le choix, il arrive que des confusions se glissent entre deux prépositions. Voici quelques cas de prépositions comparées deux à deux pour les distinguer :

- ***At / to***

1re distinction : AT indique une **situation.** TO indique un **déplacement.**

*He's **at** school.* (situation)
*He's going **to** school.* (déplacement)

2e distinction : AT « vise » quelqu'un **avec agressivité.** TO « vise » quelqu'un **sans agressivité.**

*He threw a stone **at** the dog.* (to hurt him)
*He threw the ball **to** the dog.* (to play)

- ***In / into***

IN indique une **situation.** INTO indique un **déplacement.**

*She was working **in** the garden.*
*She drove **into** the garden.*

- ***In / inside***

INSIDE désigne l'**intérieur** opposé à l'extérieur. Comparez :

*He is **in** the house.*
*Come **inside** the house, where it's warm.*

- ***Out / outside***

OUTSIDE désigne l'**extérieur** opposé à l'intérieur.

*We can't play **outside,** it's raining.*
*He's not at home, he's **out.*** (mais il peut être dans un cinéma)
*I'll be waiting **outside** the cinema.* (devant)

- ***As / like***

Ils indiquent une **comparaison,** mais LIKE est toujours **préposition** :

*He plays **like** a professional.*
groupe nominal

AS est souvent **conjonction** :

***As** they say: better late than never!*
proposition

Comment les distinguer quand les 2 sont prépositions, suivis d'un groupe nominal ?
LIKE implique une **comparaison entre deux choses différentes.** AS implique l'**identité de deux termes.**
Comparez :

*He is **not a professional,** but he dances **like one.***
***As a professional,** he knows dancing requires a lot of work.*

4. Verbes et particules verbales

Les **particules verbales** sont peu nombreuses, contrairement aux prépositions. En voici la liste complète : ABOUT, ACROSS, ALONG, AWAY, BACK, DOWN, IN, OFF, ON, OUT, OVER, ROUND, THROUGH, UP.

Remarque : Toutes ces particules sauf trois (AWAY, BACK, OUT) peuvent être aussi utilisées comme **prépositions.** Nous verrons au § 7 comment distinguer une particule d'une préposition.

Les verbes à particule ne sont pas une nouvelle catégorie de verbes ; on retrouve les catégories énumérées au § 1 :

— Verbes **intransitifs** : BREAK DOWN, GO AWAY, FALL BACK, etc.

*The car **broke down** on the motorway.*
*He **has gone away.***
*She **fell back** on the cushions.*

— Verbes **transitifs** : CARRY ON, FIND OUT, GIVE UP, MAKE UP, TAKE OVER, WRITE DOWN, etc.

*They eventually **gave up the idea.***
*He **hasn't made up his mind** yet.*
*He **has taken over his father's business.***

— Verbes **prépositionnels** : un verbe à particule peut être aussi prépositionnel. Un verbe peut donc être suivi d'une **particule et** d'une **préposition** (et dans cet ordre). La préposition est donnée entre parenthèses : CATCH UP (WITH), GET ON (WITH), HOLD ON (TO), MAKE UP (FOR), STAND UP (FOR).

Hold on to the rail.

He doesn't get on with his brother.

5. Signification des verbes à particules

Tous les verbes à particule cités dans le § 4 sont des verbes qui peuvent aussi être **employés seuls.** Il est intéressant de comparer les significations du verbe employé seul et d'un verbe à particule correspondant : les significations sont parfois proches et parfois très différentes :

a. Il n'y a **aucun rapport** de sens entre MAKE *(fabriquer)* et MAKE UP *(maquiller)*, entre CARRY *(transporter)* et CARRY ON *(continuer)* entre GIVE *(donner)* et GIVE UP *(renoncer)*.

b. On retrouve la **même idée dans les deux verbes,** même si le verbe équivalent en français est différent : RING *(sonner)* et RING UP *(appeler quelqu'un au téléphone ;* on retrouve l'idée de sonnerie), WRITE *(écrire)* et WRITE DOWN (*noter, inscrire ;* l'idée est la même).

c. Parfois le verbe à particules et le verbe seul ont la **même signification,** et peuvent être employés indifféremment : GO ou GO AWAY *(s'en aller)*.

d. Un même verbe (TAKE, par exemple) peut être associé à **plusieurs particules différentes,** chacune d'elles en modifiant le sens :

— TAKE *(prendre) : **Take** your time.*

— TAKE OVER *(prendre la suite) : **He's taken over** his father's business.*

— TAKE OFF *(enlever ;* verbe transitif) : ***Take off** your coat.*

— TAKE OFF (*décoller ;* verbe intransitif) : *The plane is about to **take off.***

— TAKE ON *(embaucher) : He had to **take on** more workers.*

— TAKE ON *(entreprendre) : She **took on** a difficult task.*

— TAKE TO *(se mettre à) : **He's taken to** drinking.*

6. Traduction des verbes de mouvement

Les **verbes de mouvement** sont souvent associés à des particules verbales exprimant le **lieu** ou le **mouvement** : GO OUT, COME IN, GET BACK, etc. En français, traduire GO OUT par *« sortir »*, et RUN OUT par *« sortir en courant »*, GO BACK par *« revenir »* et WALK BACK par *« revenir à pied »*. On remarque que la particule (qui n'existe pas en français) est traduite par un **verbe de mouvement** tandis que le verbe de mouvement est lui-même traduit par un **complément** exprimant la **manière de se déplacer** (à pied, en courant).

Comparons diverses associations possibles d'une même particule (IN) avec des verbes :

— *He drove **in*** : *Il entra au volant de sa voiture.*

— *He rode **in*** : *Il entra à cheval.*

— *He walked **in*** : *Il entra à pied.*

— *He ran **in*** : *Il entra en courant.*

— *He sneaked **in*** : *Il entra furtivement.*

7. Préposition ou particule verbale ?

a. Accent

Une **particule verbale est toujours accentuée,** alors qu'une préposition suivie d'un nom ne porte jamais l'accent.

b. Place dans la phrase

Une particule peut être **suivie d'un complément direct** (verbes transitifs) :

*He **hasn't made up his mind,***

ou bien se trouver en **fin de phrase** (verbe intransitif) :

*They finally gave **up.***

alors qu'une préposition introduit un **groupe prépositionnel ;** elle est donc **suivie d'un groupe nominal** (sauf cas particuliers, voir § **7e**) :

*He climbed **up the ladder.***

c. Place du complément

La préposition est placée **avant le complément** qu'elle introduit (sauf cas particuliers). Mais la particule peut être placée **avant ou après le complément,** si le complément n'est pas trop long :

*Take **off** your shoes.*

*Take your shoes **off.***

Attention ! Quand le complément est un **pronom,** il est obligatoirement placé **entre le verbe et la particule :** *Take it off.*

La préposition, elle, **ne change pas de place,** quelle que soit la forme du complément :

*She got **on the bus.***

*She got **on it.***

d. Le test de l'impératif

L'impératif permet de reconnaître à coup sûr une préposition d'une particule :

— La particule est un **constituant du verbe,** elle reste donc **associée au verbe** à l'impératif, même si le complément est sous-entendu :

Switch on** the machine. / **Switch on!

— La préposition **disparaît** à l'impératif quand le complément est sous-entendu :

Wait for** me! / **Wait!

e. Cas particuliers

Cas où la préposition n'est pas placée avant le complément qu'elle introduit (place habituelle) mais

en fin de phrase, parce que le complément a été déplacé vers la gauche :

— **Relatives :**
I know ***the man*** *you* ***were playing*** *tennis* ***with.***
compl. v. prép.

— **Interrogatives :**
Who *are you* ***talking about?***
compl. v. prép.

— **Exclamatives :**
What a ***beautiful house*** *you* ***live in!***
compl. v. prép.

— **Passif :**
This bed *hasn't been* ***slept in.***
compl. v. prép.

EXERCICES

A. Préposition ou particule verbale ? (voir § 7).
Remplacez le complément par un pronom, et mettez-le à la place qui convient par rapport à la préposition ou à la particule.
Ex.: *Did she take off her dress?*
→ *Yes, she took it off!*

1. Did he try on his father's suit? **2.** Did the policeman write down my car number? **3.** Did she wake up her friends in the middle of the night? **4.** Did the ghost go through the wall? **5.** Did she climb up the iron pipe? **6.** Did they ring up their teacher for a joke? **7.** Did the director sit on the broken chair? **8.** Did he cut off his daughter's allowance?

B. Significations des verbes à particules. (voir § 5).
Un même verbe *(get)* peut être suivi de diverses particules, chacune en modifiant le sens. En vous aidant au besoin d'un dictionnaire, trouvez la particule qui convient dans les phrases suivantes (une particule différente pour chaque phrase).

1. I haven't got ... that attack of flu yet. **2.** I have only just got ..., I was out all day. **3.** Where do we get ...? At Victoria station? **4.** Do you get ... well with your director? **5.** I would like to get my book ..., I need it. **6.** The rumour got ... quickly. **7.** I cannot get ... with so little money. **8.** He was locked up, we could not get ... him. **9.** I would like to get ... from here. **10.** Could you get that book ... from the shelf, I would like to see it. **11.** This car is very difficult to get ..., it is so low!

C. Thème. Les verbes de mouvement (voir § 6).

1. Il s'éloigna au volant de sa voiture. **2.** Il traversa le hall en courant. **3.** Nous sommes revenus à pied hier soir. **4.** Il sortit furtivement. **5.** Il a dû entrer en rampant. **6.** Il descendit en hâte. **7.** Nous avons longé la rivière en nous promenant.

13. LES RELATIVES

1. Définition. Liste des relatifs

Une **relative** est une **proposition subordonnée** qui donne des **renseignements sur un nom** de la proposition principale : dans ce cas, ce nom est appelé **antécédent,** et **précède** directement le **pronom relatif** qui introduit la relative :

(1) *The woman* ***who sings so beautifully*** *is an Australian "diva".*
(2) *I prefer the dress* ***which is in the window.***
(3) *The boy* ***I met at the disco last night*** *is American.*

Remarques : La relative peut être enchâssée dans la principale ((1) et (3)), ou bien juxtaposée (2). En (3), le pronom relatif n'apparaît pas après l'antécédent, et pourtant *"I met at the disco last night"* est clairement une relative, introduite par le relatif ZÉRO.

• **Liste des relatifs**

Relatifs qui remplacent des **groupes nominaux :** WHO, WHOM, WHICH, THAT, ZÉRO, WHAT, WHOSE (qui remplace un génitif).

Relatifs qui représentent des **compléments de temps, lieu, cause :** WHEN, WHERE, WHY.

2. Choix du pronom relatif

Le choix du relatif dépend de l'**antécédent (animé** ou **non animé)** et de la **fonction** du relatif dans la subordonnée qu'il introduit (**sujet** ou **complément** du verbe de la relative). La distinction animé/non animé n'existe pas en français (*l'homme* ***qui...****, le chat* ***qui...****, le livre* ***qui...***) mais elle est **indispensable en anglais :** WHO et WHOM remplacent exclusivement des **antécédents animés,** WHICH exclusivement des **antécédents non animés,** THAT et ZÉRO remplacent **les deux indifféremment.**

SUJET	WHO	*The man who wrote that song is a genius.* (animé)
	WHICH	*I prefer the dress which is in the window.* (non animé)
	THAT	*She had a coat that matched the colour of her hair.* (indiff.)
COMPLÉMENT DU VERBE	WHOM	*This is the man with whom I work.* (animé) *I went there with Julie, whom you know.* (animé)
	WHICH	*I like the house in which you live.* (non animé) *I have two pairs of boots, which I never wear.* (non animé)
	THAT	*He is the only nice policeman that I know.* (indiff.)
	ZÉRO	*The boy I met at the disco is American.* (indiff.) *The last book he wrote won the Booker Prize.* (indiff.)

Remarques :

- WHICH peut être **sujet** ou **complément.**
- WHO est toujours **sujet** et WHOM toujours **complément.**
- Seuls WHOM et WHICH peuvent être employés **avec préposition.**
- ZÉRO n'est **jamais sujet** (un relatif sujet doit toujours apparaître dans une relative).
- THAT ou ZÉRO sont **obligatoires** dans certains cas :

— en fonction **attribut** :
*He is not the champion **(that)** he used to be.*

— après un **superlatif** :
*It is not **the funniest** film **(that)** I have seen.*

— après ALL, ANYTHING, EVERYTHING, ONLY :
*This is **all (that)** I can tell you.*
*He will do **anything (that)** you say.*
*I'll do **everything (that)** you want.*
*This is the **only** song **(that)** I know.*

3. Rôle de la relative : déterminative ou non déterminative ?

Le rôle de la relative est de **donner des renseignements sur l'antécédent** : si ces renseignements sont **indispensables** pour identifier le nom, pour comprendre ce dont il s'agit, la relative est **déterminative** ; si ce sont des renseignements **complémentaires,** donc facultatifs, la relative est **non déterminative.**

a. Relative déterminative

Elle est indispensable pour **identifier l'antécédent** :
*I am **the girl who phoned this morning.***
*I prefer **the dress which is in the window.***

La relative est une des multiples façons de **déterminer** l'antécédent ***dress*** :
— *Which dress do you prefer?*
— *I prefer Julie's.*
— *I prefer the blue one.*
— *I prefer **the one which is in the window.***

b. Relative non déterminative

Elle fournit un **renseignement complémentaire** sur l'antécédent qui est déjà déterminé par ailleurs :
*Her father, **who is a rich man,** has just bought her a car.*

La personne est **déjà déterminée** par le **possessif** HER, et ce renseignement suffit pour identifier le sujet du verbe ***buy.*** La relative pourrait être supprimée sans nuire à l'information principale : *"Her father has just bought her a car."* C'est pourquoi la relative est mise en **apposition** (les relatives non déterminatives sont aussi appelées **appositives**).

c. Opposition déterminative/ non déterminative ; choix du relatif

Comparez :
(1) *I am **the girl who phoned this morning.***
(2) *Mum, this is **Liza Redfern, who phoned this morning.***

En (1) le renseignement fourni par la relative est **indispensable** pour déterminer de quelle jeune fille il s'agit.
En (2) il s'agit d'un renseignement **complémentaire,** une personne étant suffisamment identifiée par son nom.

Comparez (autre aspect de cette opposition) :
(1) ***The guests who had a long way to go** left early.*
(2) ***The guests, who had a long way to go,** left early.*

En (1) la relative **détermine** ceux qui, parmi les invités, sont partis tôt (seulement ceux qui avaient une longue route à faire) ; la relative **déterminative définit** donc un **sous-ensemble** dans l'ensemble des invités.
En (2) la relative non déterminative indique que **tous** les invités sont partis tôt *("the guests left early")* et donne une **renseignement complémentaire** : la **cause** (parce qu'ils avaient une longue route à faire). La relative **non déterminative** désigne l'**ensemble des invités.**

• **Choix du relatif**

Les relatifs en WH- s'emploient dans les deux types de relatives :

I have a pair of boots, ***which I never wear.***
The man ***who wrote this song is a genius.***

Les relatifs THAT et ZÉRO sont très courants dans les relatives **déterminatives** :

I like the pull-overs ***(that) she makes.***

Dans les **non déterminatives** THAT est **exceptionnel,** ZÉRO est **impossible.**

4. Le relatif génitif *whose*. La traduction de « dont »

Nigel's bike *broke down.*
I gave a lift to ***Nigel, whose bike had broken down.***

Le relatif WHOSE est employé comme un **génitif,** quel que soit l'antécédent, animé ou non animé (voir Fiche **3, § 3**) :

The car whose *number is GCD 7401 is stolen.*

Rappel : Le génitif prend la place du déterminant ; de même, WHOSE ne peut être suivi d'un déterminant.

• **Traduction de « dont »**

La traduction des 2 phrases ci-dessous :

Nigel, ***dont la moto*** *était en panne.*
La voiture ***dont le numéro...***

pourrait faire croire que le relatif WHOSE est un équivalent du français « dont ». Il n'en est rien. WHOSE n'est qu'**une** des traductions possibles du français « dont », qui représente des **fonctions très diverses.** En voici quelques-unes, suivies de leur traduction en anglais :

Voici le livre **dont** je t'ai parlé : *Here is the book I told you* ***about.*** (relatif zéro)
Ils ont trois voitures, **dont** deux Rolls Royce : *They have three cars, two* ***of which*** *are Rolls Royces.*
J'ai aidé Gordon, **dont** la moto était en panne : *I helped Gordon,* ***whose*** *motorbike had broken down.*

Seul le **génitif** (dernière phrase) est traduit par WHOSE.

5. Relatifs avec préposition

Les relatifs WHOM et WHICH (en fonction **complément**) peuvent être associés à une **préposition** :

This is the man ***with whom*** *I work.*
This is the room ***in which*** *I work.*

La même possibilité existe en français :

C'est la pièce ***dans laquelle*** *je travaille.*

Attention ! Il n'y a pas en anglais le changement de pronom relatif que l'on observe en français :

C'est la pièce ***que*** *j'ai retapissée.*
C'est la pièce ***dans laquelle*** *je travaille.*

On garde dans tous les cas le relatif WHICH.

En français, la **préposition précède toujours le relatif** (« dans laquelle »). En anglais, la préposition peut **soit précéder** le relatif (1), **soit s'en détacher** pour être placée à droite du verbe, immédiatement (2) ou pas (3). Quand la préposition est placée à droite du verbe elle commande souvent l'emploi du relatif ZÉRO (4) :

(1) *This is the room* ***in which*** *he plays.*
(2) *This is the room* ***which*** *he plays* ***in.***
(3) *This is the room* ***which*** *he plays the piano* ***in.***
(4) *This is the room he plays the piano* ***in.***

Attention ! Cette séparation de la préposition et du relatif est **obligatoire** avec les relatifs THAT et ZÉRO.

6. Cas particuliers de relatifs

a. *When, where* et *why*

Ils représentent les fonctions complément de **temps,** de **lieu** et de **cause** :

I remember ***the day when*** *I first met you.*
The street where *I live is very quiet.*
I don't know ***the reason why*** *they don't speak to each other.*

Remarque : Le relatif WHEN peut être remplacé par THAT ou ZÉRO :

I remember ***the day (that)*** *I first met you.*

Attention à ne pas reproduire l'expression française « le jour **où**... » (le relatif représentant d'habitude le lieu — « où » — ayant pour antécédent un complément de temps). Ceci est impossible en anglais :

The night ***when,*** *the moment* ***when...***

b. *Which*

Il peut avoir pour antécédent **toute une phrase** (« ce qui..., ce que... ») :

He gave me a lift home, ***which*** *was very nice of him.* (ce qui)
He gave me a lift home, ***which*** *I appreciated.* (ce que)

c. L'antécédent peut être « effacé »

Le relatif WHAT n'a **jamais d'antécédent :**

She doesn't want me to see ***what*** *she writes.*

Les antécédents des relatifs **WHEN, WHERE** et **WHY** sont souvent « effacés » car ils sont plus ou moins évidents : *the time when..., the place where..., the reason why...* (seul antécédent possible de WHY).

I don't know ***when*** *he will be back.*
I can't remember ***where*** *I left it.*
I would like to know ***why*** *she avoids me.*

Remarque : Ce type de phrase est souvent une **interrogative indirecte** (une question rapportée par quelqu'un d'autre. Voir Fiche **17**).

*"****Why*** *do you avoid me?"*
I asked her ***why*** *she avoided me.*

7. Autre rôle de la relative

Elle sert à **mettre en relief** un mot. Les structures « c'est... qui, c'est... que », permettent de mettre en relief un élément de la phrase :

*C'est **mon frère** qui a une B.M.W.* (sous-entendu : ce n'est pas moi, vous vous trompez)
*C'est **hier** que je l'ai vue.* (sous-entendu : ce n'est pas la semaine dernière)

On met en relief un élément de la phrase (sujet ou compléments divers) pour l'opposer à tous les autres possibles :

*It is **my brother** who drives a B.M.W.*

Le verbe BE peut aussi être au **passé** :

*It was **yesterday** that I met her.*

BE est toujours **singulier,** même si le sujet est pluriel :

*It **was my parents** who understood best.*

Les relatifs les plus couramment employés avec cette structure sont THAT et ZÉRO :

*It was the look of it **I didn't like.***

Remarque : Cette structure implique que l'on place en tête le constituant que l'on veut mettre en relief. Autre structure possible, sans déplacement du complément :

***What I didn't like** was the end.*

EXERCICES

A. Complétez avec le relatif qui convient. (Quand il y a plusieurs possibilités, indiquez-les toutes.)

— Have you seen all the people ... are waiting outside that phone-box? There is another one just opposite ... is empty, ... no one seems to want to go. Do you know the reason ... they are queuing here?
— I think I know ... . It is a telephone... doesn't work normally. There is a coin ... is permanently stuck in the machine, so that the coin ... you put in doesn't stay in the machine, you get it back. But the telephone works, and it doesn't cost you a penny!
— That is very interesting! Do you think I could make a call to the States? I have a friend ... lives there and ... I never call because it is too expensive. I'll come back tomorrow and phone from here.
— Don't wait until tomorrow. The phone will be repaired by then. Now is the time ... you should phone.

B. Vous écrivez à un ami pour lui parler de quelqu'un que vous avez rencontré :
Ex.: ***He goes to school with my brother.***
→ *He's the boy who goes to school with my brother, ...*
Utilisez les relatifs : *who, whom, whose.*

1. I met him at the "Nashville". **2.** He lives in the posh district. **3.** His motorbike is always parked near the Odeon. **4.** His name is very difficult to pronounce. **5.** I went to a concert with him last week. **6.** His brother works in "show-biz". **7.** He is always dressed in black. **8.** I am mad about him.

C. Vous avez trouvé une annonce intéressante dans un journal pour un ami qui veut acheter une moto. Vous la lui décrivez : *It's a motorbike...*

1. It is not too expensive. **2.** Its colour is not too loud. **3.** You can go very fast with it. **4.** You would not need a special licence for it. **5.** It is second-hand. **6.** Its engine is almost new, but its tyres will have to be changed.

D. Relatives déterminatives ou non déterminatives (voir § 3).
Complétez à l'aide d'une relative déterminative ou non déterminative (dans le 2e cas, ajoutez une virgule après l'antécédent).
N.B. : Vous pouvez utiliser 2 relatives coordonnées pour 1 seul antécédent.
Ex.: *I want to try a dress on. What dress? The one...*
→ *The one which is in the window.*

1. — Who can visit him at the hospital? Everybody? — No, only... **2.** — That car is very nice. — What car? — The car... **3.** Mum can I go to the pictures with a friend tonight? — What friend? — A boy... **4.** — Do you buy all the books you read? — No, only... **5.** — I have an appointment with a girl. — What girl? — The girl... **6.** Tell me, how does this game of Loto work? Who wins? — Only the people... **7.** — Don't you ever buy cakes? — No, I only eat... **8.** — Dad, there's someone at the door, wanting to speak to you. — Who? — The neighbour next door... **9.** — I saw one of your teachers yesterday on T.V. - Which one? — Mr Longman ...

E. Traduction de « dont »

1. Les chanteurs dont on connaît le mieux le nom ne sont pas toujours les meilleurs. **2.** C'est un métier dont je n'avais jamais entendu parler. **3.** A San Francisco il y a des maisons dont les murs sont peints comme des tableaux. **4.** Elle a quarante robes, dont la plupart sont démodées. **5.** Il n'y a pas beaucoup de gens dont le nom commence par un Z. **6.** C'est ce dont j'ai peur. **7.** On m'a offert la bague dont je rêvais. **8.** C'est quelqu'un dont je pense beaucoup de bien.

14. LE PASSIF

1. La transformation passive

Une phrase passive est obtenue par transformation d'une phrase active, en effectuant 3 changements : le **complément d'objet du verbe** et le **sujet** de la phrase active sont **déplacés** ; le **complément d'objet** devient **sujet** de la phrase passive, tandis que le **sujet de l'action** est transformé **en complément d'agent** ; on introduit la marque du passif : BE + **participe passé** :

(1) ***The cat*** *has killed* ***the mouse.***
s. c. objet

(2) ***The mouse*** *has been killed by* ***the cat.***
s. c. agent

Attention ! Bien que l'action décrite soit identique dans les phrases (1) et (2), ces deux phrases ne sont **pas équivalentes.** Une phrase passive et une phrase active ne sont pas interchangeables. En même temps qu'a eu lieu une transformation syntaxique (voir plus haut), le point de vue aussi a changé. Prenons l'exemple tant cité du chat et de la souris : en (1) le chat est le personnage qui m'intéresse, j'en fais le sujet d'une phrase active. En (2) c'est la souris qui occupe mon attention, j'en fais le sujet d'une phrase passive ; le sujet est placé en tête, c'est celui qui est mis en valeur :

(1) ***The cat*** *has killed and eaten the mouse. (that is why he looks both proud and guilty)*

(2) ***The mouse*** *has been killed and eaten by the cat. (poor little mouse, I had got used to it)*

• **Le passif peut être associé à tous les auxiliaires :**

— **passif + parfait** : *Your car* ***has been repaired*** *by our best mechanic.*

— **passif + modal** : *Your car* ***will be repaired*** *by our best mechanic.*

— **passif + progressif** : *Your car* ***is being repaired*** *by our best mechanic.*

Remarque : C'est l'auxiliaire BE qui porte la **marque du temps** *(the car* ***was*** *mended,* ***will be*** *mended, ...)*, le verbe *(repair)* reste au **participe passé.**

2. Le passif sans agent

Selon la transformation passive de base (voir § 1) le **sujet** doit se retrouver sous la forme de **complément d'agent,** introduit par BY. Or, beaucoup de phrases passives n'ont **pas de complément d'agent** : *Your car* ***has been repaired.***

Les phrases passives sans agent sont de loin les plus nombreuses. Voici 4 cas principaux où l'agent n'est pas mentionné :

— **L'agent est évident :**
The T.V. set ***has been repaired.*** *(by the T.V. repairman, of course!)*

— **L'agent importe peu :**
Don't worry, the dog ***will be fed*** *when you're away. (by a member of the family)*

— **L'agent est inconnu :**
S'il était exprimé, l'agent serait un **pronom indéfini** (donc inutile, n'apportant aucune information) :
I ***have been robbed.*** *(by someone)*
I ***was woken up.*** *(by something)*

— **On ne veut pas nommer l'agent :**
I ***have been told*** *that you don't approve of my management.* (**On** m'a dit que...)

3. Le passif avec les verbes prépositionnels

En français, on ne peut avoir de phrases passives qu'avec un **verbe transitif** (voir définitions Fiche **12,** § **1**). Mais en anglais, on peut avoir des phrases passives aussi avec un **verbe prépositionnel :**
He ***can be relied on.*** *(You can rely on him)*

Remarque : Le complément seul est déplacé. La préposition reste **après le verbe :**
My dog ***was*** *well* ***looked after*** *when I was away.*

Attention ! Certains verbes prépositionnels **n'admettent pas le passif** : *agree (with), care (about), run (into), stand (for), worry (about),* etc. et en particulier tous les **verbes de mouvement** : *come (from), go (to), arrive (at),* etc.

4. Le passif avec les verbes à la fois transitifs et prépositionnels

Les verbes transitifs **et** prépositionnels admettent **2 compléments,** et **2 structures** suivant l'ordre des compléments (voir Fiche **12,** § **2**) :
(1) *They gave Nigel a part-time job.*
(2) *They gave a part-time job to Nigel.*

De même, il y aura **2 structures passives** possibles :
(1) *Nigel was given a part-time job.*
(2) *A part-time job was given to Nigel.*

La structure (1) est **obligatoire** quand le 2e complément est une **proposition :**
The kid was asked ***not to tell anyone.***

La structure (1) est **la plus courante** quand la personne est représentée par un **pronom :**
He *was given a job.*

5. Verbes n'admettant pas le passif

— Quelques **verbes transitifs,** comme RESEMBLE.
— Quelques **verbes prépositionnels,** et les **verbes de mouvement** (voir § **3**).

— Les **verbes intransitifs,** sauf : LIVE, SIT, SLEEP :

*This house **hasn't been lived in** for a long time.*
*This bed **hasn't been slept in.***
*This chair **mustn't be sat on.***

Il s'agit dans ce cas de verbes intransitifs suivis d'un **complément circonstanciel** (et non de verbes prépositionnels) :

They lived in a house, slept in the bed, sat on the chair.

6. Le passif avec les verbes causatifs *have, make, want*

Dans leur sens causatif, ces verbes appellent un **participe passé à sens passif :**

(1) *I will **have** him **arrested.***
(2) *I **want** him **arrested** as soon as possible.*
(3) *I can **make** myself **understood** in Japanese.*

Remarques : (2) On perçoit bien ici l'ellipse de TO BE. (3) MAKE est toujours **suivi d'un pronom en** -SELF dans cette structure causative.

7. Quand utiliser le passif ?

Une phrase passive n'est pas l'équivalent d'une phrase active (voir § 1). On utilise le passif en anglais plus souvent qu'en français : dans tous les cas où on l'utilise en français, et dans d'autres cas (nous en citerons 4).

a. Dans les mêmes cas qu'en français

— Pour **mettre en valeur le complément d'objet,** qui passe en tête de phrase et devient sujet :

__Our beautiful beech-tree__ has been struck by lightning.

— Le passif permet de continuer de **mettre l'accent sur le complément d'objet :**

*What happened to **that poor tramp?***
***He** was drowned in the river.*

— Le passif est très utile dans les **relatives :**

*The man who **had been arrested** the week before **was released** because he **was proved** innocent.*

— Pour **se passer de mentionner l'agent** quand il est inconnu, évident ou indifférent (voir § 2) :

These shoes are made for dancing.

b. Dans des cas où on n'utilise pas le passif en français

— Pour traduire le **pronom indéfini** « on » quand il représente un **agent inconnu,** ou qu'on veut le passer sous silence (ne pas confondre avec le pronom « on » qui représente « nous » ou « les gens en général » : voir Fiche **11, § 5**), le passif traduit parfaitement l'agent inconnu « on » :

You had been warned. (On vous avait prévenu)
He needs to be told everything. (On doit tout lui dire)
Information may be obtained at the desk. (On peut se procurer...)

— Avec les **verbes prépositionnels** (voir § **3**).
— Avec les **verbes transitifs et prépositionnels** (voir § **4**).
— Pour traduire **certains verbes pronominaux français,** car les verbes pronominaux n'existent pas en anglais. (**Attention :** ne pas confondre les verbes pronominaux qui suivent avec les verbes à sens réfléchi et réciproque : voir Fiche **5**) :

This isn't done. (Cela ne se fait pas)
Nothing is lost. (Rien ne se perd)
This is easily understood. (Cela se comprend)

Attention ! Certains **verbes transitifs** très courants (« casser », « ouvrir », etc.) ont aussi un **emploi pronominal à sens passif** (*ça **se** casse, la porte s'ouvre,* etc.), mais en anglais ces verbes ne sont **pas traduits par un passif :**

This breaks easily.
The door opens automatically.

Voici quelques verbes ayant cette double valeur : *break, end, open, read, sell, wash, shut.*

EXERCICES

A. Transformez les phrases proposées selon la transformation passive (voir § 1). Mettez le complément d'agent si c'est nécessaire.

1. They asked the boy many questions. **2.** A car ran over our dog. **3.** We will give you another chance. **4.** My father repaired the T.V. set. **5.** We must not throw away empty bottles. **6.** Someone left the light on all night. **7.** The police will ask you a lot of questions. **8.** The flood destroyed a lot of houses. **9.** Something has disturbed me. **10.** The wind has blown off the roof. **11.** Nigel gave me your address.

B. Passif modal.
Répondez aux questions en utilisant un passif sans agent.
Ex.: *Where can I get information?*
→ *Information can be obtained at the desk.*
Can we feed the animals?
→ *No, animals mustn't be fed between meals.*

1. Where can I leave my umbrella? **2.** When will I know the answer? **3.** Where can I put my case? **4.** Where can I park my motobike? **5.** When will I receive my invitation?

6. Can I take my dog with me in the shop? No, ... 7. Can I finish the job tomorrow? No, ... 8. Can I make a reservation for tonight? No, ...

C. Vous partez en week-end. *« Check-list » :* Vous vérifiez que tout ce qui devait être fait a été fait, que vous pouvez partir (portes et fenêtres fermées, lumières éteintes partout, plantes arrosées, clé donnée aux voisins, etc.)
Ex.: *The back door has been locked.*

D. Le passif avec les verbes transitifs et prépositionnels (voir § 4).
Répondez en employant le passif. Mettez l'agent quand c'est nécessaire.
Ex.: *Why did he work so hard?*
→ *Because he had been promised a reward.*

Utilisez les verbes : *lend, tell, steal, give, show, offer, teach, bring.*

1. You dance beautifully. How did you learn? 2. How will she get her meals? She has a broken leg. 3. How come he has not got his bike? 4. Why did she leave the firm? 5. Why does the dog look so happy? 6. Who told you you could park here? 7. How did you manage to fix that wallpaper? It must be difficult. 8. Will I have to hire a racket?

E. Traduisez. Le passif avec les verbes prépositionnels et avec certains verbes intransitifs (voir §§ 3 et 5).
Ex.: *C'est un homme sur lequel on peut compter.*
→ *He's a man who can be relied on.*

Attention : une phrase est impossible au passif.

1. C'est quelqu'un à qui on peut tout dire. 2. C'est un enfant qu'il faut toujours surveiller. 3. C'est un directeur avec lequel il faut toujours être d'accord. 4. C'est une maison dans laquelle on ne peut pas vivre l'hiver. 5. C'est un lit très inconfortable dans lequel on ne peut pas dormir. 6. C'est une personne en qui on peut avoir confiance. 7. C'est un enfant à qui on doit parler beaucoup. 8. C'est un fauteuil très ancien, sur lequel on ne peut pas s'asseoir.

F. Répondez aux questions en utilisant le passif. Mettez l'agent quand il est nécessaire.

1. What happened to your dog? 2. Haven't you got a car? Yes, but ... 3. Does he still work in that bank? No, ... 4. Did the French win the battle of Waterloo? 5. Is the cat hungry? No, ... 6. Are these shoes brand-new? Yes, ... 7. Are we going to the Longmans' party? No, ... 8. Does the T.V. set work now? Yes, ... 9. Did you buy this tape-recorder? No, ... 10. Is it a Swiss watch? No, ...

G. Traduisez. (Le pronom « on » et les verbes pronominaux : voir § 7.)

1. On doit secouer la bouteille. 2. On ne peut pas ouvrir cette porte. 3. On ne m'avait pas prévenue de son arrivée. 4. On ne nous a pas encore donné de réponse. 5. Cette boîte s'ouvre sur le côté. 6. Cette règle se retient facilement. 7. Son livre se vendra bien. 8. L'histoire se termine bien. 9. Les vêtements en laine ne se lavent pas facilement. 10. Tout s'explique.

15. LES PHRASES INTERROGATIVES

1. La transformation interrogative. Deux types de questions

On obtient une phrase interrogative par transformation d'une phrase déclarative, en faisant passer **l'auxiliaire avant le sujet** :

— déclarative : ***They will*** *come to the party.*
s. aux.

— interrogative : ***Will they*** *come to the party?*
aux. s.

S'il y a plusieurs auxiliaires, seul le **premier est déplacé avant le sujet** :

They will *have finished by then.*
Will they *have finished by then?*

Il y a **deux types de questions.** Comparez :

(1) *Have you called the doctor?*
(2) *When did you call the doctor?*

La question (1) porte sur **toute la phrase,** et demande une réponse qui peut être « oui » ou « non » : en anglais, ces questions sont appelées YES/NO *questions* (voir § 3). La question (2) porte sur **un élément de la phrase** (ici : le temps), elle est introduite par un **pronom interrogatif** : en anglais, ce sont les questions en WH- (car tous les pronoms interrogatifs, sauf **HOW,** commencent par ces 2 lettres : voir § 4).

2. Le rôle de *do* dans les phrases interrogatives

La transformation interrogative demande que l'**auxiliaire** soit placé **avant le sujet** : si la phrase déclarative comporte déjà un auxiliaire, il suffit d'**inverser le sujet et l'auxiliaire** :

You could *come on Sunday.*
Could you *come on Sunday?*

There will *be a lot of people.*
Will there *be a lot of people?*

Si la phrase déclarative ne comporte pas d'auxiliaire (présent simple, prétérit), on a recours à l'auxiliaire **DO (DOES, DID) :**

His parents understand him.
***Do** his parents understand him?*

He still lives with his parents.
***Does** he still live with his parents?*

He came by train.
***Did** he come by train?*

Attention ! La **marque du temps** ne doit apparaître qu'**une fois** (sur le verbe dans la déclarative : *he lives, he came;* sur l'auxiliaire DO dans l'interrogative : ***Does** he live? **Did** he come?* **suivi d'une base verbale**).

3. *Yes/no questions* et réponses elliptiques commençant par *"yes"* ou *"no"*

Les YES/NO *questions* portent sur toute la phrase et demandent des réponses commençant par YES ou NO, réponses très souvent **elliptiques** reprenant le **sujet** (sous forme de **pronom,** obligatoirement) et l'**auxiliaire (jamais contracté à l'affirmation)** déjà utilisés dans la question :

***Will Nigel and Greg** come to the party?*
*Yes, **they will** / No, **they won't.***

***Has Julie** called the vet?*
*Yes, **she has** / No, **she hasn't.***

***Does he** still live with his parents?*
*Yes, **he does** / No, **he doesn't.***

Il n'est pas nécessaire de répéter tout le groupe verbal, et il est **impoli** de répondre par YES ou NO seulement, d'où les réponses elliptiques.

Schéma d'une YES/NO *question* : **aux. + s. + v. ...**
Parfois, un **adverbe** est placé entre le sujet et le verbe :

*Has **he always hated** water?*

4. Questions en *wh-* et réponses elliptiques ne comportant pas *"yes"* ou *"no"*

Les questions **introduites par un pronom interrogatif** portent sur un élément de la phrase qui peut être le **sujet** (WHO, WHAT sujets), un **complément du verbe** (WHO, WHAT compléments), un **complément du nom** (WHOSE), ou un **complément circonstanciel** (WHEN, WHERE, WHY, HOW,...) :

*I drove **Greg** to **Richmond Road** **yesterday***
(1) (2) (3)
*because **his car had broken down.***
(4)

On peut poser **quatre questions** sur cette phrase déclarative, chacune portant sur un des éléments en gras :

(1) ***Who** did you drive?*
(2) ***Where** did you drive him?*
(3) ***When** did you drive Greg there?*
(4) ***Why** did you drive him there?*

a. Le schéma d'une question en *wh-*

Il est souvent semblable à celui des YES/NO *questions* : les 4 premiers éléments sont **WH- + aux. + s. + v. ...** dans les cas suivants :

— WHO et WHAT en fonction **complément d'objet** :
***Who** have you invited?*
***What** will you have to buy?*

Attention : Le **pronom interrogatif** est **pratiquement toujours en tête de la question.** Même si l'on est tenté de le faire précéder d'une préposition, comme en français *(avec qui ? dans quoi ?),* il faut laisser la **préposition** à sa place, **après le verbe** (même phénomène avec les **relatives** : voir Fiche **8, § 5**) :

*What are you going to sit **on?*** (sur quoi ?)
*Who did you go to the exhibition **with?*** (avec qui ?)

— WHEN, WHERE, WHY, HOW (seul), WHAT TIME, WHAT... FOR: la fonction **complément circonstanciel** :

***When** did you arrive?* (temps)
***Since when** have you been here?* (temps : voir Fiche **11, § 4**)
***Where** did you leave your cases?* (lieu)
***Why** did you come so late?* (cause)
***How** did you travel?* (manière)
***What time** did the train leave?* (temps ; heure)
What** did you bring your guitar **for? (but)

Remarquez la position de FOR en **fin de phrase.**

b. Place de l'auxiliaire

Dans certains cas, le pronom interrogatif n'est pas suivi directement de l'auxiliaire.

— HOW MUCH, HOW MANY: questions sur la **quantité** :

***How much** work have you done?* (HOW MUCH + nom indénombrable + aux. + s. + v.)
***How many** invitations did you send?* (HOW MANY + dénombrable + aux. + s. + v.)

— HOW LONG, HOW BIG, HOW OLD, HOW FAR: questions sur le **degré** :

***How long** will it take?*
***How long ago** was it destroyed?*
***How big** is your house?*
***How old** will she be when she leaves school?*
***How far** did he walk you?*

— WHOSE, question sur le **génitif** :
***Whose** racket did you borrow?*

— WHICH et WHAT **déterminants,** devant un nom (« quel... ? ») : On cherche à **identifier quelqu'un ou quelque chose** parmi un ensemble de possibles : si l'ensemble des possibles est **petit et connu** de ceux qui parlent, on emploie WHICH, sinon, on emploie WHAT :

***Which disco** did you go to? The Nashville? The Scala?*

Which doctor did you call? The old one? The young one?
What flag is that?
What president is here on a visit?

c. Cas particulier

• *Who* et *what* en fonction sujet

Le pronom interrogatif étant lui-même le sujet de la phrase interrogative, le schéma se transforme : ces questions sont construites comme des **phrases déclaratives** :

(1) ***Who will** help me?*
(1) ***What is** going to happen to him?*

(2) ***Who told** you?*
(2) ***What makes** you so sad?*

Les phrases déclaratives (1) comportant **déjà un auxiliaire,** il est donc reconduit :

***Someone will** help me.*
***Something is** going to happen to him.*

Les phrases déclaratives (2) ne comportent **pas d'auxiliaire** (présent simple et prétérit), et les phrases interrogatives correspondantes non plus :

***Someone told** you.*
***Something makes** you sad.*

• Réponses elliptiques sans *"yes"* et *"no"*

Les questions en WHO et WHAT **sujet** demandent souvent des **réponses elliptiques** (voir définitions au § **3**) dont le sujet n'est pas obligatoirement un pronom, mais dont l'auxiliaire doit **toujours être sous sa forme pleine** (non contractée) :

***Who told** you?*
Nigel did
s. aux.

Who is using the bathroom?
Greg is.
s. aux.

• Cas particulier de réponses elliptiques : *so* et *neither*

Les répliques commençant par SO et NEITHER (réplique de **conformité** : « moi aussi... », « moi non plus... », « ma sœur aussi... », etc.) ne répondent pas à des questions, mais à des phrases déclaratives :

*I **have** an appointement with the manager.*
*So **have** I.* (Reprise de l'auxiliaire de la déclarative)
*I **want** to buy myself a dog.*
*So **do** I.* (Recours à l'auxiliaire DO, DOES ou DID)
*He **went** to an art school.*
So did his sister. (Le sujet peut être un groupe nominal autre que « je »)

NEITHER répond à des phrases déclaratives **négatives** :

Julie cannot come.
Neither can I.

5. Les questions elliptiques et les tags

a. Une **question elliptique** est réduite à l'**auxiliaire** et un **pronom sujet** :

— *I have met Elton John.*
— ***Have you?*** *(met Elton John)*

I don't like his music; ***do you?*** *(like his music)*

b. Le « tag »

• Forme du « tag »

Le « tag » est une question elliptique qui, placée **à la fin d'une phrase déclarative,** la transforme en **phrase interrogative.** Un « tag » est toujours inscrit **entre une virgule et un point d'interrogation** :

*You **haven't** got a car,* ***have you?*** (phrase négative → « tag » interrogatif)
He arrived *rather late,* ***didn't he?*** (phrase affirmative → « tag » interro-négatif)

• Rôle du « tag »

Une phrase avec « tag » est une **phrase interrogative,** mais n'est pas toujours une vraie question :

— Dans le cas d'une **vraie question, on attend confirmation** du contenu de la déclarative :

You aren't bored, ***are you?*** (intonation montante)
No, I am not! (réponse négative)

You will help me, ***won't you?*** (intonation montante)
Of course, I will. (réponse affirmative)

— Le « tag » peut aussi être **machinal,** ne pas demander de réponse, être ironique (intonation descendante dans les 3 exemples) :

Nasty weather, ***isn't it?***
You're a professional, ***aren't you?***
You don't like chocolate, ***do you?***

6. *Be* et *have* auxiliaires ou verbes = cas particulier

HAVE n'occupe pas la même place dans la phrase interrogative selon qu'il est **auxiliaire** ou **verbe** :

— **auxiliaire :**

Have you got *a helmet?* (avoir, posséder)
Has she phoned? (auxiliaire du parfait : voir Fiche **11**)
Had you rather *stay here?* (*had rather:* voir Fiche **10,** § **1**)

— **verbe :**

*What will you **have?*** (prendre, consommer)
*Do you **have** nice friends?* (avoir, posséder)
*Why do you **have to** leave so soon?* (obligation : voir Fiche **10,** § **2**)
*Did you **have** a nice time?*

Attention : Quand HAVE signifie « avoir », il peut fonctionner soit comme un **auxiliaire (avec ou sans** GOT**)**, soit comme un **verbe (avec** DO**)**.

BE occupe toujours la même place, qu'il soit **auxiliaire** ou **verbe** :

Are you ready? (verbe)
Is he coming? (auxiliaire présent progressif : voir Fiche **8**)
Was he arrested? (auxiliaire passif : voir Fiche **14**)

7. L'inversion du sujet dans des phrases qui ne sont pas interrogatives

a. Attention : On ne doit **pas inverser** l'ordre du **sujet et du verbe** dans les phrases déclaratives, comme on le fait souvent en français : *Il m'a indiqué où se trouvait* (v.) *la boutique* (s.) ; *Je ne sais pas où mène* (v.) *cette route* (s.).

En anglais, le **sujet** doit se trouver **avant le verbe** :

He showed me where the shop (s.) *was* (v.).
I don't know where this road (s.) *leads* (v.) *to.*

b. On trouve parfois le schéma : **aux. + s. + v.** dans des phrases qui ne sont **pas** pour autant **interrogatives** :

Never again will I *be such a fool!*
Not only did he finish *first, but he got the best mark as well.*
Hardly had I recovered *from the flu when I broke my leg.*
Little did we know *he would be such a nuisance.*
No sooner had I locked *my door than the telephone rang.*
I would hardly have recognized her, ***so*** *unaware of her* ***had I been.***
Should you feel hungry, *there is some cold chicken in the fridge.*

EXERCICES

A. Phrases interrogatives et expressions de la durée (voir Fiche 11, § 4).
On vous a volé votre moto. Quelques mois après, vous croyez la reconnaître, dans la rue. A côté d'elle, un jeune homme en train d'enlever son casque. Vous entrez en conversation avec lui, et vous lui posez un maximum de questions, pour en avoir le cœur net. Traduisez les phrases suivantes :

1. C'est un modèle récent ? **2.** A quelle vitesse peut-elle aller ? **3.** Depuis combien de temps vous l'avez ? **4.** Quand est-ce que vous l'avez achetée ? **5.** Où l'avez-vous achetée ? **6.** C'était une occasion ? **7.** Depuis combien de temps avez-vous votre permis ? **8.** Vous l'avez passé il y a combien de temps ? **9.** Depuis quand conduisez-vous cette moto ? **10.** Vous avez déjà eu un accident ? **11.** C'était quand votre dernier accident ? **12.** Depuis quand avez-vous ce casque ? Depuis votre accident ? **13.** Il y a combien de temps que vous avez repeint cette moto ? **14.** Combien de temps comptez-vous la garder ? **15.** Vous comptez la changer quand ?

B. Un truand, soupçonné de complicité, répond aux questions des policiers. Il se dit innocent. Trouvez les questions correspondant aux réponses en gras :

1. I have known Jack the Dealer **for years.** **2.** I haven't seen him **for months.** **3.** The last time I saw him was **on July 27th,** when he came out of prison. **4.** I saw him **at his place.** **5.** I went to his place **to welcome him back.** **6.** I haven't seen him since because **he played a dirty trick on me.** **7.** It's **not mine,** Inspector; I haven't seen this cigarette-case before. **8.** I have been driving a **B.M.W.** these days, though I have two other cars in my garage. **9.** Last night, I took my wife's **Mercedes.** So you see, it couldn't have been me, Inspector.

C. Place de la préposition dans les questions en *wh-* (voir § 4a).
Vous êtes d'un tempérament jaloux. Vous regardez l'aide-mémoire de votre petit(e) ami(e), et vous lui posez des questions : vous voulez savoir avec qui il/elle sort, etc.
Ex.: *Sat 9.p.m.: concert.*
→ *Who are you going to a concert with?*

1. Tues. aft.: baby sitting. **2.** Monday. 1.p.m.: Chinese restaurant. **3.** Sat. aft.: make big cake. **4.** Wed.: give my old leather jacket. **5.** Fri.: borrow a car. **6.** Sund.: tennis-match at the club.

D. Traduisez.

1. Il aimerait mieux rester indépendant, et moi aussi. **2.** Les pianistes doivent s'entraîner tous les jours, et les pick-pockets aussi. **3.** Il a pris du caviar, et tous ses invités aussi ! **4.** Il ne téléphonera pas, et elle non plus, elle est bien trop fière ! **5.** Aviez-vous déjà mangé des escargots ? **6.** Je ne sais pas où est mon chien. **7.** A peine avais-je le dos tourné, que mon chat remontait sur le canapé. **8.** Il voulait savoir à quelle heure commençait le concert. **9.** Jamais plus je n'irai seule dans une discothèque. **10.** J'ai entendu aboyer le chien des voisins toute la nuit. **11.** Non seulement les places sont très chères, mais il faut faire la queue pendant des heures.

16. LES PHRASES NÉGATIVES

1. La transformation négative

On obtient une phrase **négative** par transformation d'une phrase affirmative, en ajoutant la négation NOT **après l'auxiliaire :**

*I **will not** forget.*
*You **should not** worry.*

S'il y a plusieurs auxiliaires, la **négation** se place **après le premier auxiliaire** (même règle pour les phrases interrogatives : voir Fiche **15, § 1**) :

*He **may** not **have** heard.*
aux. 1 aux. 2
*He **could** not **be** trusted.*
aux. 1 aux. 2

Dans la langue parlée, la négation NOT est souvent **contractée** en N'T et **rattachée à l'auxiliaire :** ISN'T, AREN'T, HAVEN'T, COULDN'T, etc.

Attention : Particularités orthographiques :
— La négation NOT est toujours accolée à l'auxiliaire CAN : CANNOT ou CAN'T
— Modification orthographique des auxiliaires WILL et SHALL quand la négation NOT leur est rattachée : WON'T et SHAN'T.
— Contraction impossible pour MAY NOT (toujours écrit sous cette forme).
— Contraction de l'auxiliaire, et non de la négation, pour *I **am not** : **I'm not.***

2. Le rôle de *do* dans les phrases négatives

La transformation négative introduit la négation NOT **après le premier auxiliaire :**

*There **cannot** be any doubt.*
*You **must not** forget.*

Si la phrase affirmative ne comporte pas d'auxiliaire (cas du présent simple et du prétérit), on a recours à l'**auxiliaire** DO (DOES, DID) :

*You **do not** seem to understand.*
*He **does not** often smile.*
*He **did not** even wave to me.*

Formes contractées : ***You don't, he doesn't, he didn't.***

3. *Be* et *have* auxiliaires ou verbes

a. *Be*

Dans les phrases négatives, BE est **toujours suivi de la négation** NOT, qu'il soit auxiliaire ou verbe :

*He **isn't** ready yet.* (v.)
*There **isn't** one ticket left.* (v.)
*You **aren't** listening!* (aux. présent progressif : voir Fiche **8**)
*He **wasn't** made use of.* (aux. du passif : voir Fiche **14**)

Remarque : 2 formes de contraction sont possibles avec les formes IS et ARE :

He isn't** ou **he's not.
You aren't** ou **you're not.

mais une seule contraction est possible avec AM, WAS et WERE :

***I'm** not.* (aux. contracté)
*He **wasn't**.* }
*You **weren't**.* } (négation contractée)

b. *Have*

HAVE est suivi de la négation NOT dans son emploi d'**auxiliaire,** mais pas dans son emploi de verbe (dans ce cas là, la négation suit l'auxiliaire DO) :

— **auxiliaire :**
*They **haven't** arrived yet.* (aux. du parfait : voir Fiche **11**)
*They **had better not** be late. **I'd rather not** be invited.* (quasi-modaux : voir Fiche **10, § 1**)

— **verbe :**
*They **don't have** a car.* (avoir, posséder)
*You **don't have to** be so fresh!* (obligation : voir Fiche **10, § 2**)
*They **didn't have** lunch with us.* (prendre)

Attention : Quand HAVE signifie « avoir » (posséder), il peut fonctionner soit comme un auxiliaire (avec GOT), soit comme un verbe (avec DO). (Voir fiche **15, § 6.**)

4. Les phrases négatives sans la négation *not*

Quelques mots à **sens négatif :** NO et ses composés : NONE, NOTHING, NO MORE, NO LONGER, NEITHER... NOR, NEVER.

En français, une phrase négative contient obligatoirement **la négation « ne » (n'), associée à un autre mot** qui, lui, n'est **pas négatif :** *je **ne** vois **pas** d'issue ; je **n**'en ai vu **aucun** ; je **n**'y vois **rien** ; je **n**'ai vu **personne** ; je **ne** l'ai vu **nulle part** ; je **ne** les vois **plus** ; je **n**'ai vu **ni** l'un **ni** l'autre ; je **ne** les vois **jamais**,* etc. En anglais, une **phrase négative doit contenir une négation,** mais qui n'est **pas toujours la négation** NOT : la négation peut être contenue dans un **mot à sens négatif** et, comme il ne doit y avoir, sauf cas particulier, qu'**une seule négation par groupe verbal,** la **négation** NOT **disparaît alors.** Ces exemples suivent l'ordre donné ci-dessus (tous ces mots commencent par la lettre N de la négation) :

*There is **no** bread.* (ne... pas de)
*It is **no** bigger than I expected.*
*Was there any objection? No, there was **none.*** (ne... aucune)
*There was **none** other.*

Attention : NONE, contrairement à NO, ne peut **pas être suivi d'un nom,** mais il peut être suivi d'un adjectif.

I heard ***nothing. Nothing*** *is ready.* (ne... rien)
I spoke to ***no one. No one*** *ever invites me (ne... personne)*
It is ***nowhere*** *to be found.* (ne... nulle part)
I'll eat ***no more.*** (ne... plus)
They ***no longer*** *live here.* (ne... plus)
I wanted to give him ***neither*** *my address* ***nor*** *my phone number.* (ne... ni... ni...)
I opened ***neither*** *of them.* (ne... aucun des...)

Attention : On remarque l'**absence de l'auxiliaire** DO (DOES, DID) dans ce type de phrases négatives. La **marque du temps est portée par le verbe** (*heard, spoke, invites,* etc.). DO n'est présent que dans les phrases négatives contenant NOT.

He has ***never*** *been so depressed.* (ne... jamais)
He is ***never*** *late.*
He ***never*** *tells lies.*

Remarque : L'adverbe NEVER est toujours placé **après le 1er auxiliaire,** et **avant le verbe** s'il n'y a pas d'auxiliaire.

Attention : On ne peut pas associer deux mots à sens négatif dans le même groupe verbal. Les adverbes à sens négatif NEVER (jamais), HARDLY (à peine, presque), SCARCELY (rarement) commandent donc l'emploi de ANY et EVER (au lieu de NO et NEVER) :

I ***hardly ever*** *see him.* (presque jamais)
There was ***hardly anything*** *to drink.* (presque rien)
He ***never*** *believes* ***anyone.*** (jamais personne)
He ***scarcely*** *thinks of* ***anything*** *else.*
Is he ever wrong? ***Scarcely ever.***

5. Les phrases interro-négatives

En combinant deux transformations, on peut obtenir des phrases à la fois interrogatives et négatives : des **phrases interro-négatives,** qui attendent en général une **réponse positive :**

Aren't you *going to thank me?*
Won't you *sit down?*

— Inversion du sujet et du premier auxiliaire.
— Négation NOT accolée au premier auxiliaire.

Ces phrases peuvent aussi avoir une **valeur exclamative :**

Isn't she *pretty!*

EXERCICES

A. Mettez les phrases proposées à la forme négative **si** la phrase négative obtenue contredit la phrase proposée.
Ex.: *I drank some whisky.*
→ *I didn't drink any whisky.*
→ *I drank no whisky.*

Donnez les 2 structures quand c'est possible (*no...* ou *not any...*).

1. We had to do some cooking. **2.** He has some vague idea about it. **3.** This machine can print almost anything. **4.** He had some difficulty in finding my street. **5.** Do you have some new stories to tell me? **6.** He has spilt some wine. **7.** Someone will be held responsible for this. **8.** I had some chocolate for dessert, there was some left.

B. Complétez à l'aide d'une phrase négative contenant un (ou plusieurs) pronom indéfini *(nothing, no one, nowhere,* ou : *not anything, not anyone, not anywhere).*
Ex.: *He is a bad policeman...*
→ *He has never arrested anyone.*
He is a bad watchdog...
→ *He doesn't scare anyone.*

1. He has a very bad memory... **2.** You can't tell him a secret... **3.** This child is very shy... **4.** He is a solitary man... **5.** She is a "stay at home" kind of girl... **6.** He is very lazy... **7.** He is not a kind man... **8.** I'm not a lucky man...

C. Les choses ont changé... Expliquez pourquoi vous ne faites plus *(no longer, not any longer)* ce que vous aviez l'habitude de faire *(used to).*
Ex.: *Take tennis lessons / (I).*
→ *I used to take tennis lessons, but I don't take lessons any longer because I play better than my instructor now.*

1. Go to the cinema very often/(I). **2.** Smoke a lot/(He). **3.** Lend my records/(I). **4.** Have a cat/(I). **5.** Wear his hair very long/(He). **6.** Buy a lot of records/(She). **7.** Invite people all the time/(I).

D. Traduisez.

1. « Personne ne va nulle part. Tout le monde reste ici », dit-il. **2.** Il n'y avait pas d'autre solution. **3.** As-tu vu des traces de pas ? Non, il n'y en avait aucune. **4.** Il n'aurait pas dû la gifler. **5.** Aucune décision n'a été prise. **6.** Il se peut qu'il n'ait pas été prévenu. **7.** Il n'a pris ni son parapluie ni ses bottes, il va être trempé ! **8.** Je n'ai touché à aucun des deux boutons. **9.** Mon chien n'attaque jamais aucun autre chien. **10.** Il boit beaucoup, mais il n'est presque jamais ivre.

17. LE DISCOURS INDIRECT

1. Définitions

Il arrive souvent que l'on ait à rapporter les paroles de quelqu'un, dans des circonstances diverses : on peut le faire **directement,** ou en utilisant des guillemets : c'est le **discours direct,** où chaque mot est retranscrit fidèlement :

CLARA : *I still love Jim. Passionately!*
STEVE : *You can't!*
CLARA : *I can. And I do. And I always have. And I always will!*
STEVE : *Why did you let me hope, then?*

"George was a handsome fellow," said Mrs Curtis.
"Ah!" said Mr Curtis.
"But after he married Belinda, he never looked at another woman," said Mrs Curtis.
"Ah!" said Mr Curtis.
"She never gave him the chance," said Mrs Curtis.
"Ah!" said Mr Curtis.

On peut aussi rapporter les paroles de quelqu'un **indirectement,** en formant une phrase complexe : c'est le **discours indirect :**

(1) *Clara said/that she still loved Jim.*
(2) *Steve asked her/why she had let him hope.*
principale subordonnée

Remarques :

— Le **pronom sujet a changé** quand les paroles ont été rapportées au discours indirect :

"I still love Jim."
She said that ***she*** *still loved Jim.*

Le discours indirect impose toujours le **changement des pronoms et adjectifs représentant des personnes.**

— Le **temps a changé :**

"I still ***love*** *Jim."*
(1) *She said that she still* ***loved*** *Jim.*

"Why ***did you let me*** *hope?"*
(2) *He asked her why* ***she had let him*** *hope.*

car les paroles ont été rapportées au cours d'un récit, longtemps après avoir été prononcées, mais ce n'est pas toujours le cas (voir §§ **2** et **3**).

— **Les structures des phrases complexes (1) et (2) sont différentes :** complétive en (1), subordonnée circonstancielle en (2). Voir §§ **4, 5, 6** pour les diverses structures des phrases complexes du discours indirect.

2. Discours indirect sans changement de temps

Dans certains cas, on peut rapporter les paroles de quelqu'un au discours indirect sans avoir besoin de changer le temps : quand les paroles sont rapportées **immédiatement après avoir été entendues ou lues.** On peut, par exemple :

— Lire une lettre et la **résumer** pour quelqu'un d'autre :

"I ***will marry*** *Jim as soon as he* ***gets out*** *of prison."*
She says she ***will marry*** *Jim as soon as he* ***gets out*** *of prison.*

— **Transmettre** à quelqu'un des paroles que l'on vient d'entendre au téléphone ou dans une autre pièce :

"I'll ***be waiting*** *for you at the entrance."*
Julie says she'll ***be waiting*** *for you at the entrance.*

"I ***won't stay*** *in this house another minute."*
Cook says she ***won't stay*** *in this house another minute.*

— **Répéter** des paroles qui viennent d'être prononcées (à quelqu'un qui n'a pas bien entendu) :

"We ***ought to go*** *to another pub, this one is too noisy."*
He says we ***ought to go*** *to another pub, this one is too noisy.*

3. Discours indirect avec changement de temps. Concordance des temps

Le plus souvent les paroles sont rapportées avec un certain retard, au cours d'un récit **(donc au passé),** ce qui implique un **changement de temps** (si la personne a dit : « *Je ne* ***veux*** *pas* ***te*** *déranger* », on rapportera ses paroles plus tard en disant : *Elle m'a dit qu'****elle*** *ne* ***voulait*** *pas* ***me*** *déranger*). Le **présent** est donc rapporté au **passé (prétérit),** le **futur** au **conditionnel,** le **parfait** au **plus-que-parfait,** le **prétérit** au **plus-que-parfait :** le changement se fait toujours **vers le passé :**

"I still ***love*** *him."* → *She said she still* ***loved*** *him.*
"I ***will*** *never* ***leave*** *him."* → *She said she* ***would*** *never* ***leave*** *him.*
"You ***have broken*** *my heart."* → *He said she* ***had broken*** *his heart.*
"Why ***did*** *you* ***let*** *me hope?"* → *He asked her why she* ***had let*** *him hope.*

Attention : Quand on rapporte les paroles de quelqu'un avec un certain retard, donc au passé, il y a forcément un **décalage dans les compléments de temps.** Si une personne dit : « *Je viendrai* ***demain*** », on rapporte ses paroles en disant : *Elle a dit qu'elle viendrait* ***le lendemain.*** « *Demain* » est donc devenu : « *le lendemain* ». En anglais, le principe est le même : *"Jim came out of prison* ***last week."*** → *Clara said that Jim had come out of prison* ***the week before.***

On a donc les correspondances suivantes :

Yesterday → *the day before.*
Tomorrow → *the day after.*
Next week → *the following week.*
Last year → *the year before.*
Two days ago → *two days before.*

Les mots en gras dans la colonne de gauche **ne peuvent pas apparaître au discours indirect** avec changement de temps.

4. Phrases déclaratives

Rapportées au discours indirect, les phrases **affirmatives** et **négatives** deviennent des **complétives** introduites par THAT :

"I still love Jim." → *She said* ***that she still loved Jim.***
"I can't marry Steve." → *She said* ***that she couldn't marry Steve.***

La conjonction THAT est **souvent supprimée** :

She said ***she still loved Jim.***

Dans la principale, on utilise le verbe TELL, au lieu de SAY, quand on veut mentionner la personne à qui les paroles s'adressent :

She ***told Steve*** *she still loved Jim.*

5. Phrases interrogatives

Rapportées au discours indirect, les phrases interrogatives (voir Fiche **15**) deviennent des **subordonnées,** et **perdent** donc toutes les **marques de la transformation interrogative** (auxiliaire placé avant le sujet ; auxiliaire DO, DOES, DID ne servant qu'à la transformation interrogative ; point d'interrogation final). Le verbe de la principale est généralement ASK (ou bien : *I want to know, I would like to know):*

"What are you whispering for?"
aux. s. v.
He asked me what I was whispering for.
s. aux. v.

"Do you still love him?"
aux. s. v.
I want to know if you still love him.
s. v.

Il faut distinguer **3 types de phrases interrogatives,** qui donneront chacune une phrase complexe différente au discours indirect :

a. Les YES/NO *questions* (voir Fiche **15, § 3**).

b. Les questions en WH- (sauf WHO et WHAT en fonction sujet). (voir Fiche **15, §§ 4a** et **b**).

c. Les questions en WHO et WHAT sujet (voir Fiche **15, § 4c**).

a. Les *yes/no questions*

Elles deviennent des **subordonnées introduites par** IF OU WHETHER :

"Is George a faithful husband?" asked Mr Curtis.
Mr Curtis asked ***if (whether)*** *George was a faithful husband.*

"Will there be a lot of people at Clara's wedding?"
I would like to know ***if*** *there will be a lot of people.*

b. Les questions en *wh-* (sauf *who* et *what* sujet)

"Why did you let *me hope?"*
Steve asked Clara ***why she had let*** *him hope.*

"Who have you invited?"
I would like to know ***who you have invited.***

"Who did you go *to the exhibition with?"*
I would like to know ***who you went*** *to the exhibition with.*

"How long will it take?"
He asked her ***how long it would take.***

c. Les questions en *who* et *what* sujet

Elles n'ont à subir **aucune transformation au discours indirect,** puisqu'elles sont déjà construites comme des déclaratives.

"What is going to happen *to him?"*
I wonder ***what is going to happen*** *to him.*

"Who told you?"
I would like to know ***who told you.***

6. Phrases impératives

Rapportées au discours indirect, les phrases **impératives** *(Don't look now! Take it easy! Let's go out tonight! Let's not quarrel! Don't let's get excited!)* deviennent presque toujours des **infinitives** (voir Fiche **18**) :

— **Forme affirmative :**
"Stay with me." → *I asked her* ***to stay*** *with me.*

— **Forme négative :**
"Don't look!" → *She told me* ***not to look.***

— Le verbe de la principale peut être TELL (ORDER) s'il s'agit d'un **ordre** :

"Stay in your room and do your homework."
He told/ordered his son ***to stay*** *in his room and do his homework.*

"Don't speak until you are told."
He told me ***not to speak*** *until I was told.*

— Le verbe ASK dans la principale exprime une **demande polie** :

"Sit down." → *She asked me* ***to sit*** *down.*

— Le verbe PROPOSE (SUGGEST) dans la principale exprime une **suggestion** faite à un tiers et est suivi du verbe en -ING:

"Let's have a game of football."
He proposed ***having*** *a game of football.*

"Let's not tell him beforehand."
She suggested ***not telling*** *him beforehand.*

Voir tous les exercices de *Reporting* proposés dans l'unité de révision et dans de nombreux *Follow-up work.*

18. INFINITIF ET PROPOSITIONS INFINITIVES

1. Définitions. Formes de l'infinitif

La marque de l'infinitif est TO (ne pas confondre avec la préposition TO : voir Fiche **12**) :

Base verbale : *see*
Infinitif : *to see*

L'infinitif est **rarement isolé,** il fait le plus souvent partie d'un groupe infinitif, **une proposition infinitive** :

I would like ***to see him in concert.***

La fonction de la proposition infinitive ci-dessus est : c.o.d. du verbe « *like* ». Un infinitif, seul ou figurant dans une proposition infinitive, a toujours une **fonction de groupe nominal** (voir § **3**).

Formes de l'infinitif :

(1) *I hope* ***to see*** *him soon.*
(2) *She pretended* ***not to see*** *me.*
(3) *You ought* ***to have seen*** *his face.*
(4) *I expect* ***to be seeing*** *him.*
(5) *He didn't want* ***to be seen.***

Un groupe infinitif **ne peut pas comporter de modal,** mais il peut porter la marque de la **négation** (2), du **parfait** (3), du **progressif** (4), ou du **passif** (5).

2. Divers types de propositions infinitives

a. Infinitive complète

I would like ***all my friends to be there.***
s. v. compl.

b. Infinitive réduite

— Sans sujet : *I would like* ***to have more free time.***
v. compl.

— Elliptique : *I would like* ***to.***

c. Infinitive sans *to* (voir Fiche **19**)

a. Une infinitive complète comporte un sujet, qui est différent de celui de la principale :

I would like ***Julie*** *to look after my dog.*
s.1 s.2.

Attention : Remplacé par un pronom, le sujet (s.2.) doit être un **pronom complément** :

I would like ***her*** *to look after my dog.*
s.1 s.2.

b. Infinitive sans sujet et infinitive elliptique

Si les 2 sujets (s.1 et s.2.) représentent **la même personne,** le **s.2. disparaît** pour éviter la répétition, et l'infinitive se retrouve **sans sujet (effacement par identité)** :

I would like to go for a week. (« *I* » est à la fois sujet de « *like* » et de « *go* »)

De même on peut **éviter la répétition du groupe verbal,** et former une **infinitive elliptique** :

— *Will you go away for Easter?*
— *I would like* ***to*** *(go away), but I can't.*

— *Did he get inside the lion's cage?*
— *Yes, I told him* ***not to*** *(get inside the lion's cage), but he would not listen.*

Les infinitives elliptiques se trouvent surtout après les verbes : WANT, LIKE, LOVE, PREFER, HATE, ASK, FORCE, MEAN, HAVE (TO).

3. Fonctions des propositions infinitives

a. Infinitive complément direct du verbe principal

C'est la fonction la plus courante :

He managed ***to sell his old motorbike.***
v.

She expected ***Nigel to invite her for the week-end.*** v.

Infinitive dans une subordonnée en WH- (tous les pronoms sont possibles, sauf WHY) :

I don't know ***what to do with myself.*** (Je ne sais pas **quoi** faire)

I know ***where to find genuine "blinis".*** (Je sais **où** trouver...)

I don't know ***how to use this sophisticated machine.*** (Je ne sais pas **comment** me servir de...)

Attention : Dans cette dernière structure, « *comment* » est souvent supprimé en français : *je ne sais pas le faire, je sais m'en servir, je t'apprendrai à l'allumer,* mais HOW est **indispensable en anglais** : *I don't know* ***how*** *to do it; I know* ***how*** *to use it; I'll teach you* ***how*** *to light it.*

Remarque : Certains verbes acceptent aussi, au lieu d'un infinitif, un complément de type **gérondif** (-ING) (voir § **4**).

b. Infinitive sujet du verbe principal

To remain silent was quite impossible. (infinitive sans sujet)

For him to remain silent was quite impossible. (infinitive avec sujet : *him*)

Le sujet de l'infinitive est obligatoirement introduit par la préposition FOR, mais cette position de l'infinitive en tête de phrase est rare, et on préfère la déplacer en fin de phrase, et la remplacer par IT :

*It was impossible (possible, easy, difficult, usual, unusual, etc.) **for him to remain silent.***

Remarque : En fonction sujet, on peut aussi trouver un groupe gérondif au lieu d'une infinitive (voir § 4).

c. Infinitive en complément prépositionnel (voir prépositions, Fiche 12) :

*I am **waiting for her.*** (verbe prépositionnel + groupe nominal)

*I am **waiting for her to calm down.*** (verbe prépositionnel + infinitive)

Attention : La préposition n'apparaît que si le sujet de l'infinitive est présent. **Si le sujet est effacé, la préposition est effacée aussi** :

*wait (for) → we are waiting **to be served.***
*hope (for) → I hope **to be able to come.***
*agree (with) → We agreed **not to stay on.***
*remind (of) → You must remind me **to buy some petrol.***

Même règle quand un adjectif est suivi d'un complément prépositionnel (voir ci-dessous : d).

d. Infinitive complément de l'adjectif

*afraid (of) → He is afraid **to go near water.*** (La préposition est effacée : voir c).

*His face was interesting **to see.***

*Julie is sure **to catch a cold,** if she doesn't dress properly.*

Attention à l'emploi de l'adjectif SURE : Ce n'est pas Julie qui est sûre, c'est le locuteur qui est sûr que Julie attrapera froid : *Julie va sûrement...* Si l'on veut dire que Julie est sûre, il faut utiliser une **complétive** :

*Julie is sure **that she will catch a cold.***

e. Infinitive complément circonstanciel de but

— C'est la **seule fonction circonstancielle** que peut avoir une infinitive. Elle peut être introduite par IN ORDER :

*We went to a Russian restaurant **in order to eat some caviar.*** (Infinitive sans sujet)

Mais le plus souvent, IN ORDER est absent et le TO de l'infinitif exprime le but :

*We went to a Russian restaurant **to eat some caviar.***

— Infinitive **avec sujet,** introduit par FOR (voir aussi **b**) et **différent du sujet principal** :

*He drove a white Rolls Royce, **for everyone to see he was rich.***

*His Rolls Royce was there **for everyone to see.***

— Le sujet de l'infinitive peut aussi être le même que celui de la principale (il est alors effacé). Comparez :

*I have bought some magazines **for you to read on the train.*** (Sujets différents)

*I have some articles **to read.*** (Sujets identiques)

4. Infinitif ou gérondif ?

En **fonction sujet,** on peut employer indifféremment **un groupe gérondif ou infinitif** :

Inf.: *To wait here would be a waste of time.*
Ger.: ***Waiting here** would be a waste of time.*

En **fonction complément,** le choix de l'infinitif, ou du gérondif **dépend du verbe principal** :

a. Gérondif **obligatoire** après les verbes : GO ON (KEEP ON, CARRY ON), ENJOY, GIVE UP, (CAN'T) HELP, MIND, STOP, LOOK FORWARD (TO), BE USED (TO), etc.

*I enjoy **dancing with him.***
*He can't help **being jealous.***
*Stop **arguing!***
*I am looking forward to **going to Germany.***

Attention : La préposition TO qui suit *"look forward"* ne doit pas être confondue avec la marque de l'infinitif.

b. Infinitif **obligatoire** après les verbes : MANAGE, PRETEND, SEEM, TRY, DECIDE, EXPECT, WANT (voir **d**), WAIT, ASK, FORCE, HELP, PROMISE, TELL, etc., ainsi que les **quasi-modaux** et **formes à sens modal** : OUGHT, DARE, NEED, BE ABLE, HAVE (TO), BE (TO), BE ALLOWED (Voir Fiche 10).

*She pretended **not to see me.***
*Julie expected Nigel **to remember her birthday.***
*He promised **to do his best.***

c. Infinitif ou gérondif **indifféremment** après les verbes : BEGIN, START, (CAN'T) BEAR, RECOMMEND (et quelques autres, peu nombreux) :

I can't bear { *to see you sad.* / *seeing you sad.* }

She recommends { *to boil the potatoes first.* / *boiling the potatoes first.* }

d. Infinitif ou gérondif, mais avec **modification du sens du verbe** : après les verbes : LIKE, LOVE, HATE, PREFER, etc. Comparez :

*I love **sleeping late on Sunday.*** (en général)
*I hated **to have to get up early last Sunday.*** (ce jour-là)

Après les verbes : WANT, REMEMBER, MEAN, etc. la modification de sens est plus importante.
Comparez :

*The dog wants **to go out*** (« il veut sortir » : **désir**).
*The dog wants **brushing*** (« il a besoin d'un brossage » : **nécessité, besoin**).

De même :

The dog needs ***brushing.***

Remember ***to tell Clara.*** (« souviens-toi de dire... » : **fait non encore réalisé, à venir**).

I remember ***telling Clara*** (« je me souviens d'avoir dit... » : **passé**).

I meant ***to buy tickets,*** *but I didn't have time.* **(intention)**

Going to Wimbledon means ***queuing for hours.*** **(signification, implication)**

EXERCICES

A. Infinitives de but (§ 3).
Expliquez le rôle des choses ou des personnes (ils sont là pour... ils servent à...).
Ex.: *What's a fire-escape ladder for?*
→ *To escape by, when the house is on fire.*

1. What is a helmet for? **2.** What are traffic-lights for? **3.** What is a clock-radio for? **4.** What is radar for on the motorway? **5.** What are policemen for? **6.** What are friends for? **7.** What are these exercises for?

B. Traduisez. Infinitif, ou forme en *-ing?* Si les 2 sont possibles, proposez 2 phrases.

1. Avant de partir, on va boire un dernier verre. **2.** Je suis très heureux de l'avoir rencontrée. **3.** Elle n'a pas cessé de le regarder. **4.** Il n'y a pas moyen de lui parler. **5.** Je ne me souviens pas d'être venu ici. **6.** Je l'ai invitée pour te faire plaisir. **7.** Je vous remercie beaucoup d'être venu. **8.** Pleurer ne sert à rien. **9.** Elle aimerait ressembler à Marilyn Monroe. **10.** Il aime passer des heures sur les quais, à regarder couler la Seine. **11.** Mon amie indienne m'a appris à faire un poulet « Tandoori ». **12.** Il attend d'avoir 18 ans. **13.** Il est sûr de gagner le rallye avec cette voiture. **14.** Pour gagner, il est très important de rester calme. **15.** Je préfère mettre une robe, pour une fois ! **16.** Il a besoin d'être encouragé.

19. INFINITIF SANS *TO*

Le verbe a perdu la marque TO de l'infinitif, mais il s'agit quand même d'un groupe infinitif, comportant le plus souvent un sujet (comme dans les infinitives complètes. Voir Fiche 18, § 2).

1. L'infinitif sans *to* avec les verbes causatifs *have* et *make*

Les verbes MAKE et HAVE + **infinitif sans** TO correspondent en français à la structure **« faire + infinitif »** : *« j'ai* ***fait tomber*** *la lampe » ; « ses lunettes le* ***faisaient ressembler*** *à une chouette » ; « je vais* ***faire venir*** *le vétérinaire ».* On les appelle **verbes causatifs** car leur sujet est la **cause** de ce que : la lampe tombe, il ressemble à une chouette, le vétérinaire vient :

I ***made the lamp fall.***
His glasses ***made him look like an owl.***
I will ***have the vet come immediately.***

Remarques : En français, le verbe « faire » est suivi directement de l'infinitif ; en anglais, les verbes MAKE et HAVE sont suivis d'une **infinitive sans** TO **comportant obligatoirement un sujet** (groupe nominal ou pronom complément).
MAKE et HAVE ne sont **pas interchangeables** : l'action exprimée par MAKE est généralement **plus directe** que celle exprimée par HAVE.

Attention : HAVE et MAKE causatifs peuvent aussi être suivis d'un **participe passé à sens passif** (avec effacement de BE) (voir Fiche 14).

I can ***make myself understood.***
I will ***have this picture framed.***

2. L'infinitif sans *to* avec les verbes de perception : *see, hear, feel, watch, observe*

L'infinitif sans TO **comporte toujours un sujet** (groupe nominal ou pronom complément) :

We didn't hear ***the cat come in.***

Ces mêmes **verbes de perception** peuvent être suivis d'un **participe présent (verbe + -ING),** le plus souvent sans différence de sens :

I saw ***you pinch that book.***
I saw ***you pinching that book.*** (sous-entendu : *you were pinching that book)*

Attention : Les tournures en -ING ne sont **pas possibles pour exprimer des actions brèves** (START, WAKE UP, SLIP, DROP, etc.) tandis que l'**infinitif sans** TO **est possible** dans tous les cas. En général, on préfère utiliser l'**infinitif sans** TO pour les **actions ponctuelles** et le participe en -ING pour les **actions non terminées,** vues dans leur **déroulement** :

I saw ***her start*** *when I came in.*
I watched ***the waves crashing*** *on the rocks.*

Comparez :

We all heard **the cupboard fall.**

He watched **the leaves falling,** *and tried to count then.*

3. L'infinitif sans *to* avec le verbe *let*

LET est toujours suivi d'un **infinitif sans** TO comportant un sujet : *let* **me see,** *let* **bygones be bygones.** Les phrases de ce type sont souvent considérées comme des **phrases impératives,** avec toutes les nuances que l'impératif peut exprimer (**ordres, demandes, invitations, suggestions,** etc. : voir traductions des exemples suivants).

LET n'est utilisé qu'à la **1re et à la 3e personne :**

— **1re personne singulier :**

Let me have a look. (voyons...)

— **1re personne pluriel :**

Let us go! (« allons-y ! » : **ordre atténué**)

Let's ask him, shall we? (« et si on lui demandait ? » : **suggestion**)

Don't let's get carried away! (« ne nous emballons pas »)

— **3e personne (sing. ou plur.) :**

Let him go to hell! (« qu'il aille au diable ! » : **indifférence**)

Let Nigel be on time for once! (« qu'il soit à l'heure... » : **ordre indirect**)

Let him be! (« laissez-le tranquille » : **permission**)

Attention : Cette dernière valeur du verbe LET **(laisser, permettre)** n'a rien à voir avec l'impératif. Le verbe LET a donc **deux valeurs possibles :**

(1) Une sorte d'impératif (suppléant à l'impératif aux 1re et 3e personnes seulement).

(2) « laisser », « permettre ».

Hors contexte, certaines phrases peuvent être ambiguës : *Let her go!* peut signifier : (1) « qu'elle s'en aille, qu'elle sorte de ma vie, ça m'est égal... » ou : (2) « laissez la partir ».

4. Infinitif avec ou sans *to*

— Après le verbe HELP :

I'll help you (to) get everything ready.

— Après certaines expressions :

All I could do was (to) hold her hand.

All he ever did was (to) sleep on the sofa.

There is nothing we can do but (to) wait.

EXERCICES

A. Infinitif sans *to* avec les verbes de perception (voir § 2).

1° Vous racontez toutes les choses extraordinaires que vous avez vues faire au cirque.

Ex.: *I saw a man put his head into a lion's mouth.*

2° Dans une boîte de nuit, vous apercevez votre petit(e) ami(e), sans être vu(e), et vous l'observez pendant un long moment. Vous racontez le lendemain à un(e) ami(e).

Ex.: *I saw her look at that guy...*

B. Infinitif sans *to* avec les verbes causatifs (§ 1).

Vous avez sûrement déjà vu un prestidigitateur. Rappelez-vous tout ce qu'il peut faire et imaginez aussi ce que vous aimeriez faire si vous aviez ce talent.

Ex.: *What can a conjurer do?*

→ *He can make rabbits come out of top hats, etc.*

→ *If I were a conjurer, I could make...*

C. Traduisez (voir §§ 1 et 3).

1. Je n'ai pas fait la piqûre moi-même, je l'ai fait faire par le vétérinaire. **2.** J'ai fait attendre Greg sous la pluie pendant 1/4 d'heure, exprès. Il m'a déjà fait attendre 100 fois. **3.** Si tu ne peux pas dormir dans le train, bois un verre de Scotch, ça te fera dormir. **4.** On peut le faire rougir très facilement. **5.** L'absence de meubles faisait paraître la pièce immense. **6.** Je lui ai fait porter la plus grosse valise. **7.** Tu t'es fait couper les cheveux. C'est une bonne idée. **8.** Il a fait réparer sa moto la semaine dernière, et elle est encore en panne. **9.** Qu'elle entende notre conversation, ça m'est égal ! **10.** Laisse-moi réfléchir. **11.** Ne nous énervons pas. **12.** Qu'elle prenne ses responsabilités ! **13.** Il faut laisser les jeunes s'habiller et se coiffer comme ils veulent. **14.** Laisse-le aller où il veut.

20. FORMES EN *-ING*

Une forme en -ING (suffixe -ING ajouté à une base verbale) peut avoir quatre valeurs différentes :
— **Forme progressive** : *The birds were singing in the trees.*
— **Participe présent** : *The birds were in the trees, singing.*
— **Gérondif** : *The birds started singing.*
— **Nom verbal** : *The singing of the birds gave me a headache.*

1. Forme progressive (voir Fiche **8**)

*Julie **is talking** to Nigel on the phone.* (+ présent)
*They **were arguing** when I came.* (+ prétérit)
*You **should be working**.* (+ modal)
*I **have been thinking**.* (+ parfait)
*It **is being done**.* (+ passif)

Dans une subordonnée introduite par WHILE, on reconnaît la forme progressive malgré l'ellipse du sujet et de BE :

*Never try to read a map while (you are) **driving**.*

2. Participe présent

Un participe présent peut être **simple** (*opening:* « ouvrant »), **négatif** (*not opening:* « n'ouvrant pas ») ou **associé au parfait** (*having opened:* « ayant ouvert »).

a. Participe présent et propositions participes en *-ing*

*He stood there, **smiling**.* (part. présent)
*He went out, **forgetting to slam the door**.* (proposition participe en -ING)

Une proposition participe en -ING peut avoir une **fonction circonstancielle de temps ou de cause** (mêmes fonctions pour les propositions participe en *-ant* en français).
— Temps :
Walking past her, I noticed her perfume. (en marchant...)
Having read the letter, I threw it away. (ayant lu...)
— Cause :
Knowing there could be seats left, I waited till the last minute. (comme je savais que..., sachant que...)
Having queued for hours in the cold, we were glad to get inside. (ayant fait...)
There being no traffic-lights, accidents were frequent at that crossroads. (comme il n'y avait pas...)

b. Participe présent employé comme adjectif

(1) **Participe en position épithète devant le nom** (dans ce cas-là, on n'utilise pas un participe présent en français).

*We watched the **rising** sun.*
*She had a **bleeding** finger.*
*She was a **working** woman.*

(2) **Participes devenus de vrais adjectifs** (l'équivalent existe en français). Ils peuvent être précédés de VERY ou MORE : *amusing, charming, boring, embarrassing, exciting, frightening, interesting, moving, surprising, tiring,* etc.

*He is a **charming fellow**.*
*He is a **very charming fellow**.*
*It was even **more embarrassing**.*

Attention : VERY et MORE sont impossibles dans le cas (1) :

*She had a **bleeding** finger.*

(3) **Adjectifs composés en -ING** (l'équivalent n'existe pas en français).
— **Nom + participe en -ING** : *heart-breaking, animal loving, painstaking,* etc.

*He gave a **heart-rending** sigh.*

— **Adjectif ou adverbe + participe en -ING** : *hard-working, good-looking, sad-looking, strange-looking,* etc.

*He's **hard-working**.*
*It was a **strange-looking** assembly.*

3. Gérondif

a. Définition

Nous avons vu (Fiche **18**, § **4**) que certains verbes doivent être suivis d'un gérondif complément :

*He was used to **getting up before dawn**.*

Ce groupe gérondif était à l'origine une phrase, qui a été nominalisée pour occuper la position d'un groupe nominal, complément du verbe principal :

*He **got up** before dawn, he **is used to** that.*
(1) v. principal g.n.
*He **is used to getting up** before dawn.*
(2)

La phrase (1) a été transformée en groupe gérondif (2).

Attention : Le gérondif est très couramment employé en anglais, mais n'existe pas en français : les phrases équivalentes en français comportent soit un **infinitif** (« *il a l'habitude de **se lever*** » → gérondif **sans sujet** en anglais = voir c), soit un **subjonctif** (« *il a l'habitude **que je fasse** le petit-déjeuner* » → gérondif **avec sujet** en anglais). Comparez :

***Taking a statue from a temple** is illegal.* (« prendre une statue... est illégal », ou : « il est illégal de prendre une statue... »)
***Their taking a statue from a temple** would not surprise me.* (« qu'ils prennent une statue... ne m'étonnerait pas », ou « il ne m'étonnerait pas qu'ils prennent... »)

b. Diverses formes du groupe gérondif

After ***having been*** *rude, he apologized.* (+ parfait)
Her ***not marrying*** *Steve was a surprise to everyone.* (+ négation)
The child was afraid of ***being left*** *alone.* (+ passif)

c. Groupe gérondif avec ou sans sujet ?

— Les groupes gérondifs **sans sujet** sont les plus fréquents :

Dramatising *does no one any good.* (le sujet n'est pas mentionné, car il est « général » : *people, everyone, ...*)
She spent her time ***watching the trains.*** (le sujet n'est pas mentionné car il est identique au sujet principal : *she*)

— Les groupes gérondif **comportent un sujet** quand celui-ci est **différent du sujet principal** (le sujet du gérondif peut être un groupe nominal ou un pronom complément) :

I can remember ***Nigel telling me he would not go alone.***
I can remember ***him telling me he would not go alone.***

Le sujet du gérondif porte souvent la **marque du génitif** *(Nigel's)* ou du possessif *(his)* quand il est en tête de phrase :

Nigel's going to the U.S.A. alone *surprised everyone.*
His going to the U.S.A. alone *surprised everyone.*

d. Emplois du gérondif

— **Sujet du verbe principal :**

Making one's bread *oneself is a long process.*
Her making her own bread *impressed me.*

(Dans ce cas là, on peut avoir aussi une infinitive. Voir Fiche **18, § 3**).

On utilise souvent le gérondif dans des **comparaisons :**

Redecorating one's appartment *is cheaper than* ***having a decorator do it.***

— Après **certains verbes et expressions :**

Expression du goût (ce qu'on aime de façon générale) : *I* ***like/love*** *travelling, I* ***enjoy*** *walking, I* ***feel like*** *laughing, I* ***have a taste for*** *gossiping, I* ***am fond of/keen on*** *going to concerts, I* ***hate*** *waiting, I* ***don't care*** *for drinking, I* ***don't approve of*** *smoking, I* ***resent*** *people lying, I* ***am averse to*** *prying, I* ***can't stand/bear*** *people being rude,* etc.

Les phases de l'action : gérondif obligatoire après *go on, keep on, carry on,* et *stop;* **gérondif très courant** après *start, begin, cease, continue, finish* (voir Fiche **18, § 4**) : *She started* ***screaming.***

Autres verbes : *give up, look forward (to), be used (to), remember, apologize (for), think (of), involve, reproach (for), blame (for),* etc.

I must apologize for ***not coming yesterday.***
I remember ***giving her the key.*** (souvenir d'un fait passé : voir Fiche **18, § 4**)

Autres expressions : *How about? What about?*

How about ***stopping for a drink?*** (et si...?)
What's the use of ***telling him over and over again?*** (à quoi cela sert-il...?)
There is no point in ***leaving so early.*** (il ne sert à rien...)
There is no ***getting away from it.*** (il n'y a pas moyen de...)

Après les prépositions (toutes sauf BUT) : WITHOUT, ON, BY, AFTER, BEFORE, IN SPITE OF, INSTEAD OF, BECAUSE OF, etc.

She could spend weeks ***without looking at a mirror.***
He won her ***by being very patient.***

Nom et préposition :

You'll have ***the opportunity of getting to know her better.***

Adjectif et préposition :

He was ***afraid of not having enough money.***

Attention : Pas de préposition après l'adjectif WORTH :

This match was ***worth seeing.*** (valait la peine de...)
This set is ***not worth mending.***

4. Le nom verbal

Comparez :

(1) *His heart started* ***beating*** *loudly.* (gérondif après *start*)
(2) ***The beating of his heart*** *was very loud.* (nom verbal)

(1) Le groupe **gérondif** a une **structure proche de celle d'une phrase :** verbe suivi directement de ses compléments.

(2) Le **nom verbal** a la structure d'un **vrai groupe nominal** avec déterminant (THE) et complément en OF : Comparez :

The ***beating*** *of his heart.*
The ***size*** *of his heart.*

Attention : Un groupe nom verbal ne peut pas être négatif, ni comporter le parfait ou le passif, comme un groupe gérondif (voir § **3b**).

Exemples de noms verbaux :

From the moment I saw him, I took ***a great liking*** *to him.*
Travelling results in ***the forming of strange acquaintances.***
The wording of the letter *was insulting.*

Certains noms verbaux sont de **vrais noms** : *a building, a meeting, the cooking, the washing-up, the beginning,* etc.

Ces noms sont parfois au **pluriel** :

The meetings will be held in that hall.

Noms composés avec nom verbal :

— *swimming-pool, waiting-room, washing-machine, playing-cards,* etc. Le 2ᵉ nom *(pool, room, machine)* est fait pour... nager, attendre, laver, etc.

— *House-keeping, sightseeing, fox-hunting, stamp-collecting,* etc. : l'action de chasser le renard, collectionner les timbres, etc.

Attention : Certaines formes en -ING sont utilisées en français de manière trompeuse : en français, « un camping », « un parking » représentent des **lieux** ; en anglais, ces mêmes mots représentent des **actions** (action de camper, de garer sa voiture).

I prefer ***camping*** *in the fields.*

The parking of a car *requires a lot of patience.*

Ce que nous appelons « un parking » en français est en anglais *"a car-park"*; « un camping » en français se dit en anglais *"a camping-site"*, etc.

De même pour « le pressing » (endroit où l'on donne ses vêtements à nettoyer) :

I must go to ***the cleaner's.***

EXERCICES

A. Participe présent : complément de temps ou de cause (§ 2).

Réunissez 2 par 2 les éléments donnés en 2 colonnes dans le désordre : le verbe de la colonne de gauche est transformé en participe présent, exprimant soit un complément de temps, soit la cause ; indiquez-le entre parenthèses à la fin de la phrase que vous aurez ainsi obtenue.

Ex.: (1) *He put his key into the keyhole.*	*He had to work at night and rest during the day.*
(2) *He was a baker.*	*He realized his lock had been forced.*

→ (1) *Putting his key into the keyhole, he realized his lock had been forced.* (temps)

→ (2) *Being a baker, he had to work at night and rest during the day.* (cause)

He finished his investigation	We got no seats
I know he never pays back	The wedding was cancelled
The bridegroom was absent	The motorists slowed down
We had made no reservation	I wouldn't lend him any money
They saw policemen	He has a beautiful tan
There was a radar check	He knows how to surf
He's spent 2 weeks in Florida	He started to write his article
He's spent 2 weeks in California	They were caught speeding

B. Gérondif sujet (§ 3d)

Comparez les 2 éléments donnés en formant 2 groupes gérondif. Vous êtes libres d'utiliser le comparatif et l'adjectif que vous désirez (*more pleasant than..., as difficult as...,* voir Fiche 7).

Ex.: *Books: library or bookshop?*

→ *Borrowing books from a library is less expensive than buying them from a bookshop.*

1. Films : cinéma or T.V.? **2.** Pull-over: make it or buy it? **3.** Tennis-match: at Wimbledon or on T.V.? **4.** Portrait: draw it or paint it? **5.** Tennis: learn with a friend or take lessons? **6.** Money: save it or spend it? **7.** T.V. set: hire one or buy one? **8.** Car: in the street or in a garage?

C. Gérondif complément (expression du goût).

Vous devez aller passer un an aux U.S.A. dans une famille qui a un enfant de votre âge. Vous décidez de vous présenter à lui(elle) par lettre, de décrire vos goûts, vos préférences, etc., pour voir quel terrain d'entente vous pouvez avoir : *I like..., love..., hate..., enjoy..., etc.*

D. Traduisez.

1. Ça ne vaut pas la peine d'acheter ce journal. **2.** En entrant dans la pièce, il remarqua tout de suite sa présence. **3.** Au lieu de travailler pour son examen, il allait danser tous les soirs. **4.** Laisser son chien dehors par ce temps serait criminel. **5.** Il n'y a pas moyen de lui faire comprendre quoi que ce soit. **6.** A quoi cela sert-il d'avoir une si belle stéréo dans ta voiture ? On va sûrement te la voler. **7.** J'ai l'habitude qu'il m'appelle à n'importe quelle heure. **8.** Il a l'habitude de répéter ses histoires plusieurs fois. **9.** Il est peu vraisemblable qu'il téléphone à cette heure-ci. **10.** Garder les places pour les copains au concert, cela signifie : arriver très en avance, et se faire insulter par tous les gens qui veulent s'asseoir à ces places-là. **11.** Ce n'est pas facile de ne pas se mettre en colère. **12.** Marcher devenait de plus en plus difficile, avec toute cette neige. **13.** Aller au théâtre en banlieue implique que tu nous accompagnes en voiture. **14.** Aller au théâtre implique de réserver ses places 15 jours à l'avance.

Index grammatical

(Les numéros en gras renvoient aux fiches de grammaire.)

INDEX FONCTIONNEL

Lorsque l'on veut décrire les possibilités d'expression d'une langue, il y a deux approches.

La première consiste à décrire ces possibilités en les classant et en mettant en évidence les règles qui les gouvernent. C'est ce que nous avons fait dans la partie *Précis grammatical.*

L'autre approche consiste à partir des *besoins d'expression* des individus, en classant ces besoins à exprimer sous forme de *fonctions.* Ces deux approches ne vont d'ailleurs pas l'une sans l'autre. Prenons par exemple la forme grammaticale (ou structure) : *Sujet + be + going + to + Verbe (I'm going to buy a new TV set).* Cette *forme* grammaticale peut avoir plusieurs *fonctions :* exprimer la futurité, l'intention... dans ce cas, nous sommes partis de la *structure* pour aboutir à la *fonction.*

Inversement, et c'est là l'*approche fonctionnelle,* on peut partir des besoins à exprimer, c'est-à-dire se poser la question : « Dans telle situation de communication, quels vont être mes besoins ? De quels outils vais-je devoir me servir ? » Si l'on a besoin d'exprimer l'*intention,* on dispose à ce moment d'un certain nombre de structures et d'expressions sous la rubrique *intention :*

I'm going to change jobs.
She's thinking of gett**ing** married.
When in Greece, **we want to** visit Athens.

Toutes ces formes expriment l'*intention* à des degrés divers.

Vous trouverez donc ci-dessous un inventaire des fonctions essentielles suivies d'exemples. Nous nous sommes volontairement limités aux fonctions et aux formes qui nous semblaient répondre aux besoins les plus courants. La liste est loin d'être exhaustive ! Il vous appartiendra de compléter éventuellement vous-mêmes cette liste.

Souvenez-vous qu'une même forme peut être utilisée pour exprimer plusieurs besoins. Vous trouverez donc parfois la même structure sous plusieurs rubriques. Ainsi la forme :

Why + auxiliaire + not + sujet + verbe

peut exprimer le *regret :*

Why didn't I buy a colour TV?

le *reproche :*

Why didn't you tell him you were going away?

une *proposition :*

Why don't we have breakfast in bed for once?

un *conseil :*

Why don't you get a better pen?

Pensez également qu'à l'intérieur d'une même fonction, vous pouvez, la plupart du temps, passer à la forme interrogative ou négative. Ainsi :

— un *conseil* deviendra une *demande de conseil* à la forme interrogative :

You should really stop eating so much bread.
Should I tell them I won't be there at Christmas?

— une *obligation* deviendra une *absence d'obligation* à la forme négative :

You have to be at the station at 5.
You don't have to give your answer now.

— une *intention* deviendra une *demande d'intention* à la forme interrogative :

I'm going to tell him what I think.
Are you going to leave the firm?

De même, à l'intérieur d'une fonction, les diverses formes ou expressions ne sont pas totalement équivalentes. L'utilisation de telle ou telle forme dépendra de la situation de la personne à qui vous parlez, de votre humeur, etc. Par exemple, si vous voulez marquer votre *désaccord,* la forme :

You're not entirely wrong, however I think...

sera beaucoup plus nuancée que :

I entirely disagree with you!

sans parler de :

You must be out of your mind!

La plupart du temps, vous sentirez vous-mêmes que telle ou telle structure s'applique plus particulièrement à la situation de communication dans laquelle vous vous trouvez, et votre professeur est toujours là pour vous guider. Dans chaque exemple, nous avons mis en gras le ou les éléments qui expriment essentiellement la fonction. Ainsi dans les phrases :

You should learn another language. *(conseil)* ou
You're allowed to smoke in the hall only. *(permission),*

ce sont les éléments **You should** et **You're allowed to** qui expriment ces deux fonctions. Mais très souvent, bien sûr, sujet et temps sont variables.

Vous trouverez dans le manuel, à la suite des *Main topics* et *Follow-up work,* une rubrique *Useful functions.* Nous avons dans cette rubrique essayé d'anticiper quelques-uns des besoins qui risquent de se présenter lors de l'étude et de la discussion d'un texte ou lors d'une activité de *follow-up work.* Il vous appartiendra, au moment de l'activité (ou avant), de parcourir dans l'index les fonctions suggérées dans cette rubrique et de faire votre choix.

Functions

ACCEPTING

Yes, of course!
Yes, I will, I can, etc.
I don't mind go**ing** to this party with you.
I'd be pleased (happy) to help you.
All right! O.K.! Sure!
If you like! Why not?
That's a good idea!
That would be lovely (great/fine)!

ADMIRATION

It's really gorgeous!
What a beautiful motorbike!
How nice she is!
Isn't it marvellous?
That's wonderful! (great, terrific, fantastic, smashing, etc.**)**
You're so strong!
She's such a clever girl!
This is super!
Well done! Congratulations!
How wonderful (extraordinary, etc.**)!**

ADVICE

You should learn another language.
You shouldn't watch T.V. so often.
You ought to stop smoking before it's too late.
Couldn't you play in your bedroom?
You could read a good book instead.
You'd better look for another flat.
If I were you, I'd take a holiday now.
Why not go for a walk, you look tired.
In your position, frankly, **I'd** resign.
Why don't you go for a walk? You look tired.
He might try another doctor.
I suggest you stop behaving like a kid.
I('d) advise you to see a doctor.

AGREEMENT TO APPRECIATION

Cf. *Accepting*
So am I.
So do I.
Neither do I, etc.
I quite **agree with you.**
I think **he's right. How right** he is!
Definitely! Of course! Absolutely! Exactly!
This is quite true!
He's right to say (in saying) that this problem will never be solved.
I couldn't agree more with what you say.
I must admit (It's a fact) that she's quite bright.

CAPACITY

I bet **I can** jump higher than you.
She can speak six languages.
You'll be able to run again in about a week.
Don't worry, **I'll manage to** repair the roof.
I know **I could have bought** some butter, but the shops were all closed.
Now that the £ is stronger, **it's possible for him to** buy a house.
Money **enables** people **to** do a lot of things!
Sleeping **helps** me feel better.
They succeeded in handl**ing** the situation.

CAUSE

He stayed at home **because** he felt rather ill.
As he hadn't finished his homework, he didn't go to the cinema.
Mend that chair yourself, **since** you're so clever!
He couldn't run for too long **because of (on account of)** his asthma.
That is the reason why (That's why) she wasn't there last night.
It's precisely because I don't agree with her that I find her conversation so interesting.
I think he killed her **out of** jealousy.
In that case, I won't see her any longer.
Well... **Perhaps it's because** she's so young.

COMPARISON

You say your car's fast**er than** mine, prove it!
He was **more** determined **than** ever.
There's **more (less)** money in my bag **than** yesterday!
You eat much **more than** you used to!
It's not **as (so)** difficult **as** I expected.
He's got **the same** nose **as** his father.
She sings **like** a bird.
This house is **similar to** my grandfather's.
She plays poker **as if** she had done it all her life.
You talk **as though** you knew everything!
Don't worry, it might be **worse.**
Your father gets **more and more** irritable.
There's **less and less** sauce in their ravioli!
The more (less) I see you, **the more (less)** I love you.

COMPLAINING

Honestly! For goodness' sake!
Enough is enough!
I'm fed up with you!
I'm fed up (with) wait**ing** for him!
I'm sick of hear**ing** you!
I've (just about) had enough of all this!
I'm tired of work**ing** so much.
That drives me mad / crazy.
He (What) really gets on my nerves (is...).
You are the limit (the end)!
You make me sick!
What a nuisance you are!
How boring it was!
What are you complaining (moaning / grumbling) about?

CONCESSION

In a sense (Up to a certain point / After all), what she says is quite sensible.
That may be so, but it's a bit far-fetched.
I guess (suppose) you're right, but...
In a way (To some extent), he might be right.
You may be right, but you shouldn't tell her.
I admit that you've made a good point.
That's all very well, but I stick to my point.
You're not entirely wrong, but (however / yet / nevertheless / still)...
Although I'm (well) aware of the problem, I'd rather say that...

CONDITION AND HYPOTHESIS

If it's fine, **we'll** go to Sandy Bay.
If it was (were) cheaper, **we'd (we would/ could)** definitely travel by plane.
Supposing you won £ 10,000, what **would you** do?
If you hadn't been so careless, **you wouldn't have bumped** your head!
You touch that gun, Sheriff, **and I'll** kill you!
Suppose I were poor, **would you** help me?
You won't find it **unless** you open the box.
You can go out tonight **provided** you ask me.
Even if (though) he wanted to, **he couldn't take** himself seriously.
You'd better listen to what he says **otherwise (else / if not)** you'll regret it!

CONSEQUENCE

If she really insists, **then** I may say "yes".
It implies (means) that he's not guilty.
He's rich, **therefore (consequently / so / as a consequence / as a result)** he can afford to buy anything.
The crisis **entails** tremendous consequences.
She's **so** kind **that** she will surely welcome you.

CONTRAST AND CONTRADICTION

I haven't got a guitar, **but Jenny** has.
I didn't say she **loved** you, I said she **liked** you!
A: **You didn't** move all day! B: **I did** go for a short walk!
A: **You were** watching that girl (boy)! B: **I wasn't! (I was not).**
You weren't at the match yesterday, **I was!**
She hates watching TV **whereas (while)** her husband loves it.
A: **This is not** funny at all. B: **Yes, it is!**
On the one hand she said she would do it, **but on the other** she acted quite differently.
On the contrary! That's exactly what I said!

DESIRE AND WISHES

I want to go there with you, please.
I want you to listen carefully to what I'm saying.
I wish I had a faster bike.
I'd like to go to that Indian restaurant.
I'd love to see that film.
I wish you'd buy me that necklace.
I'd like you to throw that cigar away.
If only you weren't 7 feet tall, Georgia...
Do you feel like go**ing** to the theatre tonight?
I'm (quite) willing to dine with you, provided you take me to the restaurant!
I'm dying to meet him!

DETERMINATION

This is the girl I want to marry!
This is the very man I've been trying to find.
That's the girl I'm going to go out with!
I'm **definitely** going to divorce him!
I'm marrying him, with or without your consent!
I will live with her, whether you like it or not!
He was determined to win.

DISAGREEMENT TO CRITICISM

I don't agree with what he said.
I disagree entirely (I rather disagree) with his position on nuclear weapons!
You can't be serious! You must be joking!
I couldn't agree less with your last statement.
You must be out of your mind! She can't be so cruel!
I think **he's wrong.**
Certainly not!
I don't see it that way.
This is ludicrous! Nonsense! Rubbish!
I (can't but) object to what you've just said.
It's beside the point!
This is totally irrelevant!
This has nothing to do with the question!

DISLIKING

Cf. *Admiration* (with other adjectives).
I hate all kinds of fish.
She hates (dislikes) hav**ing** to get up early.
I don't like him **very much (at all).**
I resent be**ing** told what I've got to do.
I can't stand wait**ing** for a bus for hours!
My sister can't stand (detests) carrots.
I can't bear gett**ing** up early in the morning!
That film was **really awful... terrible... dreadful... revolting...** etc.
I really **don't care for (fancy)** those big cars.
I can't put up with this sort of life!
Your behaviour **sickens me!**
Those people are **unbearable!**

DURATION

I'm us**ing** an old bike **at the moment.** The new one hasn't arrived yet.

I'm experiment**ing** with this machine **for** a month. I hope it'll work!
I've been try**ing** to call you **for** more than an hour!
She worked for Rolls Royce **for** a month and left.
It's at least **three years since I** last **saw** them.
I've not eaten such a good hamburger **since I left** my mother!
He keeps talk**ing** all the time.

EMPHASIS

I **did** tell you he was in love with you!
She **is** a nice girl, isn't she?
Sheila made that delicious curry!
It's John **who** told me! I didn't invent it!
Those films I don't like **at all!**
Come on, your problem **isn't that** difficult!
I insist on see**ing** the manager at once!
They're **(really)** nice **indeed!**
Surely, you don't believe him!
You're **absolutely (quite)** right!
She speaks **fairly** good English.

FREQUENCY

He **often... sometimes... never... always... usually... seldom... rarely...** etc. goes out.
When my grandmother was younger, **we would** often go fishing together.
How often do you wash? **Once a** month?
Once in a while, I sleep until noon.
Most of the time, these shops will offer you a discount.
He's late... **as usual.**
She **hardly ever** reads the paper.
Do you **often** see her? — Not really, just **occasionally (from time to time).**

FUTURE

We'll buy this flat as soon as we've saved enough money.
She's going to buy a new TV set.
Careful! That rock **is about to** fall!
The new supermarket **opens tomorrow.**
They're com**ing** to see us.
From now on, I refuse to talk to him.
I'll tell you **when he comes.**
Do you know **when he will come?**
Some day (One of these days), I'll be famous.

GETTING SOMEONE TO DO SOMETHING

He wanted her to listen to him but she wouldn't!
She made me sweep the floor!
I had them write a long essay.
I'll get (force) you to confess, Bernard!
He persuaded (convinced) me to come to school today.
I had my car repaired.

GIVING ONE'S OPINION

As far as I am concerned (Personally), I think there's no other possible outcome.
I have the feeling that we're not welcome.
In my view (opinion / To my mind), she completely misses the point.
I feel (believe) that we should leave now.
At first sight (glance), I agree with you, but **on second thoughts, I should say** that you're wrong!
My view is that he's hiding his true motives.
As for me, I'd choose the other solution.
Now **I realize** how stupid I was!

INCAPACITY

It's (too) difficult (hard) for me to understand his arguments.
Sorry, sir, **it's quite impossible for us to** give you an immediate answer.
He can't even use a screwdriver!
They didn't (couldn't) manage to open the garage door.
They weren't able to finish in time.
Sorry, **I'm totally unable to** go to this interview.
When I was a child, **I couldn't** ride a bike...
She's incapable of tell**ing** the truth.
I can't help lov**ing** her...
High taxes **will not enable the** economy **to** recover.

INTENTION

He's leav**ing** tomorrow.
I'm going to change jobs.
She's thinking of gett**ing** married again!
He's determined not to give up.
What **are you planning to** do this summer?
Do you really **intend to** smoke that awful cigar?
We want to visit all the temples.

LIKING

I like watch**ing** spaghetti westerns on TV.
She enjoys go**ing** for long walks by the sea.
My sister is very fond of the Beatles.
I just love the way Robert Redford walks!
She (just) loves (adores) skateboard**ing** with her grandchildren.
Mint sauce is very nice (delicious, etc.**),** isn't it?
Are you keen on (Do you fancy) Chinese food?
I'm crazy (mad) about this book!

OBLIGATION

It's necessary for you to be at the airport at 9.
You're to stay in bed for at least a week.
But **you must** give that money back!
You'll have to take an early train.
Remember, Cinderella, **you've got to** leave the ball before midnight!
You need to see a dentist.
You're requested to leave immediately!
They were forced (compelled) to abandon the project.

ORDERS

Go away! Don't run!
Do be quiet for a minute! I'm trying to think.
You bring that ball back immediately, stupid dog!
Can't you be quiet for a second!
Will you stop arguing!
I'm telling you you must leave at once!

PAST

Cf. *Précis grammatical : Les temps.* ***(8)***
There used to be a tree there.
Kids are no longer what **they used to be...**
Long ago people were more courteous...
In the past parents were more strict.
He had **once** asked me to marry him.

PERMISSION

You may play the saxophone, but not too loud.
You can go out now, Johnny.
You're allowed to smoke in the hall only.
I hope **they'll let us** get in.
They allowed us to leave early.

POSSESSION

I have (got) twelve brothers, but **I don't have (haven't got)** any sisters.
The smaller house is mine.
Whose jeans are those?—**They're mine.**
Those trousers are yours, I suppose.
You see that pretty girl? Well, **she's an old girlfriend of mine!**
Are those **Janet's records?**—No, **they're Bob's.**
Your seat is here, but **Jimmy's** is further down.
That's my own tape-recorder I'm using.
The other record-player **belongs to** the club.
He owns at least seven hotels in Saudi Arabia!

PROBABILITY: FROM UNCERTAINTY TO CERTAINTY

It might rain tomorrow, be careful on the road.
They could arrive sooner than we expected.
They might be at home, but **I rather doubt it (it's quite doubtful).**

The railway workers may go on strike soon.
I don't really know why he's so late. **He may (can) have missed** his train.
I think (suppose, believe) they had good reasons for not coming.
It looks as if it were going to rain.
Perhaps (maybe) he's ill.

The bell's ringing: **that will be** the postman.
He should be in London by now.
It must be a mistake! This is not my umbrella!
I'm sure (certain / convinced) you're very tired after such a hard day's work.
He must have forgotten our appointment.
Our teacher can't be wrong! **He can't have made** such a gross mistake!
You're not likely (You're unlikely) to see me again in your filthy restaurant!
She's likely to arrive at any time now.
It's obvious (Obviously) he has forgotten us.
He's sure to (It's sure he will) come to the party.
I'll never come back, and **that's for sure!**
They're bound to get into trouble!
I'm positive I saw him last night!

PROHIBITION

You can't lie on the grass! **It's forbidden (prohibited/not permitted)!**
No one may borrow more than one book.
You're not allowed to open that door.
You mustn't (aren't to) touch this guitar.
Please, **do not** put litter on the grass.
No smok**ing allowed.**
No swimm**ing** beyond this point!
No, my lad, **you may not** leave that room!
You're not supposed (expected) to laugh!
I won't have (let) you talk like that!

PROPOSING

Have another pint! It won't hurt you.
Will you have lunch with us?
Won't you join us?
Would you like to go to a restaurant?
Would you like another glass of sherry?
What about go**ing** for a swim tonight?
How about a bicycle race? I bet I can beat you!
Say, **why don't we (why not)** play poker?
Let's go to Rocky Point, **shall we?**
We could have a pint after the film, **couldn't we?**
Shall we try to go on holiday in June this year?
I suggest that we leave immediately.
Don't you think we should (could) wait for her?
Shall I help you?
What shall I offer you? Flowers or chocolates?
Which cake do you prefer (would you rather have)?

PURPOSE

What did she learn Japanese **for?**
He works a lot **in order to** get a good job.
He stopped smoking **so as not to** ruin his health.
They saved $ 2 000 **to** buy a new car.
I bought these magazines **for you to** read.
I moved to the country **so that** my baby would stop coughing.

QUANTITY

Cf. *Précis grammatical : La quantité* **(2)**
Thirty people rang this morning!
A lot of (Lots of) people were there.
There's **no** tea left.
There were **few** people at the show.

I can manage with **very little** money.
It means **a great (good) deal of** trouble.
How much money have you got?
How many children has she got?
How far is it from the station?
How deep is the well?
This canyon is **three miles wide.**
The village is nearly **ten miles away.**

REFUSAL

He flatly refused to help me.
She won't come if Ted is here.
She'll never accept (agree) to leave her family.
Kissing you on a first date! **It's (completely) out of the question!**
He's quite reluctant to show his real feelings.
They were unwilling to talk about it.
I have no intention of going out tonight.

REGRET

I'm sorry I couldn't be at your wedding.
Excuse me (Forgive me / I apologize) for being so late.
I wish I had seen this film!
We should (shouldn't) have left the door open!
If only I had bought a better car, I wouldn't have had this stupid accident!
Why didn't I work at school! It's too late now...
What a pity you weren't at the party!
You missed him by an inch! **(That's) too bad...**

REPORTING

Cf. *Précis grammatical : Le discours indirect* ***(17)***
He says he will soon join the Navy.
He said he was unable to drive such a big car.
She said that she would come with you.
He asked if he could leave immediately.
She wondered whether he had understood.
He told me that I had to come at once.
They told the policeman that **they would have stopped if they had heard** him.

REPROACH

You shouldn't watch TV so late at night!
You should (might, could) have told us!
I wish you were nicer with your sister!
I wish you had been more polite!
Why didn't you stay with us?
If only you had married me instead of Ronald!
Couldn't you (Can't you) make less noise?
I'd rather you didn't answer back!
I'd rather you hadn't spent all your money!
Instead of spending your time reading comics, **you should (you'd better)** prepare your exam!
What a disgrace (a shame)!
How can (could) you?

REQUESTS

Will you help me find my umbrella, please?
Would you lend me some money?
Brother, **can you** spare a dime?
Could I have another cup of that delicious tea?
Can I leave now, sir?
May I ask your name and address, young man?
Do (Would) you mind switch**ing** that TV off?
Do you mind if I open the window?
Could you tell me where San Diego is, please?

SUMMING UP ONE'S IDEAS

Roughly speaking, I'd say he is right.
On the whole (All things considered), I feel you're not far from the truth.
In other words (In a word), he's silly!
To sum up (To conclude / In conclusion) I'd say he's both right *and* wrong...
After all (All told), she's not such a bad girl.
All in all, things could be worse.

SURPRISE

I'm surprised at her behaviour.
Really? Is that so? You don't say so!
You're (You must be) kidding (joking)!
My goodness! Good gracious (Lord / Heavens)!
That's incredible (amazing)!
Isn't that surprising (amazing)?
How incredible (amazing / surprising)!
You're not serious! Don't make me laugh!
I don't believe a word of it!
That's (a bit) hard to believe!
No! Did she (really)?
I can't believe it!/It's unbelievable!

INDEX LEXICAL

Ces **fiches de vocabulaire** présentent un **minimum nécessaire** pour un commentaire écrit ou oral sur un texte, ou pour une activité de *Follow-up work*. Bien entendu, il n'est pas question de tout y trouver. Il s'agit d'une base à laquelle doit s'ajouter le vocabulaire acquis à l'occasion de chaque texte, des diverses activités en classe, de vos lectures, etc.

Les mots suggérés ne sont pas systématiquement traduits, pour des raisons évidentes : ou bien il existe un équivalent anglais qui rend le sens clair; ou bien le mot lui-même est transparent; ou bien encore le sens peut être déduit du contraire qui vous est donné. Par exemple : *optimism* : transparent; *worship* = *adoration*; *false* ≠ *true*, le sens de *false* est transparent, on en déduit celui de *true*. Les parenthèses donnent des commentaires ou des traductions. Les usages britanniques ou américains sont signalés par G.B. et U.S.

Attention ! Donner une traduction est toujours délicat. Les mots n'ont de signification que dans un contexte et il n'est pas toujours possible de donner une solution universelle. Les traductions proposées ne sont donc que des indications possibles sur le sens.

1. Light, sounds and the senses

The eyes

n. eye, eyelid *(paupière)*, eyelash *(cil)*, eyebrow *(sourcil)*, eyeball *(globe oculaire)*, pupil — sight *(vue)*, view, vision.

a. sharp ≠ dull (*aigu* ≠ *terne*), keen *(perçant)* — (in) visible — blind *(aveugle)* — blurred *(trouble)*.

v. see, watch *(regarder ce qui est en mouvement)*, examine — glance, glimpse *(regards rapides)* — gaze, stare *(regards prolongés)* — make out *(distinguer)* — spot *(repérer)* — spy (on) *(épier)*.

Light

n. light, ray, beam *(rayon)* — sun, sunshine.

a. bright, clear, brilliant, shiny, glowing *(rutilant)*.

v. et n. flash, glow, gleam, glimmer *(faible)*, dazzle *(éblouir)*.

Absence of light

n. shade, shadow *(ombre)*, darkness *(obscurité)*.

a. dull *(terne)*, dim *(vague, à peine visible)* — dark *(sombre)*, gloomy *(sombre ou triste)* — shadowy *(ombreux)*.

v. darken *(obscurcir)* — shade *(ombrager)*.

Hearing

n. ear, hearing — sound, noise, din *(vacarme)*, racket *(id.)* — silence.

a. loud, noisy — silent, noiseless, quiet *(qui ne fait pas de bruit)* — sharp *(aigu)*, dull *(sourd)*, harsh *(discordant)*.

v. et n. bang *(explosion)*, crash *(bruit violent)*, rattle *(bruit répété)*, pop *(comme un bouchon)* — ring *(sonner)* — rustle *(bruits discrets)* — clang *(bruit métallique)*.

Human voices

n. voice — chat = conversation, speech, talk.

a. loud *(fort)*, low *(bas)* — clear, hoarse *(enroué, rauque)* — high ≠ low pitched *(aigu ≠ grave)*.

v. speak *(intr. ou avec* with *ou* to*)*, talk (*intr., ou avec* to *ou* with) say — ask, answer *(tr.)*.

v. et n. chatter (= chat) *(bavarder)*, mumble *(marmonner)*, mutter *(murmurer)*, whisper *(id.)* — stammer *(bégayer)* — shout *(cri, appel)*, call, cry *(aussi pleurer)*, scream, shriek *(cris aigus)*, howl *(hurler)*, growl *(grogner, gronder)*, yell *(cris violents, colère, douleur)* — exclaim, cheer *(acclamer)*.

Touch

n. touch, contact, feel *(sentiment au toucher)* — caress — skim = brush against *(effleurer)*.

a. soft *(doux)* ≠ hard — rough ≠ smooth (*rugueux* ≠ *lisse*).

v. touch, contact, feel, stroke = caress — tickle *(chatouiller)* — scratch *(gratter)*.

Pain

n. pain, ache *(mal de..., douleur)*, headache, toothache, back-ache, etc. — cramp.

a. painful *(douloureux)* — dull ≠ sharp (*sourd* ≠ *aigu*) — stabbing *(lancinant)*.

v. ache, hurt *(faire mal)* — pain.

Taste

n. taste, flavour *(goût agréable)*.

a. good ≠ bad — delicious, tasty *(qui a du goût, plutôt bon)* ≠ tasteless — sweet ≠ sour (*doux* ≠ *aigre*), bitter ≠ sweet (*amer* ≠ *doux*) — salty — delicious, scrumptious *(succulent)*.

v. taste = try, appreciate.

Smell

n. smell, scent *(parfum)*, odour *(déplaisante)*.

a. fragrant *(parfumé)*, perfumed *(artificiellement)* — smelling, stinking *(puant)*.

v. smell *(neutre ou en mal)* — stink *(puer)* — sniff *(renifler)*.

2. Landscapes

Flat lands

n. plain, prairie (U.S.), horizon, space — desert — expanse *(étendue).*

a. flat ≠ undulating — immense, vast, wide = large.

v. stretch *(s'étendre),* expand *(id.).*

Hills and valleys

n. hill *(colline),* slope *(pente)* — valley, gulch (U.S.: *ravin*), hollow *(creux)* — canyon.

a. undulating, hilly — ragged *(découpé).*

Mountains

n. mountain, range *(chaîne)* — ridges *(crêtes),* peaks — top, summit — volcano — glaciers, snow, ice — valleys — cliff *(falaise)* — view *(vue).*

a. mountainous — steep *(à pic),* sharp *(escarpé).*

v. climb.

Forest

n. trees, trunks, leaves, etc. — shadow, darkness.

River

n. river *(fleuve ou rivière)* — torrent, brook *(ruisseau)* — side, riverside, bank *(rive)* — spring *(source),* mouth, delta — fall, waterfall (Niagara Falls), cascade — canal — lake, pond *(mare, petit lac),* lagoon, marsh *(marais)* — current.

a swift *(rapide)* ≠ slow — wide ≠ narrow *(étroit)* — deep *(profond)* ≠ shallow.

v. cross.

Sea

n. sea, ocean — wave, surf *(vagues sur les rivages plats)* — high ≠ low tide (*marée haute ≠ basse*) — current — coast — beach, shore *(rivage),* sand, pebble *(galets),* rocks, cliff *(falaise)* — gulf, bay, cape — island.

Pollution

n. air / noise / water / land pollution — fog, smog, fumes, acid rain — oil slicks *(marée noire),* tanker *(pétrolier).* waste(s) *(déchets)* — pesticides, detergents, chemicals *(produits chimiques),* fertilizers — polluter *(pollueur),* pollutant *(polluant)* ≠ environmentalist, ecologist — conservation, ecology — disaster, damage, exhaustion *(épuisement).*

a. artificial ≠ natural — non-polluting — non-biodegradable — polluted, noxious *(nocif)* — ecological — alarming.

v. save, conserve, preserve, respect ≠ destroy, endanger, pollute, ruin, exterminate, use up (resources), upset *(bouleverser)* — prosecute *(poursuivre en justice),* demonstrate *(manifester),* pass (a law = *une loi*) — protect ≠ threaten *(menacer).*

3. The body and its activities

The head and face

n. skull *(crâne)* — hair, moustache, beard *(barbe)* — eye, nose, cheeks *(joues),* mouth, lips, teeth, tongue *(langue),* chin, neck, forehead *(front).*

a. (hair) black, dark, brown, blond(e), red, dyed *(teint),* grey, bald *(chauve),* curled *(bouclé),* straight *(raide)* — (nose) sharp *(pointu),* roman, snub *(retroussé)* — (lips) thin, full *(charnues)* — chubby *(joufflu)* — (skin) white, pale, pink, ruddy *(rouge),* brown, tanned *(bronzée)* — grey-haired, blue-eyed, etc. — ugly ≠ beautiful, good-looking, handsome *(homme),* pretty *(femme).*

v. smile, laugh, grin *(large sourire)* — weep = cry *(pleurer)* — frown *(froncer les sourcils),* make a face *(grimace)* — eye *(dévisager)* — nod *(acquiescer).*

The limbs

n. limb *(membre)* — arm, shoulder *(épaule),* elbow *(coude),* wrist *(poignet),* hand, palm, thumb *(pouce),* finger, fist *(poing),* nail *(ongle, également clou)* — leg, thigh *(cuisse),* knee *(genou),* shin *(tibia),* foot, toe *(doigt de pied),* heel *(talon),* ankle *(cheville).*

a. strong ≠ weak — supple ≠ stiff *(raide)* — long ≠ short, long-armed, short-legged, etc. — skilful *(habile)* ≠ clumsy *(gauche)* = awkward.

v. hold *(tenir),* catch, grasp *(saisir),* clench *(serrer le poing)* — strike *(frapper),* throw *(jeter)* — stretch *(s'étendre)* — point *(montrer du doigt)* — wave *(faire signe)* — kick *(donner un coup de pied),* trample *(piétiner),* tread on *(marcher sur).*

The body itself

n. trunk, chest *(poitrine),* breasts *(seins),* back, sides — (organs) stomach, liver *(foie)* — throat *(gorge),* lungs *(poumons)* — heart, (blood) vessels, arteries, veins, pulse *(pouls)* — kidneys *(reins)* — skin *(peau),* sweat *(sueur),* hair *(poil).*

a. lean, thin ≠ big, fat — tall ≠ short. (cf. health).

Activities

v. (non-activity, positions): stand, sit, lie, kneel *(être agenouillé).*

a. motionless, still, lazy, idle *(oisif)*.

v. (activity): move *(bouger ou déplacer)* — walk, run, hurry, rush, dash *(se précipiter)* — leap = jump *(sauter)*, come ≠ go, arrive ≠ leave *(partir)*, start, stop — enter *(trans.)* — bring *(apporter)*, take to *(apporter à)*, take away *(emporter)*, carry *(porter, transporter)*, remove *(enlever)* — pull *(tirer)* ≠ push *(pousser)* — open ≠ close = shut — climb *(grimper)* — shift *(déplacer)* — slip *(glisser)*.

a. quick = rapid = fast ≠ slow — active = busy.

Particules et prépositions de mouvement. about *(autour, ou sans direction précise)* — across *(au travers d'une surface)* — along *(le long de)* — away *(s'éloignant d'un point)* — back *(retour à la case départ)* — down *(vers le bas)* — in — off *(s'écartant de)* — on *(sur)* — out — over *(par-dessus, une distance à franchir)* — round — through *(à travers une épaisseur)* — up.

Sports

n. sports — athletics, gymnastics — football (G.B.: soccer), rugby (G.B.: rugger), American football — cricket (G.B. and Commonwealth), baseball (U.S., Japan, Cuba) — tennis, hockey — skiing, swimming, surfing — team *(équipe)*, coach *(entraîneur)*, referee *(arbitre)*.

a. indoor ≠ outdoor — violent ≠ quiet — amateur ≠ professionnal.

v. win *(gagner)*, lose *(perdre)*, draw *(faire match nul)*.

Disease

n. disease = illness *(maladie)*, sickness *(surtout U.S.)*, epidemic, complaint *(ce dont on souffre, affection)* — pain = ache (*douleur, surtout dans composés* headache, tooth-, back-) — temperature, fever — doctor, nurse — health *(santé)*.

a. healthy *(bien portant)* ≠ ill = sick (U.S.), well (better) ≠ unwell (worse) — painful, sore, aching — sickly *(maladif)* — unhealthy *(malsain)*.

v. cough *(tousser)*, sneeze *(éternuer)*, blow one's nose *(se moucher)* — choke *(suffoquer)* — vomit = be sick — ache = hurt *(faire mal)*.

4. People, their ways and characters

Characterisation

n. person, individual, character — type — personality, look — quality, feature *(trait)*, characteristic.

a. characteristic, proper *(propre à)*, individual, specific, typical — commonplace, common — particular, exceptional, unusual.

v. characterize, mark.

Characters

n. behaviour, character, disposition, temper, mood *(humeur)*.

a. easy-going *(facile à vivre)*, quiet — happy, cheerful *(gai)* — anxious, depressed, irritable — sad, miserable — proud *(fier)* ≠ ashamed — strong ≠ weak — timid, shy, self-conscious *(intimidé)* — reckless *(insouciant)* — fickle *(inconstant)* — bold = daring *(audacieux)*, courageous ≠ cowardly — kind, generous, helpful ≠ selfish, self-centered, stingy *(avare)*, greedy *(avide)* — emotional *(émotif)* — cruel, cynical — touchy *(susceptible)* — canny = cunning *(rusé)* — vain = conceited *(vaniteux)*.

Temper *(humeur)*

a. good ≠ bad — hot ≠ cold — awful, terrible — pleasant, charming — quick-tempered *(vif)*.

Habits

n. habit *(habitude)*, tendency, inclination.

a. normal, habitual, usual (and the adverbs) — mechanical, automatic — prone (to) = inclined (to) *(enclin à)*, liable (to) *(sujet à)*.

v. will, would (see grammar) — tend (to).

Wanting

n. hope, expectation — will, desire, want *(besoin)* — lack *(manque)* — optimism ≠ pessimism.

a. wilful *(volontaire)*, willing to *(disposé à)*, resolute, determined to.

v. want (*vouloir = désirer*), demand *(exiger)*, wish *(souhaiter)*, long for = aspire = dream of, care (for) *(aimer)*, fancy *(aimer dans les interrogatives, vouloir)* — miss *(ressentir l'absence)*.

5. Emotions

Joy and pleasure

n. joy, pleasure, delight *(plaisir à)*, enjoyment *(id.)*, satisfaction, contentment.

a. content *(satisfait)*, glad *(content)*, pleased (with) *(content de)* — joyful, carefree *(insouciant)* — happy, delighted, cheerful *(gai)* = light-hearted.

v. enjoy (something) *(prendre plaisir à)* — please (s.thing pleases s.one) — delight *(ravir)*, satisfy.

Sadness

n. sadness *(tristesse)*, sorrow = grief *(chagrin)*, misery *(grand chagrin)* — anxiety, worry *(inquiétude)*, distress — despair, depression.

a. sad, unhappy, miserable *(très malheureux)* — depressed *(déprimé)* = dejected — anxious, worried *(ennuyé)*, distressed — hopeless, desperate, gloomy, down-hearted.

v. sadden *(rendre triste)* — worry, disturb *(troubler)* — distress, depress — despair, grieve *(être chagriné)*.

Anger

n. anger *(colère)*, bad temper *(mauvaise humeur)*, irritation, rage.

a. angry, wild *(furieux)*, furious = mad (U.S.), infuriated (by), outraged — irritating, annoying *(agaçant ou plus fort)*.

v. anger, provoke *(irriter)*, annoy — enrage, infuriate — quarrel *(se disputer)* — blow up *(éclater)*.

Fear

n. fear, fright *(grande peur)*, scare *(souvent collectif = panique)*, terror.

a. (causing fear) fearful, frightful, awful = terrible = horrific, dreadful (*sens atténué :* an awful, a dreadful dress) — (feeling fear) afraid, frightened, scared *(les deux forts)*, nervous *(inquiet)*, anxious, shocked *(pas forcément moral, p. ex. par une explosion)*.

v. frighten, scare, terrify — strike (with) *(frapper de)*, paralyze — be afraid (*souvent très faible :* I'm afraid the coffee is just warm) — shrink (back) *(avoir un mouvement de recul)* — dread *(redouter)* — shudder *(frémir)*.

6. Activities of the mind and communication

Thinking

n. thought *(pensée)*, mind *(esprit)*, brain *(cerveau)* (brains = *intelligence*), reason, reflection, logic *(v. plus bas)* — judg(e)ment — idea, notion — awareness *(conscience)*.

a. mental, intellectual — logical, abstract — thoughtful *(réfléchi)*, rational, wise *(sage)* — clever = intelligent, bright = brilliant, smart (often U.S.: clever) — stupid, silly, mad.

v. think, meditate, reason, reflect — suppose, guess (*deviner ;* U.S. : *penser* = *croire*) — conceive — judge, estimate, assess, weigh *(peser)* — understand, realize *(se rendre compte)*, be aware *(conscient)*.

Reasoning

n. reason, reasoning, wisdom *(sagesse)* — logic, deduction, conclusion — hypothesis, theory — intuition — cause, consequence — paradox — point of view, viewpoint, argument, debate — synthesis — proof, evidence.

a. balanced, coherent, wise *(sage)*, obvious *(évident)*, careful, logical, sensible *(sensé)*, sound *(solide)* ≠ unsound — true ≠ untrue — commonplace.

v. reason, deduce, conclude — prove, demonstrate, show.

Memory

n. memory, memories *(souvenirs)* — reminder *(rappel)*.

v. remember = recall, recollect ≠ forget — remind (s.one of s.thing) *(rappeler qqch à qqn)* — overlook *(négliger)*.

Imagination

n. imagination= fancy, fiction, fantasy, image.

a. imaginative, dreamy — imaginary, fanciful *(fantasque)*, fabulous.

v. imagine, fancy *(imaginer ou aimer)*, dream, foresee *(prévoir)*, picture.

Communication (speech)

n. speech *(la parole en gén.)*, statement *(déclaration)*, language — voice — words *(paroles)*.

a. low ≠ loud *(volume)*, low ≠ high *(hauteur)* — silent ≠ talkative.

v. talk (to *ou* with someone), speak *(intr.)* — tell (s.one s.thing) = inform, say (s.thing to s.o), tell (a story) — pronounce, utter *(prononcer)* — deliver (a speech) — state *(déclarer)* — address (s.o) — assert *(affirmer)*.

Communication (exchange)

n. conversation, talk *(petite conférence)*, talks *(entretiens, négociations)*, chat *(conversation familière)* — discussion = argument *(discussion ou dispute)* — question ≠ answer — advice.

a. objective ≠ subjective — quiet ≠ lively, hot (debate) — partial, biassed ≠ impartial, unbiassed.

v. discuss, debate, argue *(discuter avec des arguments)* — suggest, propose, insinuate = hint — advise, persuade, convince — contradict, refute — question *(questionner ou mettre en question)* ≠ answer — agree *(être d'accord)* ≠ disagree — admit *(reconnaître, avouer)* ≠ deny — interrupt.

Learning

n. learning ≠ teaching, education — knowledge, culture — permanent education, retraining.

a. literate ≠ illiterate — ignorant — educated — erudite = learned = well-read — self-taught.

v. learn ≠ teach — educate — explain, expose — understand, remember, know.

7. Feelings and appreciation

Feelings

n. sentiment, instinct, feeling.

v. feel.

Positive feelings

n. love *(amour)*, liking *(moins fort)* — fondness, affection *(degrés divers)* — desire, passion — preference — admiration, respect — confidence *(confiance)* = trust.

a. loving, affectionate, fond of *(sentiment moyen)*, devoted *(dévoué)*, partial (to) *(un penchant pour)*.

v. like, love, be fond of (*comme* like), be keen on *(intérêt fort pour des choses)*, fancy (*comme* like, *familier, souvent négatif*) — appreciate — prefer = like better — trust *(faire confiance)*.

Inspiring positive feelings

n. attraction = appeal — charm, beauty, interest.

a. attractive, appealing *(attirant)*, enchanting, fascinating, captivating, charming — popular *(aimé de tous)*, interesting — likeable, lovable, adorable, touching, moving.

v. attract, appeal (to), charm, fascinate — interest.

Negative feelings

n. dislike (*moins fort que* hate = hatred), disgust, repulsion *(très fort)* — indifference — jealousy, envy — spite *(dépit, malveillance)* = malice, resentment *(rancune)* — contempt *(mépris)* = scorn.

a. hostile, hateful — indifferent, reserved, cool, cold — jealous — spiteful *(malveillant)* — scornful, haughty *(hautain)* — cruel, pitiless.

v. dislike, detest, hate *(haïr, détester)* — can't stand, can't bear *(ne pas pouvoir supporter)* — despise *(mépriser)* = scorn — laugh at *(se moquer)*.

Inspiring negative feelings

a. unattractive, unappealing — unpopular, uninteresting — disgusting = revolting = repulsive *(répugnant)* = repellent.

v. disgust, repel *(repousser)*, put off *(dégoûter)*.

8. Judgements and evaluation

Judgement

n. assessment, analysis — criticism *(une critique)*, critic *(un critique)* — examination — admiration.

a. favourable ≠ unfavourable — indulgent = lenient ≠ severe — fair ≠ unfair — legal ≠ illegal.

v. like, dislike, prefer (*v.* **7**) — judge, criticize, assess — admire — despise *(mépriser)*, run down *(dénigrer)*.

Motives of judgement

n. motive, reason = grounds — arguments.

a. false ≠ true — good ≠ bad — right ≠ wrong (*juste* ≠ *faux*).

Moral judgement

n. morals *(morale ou moralité)* — approval ≠ disapproval, dismissal *(rejet)* — blame, accusation, denunciation — fault, defect — indulgence, permissiveness — severity = harshness.

a. moral ≠ immoral — right ≠ wrong (*bien* ≠ *mal*) — good ≠ bad = evil = wicked *(méchant)* = heartless, honest ≠ dishonest, sincere ≠ insincere — permissive ≠ strict = harsh, severe — perfect = faultless — unscrupulous.

v. approve (of), be in favour (of) — allow *(permettre)*, accept — blame, condemn, denounce, accuse, forgive *(pardonner)* — lie *(mentir)*.

Artistic judgement

n. art — manner, style, method — appreciation, criticism = review.

a. beautiful, fine *(beau)*, lovely *(beau, joli)*, picturesque *(pittoresque)*, original — great, unique, splendid, superb *(plus vague qu'en français)* — (artist) gifted *(doué)*, clever *(habile)*, intelligent, sensitive*(sensible)*, strong, delicate, etc.

v. appreciate, admire — review *(écrire une critique)* — praise *(louer)* ≠ criticize.

Intellectual judgement

n. intelligence, gift *(don)* = knack, talent, cleverness, capacity, skill = ability *(habileté, compétence)* — idiot, genius — insight *(perspicacité)*.

a. intelligent ≠ stupid, clever *(plus ou moins intelligent)*, perceptive *(perspicace)*, bright = brilliant, gifted *(doué)*, talented, competent, capable, skilled — efficient — awkward *(maladroit)*, foolish *(stupide, étourdi)*, silly *(bête)*, absurd — mad *(insensé)*, crazy.

9. Social attitudes

Acceptance

n. acceptance, tolerance ≠ intolerance, understanding, agreement ≠ disagreement, approval ≠ disapproval, hostility — peace, compromise — belief.

a. negative — tolerant ≠ intolerant — understanding *(compréhensif)* — liberal, open, open-minded *(à l'esprit ouvert)* ≠ narrow-minded — conventional, dutiful, law-abiding *(respectueux des lois)*.

v. tolerate, understand, accept, believe — have blinkers *(œillères)* — obey, conform.

Friendliness

n. friend, acquaintance *(une connaissance)*, (social) mixer, neighbour *(voisin)* — ally *(ami, allié)*, partner, associate — friendliness, sympathy, compassion, agreement, friendship.

a. friendly, amiable, sympathetic — intimate = close (friend) — sociable — warm, cordial.

v. be friends (with), make friends (with) *(se lier d'amitié)*, mix with, get along (with) *(s'entendre bien avec)* — welcome *(accueillir avec sympathie)*, greet *(accueillir)* — sympathise *(compatir)*, comfort *(réconforter)*, encourage, support — share *(partager)* — owe *(devoir)*.

Isolation

n. loner, outsider, misfit *(marginal)*, non-conformist, rebel — isolation, loneliness, solitude, rejection, segregation, distance, diffidence *(méfiance)*.

a. lonely, solitary, lonesome (cow-boy, *par exemple*) — reserved, diffident *(méfiant)* — distant, remote *(lointain)*, cool, cold.

v. forget, ignore, avoid *(éviter)*, keep away (from), reject = cast away, separate, set apart, exclude.

Hostility

n. enemy, opponent, antagonist, contender — enmity *(inimitié)*, hostility, antagonism — prejudice (*préjugé ;* be prejudiced against).

a. hostile, unfriendly, unsympathetic — nasty *(méchant, mauvais)*, malicious *(méchant)* — opposed, contrary, unfavourable, subversive, rebellious, provocative.

v. rebel, reject, defy.

Violence

n. aggression, violence, hate *(haine)* — anger, rage, passion, fury — mugging *(agression armée)*.

a. brutal — aggressive, violent, offensive.

v. attack, assault — kill, injure *(blesser)*.

10. Religion and other beliefs

Religions

n. Christian (-ity), Catholic (-ism), Protestant (-ism), Orthodox *(n'est pas un nom)* — Jew (Judaism), Moslem, Muslim (Islam) — Buddhist (Buddhism), Hindu (-ism) — fetishist, heathen = pagan *(païen)*, idol — church, temple, synagogue, pagoda — faith *(foi)* — doctrine, belief = creed *(croyance)* — cult — believer ≠ unbeliever, atheist — fanatic, fanaticism — follower, disciple.

a. *comme ci-dessus sauf* Jewish *et* Islamic — religious, devout, pious, faithful *(fidèle)*.

v. believe (in) — worship = adore — follow.

Christianity

n. God, Jesus (Christ), the Lord, the Holy Ghost *(le Saint-Esprit)* — the Virgin Mary, the Saints — (Catholicism) priest *(prêtre)*, bishop *(évêque)*, archbishop, the Pope, monk *(moine)*, nun *(religieuse)*, convent, abbey, mass *(messe)*, heaven = paradise ≠ hell, angels, church — (Protestantism) temple, chapel, minister, preacher, evangelist — (common to both) the Bible (Old ≠ New Testament), the Gospel = New Testament, soul *(âme)*, spirit, sin *(péché)*, virtue, grace, salvation — Satan, the Devil.

v. believe, worship *(adorer)* — pray, confess, preach — baptize = christen.

Religious practice

n. prayer, worship *(adoration)*, Sunday school *(catéchisme)*, teachings — church-going, church-goer.

a. religious, faithful, pious, charitable.

v. go (to church, chapel, etc.), attend (mass) — pray, confess — convert — repent — save — forgive.

Other beliefs

n. belief, faith — superstition, (black/white) magic, myth(ology), fanatic(ism), witchcraft *(sorcellerie)* — opinion, sect — pagans — witch *(sorcière)*, warlock *(sorcier)*, witch doctor, wizard *(magicien)*, medicine man (Indian, U.S.) — political belief — personal conviction.

a. superstitious — magical, mythical — faithful — fanatical, tolerant.

v. work (a miracle), conjure up (a spirit) *(faire apparaître)*, cast a spell *(jeter un charme)*, curse *(maudire)*.

11. Human communities

The family

n. parents, father (husband), mother (wife) (parents: only father and mother), dad (G.B. *et* U.S.), pop (U.S.), mum (G.B.), mom (U.S.) — child(ren), son, daughter — brother, sister — relatives *(autres parents)*, uncle, aunt *(tante)*, nephew, niece, in-laws *(beaux-parents)* (father-in-law, mother-in-law, etc.) — grandfather (-mother), grandchildren, grandson (-daughter) — authority, permissiveness — link *(lien)* — widow (veuve), widower *(veuf)*, bachelor *(célibataire)*.

a. parental, paternal, maternal, familial — strict ≠ permissive — (closely) knit *(très unis)*.

v. bring up = raise (U.S. : *élever*) = nurture — adopt — marry (s.o.), get married (to s.o.), divorce (s.o.) — be single *(célibataire)*.

Nations

n. nation(ality), country *(pays ou campagne)*, land, state *(état)* — citizen, citizenship — flag *(drapeau)* — nationalism, patriotism — homesickness *(mal du pays)* — (parts of the country) region, province, district, county (G.B.), state, county (U.S.) — town, city, village, community — foreigner *(d'un autre pays)*, stranger *(d'un autre endroit)*.

a. national — native ≠ alien = foreign — regional, local, provincial.

v. belong (to) *(appartenir)* — immigrate, emigrate.

Classes

n. et a. social class, social background *(origine)*, upper class — nobility, aristocracy — middle class, bourgeoisie, bourgeois, suburban (G.B. : *petit bourgeois*), lower class *(péjoratif, peu usité, préférer le suivant)*, working class — the proletariat, the masses, underclass — class struggle *(lutte)*, class barriers — social status — unemployed, jobless — the rich ≠ the poor — rich, wealthy, well-off ≠ badly off, needy.

v. look up to ≠ look down upon, envy, hate = resent, despise *(mépriser)*, ignore, reject, isolate.

Work communities

n. job, occupation *(métier)*, position — farmer, agricultural worker (peasant *ne s'emploie plus pour* G.B. *ou* U.S.) — industrial worker ("blue collar"), miner — truck driver *(camionneur)* (U.S. also teamster), lorry driver (G.B.) — (the professions) doctor, lawyer, etc. — "white collar", employee, (bank, etc.) clerk — secretary, typist *(dactylo)* — civil servant (G.B. : *fonctionnaire*), the Civil Service — management, manager, director, executive staff *(les cadres)*, staff = personnel.

conflicts. (Trade) Unions, labor unions (U.S.) *(syndicats)*, the Railway Union (G.B.), T.U.C. = Trades Union Congress (*centrale syndicale unique*, G.B.) — strike (*n. et v., grève, faire la grève, souvent appelée par euphémisme* "industrial action"), strike-breaker *(jaune)* = scab, dispute (settle a dispute: *régler*).

Civilization

n. culture *(sens de « une » culture)* — society, civilization, community.

a. traditional, primitive = backward ≠ advanced, technically developed — industrial — ancient ≠ modern civilizations — agricultural societies.

Races

n. attitudes towards different people (the Blacks, the Indians), racialism (G.B.), racism (U.S.), racialist, anti-racialism, etc. (cf. **9**. Social attitudes).

12. Towns, small and large

Things

n. blocks (U.S.: distance between two streets, two blocks from here) — apartment blocks, office blocks, luxury hotels — skyscrapers, story (*étage*, G.B.: floor, storey), elevators (G.B.: lifts).

Along the streets

n. sidewalk (*trottoir*, G.B.: pavement), curb (*bord du trottoir*, G.B.: kerb), mailbox (G.B.: letter box) — pedestrian crossing, traffic lights, billboards (G.B.: hoardings) for advertisements (adverts), neon signs — buses, cabs = taxis, subway (in London: tube), expressway, freeway (G.B.: motorway), highway (U.S.; trunk road: G.B.), speed limit, ticket *(P.V.)* = fine *(amende)*.

The city

n. district, city center (G.B.: centre), inner city *(centre ville)* = downtown ≠ uptown (U.S.), suburbs — town planning, town planner *(urbanisme, urbaniste)* — shopping-center, department store — ghetto.

v. build ≠ destroy, pull down — widen *(élargir)* — turn into *(transformer en)*.

People

n. passer-by (pl. : passers-by), pedestrian, driver, motorist, taxi-driver, policeman (slang: cop) — businessman, white-collar or blue-collar worker, artist, bum (*clochard;* G.B.: tramp) — Salvation Army Centers, Rescue Centers.

Problems

n. strike, blizzard, cold wave, heat wave, power failure — traffic, traffic jam (U.S.: tie-up) — crime, delinquent, delinquency, mugger, mugging, drugs, racial problems or tensions, unemployement, safety = security ≠ unsafety = insecurity — gang, gangster — police, police headquarters, police precinct (U.S.), police station (G.B.), police car, etc. — slums *(taudis)*, housing problems.

a. filthy *(dégoûtant)*, badly-kept, rundown *(en ruine)*, overcrowded *(surpeuplé)*, dilapidated *(délabré)* — unsafe.

Actions

n. crowd, mob, line (G.B. : queue), commuter *(celui/celle qui se déplace de la banlieue à la ville pour son travail, ou vice-versa)*, jogger — peak / rush / business hours.

a. busy *(animé)*, noisy, lively (= busy), crowded, crammed *(bondé)*.

v. hurry, move along, rush, dash *(se ruer)*, race *(courir)* — commute, ride *(prendre)* (bus, taxi or train) — hang about *(flâner)*, gather *(se rassembler)* — sell ≠ buy, shop, go shopping — beg *(mendier)* — steal (from s.o.), rob (s.o.), attack, mug *(agresser)*, kill, injure *(blesser)*, insult — knock down *(renverser)*, run over *(écraser)* — bump into *(bousculer)* — be lost, ask one's way.

13. Developed and developing countries

The world

n. West ≠ East, capitalism ≠ socialism (communism) — North ≠ South (underdeveloped countries *ou* developing *par euphémisme*), the Western World ≠ the Third World — ally *(allié)*.

a. socialist ≠ capitalist — imperialist — neutral, non-aligned ≠ aligned.

Some geography

n. Europe, Britain, the United States of America — Japan — the U.S.S.R. — North, Central, South America — Cuba, Salvador, Nicaragua, Brazil — the Middle East, the Far East, Vietnam, Israel — Africa, North Africa, South Africa — India — China.

a. European, British (English, Welsh, Scottish, Northern-Irish) — North / South American — Japanese — Russian — African — Asiatic.

Political regimes

n. regime, political system — head of state, sovereign, king, queen, president, dictator — kingdom, republic — democracy — government, assemblies, elections — (military) coup.

a. autocratic — military — totalitarian, fascist — communist, socialist — free, democratic.

v. govern, rule *(diriger)* — oppress — administrate (U.S.), administer (G.B.) — run (for the presidency, office, a seat: *siège*), vote, elect — take (office) — seize (power), overthrow *(renverser)*.

International relations

n. ally, alliance, treaty — isolationism, protectionism, commitment *(engagement)*, intervention, invasion — commando, raid, occupation — blockade *(blocus)*, embargo, sanctions — aircraft carriers *(porte-avions)*, fleet *(flotte)*, marines, paratroopers — victory ≠ defeat.

a. friendly ≠ hostile.

v. wage / make war, win ≠ lose, resist ≠ surrender — invade, colonize.

Revolt and revolution

n. riot *(émeute)*, revolt, rebellion, subversion, revolution, guerrilla, national liberation (front) — rebel, revolutionary, partisan, terrorist, saboteur — terrorism, sabotage.

a. revolutionary, subversive.

v. rebel, revolt, rise *(se soulever)* — resist, fight.

Developed countries

n. wealth *(richesse)*, affluence, luxury — consumer *(consommateur)*, consumer society, consumer goods *(biens de consommation)*, consumption *(consommation)*, mass-consumption — material comfort, (high) technology — energy crisis, energy sources (solar / nuclear power) — employment ≠ unemployment = recession, poverty level = poverty line (below / above the poverty level line) — the computer revolution — arms race *(course aux armements)*, atom bomb, deterrence *(dissuasion)*, nuclear weapons — aid.

a. well-off = wealthy = rich — overfed *(surnourri)* — mechanized, technical, sophisticated, artificial.

v. invest — produce — consume — export, sell.

Developing countries

n. poverty — famine = starvation, hunger *(faim)*, drought *(sécheresse)*, epidemic — over-population, birth-control, population growth — shanty town *(bidonville)*, rural exodus — agrarian / land reform, urbanisation, industrialization — corruption, exploitation, inefficiency *(manque d'effica-*

cité) — literacy ≠ illiteracy *(analphabétisme)* — foreign aid = help, medical / food supplies — debts ≠ loans *(emprunts)* — growth *(croissance),* independence, survival.

a. backward = primitive — tribal, communal — illiterate *(analphabète),* exploited, starving *(affamé),* hungry, over-populated — poor, destitute *(miserable),* homeless, jobless — industrialized, urbanised, modernized, independent, self-reliant = autonomous = self-sufficient.

v. nationalize, reform, provide *(fournir),* feed *(nourrir),* improve *(améliorer),* carry through (a programme) — increase *(accroître)* — emigrate — import.

14. Education and sciences

Education in general

n. youngsters, youths, teenagers — school, education, instruction, culture, learning — head (master / mistress), master, teacher, pupil, schoolboy, schoolgirl, schoolchildren — staff *(personnel)* — curriculum *(programme),* exam (*ou* examination), mark *(note),* essay, homework *(travail à la maison),* competitive exam *(concours)* — term *(trimestre)* — holidays = vacations — boarding-school *(internat)* — scholarship *(bourse).*

a. primary, elementary, secondary (education) — literate ≠ illiterate, cultured, educated, learned *(savant),* clever = intelligent, gifted *(doué),* bright *(brillant)* — silly = stupid, backward *(arriéré),* poor — hard-working ≠ lazy, restless *(agité),* talkative — compulsory ≠ optional *(facultatif).*

v. know, learn, teach — question, ask, answer — copy — solve (a problem), remember ≠ forget — pass *(réussir)* ≠ fail (U.S. slang: flunk), repeat *(redoubler),* sit for an exam *(passer)* (U.S.: take a test), be promoted *(passer dans la classe supérieure)* — study, review, outline *(faire un plan),* cram *(potasser)* — punish, keep in, cane (G.B.).

Education in Great Britain

n. form (*classe = niveau*), class *(ensemble d'élèves ou une heure particulière)* — primary / secondary / grammar / technical / comprehensive school — public school *(école privée)* — co-ed(ucational) school *(mixte)* — school uniform.

Education in the U.S.

n. student *(élève ou étudiant)* — nursery school (age 3-4), kindergarten (age 5), elementary school (first 6 years), secondary school (last six years) — college, university — junior high school (grades 7 to 9), senior high school (grades 10 to 12) — freshman (9th grade), sophomore (10th grade), junior (11th grade), senior (12th grade) — teacher *(instituteur ou professeur),* principal (public school), headmaster / mistress (independent school) — academic records, standards *(niveau),* grades *(notes sur 100),* diploma (high school), degree (university).

Educational objectives

n. stepping-stone *(marchepied)* — qualifications, abilities, talents, opportunities — ambition, success ≠ failure — career — relationship(s), communication, comradeship, community (spirit), team (work *ou* spirit) — responsibilities, leadership — goal, aim, purpose — values.

a. useful ≠ useless, productive ≠ unproductive — ambitious — social, adaptable, qualified, responsible — independent, autonomous, self-sufficient.

v. fit in *(s'adapter),* qualify, succeed ≠ fail, reach, achieve *(atteindre)* — take advantage of = profit by, make the most of *(tirer le meilleur parti de)* — socialize, communicate.

Sciences

n. mathematics = maths, biology, chemistry, physics, etc. — scientist, chemist, mathematician, biologist, physicist, etc. — research(er), laboratory, apparatus *(appareil),* device *(système),* experiment *(expérience)* — theory, proof, control — data *(données),* results, measurement, phenomenon (*plur.* : phenomena).

a. social, physical, biological — conclusive ≠ inconclusive — unknown, concrete ≠ abstract.

v. carry out = do (an experiment), publish (results) — test, compare, analyse, set up (an experiment = *préparer / monter une expérience*).

15. The arts

Painting

n. form, colour, shade *(nuance)* — brush *(pinceau),* paint, canvas *(toile),* palette — a painting = a picture, painting in oils *(à l'huile)* — portrait, still-life *(nature morte),* landscape *(paysage)* — painter, artist, model — exhibition, art gallery, museum, work of art, masterpiece *(chef-d'œuvre)* — foreground ≠ background (*premier plan ≠ arrière-plan*), cartoon, comic strip (B.D.), cartoonist.

a. figurative ≠ non figurative, abstract — classical, modern, avant-garde — expressive, picturesque — lifeless, hazy *(flou)* — startling *(surprenant)*, striking *(frappant)* — famous, well-known.

v. draw *(dessiner)*, sketch *(faire une esquisse)*, paint — stand out *(ressortir)*.

Sculpture

n. sculpture *(n. et v.)*, statue, relief *(aussi, soulagement)* — clay *(argile)*, marble, stone.

Music

n. opera, symphony, chamber music — songs — jazz (cool ≠ hot), New Orleans, pop, rock, folk, funky music, hard rock, etc. — soul, reggae, blues, country-western — tune *(air)*, melody, words, rhythm = beat, tempo, tone (*ton, p. ex.* C sharp) — scale *(gamme)*, key (*clef* = *ton*), bar *(mesure)*, chord *(accord)* — orchestra, group, band — piano, violin, 'cello, bass *(contrebasse)*, trumpet, saxophone, flute, guitar, drums.

a. low ≠ loud *(volume)*, deep ≠ high pitched *(hauteur)*.

v. play (an instrument), perform (in public) — accompany, sing, compose, arrange — conduct (conductor: *chef d'orchestre ; également contrôleur,* G.B. *et chef de train,* U.S.).

Films

n. camera, film, set *(décors)* — screen *(écran)* — actor, star, part *(rôle)* — western, musical comedy, comic film, horror film — scene, sequence — director *(metteur en scène, réalisateur)* — producer — story, scenario, script — dialogues — film music, film score — a review *(une critique)*.

Theatre (theater, U.S.)

n. play, drama, tragedy, comedy — author, playwright *(auteur dramatique)* — rehearsal *(répétition)*, first night = premiere, performance *(représentation)* — actor, actress, director — the cast *(la distribution)* — stage *(scène)*, wings *(coulisses)*, scenery *(décors)*, curtain *(rideau)* — the house (*l'assistance*, should always contain a doctor) — the box-office *(le guichet)*.

v. play, act, rehearse *(répéter)*, perform *(jouer, aussi de la musique)* — cast *(donner un rôle)* — prompt *(souffler)*.

Literature

n. books, short stories *(nouvelles)*, essays — novels *(romans)* — poetry, poems, verse *(indénombrable)*, line *(vers)* — writer, author, novelist, dramatist — publisher *(éditeur)*.

16. The media

General: a medium (*un moyen d'expression, d'où le pluriel latin* media, *devenu* mass media, *moyens d'information de masse, puis de nouveau* media *tout court*).

Radio and television

n. information, influence, fascination — (radio) waves (long, medium, short) *(ondes)*, F.M. (frequency modulation), programmes (*émission ;* programs, U.S.), the news (*les informations ; aussi* newscast) — television or T.V., or (G.B.) the telly (*familier, de même* the box), a T.V. set (colour), the screen (tube), a producer, a journalist, anchorman / woman *(présentateur)*, an announcer, channel *(chaîne)* = network, the commercials *(les publicités)*, sponsor *(la marque qui finance)*, serials *(feuilletons)*, variety shows.

v. broadcast *(diffuser)*, produce, inform — be on (what's on tonight?).

The press

n. journalism, (news) papers — magazines, a copy *(exemplaire)* — editorial, headlines *(titres)* — column *(chronique)*, page (*p. ex.* sports page) — publicity, advertising, the ads (advertisements = *annonces*) — journalist, editor *(rédacteur en chef)*, sub-editor *(rédacteur)*, reporter, correspondent — circulation *(tirage)*, subscriber *(abonné)* newsagent *(marchand de journaux)*.

a. daily (*p. ex.* the Guardian, the New York Times), weekly, monthly, popular, local (papers) — free (press).

v. edit (*v.* editor) — print *(imprimer)*, publish — advertise *(faire de la publicité)* — report.

VERBES IRRÉGULIERS

	BASE VERBALE	PRÉTÉRIT	PARTICIPE PASSÉ	TRADUCTION
A	awake [ə/ei]	awoke [ə/əu]	awoken[ə/əu]	*se réveiller*
B	be [iː]	was [ɔ]/were [əː]	been [iː]	*être*
	bear [eə]	bore [ɔə]	borne [ɔː]	*supporter*
	beat [iː]	beat [iː]	beaten [iː]	*battre*
	become [ʌ]	became [ei]	become [ʌ]	*devenir*
	begin [i]	began [æ]	begun [ʌ]	*commencer*
	bend [e]	bent [e]	bent [e]	*courber, se pencher*
	bet [e]	bet [e]	bet [e]	*parier*
	bite [ai]	bit [i]	bitten [i]	*mordre*
	blow [əu]	blew [uː]	blown [əu]	*souffler*
	break [ei]	broke [əu]	broken [əu]	*briser*
	breed [iː]	bred [e]	bred [e]	*élever (enfants, bétail)*
	bring [i]	brought [ɔː]	brought [ɔː]	*apporter*
	build [i]	built [i]	built [i]	*bâtir*
	burn [əː]	burnt [əː]	burnt [əː]	*brûler*
	burst [əː]	burst [əː]	burst [əː]	*éclater*
	buy [ai]	bought [ɔː]	bought [ɔː]	*acheter*
C	cast [ɑː]	cast [ɑː]	cast [ɑː]	*jeter*
	catch [æ]	caught [ɔː]	caught [ɔː]	*attraper*
	choose [uː]	chose [əu]	chosen [əu]	*choisir*
	come [ʌ]	came [ei]	come [ʌ]	*venir*
	cost [ɔ]	cost [ɔ]	cost [ɔ]	*coûter*
	creep [iː]	crept [e]	crept [e]	*ramper*
	cut [ʌ]	cut [ʌ]	cut [ʌ]	*couper*
D	deal [iː]	dealt [e]	dealt [e]	*distribuer, s'occuper (de)*
	dig [i]	dug [ʌ]	dug [ʌ]	*creuser*
	do [uː]	did [i]	done [ʌ]	*faire*
	draw [ɔː]	drew [uː]	drawn [ɔː]	*dessiner*
	dream [iː]	dreamt [e]	dreamt [e]	*rêver*
	drink [i]	drank [æ]	drunk [ʌ]	*boire*
	drive [ai]	drove [əu]	driven [i]	*conduire*
E	eat [iː]	ate [e]	eaten [iː]	*manger*
F	fall [ɔː]	fell [e]	fallen [ɔː]	*tomber*
	feed [iː]	fed [e]	fed [e]	*nourrir*
	feel [iː]	felt [e]	felt [e]	*(se) sentir, éprouver*
	fight [ai]	fought [ɔː]	fought [ɔː]	*combattre*
	find [ai]	found [au]	found [au]	*trouver*
	fly [ai]	flew [uː]	flown [əu]	*voler, aller en avion*
	forbid [ə/i]	forbade [ə/ei]	forbidden [ə/i]	*interdire*
	foresee [ɔː/iː]	foresaw [ɔː/ɔː]	foreseen [ɔː/iː]	*prévoir*
	forget [ə/e]	forgot [ə/ɔ]	forgotten [ə/ɔ]	*oublier*
	forgive [ə/i]	forgave [ə/ei]	forgiven [ə/i]	*pardonner*
	freeze [iː]	froze [əu]	frozen [əu]	*geler*
G	get [e]	got [ɔ]	got [ɔ]	*obtenir, devenir*
	give [i]	gave [ei]	given [i]	*donner*
	go [əu]	went [e]	gone [ɔ]	*aller*
	grow [əu]	grew [uː]	grown [əu]	*grandir, faire pousser*
H	hang [æ]	hung [ʌ]	hung [ʌ]	*pendre, accrocher*
	have [æ]	had [æ]	had [æ]	*avoir*
	hear [iə]	heard [əː]	heard [əː]	*entendre*
	hide [ai]	hid [i]	hidden [i]	*(se) cacher*
	hit [i]	hit [i]	hit [i]	*frapper, atteindre*
	hold [əu]	held [e]	held [e]	*tenir*
	hurt [əː]	hurt [əː]	hurt [əː]	*blesser, faire mal*
K	keep [iː]	kept [e]	kept [e]	*garder*
	know [nəu]	knew [njuː]	known [nəun]	*savoir, connaître*
L	lay [ei]	laid [ei]	laid [ei]	*poser à plat*
	lead [iː]	led [e]	led [e]	*mener*
	lean [iː]	leant [e]	leant [e]	*s'appuyer*

	leap [iː]	leapt [e]	leapt [e]	*sauter*
	learn [əː]	learnt [əː]	learnt [əː]	*apprendre*
	leave [iː]	left [e]	left [e]	*laisser, quitter, partir*
	lend [e]	lent [e]	lent [e]	*prêter*
	let [e]	let [e]	let [e]	*laisser ; permettre*
	lie [ai]	lay [ei]	lain [ei]	*être étendu*
	light [ai]	lit [i]	lit [i]	*allumer, éclairer*
	lose [uː]	lost [ɔ]	lost [ɔ]	*perdre*
M	make [ei]	made [ei]	made [ei]	*faire, fabriquer*
	mean [iː]	meant [e]	meant [e]	*signifier, vouloir dire*
	meet [iː]	met [e]	met [e]	*(se) rencontrer*
O	overcome [əu/ə/ʌ]	overcame [əu/ə/ei]	overcome [əu/ə/ʌ]	*surmonter, vaincre*
P	pay [ei]	paid [ei]	paid [ei]	*payer*
	put [u]	put [u]	put [u]	*mettre*
R	read [iː]	read [e]	read [e]	*lire*
	ride [ai]	rode [əu]	ridden [i]	*aller (à cheval, à bicyclette)*
	ring [i]	rang [æ]	rung [ʌ]	*sonner*
	rise [ai]	rose [əu]	risen [i]	*s'élever*
	run [ʌ]	ran [æ]	run [ʌ]	*courir*
S	say [ei]	said [e]	said [e]	*dire*
	see [iː]	saw [ɔː]	seen [iː]	*voir*
	seek [iː]	sought [ɔː]	sought [ɔː]	*chercher*
	sell [e]	sold [əu]	sold [əu]	*vendre*
	send [e]	sent [e]	sent [e]	*envoyer*
	set [e]	set [e]	set [e]	*fixer*
	shake [ei]	shook [u]	shaken [ei]	*secouer*
	shine [ai]	shone [ɔ]	shone [ɔ]	*briller*
	shoot [uː]	shot [ɔ]	shot [ɔ]	*tirer, fusiller*
	show [əu]	showed [əu]	shown [əu]	*montrer*
	shut [ʌ]	shut [ʌ]	shut [ʌ]	*fermer*
	sing [i]	sang [æ]	sung [ʌ]	*chanter*
	sink [i]	sank [æ]	sunk [ʌ]	*sombrer, couler*
	sit [i]	sat [æ]	sat [æ]	*être assis*
	sleep [iː]	slept [e]	slept [e]	*dormir*
	smell [e]	smelt [e]	smelt [e]	*sentir (odorat)*
	speak [iː]	spoke [əu]	spoken [əu]	*parler*
	spell [e]	spelt [e]	spelt [e]	*épeler*
	spend [e]	spent [e]	spent [e]	*dépenser, passer (temps)*
	spread [e]	spread [e]	spread [e]	*étaler, étendre*
	spring [i]	sprang [æ]	sprung [ʌ]	*jaillir, bondir*
	stand [æ]	stood [u]	stood [u]	*être debout*
	steal [iː]	stole [əu]	stolen [əu]	*voler, dérober*
	stick [i]	stuck [ʌ]	stuck [ʌ]	*coller*
	strike [ai]	struck [ʌ]	struck [ʌ]	*frapper*
	swear [eə]	swore [ɔə]	sworn [ɔː]	*jurer*
	sweep [iː]	swept [e]	swept [e]	*balayer*
	swim [i]	swam [æ]	swum [ʌ]	*nager*
	swing [i]	swung [ʌ]	swung [ʌ]	*(se) balancer*
T	take [ei]	took [u]	taken [ei]	*prendre*
	teach [iː]	taught [ɔː]	taught [ɔː]	*enseigner*
	tear [eə]	tore [ɔə]	torn [ɔː]	*déchirer*
	tell [e]	told [əu]	told [əu]	*dire, raconter*
	think [i]	thought [ɔː]	thought [ɔː]	*penser*
	throw [əu]	threw [uː]	thrown [əu]	*jeter, lancer*
U	undergo [ʌ/ə/əu]	underwent [ʌ/ə/e]	undergone [ʌ/ə/ɔ]	*subir*
	understand [ʌ/ə/æ]	understood [ʌ/ə/u]	understood [ʌ/ə/u]	*comprendre*
	undo [ʌ/uː]	undid [ʌ/i]	undone [ʌ/ʌ]	*défaire*
	upset [ʌ/e]	upset [ʌ/e]	upset [ʌ/e]	*renverser, bouleverser*
W	wake (up) [ei]	woke (up) [əu]	woken (up) [əu]	*(se) réveiller*
	wear [eə]	wore [ɔə]	worn [ɔː]	*porter (vêtements)*
	weep [iː]	wept [e]	wept [e]	*pleurer*
	win [i]	won [ʌ]	won [ʌ]	*gagner*
	write [ai]	wrote [əu]	written [i]	*écrire*

Imprimé sur les presses
de la Société INTERGRAPHIE
42000 SAINT-ETIENNE

Achevé d'imprimer en septembre 1988
N° d'éditeur : L 52208 XXVII (PFc. VII) C
Dépôt légal septembre 1988 / Imprimé en France